ECCENTRIC EXPLORERS

Being the amazing Adventures of fanatical & fearless Explorers & barmy Visionaries on the Rooftop of the World & their sometimes-painful Peregrinations as they attempt to unlock the Secrets of Tibet—closing in on the enigmas of Trance-runners & Monks with occult Powers, stumbling into long-lost Kingdoms, hunting for rare Butterflies & exotic Flora, or heading into unknown Terrain in the deepest Gorges & the highest Mountains on Earth— the latter Forays incurring the Wrath of the Goddess of the Snows— in Tales related by the Author, who followed in their Footsteps…

Michael Buckley

Published by CrazyHorse Press
Vancouver, Canada
Email: buckeroo555@yahoo.com

To order this book online, go to: www.itmb.com
For publishing inquiries & agent liaison:
contact Robert Mackwood
Email: rmackwood@seventhavenuelit.com

Book design: Michael Buckley
Typesetting: John McKercher
Cover design: Diane McIntosh
Maps, artwork: Naz Ali, Teresa Nightingale

Eccentric Explorers
ISBN 978-0-9693370-2-7
Travel: Adventure | Biography | History: Tibet

Library and Archives Canada Cataloguing in Publication
Buckley, Michael
Eccentric explorers: being the amazing adventures of
fanatical & fearless explorers & barmy visionaries on the
Rooftop of the World / Michael Buckley.
Includes bibliographical references.
ISBN 978-0-9693370-2-7
1.Explorers—China—Tibet—Biography.
2.Tibet (China)—Description and travel. I. Title
DS786.B833 2008   915.15   C2008-906417-8

Printed in Canada by Friesens

ECCENTRIC EXPLORERS

MICHAEL BUCKLEY

If we are facing in the right direction,

all we have to do is keep on walking

—Buddhist saying

Contents

TEXT NOTES

The British imperial system of miles, feet, inches, pounds and other abnormalities has been used throughout in this book. A splendid reason for this is that the British were heavily involved in mapping and exploration of pre-1950 Tibet. Names like Calcutta (instead of Kolkata) and Peking (instead of Beijing) have been used because those were the names current at the time. The $ symbol appearing in this book indicates US dollars; the £ symbol indicates British pounds sterling.

ABBREVIATIONS
HQ—headquarters
PLA—People's Liberation Army, the national army of China
POW—prisoner of war
RGS—Royal Geographical Society, UK
WWII—World War II

Heading into the Unknown

The Tibetan plateau is a bizarre place—a world unto itself. It is a place that was long cut off from the rest of the world—never colonised until the Chinese invaded in 1950. A place where the accumulating of wealth and material goods was of little importance—where the attainment of enlightenment was the ultimate goal. Ruled by a line of reincarnate 'god-kings', the Tibetans believed that the world was flat—and that a huge mountain lay at the centre of the universe, with a glittering city of the gods crowning it.

The exploration of Tibet has long fascinated the West. During the Victorian era, with the mysteries of the Nile solved and Africa trampled over, Tibet's rivers and mountains remained untouched. Tibetan hosted a wealth of unknown fauna and flora—due to startling adaptation to the harsh environment and the rigours of high altitude. This was *Terra Tibetana Incognita*. With the discovery in 1856 that Mount Everest was the highest mountain yet sighted, fascination increased. The imperial powers of Great Britain and Russia had their eyes on Tibet for other reasons: for strategic and trade purposes. Neither power had adequate maps of the region—explorers were recruited to gather this intelligence.

Tibet held a host of strange riddles and secrets to unlock. Very little was known about arcane Tibetan Buddhist rituals, or Tibetan art—or, indeed, much about this reclusive culture at all. Can monks run non-stop—for days on end—in a trance? Can High Lamas direct their reincarnation? What do Tibetans believe about the goddess of Everest? Do yetis trample the foothills of Himalayan peaks? Where does the wondrous wool *tus* come from? What new mammals and birds might be discovered in Tibet? What miraculous medicinal plants? Is there any truth to the ancient story of the gold-digging ants of Tibet? Is there a huge waterfall lying along the Tsangpo river? Where do the sources of Tibet's major rivers lie? Some explorers found answers—but others came back with more questions. And they all had strange tales to tell.

In this book, the rich culture and history of Tibet are viewed through a rather special lens—through the eyes of these eccentric explorers. The book encompasses the curious encounters—some might say clashes—of two very different civilisations: East and West. And in the end, who has more to learn? The west is far advanced in technology, but the Tibetans are more highly evolved in the quest for 'inner space'—studies of the nature of the mind, of compassion, of inner peace. Tibet is like the Black Box of Central Asia, if you take in the broader definition of 'black box'—a kind of complex equipment not normally maintained or modified by its operators, yet vital to their existence. For over a thousand years, Tibet was the 'black box' of Buddhism. Tibetans were the custodians of its teachings and sacred texts after the faith was snuffed out by Muslim invasion in the place of its birth, India. Mongolia drew on the black box. India respected it. China attempted to smash it. And if this legacy disappears, the world will be a much poorer place without it.

With its bizarre culture and beliefs, Tibet became a magnet for the most eccentric explorers. Missionaries, mystics, batty spiritualists, moody mountaineers, geographers, spies, secret agents, charlatans, serious scholars, wacky misfits—and plain sensationalists: Tibet drew them all. It is quite possible that these eccentrics felt quite at home there because of the oddball nature of Tibetan culture itself. And conversely, time spent in high altitude zones has been known to amplify eccentric traits. A number of these explorers, agents and misfits make an appearance in cameo roles in this book—crossing paths with the main explorers profiled, inspiring them, or triggering fierce rivalry.

Tibet is a land of extremes: extreme altitude, extreme weather—and extreme people. To the northeast of Lhasa live the Amdowas, called 'people of the extremes' by sophisticated Lhasans. By this, they mean people living at the extremities of the plateau, but from the way the Amdowas dress—with wild unkempt hair and dishevelled sheepskin cloaks—you might also be led to believe these are extreme people. The nomads from this area must be among the hardiest in the world, living in conditions of harsh cold and wind. One of the major reasons that explorers could not make headway into Tibet was because of nomads like this—whose favourite pastime was banditry. On the fringes of Tibet, several explorers met a grisly end at the hands of the much-feared Golok or Khampa tribesmen. Anyone who made it through the bandit-infested extremities of the plateau would invariably be spotted and captured by Lhasan soldiers, and turned back with a stern warning. The government of Tibet was fanatically vigilant in preventing foreigners from reaching Central Tibet.

As a consequence, the explorers in this book all—at one time or another—travelled in disguise, freely dispensing any lies necessary to reach their goal. And given the chance, they kept firearms handy. The skill of bluffing was high on the survival agenda. Thomas Manning, dressed in long Chinese gowns, pretended to be a Chinese physician—though nobody took his disguise seriously. Peter Aufschnaiter first bluffed his way out of a prisoner-of-war camp in India, and then bluffed his way past Tibetans keen on keeping foreigners out. Alexandra David-Néel travelled disguised as a beggar, but one who packed a pistol in her purse—and wasn't shy about using it if the going got rough.

The explorers profiled are driven by a restless curiosity—a wander-lust that renders them unable or unwilling to stay in one spot for long. They are largely self-taught—learning along the way because they are venturing into realms where no Westerner had been before. And they're gifted 'code crackers'—some are master linguists—intrigued by riddles, obsessed with getting the answers. Some came looking for rare plants or animals, some tackled riddles of geography, and others came to decode the secrets of Tibetan religious knowledge.

For all these adventurers, Tibet felt like home. No matter that it was full of dust and bandits and the food was terrible. No matter that you could perish in extreme cold or die from altitude sickness. It felt like home. Alexandra David-Néel left her heart there, and were it not for her arthritis and the Chinese invasion of Tibet, she would have gone back. Joseph Rock, on his brief visits to America, would complain about an 'automobile-crazy society' and scamper back, ego bruised, to the remote regions of the Tibetan plateau, where he could play at being king. Peter Aufschnaiter hoped to live out his days in Tibet as an estate-owner. Michel Peissel has been drawn back time and again.

The ten explorers presented include some who are famous—and some whose tales have not seen much print at all. They are united by their obsessive infatuation with Tibet, by their loner approach, and by their eccentric character and methods of exploration. Other adjectives that would apply: cantankerous, hot-headed, bad-tempered, stubborn, crackers, and absolutely fearless. The word 'impossible' does not figure in their vocabulary—even when impossible means life-threatening. They are all tough as nails, and unwavering in their quests—drawing on an incredible inner well of strength in the face of great hardship. *Eccentric Explorers* is a tome about the hilarious escapades of these quirky adventurers.

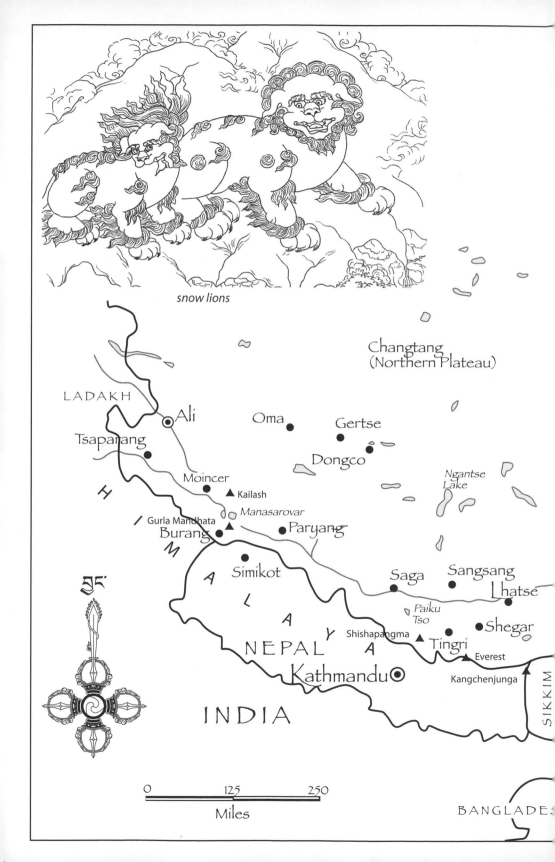

snow lions

Changtang
(Northern Plateau)

LADAKH

Ali

Tsaparang

Oma

Gertse

Dongco

Moincer

Ngantse
Lake

▲ Kailash

Manasarovar

Gurla Mandhata

Paryang

Burang

Simikot

Saga

Sangsang

Lhatse

Paiku
Tso

Shegar

Shishapangma

▲ Tingri

NEPAL

Kathmandu◉

▲ Everest

Kangchenjunga

SIKKIM

INDIA

0   125   250

Miles

BANGLADES

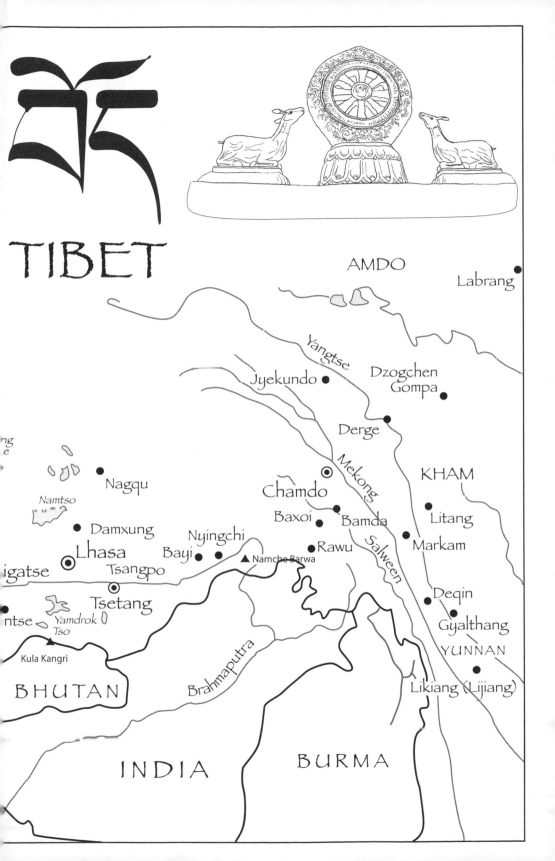

TIBET

AMDO
Labrang

Yangtse

Jyekundo
Dzogchen
Gompa

Derge

KHAM

Nagqu

Chamdo

Namtso

Baxoi
Bamda
Litang

Damxung
Nyingchi
Rawu
Markam

Lhasa
Bayi

igatse
Tsangpo
Namche Barwa

Tsetang
Deqin

ntse
Yamdrok
Tso
Gyalthang

YUNNAN

Kula Kangri

BHUTAN
Brahmaputra
Likiang (Lijiang)

INDIA
BURMA

Mekong
Salween

Manning in his clean-shaven days, before Sinomania
set in—redrawn from a portrait, artist unknown

 # Thomas Manning
1772–1840

linguist, scholar, Sinomaniac &
comedian of the Land of Snows

Blundering
into Tibet

A zany Englishman bags
the explorer's trophy—by accident

In the 19th century, Tibet was a blank on the map. This huge
blank was particularly annoying to the British, seeking trade
links beyond India—and perhaps with colonial expansion in
mind as well. The exact altitude and location of Lhasa was
unknown. Six of Asia's great rivers—the Brahmaputra, Indus,
Mekong, Salween, Sutlej and Yangtse—were known to have
their sources in Tibet, but none had been adequately mapped.
Worse yet, between 1783 and 1903, only one Englishman
managed to enter Tibet. And he refused to say anything...

 IN THE WINTER OF 1811, British scholar Thomas Manning blundered into Tibet. His dream was actually to reach Peking, where he hoped to advance his study of the Chinese language. Manning was a classics scholar who, having exhausted the study of Latin and Greek—and mathematics and philosophy—had turned his mind to the ultimate linguistic challenge. He decided to tackle the entire literature of China. After a spell at the centre for oriental studies in Paris, he was determined to get to the source—he set sail on an East India Company ship in 1806 for Canton. There was only one snag: the Celestial Empire was closed off to foreigners by the xenophobic Manchus. In fact, even the study of Chinese language was forbidden to foreigners—Manning got around this by enlisting a Chinese tutor from Macau.

Dressed in a long Vietnamese gown, Manning mounted a bizarre attempt to disembark from a boat on the coast of northern Vietnam and enter southern China, but this plan was aborted. Frustrated in his attempts to get to Peking from Canton, the tall, brooding Englishman decided to try his luck from India. He hatched the harebrained scheme of travelling through Tibet to Sining, and thence to Peking. The distance was over 3,000 miles—something that the wildly impractical Manning didn't dwell upon at the outset. At the time, the only foreigners allowed into Tibet were Chinese diplomats and troops. After the outbreak of war between Tibet and Nepal in 1788, the position of the Chinese in Tibet was greatly strengthened, and Tibet's doors became as tightly closed as China's, with Chinese troops garrisoned in Lhasa and other large towns.

The Holy City of Lhasa was one of the most secret places on earth. It had attained a mythical aura—reaching it proved the ultimate explorer's challenge, on a par with sneaking into Mecca. Although 19th-century explorers crisscrossed the Tibetan wasteland, attempts to gatecrash Lhasa were firmly repulsed.

Manning hated travelling, had no financial backing, and made no preparations. He did, however, take along a pair of ice-skates in anticipation of winter sports in the Himalayas. For company he had a Chinese valet—the same man he'd employed as his Chinese tutor in Macau and had dragged along for the ride. In his diaries, he doesn't name him: he starts off referring to him as 'the Chinaman' and then switches to 'the Munshi' or 'my Munshi' (*munshi* is the Hindi term to describe a teacher of native languages or interpreter—and also a term denoting a native secretary). The valet was a sullen character with whom Manning argued much of the way, and who finally parted ways with him in Lhasa—under dire circumstances. The two argued in Latin, and Manning made footnotes in his journal about his servant's misuse of Latin grammar: 'In Latin he used the words *non potes*. He ought to have said, *non licet*. My response was, *at verberabo*.'

Some background here: Manning was a master linguist who could've carved out a brilliant career as a scholar in England. He was born in 1772, the son of a clergyman in Norfolk. At Cambridge, he struck up a friendship with Charles Lamb, who thought him more extraordinary than Wordsworth or Coleridge. Though brilliant at his studies, Manning left Cambridge without a degree because he disliked the oaths and religious tests required. As a tutor he published a highly regarded book, *Introduction to Arithmetic and Algebra*. Around 1800, he abandoned all interest in mathematics and did a complete about-face: he decided to pursue the study of Chinese literature. That meant decoding complex Chinese characters—a task akin to cracking Egyptian hieroglyphics.

England has produced more than its fair share of eccentrics over time—indeed, the country prides itself on fostering such characters. And here Manning was definitely an innovator: his obsession with China and things Chinese was an eccentricity completely unknown in England at the time. He was suffering from a condition that could best be described as 'Sinophilia' or 'Sinomania'. He qualifies for the dubious privilege of being England's very first Sinomaniac. He simply had to get to the source—he had to get to China. His friend Charles Lamb, trying to dissuade him from such foolish purposes, wrote in a letter:

> Believe me, 'tis all a poets' invention. Pray try and cure yourself. Take hellebore. Pray to avoid the fiend. Read no more books of voyages, they are nothing but lies.

But Manning could not be swayed. Manning was a skilled and witty writer with a keen eye for detail: his writing is tempered with a fine sense of humour. But he refused to tell a soul of his Tibetan exploits: the only records are letters, and a short journal that surfaced after his death. Although he was considered the foremost Chinese scholar in Europe, Manning published only a slim tract of Chinese jokes in translation. Among the unpublished material was a paper on the consumption of tea in Bhutan, Tibet and Tartary, and his Tibetan journal.

The journal was never intended for public consumption and mostly contains trivia of a personal nature. It had to be reassembled posthumously to make it somewhat coherent. Manning's scrawl was copied out in clearer longhand script by his sister. Much later, the text was passed along from Reverend Manning (nephew to Thomas Manning) to Clements Markham, of the Geographical Department of the India Office. Markham cobbled together Manning's scattered journal and notes, along with accounts of several other pioneering explorers in Tibet, and packaged everything under the unwieldy title *Narratives of the Mission of George Bogle to Tibet and of the Journey of Thomas Manning to Lhasa*. Manning's account runs to 80 pages. Markham's book was published in 1876, which was 36 years after Manning died and 64 years after his Tibetan adventure. But the journal—though brief and fragmented—reveals an extraordinary story.

Reading that story is a bit like watching a stand-up comic. Manning is the comedian of the Land of Snows, delivering some classic one-liners and delightful double-entendres—but failing to deliver anything of geographical substance. The prose is not the chest-thumping bravado of a great explorer on a momentous mission: it is a whimsical account of a man distracted by gossip and petty problems—and occasionally addressing the more serious issue of his own survival. As the editor responsible for bringing this ground-breaking account to the public, Markham must've pulled his hair out. Manning was the jester in the court of the Geographical Department of the India Office. Markham was so frustrated by Manning's lack of attempt to furnish pertinent geographical data, or stray bits of scenery—or even an attempt at describing a Tibetan temple—that he felt obliged to insert footnotes to cover these black holes in the text. Because Markham was editing Manning's work some 60 years after the actual journey, he was able to draw on details furnished by Indian pundits sent in disguise by the British to spy out the land.

Lhasa

Tsangpo

Shigatse

TIBET

Nagartse

Gyantse

Yamdrok
Tso

Phari

SIKKIM

Tassisudon (Thimphu)

NEPAL

Gangtok

Paro

BHUTAN

Duna

Buxa Duar

Cooch Behar

Brahmaputra

Rangpur

Dinapur

Ganges

BANGLADESH

INDIA

Murshidabad

Calcutta

0   50   100 Miles

Bay of Bengal

Thomas Manning's haphazard route into Tibet, 1811–1812

Pallast von Tassisudon in Bootan

An engraving from 1811 showing the grand fort of Tashichodzong, seat of the ruler in the Bhutanese capital of Tassisudon.

Manning and his valet started this lunatic trip in September 1811, departing from Calcutta. Calcutta was, at the time, the capital and chief port of the British territory of Bengal. Bengal had started life as the personal fiefdom of the East India Company, which held a monopoly on the India trade until 1813. The transport modes open to Manning and his valet: travel on horseback, on foot, or by 'chair'. A chair was simply strapped to the back of a porter. This was rather like sitting on a train: the person being transported could read a book to pass the time if it was not raining and if the going was not too bumpy. Manning was a hopeless horse-rider: more than once on the journey his steed bolted—with himself hanging on for dear life. The pair of travellers made their arduous way by horse up through Tassisudon, the old capital of Bhutan and site of present-day Thimphu. Then they moved on to Paro. The clans of these parts were partial to kilt-like robes, an oddly Scottish touch. Some wore tam-o-shanters decorated with yak-tails dyed red. The Bhutanese were very keen on textiles—and to Manning's chagrin, they took most of his textile stock, intended as gifts for Tibetans.

Despite setbacks like this, Manning was actually in a fine mood. After being cooped up so long in the city of Calcutta, the trip north was a breath of fresh air for Manning. The change of people, the change of scenery and weather: all this was a tonic. Manning revelled in the changes, finding himself in a peculiar emotional condition—perhaps due to the effects of altitude:

> Strange sensation coming along: warm and comfortable. Horse walking in a lane between two stone walls. The snow! Where am I? How can I be come here? Not a soul to speak to. I wept almost through excess of sensation, not from grief.

Ahead lay more strangeness—at Phari, the Tibetan border town. Phari provided a macabre introduction to the ways of the Tibetans. The village consisted of a fort, a few hundred hovels, and a couple of centuries of garbage. The people of this town—clothed in greasy rags and sheepskins—with faces blackened and ingrained with dirt—were in the habit of throwing all their refuse immediately outside their doors. The garbage was so high that holes had to be dug to give access to doorways, leading to subterranean cellars. The air was rank; the stench was pervasive. Eagles, kites, ravens and vultures wheeled around an open-air funeral site, where chopped-up bodies were offered to the birds. But contrasting with the filth and stench of the place were sublime views of distant snowcapped peaks.

Manning glossed over Phari in his journal, but later European travellers fill in the gaps here. John Noel, pioneer of the early British Everest expeditions tells us that Phari's hovels were built of mud reinforced with the horns, hair and skin of dead cattle. Everything was coated with greasy soot from yak-dung fires; children were dressed in rags and matted in filth. This extreme filth seemed to be lovingly cultivated—and topped off with the smell of rancid yak-butter. What Noel did not know was that the face-blackening layer derived from a red paste smeared on the face: the paste turned black as it oxidised—and was intended to protect the skin from damaging rays of the harsh sun. There was one redeeming facial feature that defied explanation: no Tibetans used anything remotely resembling a toothbrush, but when they laughed, they showed off exquisite pearly-white teeth. These teeth greatly impressed Europeans—who could not fathom how this was possible in a place where the concept of dentistry revolved around yanking out any tooth that caused pain.

It's not clear why Phari was so spectacularly filthy compared with other towns like Gyantse, which were relatively clean. Noel describes two governors of Phari, outstanding because they wear gorgeous flowing robes of Chinese silk:

> One wears a headdress that is nothing other than an enormous purple lampshade. They hold the rank of the Backward-sloping Peacock Feather and the Order of the Crystal Button. They wear their sleeves long, reaching almost to the ground and hiding their long, carefully manicured nails. Such are the marks of their dignity. They sit in their castle and extract taxes, for which there is no fixed scale or rule, from the traders who collect here from India, Bhutan, Nepal and Tibet.

On arrival in Phari, Manning ran into Tibetan officialdom. He immediately claimed to be a pilgrim from Bengal. The local officials had no idea what to make of the pale-skinned apparition that had arrived on their doorstep—due to Manning's Chinese attire, they assumed he was a tall, strange Asian with a big nose and a beard. They left the matter to be decided by a Chinese mandarin—a high-ranking military officer who was due to arrive shortly. An advance guard of the mandarin showed up, causing Manning and his companion to be bumped out of their humble lodgings to make way for them. Manning describes his new digs thus: 'Dirt, dirt, grease, smoke. Misery, but good mutton.' Several days later, the big man himself appeared: Manning refers to him as 'the General'.

Although Manning was woefully unprepared for a winter trip to the Tibetan plateau, he possessed two skills that dazzled the General. He spoke good Chinese, and he seemed to know a lot about medicine. The Chinese troops badly needed medical attention: Manning set up an impromptu clinic. There was perhaps some method to Manning's madness. Back in Cambridge, before he embarked on a serious study of Chinese, Manning had taken a course in medicine, figuring that this skill would prove useful in the Orient. Though minimal, his knowledge of Western medicines and techniques indeed gained him considerable status in the eyes of the Chinese.

As luck would have it, the General and his entourage were on border patrol: they were headed back for Gyantse. Two bottles of cherry brandy donated to the cause got Manning a passage that far. The General even persuaded Manning to have some warmer Chinese clothes made up, as they were heading into the bitter Tibetan winter. His new robe was made up by the general's soldier-tailors:

> It was an ample coarsish red woollen-cloth robe with fur cuffs; it was lined with cotton cloth, and upon the cotton cloth was stitched a dressed sheepskin with all the wool on. I had also brought stockings of the same kind of sheepskin, under which, if I pleased, I could put one or two pairs of common worsted or cotton stockings, and over all draw my Chinese boots, so that I was able to keep my feet cosy whatever weather might ensue. I had a sort of fur tippet, and a quilted cap to defend my face and ears...

Between Phari and Gyantse, Manning mentions a lake which he sized up for skating, though this might have proved difficult given the foregoing ponderous mass of clothing he had acquired:

> The lake was frozen; at least that part we were next, and would certainly have borne me. My skates were not many miles off... We stopped but a few minutes and proceeded on to where the lake becomes a river...There were many fine, fat ducks on it, which were very tame, and let us come close to them. The people of Tibet never disturb them: they eat no birds, but, on the contrary, let the birds eat them.

Manning was referring to the Tibetan custom of sky burial, which involves chopping up the body and crushing the bones, and then feeding the pieces to the vultures. Manning now assumed a role as a Chinese physician, complete with long Chinese gown and Chinese spectacles—although nobody took his disguise seriously. His copious beard was out of character with the disguise but he couldn't bring himself to part with it:

> He [the Chinese General] was greatly taken with my beard, and seemed as if he could never sufficiently admire it. He adverted to it both then and afterwards on other occasions. He named such and such a mandarin, such a one he thought had better moustaches; in fact, I had kept mine cut short in India, for convenience of eating soup and drink, and they were not yet full grown.

Although he was 39 years old at the time, Manning must have appeared somewhat older to both the Chinese and the Tibetans due to the length of his beard—normally associated with much older men. Night rests were at wayside inns—which were smoky, dirty and dusty, and windowless. Many families would share the inn. Manning noticed, to his delight, that women and girls would come in, make up their beds and then strip without any concern for modesty. The Tibetans slept naked under the covers. 'I now and then took an impertinent peep, but the smoke was so thick and the light so bad, I could discern nothing.' Manning himself didn't bother to undress—he slept fully clothed, claiming it was too cold to do otherwise. At any event, he quickly became preoccupied with another bedtime problem: bedbugs. He had picked them up from the soiled bedding and couldn't quite get rid of them.

Manning devoted two pages in his journal to problems with his horse and saddle—the journey was obviously a pain in the butt. He was a poor rider: at one point his horse bolted, leaving him grimly hanging on for dear life. The entourage finally reached Gyantse. Setting up shop in Gyantse, Manning dispensed herbal remedies, opium and solution of arsenic to needy patients, mostly Chinese. Gyantse Dzong was the major defense fort on the southern approach to Lhasa.

The last Englishmen to get this far were George Bogle and Samuel Turner, East India Company envoys dispatched on separate trading missions in 1774 and 1783. These missions managed to fill in some details about the route from Bhutan to Shigatse. Maps of the plateau were exceedingly rare. Between 1725 and 1735, independent Dutch adventurer Samuel Van der Putte had twice crossed Tibet in caravans— from Ladakh via Lhasa to Peking, in disguise. But despite their value to colonial powers desperate to fill in blank spaces on the map, Van der Putte ordered all his notes destroyed: all that remains from the journeys is a rudimentary sketch-map (now in a Dutch museum) and some indecipherable bits of paper.

The only thing that came close to real cartography of Tibet was the D'Anville map of 1733. This effort was published by French cartographer Jean D'Anville as part of a collection on China—based on the Great Lama Survey ordered by Chinese Emperor Kangxi in 1717. The lamas had been trained by Jesuit missionaries, but the map was rather vague when it came to details like the rivers of Tibet, which tapered off in the middle of nowhere. When George Bogle entered Tibet in 1774, he carried the D'Anville map.

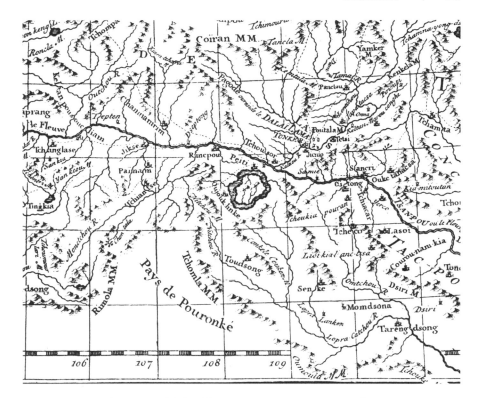

Section of a map published by cartographer Jean D'Anville in Paris
in 1733, shows Lake Yamdrok Tso (to the southwest of Lhasa) as a
circular shape—when it is actually shaped like the claws of a crab.
Passing by the lake in 1811, Manning could easily have corrected this
data, but the error continued with all maps of Tibet prior to 1880.

The British saw Tibet as a back door for trade with China—with
its treasures of silk and tea, which the British wanted to trade for English cloth and woollens. And they were interested in direct trade with
Tibet for items such as sheep-wool (known to be of fine quality), goat-
wool, minerals such as borax, and medicinal plants. Highly prized for
its medicinal properties at the time in both England and Russia was
rhubarb, which was only available in the East: Tibet was rumoured to
be a place where a giant variety of this plant grew. If Tibet was a blank
on the map, so was its high-altitude fauna and flora and culture—there
was a possible treasure-trove of new drugs to be derived from unusual
plant life.

Added to this was the tantalising prospect of finding gold. The
ancient Greek historian Herodotus recounted a strange riddle about

'gold-digging ants' coming from the Tibetan region (the solution to this riddle can be found toward the end of this book). There were indeed gold and silver mining fields in Tibet, but the Tibetans were not greatly interested in mining these precious metals other than using them for decorating religious statues. They believed that gold nuggets were the 'parents' of gold dust: if a nugget was accidentally excavated, it was to be re-buried.

Bogle was charged with bringing back any rare plant or seed samples, particularly those of walnuts, rhubarb and ginseng, and to keep an eye out for any curious natural products or animals. Prior to his departure, Bogle was given a pashmina shawl to keep him warm on the journey—and to act as a reminder that he was to commandeer a live pair of the animals responsible for 'tus', the wondrous wool used to make high-quality shawls in Kashmir. The textile-crazed English desperately wanted to find the source of it. And he was to procure two musk deer, valued for their musk-sacs.

Adding to this small zoo, if he could manage, he was to bring back one or more pairs of 'cow-tailed cattle', much admired for their rich meat and their bushy tails. The fine-haired tails of this animal were sought after by wealthy Indians and Nepalis as fly-whisks and dusters. They were also used for making tassels and helmet ornaments—tassels of yak-hair dyed red were treasured by Samurai warriors in Japan. The Tibetans rely on the yak for their survival, with ingenious uses of all parts of the animal: yak-hair is woven into cloth and rope used to make nomad tents, for instance. But nomads are not fashion-conscious—yak-hair was found to be too harsh in quality for Europeans. It would take time for the full potential of yak-hair to be realised—in the entertainment industry, where it is valued for making opera wigs. Dyed bright orange-red, yak-hair is also used to make wild-looking circus-clown wigs. In the pre-synthetic era, yak tails were considered the best material for making Santa Claus beards.

'Cow-tailed cattle' was an early reference to the yak: there was no specific word for the animal in Bogle's time. It's not clear where the 'cow-tailed' part came from, since the yak's tail more resembles that of a horse. The Latin or scientific name assigned to this high-altitude bovine was *Bos grunniens*, or grunting ox—a reference to the grunting sounds the yak makes when agitated, hungry or calling its young. This comical creature—a cow with a shaggy skirt—was known as 'gyagk' in Tibetan. A German book of 1811 called it 'buffalo with horsetail', while

Der Büffel mit dem Pferdeschweife. (Bos grunniens.)

This engraving—from a book printed in Leipzig (Germany) in 1811—identifies the yak as a 'Buffalo with a Horsetail'

it was identified in a letter of 1824 by British naturalist Brian Houghton Hodgson as a 'yak-cow'. Bogle was on an intelligence-gathering mission: he was to keep a pocketbook journal with a pencil, and take copious notes on the people, the land and the customs, and to inquire about what kind of trade the Tibetans conducted, and with whom. Further, he was to take samples of trade items along and show these to the Tibetans to whet their appetite for English goods like cloth, cutlery and glassware.

Bogle proceeded into Tibet at the invitation of the Tashi Lama, spiritual leader of Tashilhunpo Monastery at Shigatse. Though he stayed in Shigatse for four months, he could not obtain permission to continue to Lhasa: he was informed that any trading would have to be arranged through the Chinese court. The xenophobic Chinese, fearing competition from the British and the Russians, had convinced the Tibetans that these two super-powers were aiming to destroy Tibetan Buddhism. Bogle whetted the appetite of the East India Company for trade with Tibet with his detailed descriptions of trade items. And then there was the question of gold and silver: upon his departure,

Bogle was given purses of gold dust and silver talents (coins) by the Tashi Lama. Later in the year of 1775, the Tashi Lama sent an envoy to Warren Hastings, the Governor of Bengal and head of the East India Company, bearing silver ingots and gold dust as presents.

In Tibet, gold-mining operations were permitted on small scale if located well away from religious centres in Tibet. Bogle had seen numerous votive objects and large images of Buddha coated with real gold at Shigatse: this information would certainly have excited the interest of the East India Company. Bogle hunted the musk deer, and he saw numerous 'cow-tailed cattle' (yaks), but he failed to bring back the live animal samples he had been requested to get: the Tashi Lama promised he would send some animals along later.

As for the animal that produced the shawl wool, Bogle was still foggy about its identity—although he'd been told it was the highest priority to bring back live specimens. In Kashmir, the underwool of cashmere goats was used in making pashmina shawls. The animal was thus known as the 'shawl goat'. North of Kashmir, the regions of Gar and Rudok in far-west Tibet did a roaring trade in supplying shawl-wool from domesticated cashmere goats. By the early 18th century, shawls from Kashmir were much sought-after by the élite in Europe, particularly in France where Empress Josephine was crazy about them. The biggest supplier of Kashmir shawls was the East India Company, shipping from Bombay. But something eluded the British traders. The finest shawls made in Kashmir used a mysterious high-grade wool from Tibet which was not from a domestic goat. Such are the secrets of the Tibetan plateau that it would take another few centuries before the wild animal that bore the *tus* wool would be identified—you have to read to the end of this book to find it.

In 1774, just getting into Tibet and dining with the Tashi Lama was a feat in itself. Bogle discovered much about the strange customs and beliefs of the Tibetans—he is credited with coining the word 'polyandry' to describe the occasional practice of Tibetan women having several husbands—usually brothers. The Tibetans also practice polygamy (more precisely: polygyny)—one man having several wives, usually sisters who wanted to keep the family wealth together. Tibetan society was remarkably tolerant of relationships between unmarried men and women, and Bogle noted in his journal that 'Tibetan women are kind, tender-hearted and easily won.' Bogle's account does not elaborate on whether he availed himself of the charms of young Tibetan women, but he certainly had ample opportunity—being introduced to high-spirited females of the Tashi Lama's entourage. Shortly after Bogle returned from his Tibetan mission in 1774, Hamilton advised him on how to deal with an inconvenient sexually transmitted disease—contracted either in Tibet or Bhutan.

Other interactive hi-jinks: Bogle can be blamed for starting up the Tourist Curse of Tibet. A number of times, he dispensed sweets to Tibetan children as gifts. Naturally, he was besieged by unruly urchins when this happened—a practice that endures to this day, when Tibetan children mob visitors in Landcruisers, demanding sweets or pens. But overall, Bogle got off to a grand start as England's first ambassador to the Land of Snows: he established cordial relations with the court of Shigatse. He counted his six months in Tibet the happiest time in his life. On his departure, he wrote:

> Farewell ye honest and simple people, may ye long enjoy that happiness which is denied to more polished nations, and while they are engaged in the endless pursuit of avarice and ambition, defended by your mountains, may ye continue to live in peace and contentment, and know no wants but those of nature.

Odd words indeed for a Scot in the employment of the decidedly avaricious East India Company with designs to exploit the Tibetans. Bogle saw great possibilities for India-Tibet trade but nothing became of his mission. In November 1780, the Tashi Lama died of smallpox in Peking, aged around 45 years old. Within five months, Bogle was struck down with cholera, dying in Calcutta in April, 1781. The important link with the Tashi Lama was lost.

Back in Calcutta, Warren Hastings decided to reforge the link by sending in another mission to congratulate the newly appointed Tashi Lama upon his reincarnation. The Tibetans believe that all high lamas can direct their rebirth. In December 1783, British envoy Samuel Turner had an audience with a child of 18 months—the reincarnate—in Shigatse. According to Turner, the child looked steadfastly at him with the appearance of much attention, and nodded repeatedly as though he understood every word. The handsome child conducted himself with 'astonishing dignity and decorum.' Decision-making from an 18-month-old was limited, and Turner was not allowed to proceed to Lhasa: his brief mission to Tibet did little to break the stranglehold of the Chinese and Kashmiris over trade with Tibet. But Turner's report, published in 1800, was used as a reference work on Tibet for a century. Oddly, Bogle's notes did not see the light of day until their publication double with Manning's notes in the 1876 volume edited by Markham.

Bogle was only 34 when he died. He left behind two young daughters who were sent to be educated in Scotland at the Bogle family estate. And herein lies a mystery: the ethnic origin of their mother is not revealed in any papers left by Bogle. By some accounts, she was a 'souvenir' from his Tibetan visit; others claim she was Bogle's Indian mistress. Bogle's family descendents believe he acquired a Tibetan wife: although there is no trace of such a liaison in his journals or correspondence, women of concubine status often went unrecorded in British India.

In 1810, Manning had found his way to Calcutta through the assistance of the East India Company, but there was a falling-out of sorts. The Company probably figured that a man as wacky as Manning would never make it through to Lhasa. And if he did, would they want maniacal Manning to negotiate deals for them? The upshot of all this was that the Company would not back Manning or provide any assistance.

When he set off for Tibet in September of 1811, Manning was on no official mission: he had no agenda in Tibet save his own. He was driven by intellectual curiosity and his desire to get to Peking. He must have appeared harmless to the Tibetans, and the General was delighted with Manning's apothecary skills. Manning requested permission to be allowed to proceed to Lhasa—astonishingly, he was permitted to do so, in the company of Tibetan guides. Manning even acquired a new servant as cook—a young man with the improbable name of Sid, a Chinese Moslem in the service of the general who wished to return to Lhasa. While in Gyantse, Manning was greatly impressed by the Chinese meals he was served. Sid claimed full credit for these culinary delights—trying to curry favour to get himself back to Lhasa. It would later turn out that a Tibetan woman in the kitchen was the real talent. Sid couldn't cook worth a damn.

The General accompanied Manning's retinue partway and turned back to Gyantse. Manning was on his own. At this point, Manning was on hallowed ground: the last Europeans to see Lhasa were Capuchin

What Manning calls a 'whirligig' is a large prayer-wheel, spun by pilgrims at monasteries to send prayers heavenwards

friars, who were expelled from Lhasa in 1745 after the failure of their mission. Manning was on new ground, in a new world. There was no English vocabulary for the phenomena that Manning was seeing and experiencing, so he improvised. 'Whirligigs' (an oblique English reference to a child's toy) was the term he irreverently used to describe the portable prayer-wheels twirled by pilgrims on their way to sacred sites, or else to refer to large fixed wheels found at temples and entrances:

> There were whirligigs set up in the house, which the conductor piously twirled as he passed them. I do not know whether it was expected of me to twirl these machines. I certainly never did all the time I was in Tibet...

In his journal, Manning records a historic crossing of the Tsangpo, the river that was to preoccupy British geographers for a century. The anxiety-ridden Manning, however, is more concerned with seating arrangements than with geographic riddles:

> I could not sit still, but must climb about, seat myself in various postures on the parapet, and lean over. The master of the boat was alarmed, and sent a steady man to hold me tight. I pointed to the ornamental prow of the boat, and assured them I could

The Potala Palace shimmers in the distance like a castle from a storybook

> sit there with perfect safety, and to prove to them how commo-
> diously I was seated, bent my head and body down the outside
> of the boat to the water's edge; but finding, by their renewed
> instances to me to resist, that I made them uneasy, I went back to
> my place and seated myself quietly.

Manning appears to have suffered from restless-leg syndrome, which makes it impossible for a person to sit still during the day—and can cause jumpy legs during sleep at night. The Tibetans must have thought Manning a strange bird indeed.

In December 1811, Manning finally reached the outskirts of Lhasa. In the distance, he sighted the lofty Potala Palace:

> The road here, as it winds past the palace is royally broad; it
> is level and free from stones, and combined with the view of
> the lofty towering palace, which forms a majestic mountain of
> building, has a magnificent effect. The roads about the palace
> swarmed with monks; its nooks and angles with beggars loung-
> ing and basking in the sun. This again reminded me of what I
> have heard of Rome. My eye was almost perpetually fixed on the
> palace, and roving over its parts, the disposition of which being
> irregular, eluded my attempts at analysis. As a whole it seemed
> perfect enough; but I could not comprehend its plan in detail. Fif-
> teen or twenty minutes now brought us to the entrance of the
> town of Lhasa.

Apart from the Potala description, Manning's journal records the momentous arrival in the Forbidden City with these words: 'Our first care was to provide ourselves with proper hats.' Thus starts the first eyewitness account of Lhasa by an Englishman. Off they went to the hatter, who measured their heads for custom-made headgear. It is not clear from the diary whether Manning was aware that caps, hats and intricate hairstyles were part of a complex dress code denoting rank and social status. A minister, for instance, wore a brocade cap with a tassel for ceremonies, and a round fur cap while in his office. Servants could wear a wide-brimmed hat with red tassels around it, but only a minister could wear the same hat ringed with fur. Aristocratic women were weighed down with jewellery—their elaborate headdresses decorated with coral and pearl, their ears bearing ornaments of turquoise. Lhasa's streets were crowded with pilgrims and traders dressed in a wide array of costumes from various parts of the Tibetan realm—with competition and jostling in the noisy downtown bazaar.

While the Holy City impressed from a distance, up close it stank. Garbage piled up in the streets—which also served as sewers since there was no plumbing system. Dead animals were tossed into refuse piles to be fought over by ravens and other scavengers. The refuse was only removed once a year—transferred to the fields as fertilizer. Mangy dogs infested with lice roamed the streets. Not exactly Shangri-La, as Manning noted:

Hairstyles in old Tibet denoted a complex system of rank. This movie actress models aristocratic Gyantse-style haute coiffure, supported by a bamboo frame—which takes the cake for patience, due to large number of hours required in preparation time.

Monastic hat to ward off the fierce sun

The magnificent masonry of the Potala Palace towers above Lhasa

> If the palace exceeded my expectations, the town as far fell short
> of them. There is nothing striking, nothing pleasing in its appear-
> ance. The habitations are begrimed with smut and dirt. The
> avenues are full of dogs, some growling and gnawing bits of hide
> which lie about in profusion, and emit a charnel-house smell;
> other limping and looking livid; others ulcerated; others starving
> and dying, and pecked at by the ravens; some dead and preyed
> upon. In short, everything seems mean and gloomy, and excites
> the idea of something unreal.

In Lhasa, Manning's bluff was almost called on a visit to the Chinese
amban's entourage. The amban was the representative of the Chinese emperor in Lhasa. Appearing in the court of the Tartar mandarin, Manning promptly performed a kowtow—falling to his knees and
touching the floor with his brow. It was well-known that Englishmen
were far too proud to kowtow to any Chinese, so this immediately
allayed suspicion. The very first Chinese mission to China, in 1793,
is said to have failed because British envoy Lord McCartney refused
to prostrate himself before Emperor Qianlong. Imperial Chinese protocol demanded that he touch the ground with his forehead no less
than nine times in the manner expected of ambassadors from vassal
states—and McCartney would have none of it.

Manning didn't care about pride—he would do whatever protocol demanded. Fortunately for Manning, the Tartar mandarin was half-blind. But there was a heart-stopping moment when one of the high officers stared at Manning for a long time and asked if he'd ever been to Canton. Manning was struck speechless by the question, but the Munshi quickly replied on his behalf that he had never seen the city—which got Manning off the hook. The Munshi came in handy sometimes.

Kowtowing was among Manning's survival tactics. He had no qualms about doing whatever was necessary in local custom to make his presence acceptable, whether it be kowtowing or throwing himself full-length on the floor—as was the Tibetan custom in temples. 'When in the temples of Bengal, if there were natives about, I always made a salam'. Salaam-ing here means full-length body prostration with face to floor—excellent practice for Tibet. Manning enthusiastically embraced Asian clothing habits and any customs involving religious formalities, but it was all cosmetic. Although he had no desire to embrace Tibetan religion (or any other religion), Manning threw himself to the ground before the principal statue in the Jokang, Lhasa's holiest temple.

Such practices endeared him to the holiest man in Tibet: the Dalai Lama. Shortly after his arrival in Lhasa, Manning obtained an unprecedented audience with the 9th Dalai Lama, a boy of seven years old. Summoned to the Potala, Manning frantically searched in his bags for suitable gifts to present. He looked for things that would be rare to find in Lhasa: Smith's lavender water, Nankin tea, fine broadcloth, and a pair of brass candlesticks. These actually belonged to the East India Company and had been lent to Manning in Calcutta: somehow they had been accidentally packed in his baggage by his valet. Manning wrote in his journal that he hoped the East India Company would not only acquit him of fraudulent practices, but would be very pleased with the honourable use to which their candlesticks had been put. He was offering the Dalai Lama stolen goods.

With the Munshi acting as his valet and interpreter, Manning made the long and tedious ascent up the 400 steps of the Potala—exhausting at this altitude—and eventually arrived at the Dalai Lama's Audience Hall. When he was finally ushered into the presence of the god-king, Manning faced a delicate protocol problem: ahead was the youthful Dalai Lama, seated on his high throne, while beside him on a lower seat was the powerful Regent, a middle-aged monk in maroon and yellow dress. Not sure how much ceremony was required, or what kind, or to whom, Manning immediately flung himself in front of the Dalai Lama's throne and performed three kowtows, touching the ground three times with his head. And for good measure, he repeated the same kowtows for the Regent. This performance seems to have passed muster with the rulers of Tibet. Manning was probably not aware of the exact protocol, but in the 17th century, the first Westerners to ever reach Lhasa—the Jesuit missionaries Grueber and d'Orville—did not meet the Dalai Lama of the day because they made it very clear that they would not prostrate themselves before the god-king.

Manning proceeded to offer his gifts, putting silk scarves with his own hands into the hands of Dalai Lama and the Regent. While he was doing so, he heard an ominous sound in the background: the Munshi, his nervous servant, had fallen and caused one of the gifts—the bottle of lavender water—to smash. Manning noted that the air was perfumed with lavender water, but he ignored the incident. Manning then took off his new hat, and humbly offered his clean-shaven head for the Grand Lama to lay his hands upon—the highest blessing possible in the Land of Snows:

> The Lama's beautiful and interesting face and manner engrossed almost all my attention. He was at that time about seven years old: had the simple and unaffected manners of a well-educated princely child. His face was, I thought, poetically and affectingly beautiful. He was of a gay and cheerful disposition; his beautiful mouth perpetually unbending into a graceful smile, which illuminated his whole countenance.

What the Dalai Lama made of Manning's face we will never know, but with his clean-shaven head, long beard, long nose and Chinese spectacles, he must have looked quite arresting. Seated on cushions placed well below the level of the Dalai Lama's throne, Manning and the Munshi were served some buttered tea, and while Manning rated this 'most excellent', he was astonished to see the cup whipped away from him before he was able to drain it.

The interview must've been quite circuitous: questions were posed by Manning in Latin, which was translated by the Munshi into Chinese, then picked up by a second translator and rendered into Tibetan. Replies were returned through the same language chain. Discussion was mostly small talk, although Manning sensed that the Regent was highly curious about the outer world. When asked by the Dalai Lama if he had met with 'molestations and difficulties on the road', Manning replied that he had encountered many, but now that he was in the presence of the Grand Lama, his troubles were amply compensated. Manning notes that the Grand Lama was most pleased by this answer. After making a request for assistance in learning more about the religion and history of Tibet, Manning and his valet took their leave, making their way backward out of the presence of the Grand Lama:

> I was extremely affected by this interview with the Lama. I could have wept through strangeness of sensation. I was absorbed in reflections when I got home… I strove to draw the Lama; and though very inexpert with the pencil, I produced a beautiful face, but it did not satisfy me. I drew another which I could not make handsome, yet there was in some respects a likeness in it which the other wanted. From the two together, and instructions from me, a skilful painter might make a good picture of him.

Unfortunately, the sketches mentioned did not survive, or else Manning kept them secret. The rich visual knowledge that Manning possessed—about the inside of the Potala, the face of the Dalai Lama—could easily have been passed on to a huge audience in Europe, but Manning dodged the task.

The journal at this point shows a change of heart in Manning's attitude toward the Tibetans. He had arrived bearing the Chinese disdain of the 'barbarian Tibetans' but now he was becoming charmed by their frankness and their bizarre ways. He was soon charmed by Tibetan women too: a few of them visited to consult him on medical matters, or so it seemed:

> I had two handsome, well-dressed, clean-washed lasses come to my lodging with their mother to consult me. I could not find out that there was anything the matter with them, except superabundance of health and spirits. It was so long since I had seen female charms of this order that feeling their pulses rather disordered my own.

Manning asked many questions through his interpreter and gave the giggling young women 'something innocent' to take as medicine. A few days later they returned, bringing him a present of excellent mutton. Manning informed these high-spirited damsels that they were welcome to come back as often as they wanted, 'without bringing mutton or anything but their own pretty faces.'

It appears that the curiosity was mutual: the Tibetan damsels were from a rich merchant family and wanted to see Manning with their own eyes. That was Manning's appeal: he was the talk of the town—a great novelty for Tibetan monks and aristocrats. Everybody was keen to see this tall, long-nosed, fair-skinned phantom. With his flowing beard and Chinese gowns, he must've looked like Merlin the Magician—or, to give that a more Tibetan slant, Merlin the Grand Wizard.

Italian photographer Fosco Maraini summed it up this way:

> The Tibetans are really xenophobes of a most curious kind. Their xenophobia is exclusively abstract and theoretical. They close their country to foreigners, and the most rigorous laws are issued from Lhasa to keep them out, but when a white man arrives in their midst they greet him with enthusiasm and make a tremendous fuss of him.

Manning was allowed to remain in Lhasa for several months. Having contracted rheumatism, he never put on his skates—indeed, he seems to have forgotten about them. The rheumatism reached the point where Manning had to administer drugs to himself. And slowly he recovered. He was now running very low on funds, though his medical practice in Lhasa provided some handy income. For simple cases he provided free consultations, but for more complex cases—such as venereal disease—that involved 'expensive drugs', he charged the patient. Once, when a 'Chinaman' tried to settle for a lesser amount with a few coins, Manning took his money and flung it out the door, bidding him to go after it:

> He turned pale with anger; he advanced toward me in a menacing manner. I was on my legs in a moment and fronted him firmly. I told him if he came near me with his insolence, by heaven! I would knock him down. I believe I spoke English or Latin in my anger; but he pretty well understood me... The man poured out a torrent of abuse against me and my Munshi, very little of which I understood...

Luckily, the man's servants held him back, and then bore him off. The story spread around town, and from that time on, says Manning, he had no trouble in Lhasa 'with any man, Chinese or not.'

Manning's medical practice brought him into closer contact with the Tibetans. There was great rivalry between Tibetan and Chinese-style physicians in the capital: Manning introduced a third, untried option—Western medicine. He was able to visit Tibetan nobles, eager to try the novel cures. Language proved a major headache for Manning. On arrival in Lhasa, the Munshi had suddenly reverted to speaking only Latin, claiming that Manning spoke poor Peking-accented Chinese, which was an embarrassment. The real reason was probably that the Munshi thought it too dangerous to continue their Chinese lessons. Whatever the case, Manning was by now pretty much on non-speaking terms with the Munshi. In any case, the Munshi was contemptuous of Tibetans, so on these sorties Manning would usually take Sid, who spoke an atrocious pidgin Tibetan, or a Tibetan servant boy, who spoke vile Chinese.

Not all of Manning's patients benefited. The problem was that his patients—not familiar with his pills and potions—would rarely follow his prescriptions to the letter. He mentions in his journal that one of the Dalai Lama's personal physicians summoned him—sending two horses to bring Manning and servant up the back path to his apartment at the Potala Palace. The man complained of 'general debility.' Manning prescribed an oily mixture, a glass of wine, and a Spanish-fly blister. Manning visited several times, but found that the physician had either taken only half the prescribed medicine, or none at all. 'He was childish, they said; he did not like the taste or the smell [of the medicine].' Some time later, when Manning inquired after his health, an aide held out four fingers, indicating that he'd been dead for so many days.

Not that Tibetan medicines would have been much better. In Lhasa, pills made from the urine of the Dalai Lama were highly regarded to cure diseases, and the faeces—mixed with fragrant musk—was made into golden pills that were dispensed to believers (these might be worn as amulets). Tibetan medicine was based entirely on herbal cures, allied to belief in the curative powers of the Medicine Buddha. If a healing lama could not lay his hands on the required medicine, he would write the prescription on a piece of paper, burn it, and make the patient swallow the ashes; in other cases, a cure was sought by getting a high lama to spit on the affected part.

Another patient playing Russian roulette with remedies was an important Chinese official. He was old and decrepit, and had long

By dispatching envoys like Bogle to Tibet, the British East India Company was seeking new commercial opportunities. The musk deer was little known at the time. Tibetans used its hide for making saddlebags. Much later, the musk deer would become almost extinct due to excessive hunting for the male's musk pod. Musk is prized for its medicinal qualities and is used for the preparation of perfume.

Tibetan saddle rug, with musk-deer saddlebags, from the region of Mustang

been unwell, but the Munshi convinced Manning that if he could affect a cure, it would be easy to have himself admitted to Peking on account of the official's well-connected family. Manning was all ears. His medicine-man skills had got him this far—so why not all the way to Peking? There was, however, a slight problem: the mandarin was quite mad. Manning refers to him as 'the crackbrained mandarin' when describing their first meeting:

> He was uncombed, unwashed, beslimed with his own spittle and dirt, storming and scolding, and almost intractable.... The mad mandarin seemed rather to take a liking to me; he had me sit down, ordered tea for me, told me long unintelligible stories, and when I offered to go was uneasy, and bid me stay awhile. Sometimes he broke out into exclamations against his servants, and ordered them out of the room.

With a passage to Peking in mind, Manning set about applying a cure. But after trying a few drugs in vain, he decided that the chances of the patient becoming sane enough to help him reach Peking were extremely remote, so he didn't pay any more house calls. As it turned out, a month later, the crazy mandarin's condition deteriorated and he died.

Critically low on funds at this point, Manning started selling off his personal effects. He got rid of his useless servant, Sid, giving him a small donation to set up trade as a butcher. Manning managed some more audiences with the Regent and the Dalai Lama—at one of these, he presented the Dalai Lama with a telescope. In parting with the telescope, Manning was apparently trying to divest himself of any objects that could be considered spy gear. It's not clear whether he parted with his ice-skates.

By now, Manning's situation with the Chinese had taken a strange turn. As a minor, the Dalai Lama was under the austere control of the Regent, whom the Chinese delegates were attempting to manipulate. And the Chinese mandarin from Canton hated Europeans. A lot of questions were being asked about Manning. Who was he, and what was he doing in Lhasa? Manning had never revealed he was English: he was now posing now as a light-skinned trader from Calcutta—though everyone knew Calcutta was British, and they knew Manning was not of Indian blood. The man was under suspicion of being either a spy for the British, or, worse, a missionary—come to do the work that the Capuchins had been expelled for 60 years before.

Suddenly, around mid-February 1812, the journal stops after some ominous reflections on the prospect of torture. His valet, the Munshi, turned up on his doorstep in chains with a Chinese guard escort: this was the Chinese way of scaring Manning. It's not clear from the journal why the valet was arrested, but most likely on the grounds of associating with a foreigner and tutoring him in the forbidden Chinese language. In any case, Manning got the message: his number was up. His bizarre quest to reach Peking was at an end. And his life was in grave danger. He decided to repair, post-haste, to India. He saddled up and thundered off southward, retracing his path back through Bhutan to Calcutta.

Manning did not tarry long in Calcutta. Having failed to win the backing of the East India Company for his Tibetan venture, he was by now so mad at them that he refused to say anything about his trip. He moved along by boat to Canton.

The prize of Lhasa had fallen to a man who never wanted it—Lhasa was simply a stepping-stone en route to his dream destination: Peking. He had by no means given up on that dream. It caused him to linger a few years in Canton instead of setting sail for England again. He bided his time. In 1817, the chance finally came his way. He was offered a place to join a British Embassy delegation to Peking as an interpreter. The East India Company was banking on this delegation to open China to trade. But Manning's Chinese gowns and long beard were considered un-diplomatic material by the some in the British camp, and negotiation opened up on this. It was decided one or the other had to go: Manning agreed to dispense with his long Chinese gowns for English dress on the condition that he be allowed to keep his flowing beard.

Manning finally reached the city of his dreams—Peking—but only stayed briefly, as the mission was aborted following an argument over protocol. Upon arrival in Peking, the British were immediately rushed into a meeting with the Emperor: however, as they were tired, they refused to go. Following this, the temperamental Emperor decided to call off the meeting entirely. That meant Manning had very limited time to explore Peking. But he did try to get around. Impeded by a river with no bridge, he started swearing in Chinese. Sir John Davis, a member of the British mission, picks up the story:

> Being one day roused by strange shouting, I went out and discovered it was Manning who, wishing to cross the water, and finding nobody who would attend to him, commenced a series of howls like a dog, supplemented by execrations derived from the Chinese vernacular. This led our attendant mandarins very naturally to infer that he was mad, and they lost no time in conveying him over the river to the other side, which is all he wanted.

Sorely disappointed by his Peking venture, Manning set sail again for England, stopping en route to interview the exiled Napoleon on the island of St Helena (Manning reminded Napoleon that he was the only Englishman to whom he granted a passport in 1803). On his return to England, Manning lived in a cottage devoid of furniture but containing the best Chinese library in Britain. Through his good friend Charles Lamb, Manning mixed with high literary circles—Lamb's soirées included Wordsworth and Coleridge. But at these people were puzzled by Manning, who had committed nothing to paper. In 1826, he finally got round to contributing something to a magazine—he wrote up some Chinese jokes in translation. This was Manning the joker's idea of sharing his wealth of knowledge. Quixotic to the end, Manning spent his time in study and meditation. His mighty beard, now waist-length, had turned white. He died in 1840. His great Chinese library was donated to the Royal Asiatic Society, where it was showcased as 'The Manning Collection'.

Manning added zero to geographers' knowledge of Tibet, which was embarrassingly slim. But although Manning did not map or measure, this accidental explorer succeeded where many others failed: he reached Lhasa, the most elusive prize of Asian exploration. And while Manning considered his Tibetan venture a total failure, the journey would easily have catapulted him to the first ranks of English explorers—if he had bothered to speak about it, or write a detailed account. Even the greatest explorers of the era, travelling in disguise, failed to reach the sacred city of Lhasa. The famed Russian explorer Nikolai Prejevalsky and the legendary Swedish explorer Sven Hedin were both unmasked and repulsed close to Lhasa.

Toward 1900, Western explorers intensified efforts to bluff their way through to Lhasa. Two of them managed to break through.

Japanese Buddhist monk Ekai Kawaguchi set off into Tibet from Mustang in 1899, with two sheep for company. Kawaguchi sometimes posed as a Chinese doctor—using the same ploy as Manning—and sometimes posed as a Tibetan pilgrim. Since Kawaguchi possessed an Asiatic face—a natural disguise—he was given scant credit for his feat, even though his journey through Tibet took three years and he reached both Lhasa and Mount Kailash.

Around the same time—in 1901—a Russian student, Gombozhab Tsybikov, reached Lhasa and a number of monasteries in central Tibet. Tsybikov worked from the Mongolian end of things—he was a member of the Buriat intelligentsia. On a mission for the Imperial Geographical Society of St Petersburg, Tsybikov travelled from Amdo disguised as a Buriat lama and stayed for a year in Tibet undetected. Remarkably, he used his camera surreptitiously and returned to Russia with some of the earliest images of Lhasa ever captured. He also brought back a number of Tibetan texts, and made notes on the Tibetan practices of polyandry, and on population, army and government. All of which earned him the Imperial Geographical Society's Prejevalsky Medal.

Apart from those efforts, in the entire 19th century only two other Europeans succeeded in reaching Lhasa—French missionaries Huc and Gabet in 1846. Disguised as Tibetan lamas, the two priests launched an epic two-year effort to reach Lhasa from the northeast, on a mission to convert Tibet to the Lazarist faith.

Remarkably, they survived a crossing of the Northern Plateau, known as the Changtang—a vast windswept region with one of the harshest climates on the planet. Huc and Gabet later described how they lived for two months off the bland Tibetan diet of barley flour dipped in yak-butter tea and rolled into balls. To prevent the balls from freezing, the Frenchmen put them in pouches, which were kept next to their bodies inside a woollen garment, wrapped in a fox-skin garment, enclosed in a lambskin jacket, enclosed in a thick sheepskin robe. And their balls still froze. Lhasa for Lazarists was not to be: after spending less than two months in the sacred city, the two missionaries were expelled on the initiative of the Chinese Resident—repeating a pattern that occurred with Manning.

Among the roll call of explorers who tried to get to Lhasa in the late 19th century are the Russians (Prejevalsky, Kosloff, Ruborovsky), the Americans (the Littledales, Rockhill), the French (Bonvalot, d'Orleans, Grenard) and Swedish explorer Sven Hedin. None got within ten days' march of the sacred city. The second Englishman to enter the 'ground of the gods' was Colonel Francis Younghusband, who reached Lhasa in August 1904. His style was rather different from Manning's: he rode through the West Gate of Lhasa at the head of a long column of troops. The British invaded Tibet with a force of 100 Englishmen, 1,150 Gurkhas and Sikhs, 10,000 porters, and some 20,000 beasts of burden—on the pretext of opening the place to trade.

Kintup
1849–1914

Tinker, Tailor, Pilgrim, Spy

Portrait of a forgotten hero: Kintup in later life, with bare feet, scraggly goatee—and prayer-beads around his neck. This rare photograph was taken in Simla in 1914, when Eric Bailey interviewed Kintup about his Herculean feats.

Mission Impossible on the Tsangpo

❖ The case of the phantom waterfall ❖

By the 1870s, the riddle of where Tibet's mighty Tsangpo River flowed had bedevilled British geographers for a century. Intent on unlocking the secrets of the Tsangpo, the British dispatched an undercover agent codenamed KP—short for Kintup, a tailor from Sikkim. He was outfitted with surely the strangest equipment ever used by the Survey of India. Faced with huge setbacks and insurmountable odds, the courageous explorer battled on. Here is the tale of Kintup the lion-hearted, a man who just wouldn't give up. Kintup charted unknown swathes of the Tsangpo through massive gorges, but instead of solving the problem of where the mighty river flowed, he inadvertently sparked another chase—the quest for a giant waterfall.

ON NOVEMBER 17, 1884, a bedraggled figure showed up in the bazaar of Darjeeling in northeast India. His face bore the look of a man who had been out in the sun far too long. He had an incredible tale to tell. His name was Kintup: he had been dispatched by the British on a top-secret mission into eastern Tibet under the codename KP. Because he'd been gone more than four years, Kintup was given up for dead. It was assumed that agent KP had met some sort of grisly end—arrested or executed by the Tibetans, killed by bandits, or simply perished in some high-altitude accident. But Kintup had miraculously made it back, ready to deliver his report to his British spymasters.

If Kintup was hoping for a silver handshake, a gold watch, a few medals and a generous pat on the back, he was in for a rude shock: he met silence. Somehow his mission had gone tragically wrong. The man who had launched the mission—his trusting British overseer, Captain Harman of the Survey of India—had died. Kintup burbled some fantastic story about launching 500 logs into a river in Tibet, but nobody seemed to believe him. Devastated, Kintup beat a humble retreat to the bazaar and resumed his former trade: tailoring.

Kintup was a player in what was dubbed the 'Great Game'. Actually, he was an unofficial employee with the Survey of India. Back in the 1860s the chaps at the Survey of India were very annoyed with the upstart Tibetans, who kept ruining their gigantic map-making project by rebuffing their surveyors. The Tibetans themselves had no need for maps—they navigated by landmarks and key monasteries. By 1860, the British, who had taken the lead as topographers in Tibet, still had no precise location or elevation for Lhasa. While mapping of India was proceeding at a brisk pace, knowledge of Tibet had not advanced much beyond the D'Anville map of 1733, apart from a few morsels thrown in by Bogle and Turner.

In a huge enterprise, starting around 1800, the British set about mapping the entire Indian subcontinent. In 1818, the project was officially named the Great Trigonometrical Survey of India (abbreviated in this text as the 'Survey of India'). The project was more than 80 years in the making—and must have confounded Indians as they watched Brits roving around on camels or elephants measuring things with huge telescopes, and using the new-fangled method of triangulation. The scope of the project was flabbergasting: a precision instrument known as The Great Theodolite was imported from England—it weighed half a ton and required a dozen men to shift it. The Great Theodolite suffered the indignity of several disastrous falls when being hauled to higher ground, and had to be rebuilt several times. For a single mapping reconnaissance into the difficult region of Hindustan in 1833, George Everest set off in command of five assistants, four elephants, 42 camels, 30 horses—and some 700 natives (this number dwindled after natives abandoned their posts when chased by wild tigers and rogue elephants).

By the early 1880s, the principal triangulation of the subcontinent was finished: the British had mapped most of India, except for the far north where the Himalayas lay. Triangulation provided accurate delineation of river valleys, mountain ranges and passes—the foundation for more minute topographical surveys needed for military purposes. Indeed, the principal motivation behind the creation of such massive mapping data was not the noble quest of exploration, or a love of valleys and mountains. It was driven purely by military objectives.

Throughout the 19th century, the colonial juggernauts of Tsarist Russia and British India had been jousting with each other across Central Asia. At the beginning of the century, vast distances separated the two, but by the 1890s only a thin strip of Afghan territory prevented Russian and India from sharing a common frontier. In the intervening years, a struggle for military and political supremacy— dubbed the 'Great Game'—was under way in Central Asia. This cat-and-mouse intrigue was played out in Afghanistan and Persia, in the vast deserts of Turkestan, and in frozen wastes of the Pamir and Hindu Kush ranges.

Bar the Canadian-American border, the border of British India was the largest in the British Empire. No firm boundaries had been established by India, Afghanistan, Persia or Tibet. With the Tsarist Russians steadily advancing into Central Asia—capturing the khanates of Khiva, Kokand and Bukhara by the 1880s—the British feared a possible Russian invasion of India. Or a Russian take-over of Tibet. And Tibet shared a border with British India that stretched almost the entire length of the Himalayas—apart from the border shared with the independent kingdom of Nepal.

Tibet was a mysterious buffer zone—a great blank on the map, lying strategically between the great powers of Russia, British India and China. The Chinese knew that if the British or colonial arch-rivals the Russians drafted maps of the region, it would enable them to extend their influence there. On xenophobic Chinese advice, the Tibetans enforced a policy that no European should enter Tibet unau-thorized—on pain of death. It seemed that no Brit in disguise could fool the Tibetans (these were the days before coloured contact lenses). Besides which, a British agent might get himself killed or mutilated, which would be cause for a costly and tiresome revenge mission by the military.

In 1862, Captain Thomas Montgomerie of the Survey of India devised an ingenious strategy. Having observed that Indian pilgrims were permitted to visit sacred places in Tibet, and that Indian traders were allowed to venture across the border, he hit on the idea of train-ing Indian agents to gather intelligence. This notion had in fact been put into practice much earlier by British surveyors: what distinguished Montgomerie's approach was the ingenuity of the surveying equip-ment devised—and the ambitious scope of his plan.

These native explorers—later to become known as 'pundits'—were codenamed by letters or numbers to protect their identity. They were known as Agent A, or Agent B, or Number 9. If that sounds like a James Bond precursor, these men were not trained in martial arts or firing weapons—their self-defence method consisted entirely of the fine art of camouflage. Their training was with compass, sextant and boiling-point thermometer.

But their main mapping equipment was their feet. They trained to accurately pace out a mile with even steps. To blend in and escape detection, they posed as Hindu pilgrims or traders, carrying the strang-est equipment ever used by surveyors. A Tibetan pilgrim normally car-ries an amulet, a prayer-bead rosary and a prayer-wheel. Amulets are usually worn around the neck on a string, and might show (or enclose) a picture of a high lama or religious figure. The rosary is used for counting off recitations of sacred prayers, known as mantras, and has 108 beads. And the prayer-wheel is a hand-held device, mounted on a short stick: the rotating head is embossed with the sacred mantra *Om Mani Padme Hum*, and inside this are similar scriptures on paper. Turn-ing the wheel constantly is believed to replicate reading the sacred scriptures inside.

The only wheel in use in old Tibet was the eight-spoked Wheel of the Law, parked on top of temple entrances, framed by two deer

The prayer-wheel was the only wheel in constant use in old Tibet—either as a huge fixed prayer-wheel—embossed with sacred mantras that were spun by pilgrims at monasteries—or the miniature handheld version. Here was a culture that knew about the wheel and knew what it could do, but chose to ignore this technological advance because the wheel happened to be a sacred symbol. The eight-spoked wheel of the dharma is seen atop all Tibetan monasteries, symbolic of the teachings of Buddha. Inside a monastery are likely to be frescoes to assist with meditation—including the six-spoked Wheel of Life (showing the six realms of karmic reincarnation) and various mandalas—often circular in form. But the wheel was not used for any practical purpose in Tibet—ancient prophecy held that the use of the wheel would scar the surface of the earth, releasing evil spirits.

The Indian explorers carried the regular pilgrim gear, but instead of the 108-bead Tibetan *mala* (rosary) theirs had 100 beads, with certain modifications. Every tenth bead was slightly larger than the rest—but since pilgrim malas often employ divider beads of a different colour, there was nothing really unusual in this.

The explorer's rosary beads were used for counting off regular paces to determine distance covered. Here's how the system might work. After walking 10 paces, the 'surveyor' would drop a single bead. Counting off the beads this way, after 100 paces he would drop the larger bead. He would plod on until he measured off a full circuit of the rosary, marking 1,000 paces. Flipping the rosary around and counting in reverse order, two full turns around the rosary would then be equivalent to 2,000 paces—which translated into exactly one mile for a walker who had painstakingly practiced such pacing. Each mile could then be 'recorded' in a set of tiny silver beads that formed a small extension of the rosary.

Tibetan rosaries usually have a pair of counter strings attached to count tens and hundreds of completed *mala* cycles—each string is a double-plaited cord threaded with 10 tiny ring beads of silver. Once a mile had been walked, drop a silver ring bead. So 10 miles could be recorded this way. And on the second set of silver ring beads, multiples of 10 miles could be racked up—with a maximum capacity of 100 miles. It was akin to using an abacus in a kind of focused walking meditation—a monotonous and maddening method to obtain survey data, but somehow it achieved fairly accurate results. Another version of the bead counting used 100 paces before dropping a single bead, so the full rosary would represent 10,000 paces, or five miles.

Call it the mapmaker's mantra. Constantly counting beads like this for weeks on end would not raise a single eyebrow in a land where pilgrims may aspire to reciting a certain mantra as many as 100,000 or even a million times. The mantra could be a sacred syllable, or series of syllables, recited in silent fashion, or whispered or mumbled under the breath. Apart from counting mantra recitations, the Tibetan rosary is used for counting prostrations, circumambulations and other devotional practices. The rosary aids in focusing concentration and awareness: the regular 108 beads of the Tibetan *mala* ensure that at least a hundred mantra recitations have been completed in a full rosary turning (the eight extra beads are to allow for forgetfulness). Rosaries are usually made of wood, lotus seeds or Bodhi seeds, but can be made of many other materials—crystal, lapis lazuli or mother of pearl. Some rosaries are intended for specific purposes: for 'power activity', for instance, a *mala* of 50 beads of coral, copper or red sandalwood is recommended. And a *mala* made of human bone or animal bone is intended for use only by accomplished yogins—since ritual objects crafted of bone are believed to harbour karmic influences.

The native explorer's neck-amulet cleverly concealed a miniature compass for recording bearings of rivers and mountains passed. A hollow walking-stick hid a miniature boiling-point thermometer, used to determine elevation. The inside of a Tibetan prayer-wheel normally holds a long scroll of paper with the sacred mantra *Om Mani*

Padme Hum inscribed on it: by spinning the wheel, the pilgrim is setting
that prayer in motion. Hidden inside
the explorer model was a blank scroll
on which measurements and map
data could secretly be recorded: this
secret logbook could easily be gotten
at by removing the top of the prayer-
wheel cylinder—discreetly, of course.
An explorer could be gone for several
years, with some cash advanced, and
a bonus promised if he returned with
the goods—if he returned.

Montgomerie set about training
the first batch of native explorers at
the Survey of India HQ in Dehra Dun
in 1863. Showing great promise was
Nain Singh, a schoolmaster from the
village of Milam, nestled at over 11,000

Hand-held prayer-wheels are commonly twirled by Tibetan pilgrims:
the inside of the prayer-wheel was
modified to store secret data by the
pundit-explorers

feet in the region of Kumaon, near the Tibetan border. The British had
annexed the Kumaon region in 1816, giving them a border with Tibet
for the first time. Nain Singh was a Bhotia—ethnically from a tribal
group of Tibetan origin who traded with Tibetans in the west. Bho-
tias were hardy—able to carry heavy loads at high altitude—and Nain
Singh could read and write Tibetan. He was about 33 when he was
recruited and dispatched to Dehra Dun for training. To preserve ano-
nymity, he was codenamed 'the pundit' (meaning 'schoolmaster' or
'learned Hindu'). The term *pundit* was later generalised to embrace all
Indian explorers of the Survey of India.

After two years of training—during which Nain Singh perfected
the art of walking a mile in an even 2,000 paces—Montgomerie figured the 'pundit' was ready. Nain Singh was advanced several years'
salary. In January 1865, he joined a caravan heading toward Lhasa. An
arduous year later, he walked into the Sacred City. Using his secret
thermometer to take the temperature of water he boiled for tea, he
calculated the elevation of Lhasa at 11,700 feet—not far off its correct
height of 11,800 feet. Posing as a pilgrim, Nain Singh survived by begging—he managed to stay in Lhasa for three months. He had to dodge
detection—and after witnessing the execution of an interloper without permission to be in Lhasa, he decided it was time to move on. In

April 1866 the pundit joined a westbound caravan, charting a 500-mile route along the Tsangpo River on his way westward to India. Then he slipped across the border, back to Survey of India HQ in Dehra Dun.

The British spymasters were thrilled with the success of Singh's mission—in particular, the prize of reaching Lhasa. He had covered over 1,200 miles on foot and calculated precise locations of more than 30 sites. Nain Singh was given a gold watch by the RGS in 1868—but this was stolen from him six months later by a Pathan he was training. His survey notes enabled Captain Montgomerie to compile, in 1868, a rudimentary route map from Nepal to Lhasa. Captain Montgomerie was promoted to deputy superintendent of the Survey of India. He was, in addition, appointed the official 'in charge of trans-Himalayan exploring parties'—which gave him carte blanche to send in more pundits. Due to failing health, however, Montgomerie was not able to see many of his plans for exploration come to fruition. He left India in 1873, never to return—he died in England in 1878. Montgomerie's work with the pundits was carried on by his protégé, General James Walker, and by Captain Henry Trotter of the Survey of India. The pundits, who must qualify as the most patient champion walkers of all time—counting beads and surveying on foot—were trained by men with names like Walker and Trotter.

Nain Singh had bought back answers about the map of Tibet, but also brought back questions and conundrums. Chief among them was the course of the Tsangpo River: did it flow through the mountains to turn into the mighty Brahmaputra River? The riddle of the Tsangpo had bedevilled British geographers already for over a century. The 18th-century D'Anville map from France showed the Tsangpo flowing into the Irrawaddy, descending into Burma. This view was supported by missionaries in China. A second school of thought vigorously backed the idea that the Tsangpo carved a huge southward turn and flowed into the Brahmaputra and out through the Bay of Bengal. The question had provoked considerable debate between English and French scholars from the 1820s onward. And there was always the possibility that neither link was correct: to the eastern fringe of the Tibetan plateau, in a space of less than sixty leagues, the Brahmaputra, the Irrawaddy, the Salween, the Mekong and the Yangtse run all bottled together, carving deep furrows as they charge down from the highlands off the plateau.

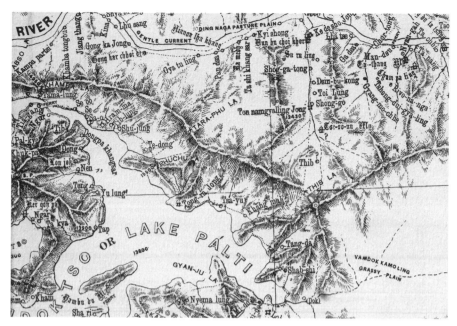

Using new intelligence collected by pundit-explorers, this 1885 British map shows Lake Yamdrok Tso (aka Lake Palti) as pincer-shaped, rather than circular as on all previous maps of Tibet. Other parts of the map indicate 'unexplored', or 'probable course' (for a river).

Nain Singh's next mission was to tackle this riddle. He was dispatched from India in 1874 with a rather tall order: to follow the length of the Tsangpo. Starting in the far west, he managed to trace the river all the way to Tsetang, east of Lhasa—a remarkable feat. In Tsetang, he ran out of energy and funds and headed home, south over the Himalayas. Worn out from his travails, Nain Singh decided to throw the towel in and retire to training other pundits.

Luckily for those he was training, the Tibetans had no counter-intelligence. In an amazing breach of security, Montgomerie had sent full details of the 1865 reconnaissance of Nain Singh and his fixing of the position of Lhasa for publication. The results appeared in the Journal of the Royal Geographical Society in early 1868. The pundit's name was not revealed, but his methods were. The magazine was distributed to members only, but it had international subscribers—including Russian rivals, who followed it for news about Tibet.

One of those Russians, Colonel Nikolai Mikhailovich Prejevalsky, showed the RGS Journal to the Tibetans. In 1870, Prejevalsky (also rendered as Przewalski, Prjevalski or Przhevalsky) was dispatched by the Imperial Geographical Society of St Petersburg on a mission to the unknown region of southern Mongolia. Prejevalsky was a man of many talents—explorer, naturalist, crack marksman. He teamed up with fellow army officer, Lieutenant Pyltseff. The mission ended up taking three years, covered 7,000 miles and encompassed much more than Mongolia—Prejevalsky continued on from Mongolia into China and northeastern Tibet. Camels loads of scientific instruments yielded valuable survey information, botanical collections and other data.

By 1872, Prejevalsky had reached the destination of his dreams—Lake Kokonor, at on the northeast fringe of Tibet. Here he stalked wild yaks—it took 13 bullets from this sharpshooter to bring down one enormous bull. The expedition had gotten much further than anyone ever expected, and while he was on a roll, Prejevalsky decided to gamble and shoot for Lhasa. He lost, heavily. He was defeated by the approach of a harsh winter—many of the camels in his caravan died. A glutton for punishment, Prejevalsky then chose to cross the Gobi Desert by an unexplored route, on the return trip to Russia. The party got lost in a sandstorm and nearly died of thirst—and suffered the loss of faithful expedition dog Faust, a robust hound that had accompanied them all the way. Prejevalsky was deeply affected by the loss of Faust.

In 1879, Prejevalsky was back to tackle Lhasa again. This time, he came along better prepared: he set off with the blessing of the Czar and with seven Cossack sharpshooters in his entourage—and he brought along pictures of Russian actresses to seduce officials. The officials were not impressed. A week's march from Lhasa, Prejevalsky was stopped by hundreds of warrior-monks: after a showdown with Tibetan officials, realised that he could not shoot his way through. But Prejevalsky's mission triumphed when it came to specimens of rare flora and fauna returned in the Russian's saddlebags. He came back with a great harvest of new plants, of which a handful are named after him—*Rhododendron przewalskii*, *Rosa przewalskii*. And in Mongolia, he discovered a species of primitive wild horse, christened *Equus przewalskii* in his honour.

Prejevalsky's disclosure of the RGS contents to the Tibetans was part of Great Game strategy—but also a case of sour grapes because he could not make it to Lhasa himself. Had the Tibetans realised the true worth of the RGS news that Prejevalsky had leaked, they could've easily acted upon it. But the Tibetans either overlooked or ignored the news. It would've been a simple matter for Tibetan frontier posts to start taking apart prayer-wheels and to check travellers' chests for false bottoms, but somehow this never occurred to them.

The RGS published more material on the native explorers in 1876, even revealing the name of their pundit prototype, Nain Singh.

The complete lack of Tibetan intelligence was an extremely lucky stroke for Nain Singh's trainees: had they had been unmasked, they most likely would have been imprisoned, tortured or executed—or suffered all three dire consequences. Incredibly, the pundit missions continued unhindered right through the early 1880s. The Russians, meanwhile, dispatched their own pundits—they put visiting Mongolian lamas to good use. Prejevalsky died in 1888 in the Tien Shan mountains while mounting yet another attempt to reach Lhasa: his research work in Central Asia was carried on by a rum bunch of Russian travellers—Pievzov, Potanin and the Grum-Grchimailo brothers.

Nain Singh was given a generous pension and a grant of land. In Calcutta in January 1878, he was officially presented with a gold watch from the Paris Geographical Society and the prestigious gold medal from the Royal Geographical Society. Considerable dissent was created in the ranks of the RGS over whether Nain Singh or his spymaster, Captain Trotter, should be eligible for the gold medal. The same day, Nain Singh was gazetted a Companion of the Order of the British Empire.

Although Nain Singh retired, exploring for the British blossomed into a family business for the remarkable Singh clan. Lots of exercise and fresh air, low pay—and the ominous threat of torture or execution if discovered. But the prospect of an empire medal or gold watch if return with secret cartographic data was successful.

There followed a profusion of agents with the surname Singh: among the high achievers were Nain Singh's brothers Kalian Singh (codenamed GK) and Nem Singh (codenamed GMN, using consonants from his name in reverse order), and Nain Singh's cousin Kishen Singh (codenamed AK).

In 1878, the Survey of India sent in GMN with a companion known as KP. The codename KP was comprised of the first and last letter of Kintup, a native from the mountains of upper Sikkim who worked as a tailor in Darjeeling. Kintup had an excellent command of Tibetan.

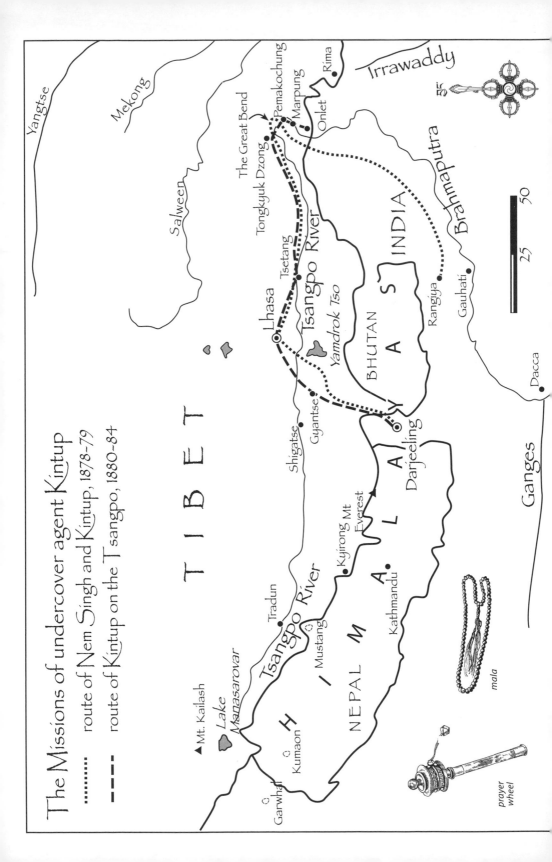

The Missions of undercover agent Kintup
········· route of Nem Singh and Kintup, 1878-79
▬ ▬ route of Kintup on the Tsangpo, 1880-84

prayer wheel

mala

25   50

Their quest was to report on uncharted sections of the Tsangpo. Starting from Darjeeling, the pair reached the upper end of the Tsangpo gorge in Tibet and the hamlet of Gyala, but impenetrable terrain beyond this caused them to abandon the quest.

Along the way, they discovered that the Tsangpo performs a very neat trick—it loops around and completely changes direction. This sharp U-turn in the Tsangpo became known as the Great Bend. The discovery of the Great Bend was the final piece of the geographer's jigsaw—the connection between the Tsangpo and the Brahmaputra made sense. But this still left the question of waterfalls. The Tsangpo thunders down deep canyons carved between two Himalayan giants—the peaks of Namche Barwa and Gyala Pelri. Comparing known elevations of the Tsangpo on the Tibetan plateau and its sister rivers in Assam, geographers calculated a seven- or eight-thousand foot drop. That could mean some spectacular waterfalls en route.

The forays by GMN and KP narrowed the unexplored gap on the Tsangpo River to about 100 miles, from Gyala in Tibet to Sadiya, a British outpost in Assam. Three rivers converged near Sadiya—the Dihang, Dibong and Lohit Brahmaputra—and any of these could be connected to the Tsangpo as far as was known in the 1870s.

Working upriver from Assam, British survey parties encountered a wall of dense jungle vegetation, as well as hostile Abhor tribesmen whom they described as nearly naked—with a flimsy covering over the lower part of the body—and always armed with a sword and bow. Lieutenant Henry Harman, of the Survey of India, who was in charge of the project, suffered from severely frostbitten feet after camping out at night on a pass on the Sikkim-Tibet border.

By the summer of 1880, Lieutenant Harman had given up on the survey parties from Assam. He decided to send in Kintup from the Tibetan end of things to investigate. Kintup was around 32 when he set off for the Tsangpo Gorges. He was briefed on two plans. The first was to follow the Tsangpo from Tibet all the way into India. Should that prove not possible, there was a contingency plan. For this part, Kintup was provided with the strangest kit of all. Apart from the standard pilgrim-spy-supplies, he was given a number of small metal tubes containing written papers, and a drill for making holes to fix the tubes into small logs. KP's mission was to cut up and mark 500 small logs, attach the metal tubes to identify them—and then launch them into the Tsangpo river over a period of a week, at a rate of 50 logs per day. If the logs found their way into India, the British could determine which river the Tsangpo flowed into when it reached the south.

Around this time there were a number of pundits secretly fanning out across Tibet to gather intelligence, mostly trained by Nain Singh. In 1880, Agent AK (Kishen Singh) reached Lhasa and made a detailed map of the sacred city and its surroundings. In 1881–82, SCD and UG were off exploring toward Lhasa. Agent SCD was Sarat Chandra Das, who was thrilled to be following in the footsteps of Thomas Manning. In 1876, Das had been given a copy of the newly published account by Clements Markham that included Manning's journals. Das says the book changed his life: he read it over and over again, kindling in his mind a burning desire to see Tibet and explore its vast unknown tracts.

Sarat Chandra Das was headmaster of Bhutia Boarding School, established in Darjeeling in 1874. The school was set up to educate Sikkimese boys in English to facilitate trade with Tibet, should Tibet open to the British—so they could work as interpreters and head sirdars. But a more secret object was to train spies of the geographic kind—the curriculum included lessons in surveying. Agent SCD had himself been given a course in surveying and observing by Nain Singh in 1879.

Few of the school's graduates ever entered Tibet on spying missions. The most celebrated agents from the school were headmaster Sarat Chandra Das himself, along with the school's teacher of Tibetan, Lama Ugyen Gyatso (codenamed UG). Disguised as pilgrims, they launched two long forays into Tibet in 1879 and 1881–82. Each carried surveying equipment, plus a gun and an umbrella. Both were highly educated: Sarat Chandra Das originally trained as an engineer and Ugyen Gyatso had been rigorously educated in a monastery in Sikkim.

In March 1882, at Drongtse in Central Tibet, Das met a beautiful 30-year-old woman called the Lhacham. She was married to two brothers of the powerful Palha family. He described her in glowing terms:

> At the foot of the ladder in the courtyard a white pony, with handsome housings of embroidered cloth and a Tartar saddle, awaited the Lhacham. With her pearl-studded headdress, her gold and ruby charm-boxes, her necklaces of coral and amber, and her clothes of satin and kinkab, she looked like a heroine of romance or a goddess.

Rare for the time, Das even took a photograph of the Lhacham—which lives up to the gushing prose. As the Lhacham was headed for Lhasa, she invited Das to ride with her small entourage and took him under her wing. When he fell seriously ill on the first leg of the journey, she arranged for him to rest up in the care of her half-sister, the abbess of Samding Monastery. Were it not for these guardian angels, Das might not have survived the journey—let alone have made it to Lhasa. Das visited the lovely Lhacham again at her opulent residence in Lhasa, but his time in Lhasa was cut short. He quickly turned back for India for two reasons: one was a smallpox outbreak; the other was the ominous rumble of a rumour that he was a spy for the British.

It was the reconnaissance of SCD and UG in Tibet that provided the backbone of intelligence for the British invasion some 20 years later. As well as being an eminent explorer, geographer, surveyor, lecturer and writer, Sarat Chandra Das was a master linguist whose voluminous Tibetan-English dictionary, first published in 1902, is a classic in its field.

Rudyard Kipling immortalised the pundits in the novel *Kim*: the character of secret agent Hurree Chunder Mookerjee (alias 'the Babu' or agent R17) was undoubtedly based on Sarat Chandra Das, while the character of Colonel Creighton was most likely based on Captain Thomas Montgomerie. Published in 1901, *Kim* is credited by many as the first spy story in the history of Western literature

The character of Mookerjee was revived much later in another classic book, *The Mandala of Sherlock Holmes: the Missing Years—His Exploits in India and Tibet as Faithfully Recorded by Hurree Chunder Mookerjee, CIE, FRS, FRGS, Rai Bahadur* by Jamyang Norbu (editor). Literature comes full circle: amazing but true, this novel is written by a Tibetan, Jamyang Norbu, with a mastery of Baker Street English. Arthur Conan Doyle, sick of his famous character, killed him off in 1891, and then, when tempted by a large amount of money to revive him, explained that Holmes had travelled in Tibet for two years, where he 'amused himself by visiting Lhassa.' But Conan Doyle did not elaborate any further.

Tibetan scholar and iconoclast Jamyang Norbu decided to fill in this two-year gap. Since it was well-known that Dr Watson did not make the trip over the Himalayas, Norbu borrowed Kipling's Mookerjee to serve as the great detective's sidekick, appropriately for a clandestine trip to Tibet. Their mission is to confront an arch-enemy who wields occult powers and who is bent on destroying the power of the

Dalai Lama. Generous snippets of Great Game politics embellish the story. The book is presented under the guise of a long-lost manuscript written by the great spy Sarat Chandra Das (alias Mookerjee) as discovered many years later among his papers in Darjeeling—by Jamyang Norbu, of course.

In 1887, when the Tibetans unmasked the true identity of the real-life spy Sarat Chandra Das, they severely punished those who had helped him. And this really marked the end of the pundit era. Sengchen Tulku, chief minister at the court of the Panchen Lama in Shigatse, was beaten, flogged daily in the marketplace, and then tossed in the Tsangpo River with his hands tied behind his back. This was the Tibetan way of avoiding the topic of killing—by saying that the river took him away. The Palha family of Gyantse had all their property confiscated: one family head was sent into exile, another was imprisoned for life; the family's servants were mutilated and left to die. The chief of Drongtse and his son were thrown into a dank dungeon in Lhasa—and only saw the light of day when discovered by the British forces in 1904, after spending many years in chains. Frontier officials were severely punished. As well as condemning the souls of these perpetrators to hell, the Tibetans even went after their reincarnations. The fate of the beautiful Lhacham, who so charmed Sarat Chandra Das, is unknown. By some accounts she perished in prison; by another account, she was sent into exile.

Rewinding to the summer of 1880 and Kintup's Tsangpo expedition: there were actually two agents dispatched by the Survey of India. Kintup was paired up with a Mongolian lama. Details about the lama are sketchy, but there are good descriptions of Kintup. Major Waddell of the Indian Medical Service—which later employed Kintup—described him as 'a thick-set active man with a look of dogged determination on his rugged, weather-beaten features...' He was of medium height, with a deep voice. But what set him apart was his character: determined, dependable, and with sturdy courage, the alertness of a mountaineer—and the strength of a lion. At the time of the 1880 mission, Kintup would have been around 30 years old (his exact date of birth is uncertain).

Kintup left Darjeeling acting as servant and assistant to the Mongolian lama. This team was apparently created because Kintup was illiterate and could thus not take down field observations. They crossed into Tibet unnoticed on August 7, 1880, and joined a caravan bound for Gyantse. After passing through Lhasa, they headed east for Tsetang.

The Mongolian lama turned out to be a poor choice—he was a complete rogue who quickly lost all interest in exploration. At Tsetang, the lama fell ill for three weeks and treated Kintup with contempt and sometimes brutality. Relations went from bad to worse. The lama was evidently more worldly than most monks: he squandered the expedition funds on women and drink. Further downriver, at the village of Thun Tsung, the pundits found lodging with an innkeeper. The lama immediately struck up an affair with the innkeeper's wife—because of this, the explorers tarried at this unimportant village for four months. Eventually, the dim-witted innkeeper discovered the adulterers under his nose: only after a sum of 25 rupees was paid to the cuckolded husband were the pundits allowed to proceed.

Kintup and the lama were posing as pilgrims. Although pilgrims were not common in these parts, the Tsangpo was regarded as sacred, and venerated as the abode of the goddess Dorje Phagmo. The area was known as Pemako, the 'land that opens like a lotus.' In Tibetan Buddhist lore, Pemako is one of the hidden or pure lands to be sought as sanctuary in times of disaster. There were a few small monasteries catering to the faithful—one was at Pemakochung, another at Marpung.

By March of 1881, Kintup and the lama had reached Gyala, at the start of the unexplored 100-mile gap in the mapping of the Tsangpo. Kintup had reached this point before, in his explorations of 1878. They trekked beyond Gyala a further 15 miles to the tiny monastery of Pemakochung. A few miles below the monastery, according to Kintup's report, the Tsangpo cascaded over a cliff about 150 feet high. Beyond this point, the trail to the river below disappeared, leaving only a higher trail with steep, rhododendron-choked slopes above.

Kintup and the lama could go no further and retraced their steps to Tongkyuk Dzong, north of the Tsangpo, where the *dzongpon* (governor) allowed them shelter in the fort. Kintup hid his pistol and three compasses: shortly afterward, he was shocked when one of the dzongpon's servants forced him to disclose the hiding place. The Mongolian lama had evidently leaked news of Kintup's exploring activities to the *dzongpon*. At this point, the lama must've decided he was not cut out for this kind of work. He told Kintup to wait for him—he would be gone

Adventurers today get a rush from whitewater rafting on the Drigung River

for a few days. But he never returned. Kintup was held in detention for two months at the fort before he discovered, to his horror, that the lama had sold him down the river: he had sold him into slavery to the *dzongpon*. The lama had most likely decided to journey onward and upward into China, or perhaps Mongolia.

On the evening of March 7, 1882, Kintup managed to escape. He pressed southward to Marpung, where his pursuers caught up with him. The monastery of Marpung housed 30 monks. Kintup pleaded with the head lama that he was on a pilgrimage and not to hand him over to his pursuers from the dzongpon. The lama paid 50 rupees to the dzongpon's men for Kintup, but this now meant that Kintup was now a servant of the head lama at Marpung— which was the same as being a slave again, except that the new master was more congenial.

After four months of hard work, Kintup asked the head lama for leave so he could make a pilgrimage. Impressed with his hard work and piety, the lama agreed. But the real reason for Kintup's leave-taking was to carry out his mission for the Survey of India. At Giling, about ten miles from Marpung, he spent probably the better part of a month cutting and stacking logs about a foot long, shaped in a peculiar fashion—and hiding them in a cave. During his misadventures, Kintup had lost the drill for the logs, but had kept the 500 small tin tubes. Unable to drill the logs to attach the tubes, he simply lashed them to the logs with strips of bamboo. The logs were ready, but Kintup realised that if he just dumped them into the Tsangpo, they could pass unnoticed. He had to somehow inform the Survey of India to be on the look-out at a specific time.

Kintup returned to Marpung and worked for another two months. He then asked for another leave of two months to go on pilgrimage

Kayak-explorer is dwarfed by rapids on the Tong Chu, a tributary of the Tsangpo in east Tibet

again. This leave was granted: Kintup reached Lhasa around December 1882 and had a letter written up to dispatch to Nem Singh, asking him to inform the Survey of India that 50 marked logs would be thrown into the river daily from a certain date. The fateful letter was dictated by Kintup to a Sikkimese judge in Lhasa, whose wife was about to return to Darjeeling. Kintup's note read as follows:

> Sir, the Lama who was sent with me sold me to a Jongpon as a slave and himself fled away with the Government things that were in his charge. On account of which the journey proved a bad one; however, I, Kintup, have prepared the 500 logs according to the order of Captain Harman, and am prepared to throw 50 logs per day into the Tsang-po from Bipung in Pemako, from the 5th to the 15th of the tenth Tibetan month of the year called Chhuluk [year of the Water-Sheep], of the Tibetan calculation.

The date Kintup had set for release of the logs was the year of the Water-Sheep, or 1883, of which the tenth Tibetan month would have been November. That allowed nine months for Kintup's message to get through to India. However, the messenger—the judge's wife—reached Darjeeling much later than planned. The letter eventually reached Nem Singh in Darjeeling, but it was never passed along to

Harman. Because his health had given out, Harman had left India in December 1882, never to return. He died in Florence in April 1883 of tubercular pneumonia. Nem Singh either failed to pass along the letter to anyone else at the Survey of India, or else no-one paid any attention to it. Many years later, Eric Bailey claimed that by the time Nem Singh received Kintup's letter, the date for throwing the logs into the Tsangpo had passed, so he simply threw the letter away.

Returning to Marpung, Kintup worked for the lama for another nine months. The head lama was so impressed by Kintup's devotion to pilgrimages that he set him free. A month later, Kintup headed for the cave where he had hidden the logs, retrieved them, and launched them into the river at the rate of fifty a day, right on schedule. With this mission finally accomplished, Kintup turned his mind to Harman's initial directive: to follow the Tsangpo all the way into India. Pressing downstream to Onlet, Kintup made a valiant effort, but this region was inhabited by fierce Abhor tribesmen, who were particularly aggressive toward outsiders. If he managed to find a berth for the night in a native hut, Kintup had to give a handful of salt to every man and woman in it, probably to spice up the catch of the day—whether that be snake, tiger, leopard or bear. Kintup evidently had second thoughts about trying to make it through an area bristling with murderous Abhors: he turned back and retraced his steps northward via Lhasa to finally return to India. There he discovered his mother had died during his absence—it took him several months to complete funeral arrangements. Finally, he ran into Nem Singh at the monastery of Namchi, and presumably found out about the failure of the letter.

Nobody that Kintup had trusted to pull their weight on this mission had come through—not the Mongolian lama, not the judge's wife, not Nem Singh, not even Lieutenant Harman of the Survey of India. The scoundrel who had sold him down the river—the Mongolian lama—was not heard from again. Wisely, he either disappeared into China or else kept a very low profile. And the marked logs that Kintup threw in the river? Those seem to have vanished without trace too.

Kintup was illiterate, which might account for his prodigious feats of memory. He must've had a photographic memory: he 'downloaded' all the geographic intelligence he'd gleaned purely from his head. Ironically, though this account later proved extremely accurate, some important details went astray with the transcribers. Kintup was dogged by typographical errors.

In 1884, Kintup related his tale in detail to Lama Ugyen Gyatso, the Tibetan teacher at Bhutia Boarding School. This was later translated into English by a scribe called Norbu, an employee of the Survey of India. But it was not until five years after Kintup's return that his full narrative was published in an official report (1889), complete with the first map of the lower Tsangpo ever drafted, as drawn up by Colonel Tanner of the Survey of India. On that map, the 'Falls of the Sangpo' appear for the very first time, located near Pemakochung. Kintup's report indicated a waterfall of 150 feet on the Tsangpo where the river:

> ...falls over a cliff called Sinji-Chogyal from a height of 150 feet. There is a big lake at the foot of the falls where rainbows are always observable.

The prospect of a major set of falls excited geographers. Colonel Tanner took the lamas' transcription and wrote up Kintup's report for publication. He commented 'I have no doubt that his account is a *bona-fide* story of his travels'. The following year, however, this statement was slightly changed to read that Kintup's information 'can only be regarded as a *bona-fide* story of his travels.' The addition of the word 'only' was significant—it implied that little faith could be placed in his observations because of his lack of training and his illiteracy. Kintup had returned without field notes, route bearings or any notations on temperature and altitude—so how could he possibly be accurate? The official report was buried in the archives and forgotten.

For his astonishing travails and his devotion to his mission at great risk, Kintup was eventually rewarded with a grant of 3,000 rupees. But his dedication—well beyond the call of duty—and his amazing perseverance under conditions of extreme hardship were qualities never recognised by the Survey of India.

Kintup took part in a few more clandestine missions at the Tibetan frontier, serving under Dr Laurence Austine Waddell, stationed for many years with the Indian Army at Darjeeling.

Along with a Sikkimese cook called Achum, Waddell said they 'tramped hundreds of miles of mountain track from Garwhal and Nepal in the west to Assam in the east, often at great altitudes, sometimes sleeping in caves to evade the frontier guards...'

Waddell dispatched Kintup across a pass in eastern Sikkim to scout a route. Kintup crossed into Tibet and managed to walk seven days further before being captured and imprisoned. He managed to escape back to Sikkim. In 1892, Waddell, Kintup and Achum set off in disguise to try and reach Lhasa, but Waddell's blue eyes proved their undoing and they were soon turned back.

When Waddell took part in the 1903 invasion of Tibet, his trusty assistants Kintup and Achum were there—along with a young Sikkimese-Scottish from Kalimpong named David MacDonald, who served as a Tibetan interpreter. Waddell's personal entourage was nothing compared to that of expedition leader, Colonel Younghusband, whose supplies were supervised by Mahmud Isa, a legendary caravaneer who had overseen expeditions with Swedish explorer Sven Hedin and French adventurer Dutreuil de Rhins. The mission must have taxed his patience with its strange cargo: in Younghusband's personal kit were 67 shirts, 19 overcoats and a dozen hats—pith helmets, brown felt hat, panama hat, and a gold-embroidered beaver-skin cocked hat for ceremonies. The Colonel had to keep up appearances, after all.

After the invasion, Kintup returned to work as a tailor in Darjeeling, with occasional forays as a guide and assistant to British sportsmen and travellers. Details about Kintup's personal life are very scarce—it is not even known if he was married.

It would be 30 years before the record was set straight on Kintup's exploration. He would've died completely forgotten had not one explorer covered his tracks in quest of the riddle of the Tsangpo. In 1913, Captain Eric Bailey explored the area in detail: he was carrying Kintup's report and he found it spot-on, except that he could find no large waterfall as Kintup described.

In 1914, Bailey who was in Simla to take part in a conference about the borders of Tibet, asked after Kintup. The Survey of India had no idea where he was—and no interest in the matter either. Bailey persisted—he wrote to a friend in Sikkim who sent him the good news that Kintup had been found, working as a tailor in Darjeeling. Bailey promptly sent funds for Kintup to come to Simla. At last the two met in May 1914: the ageing pundit and the young master, the explorers of the Tsangpo. They talked well into the night.

Phantom waterfall: this sketch of the Falls of the Tsangpo appeared in an article by Waddell in the *Geographical Journal* (1895) and again in his book *Lhasa and Its Mysteries* (1905). Waddell says he commissioned the sketch from a Tibetan lama on pilgrimage to the Tsangpo. In the sketch, the image of a deity is just visible behind the falls, carved in the rock. Waddell believed the 100-foot falls to be situated on the main river, but Eric Bailey, after talking with Kintup in 1914, determined that this was a 150-foot stream on a side-route near Gyala. Singji-Chogyal, the deity carved behind the falls, is only visible when the volume of water is lower.

It soon became clear to Bailey that Kintup had never said there were any great falls on the Tsangpo. He had talked about a 150-foot *stream* on a tributary falling over a cliff near Gyala. Behind the stream was hidden either a carved or painted image of the deity Sinji-Chogyal, sacred to pilgrims. And Kintup talked about a 30-foot waterfall on the Tsangpo near Pemakochung, which Bailey had seen himself. Somehow, the scribe he dictated his account to, or the person who translated it into English, had put the two falls together, making a 150-foot fall on the Tsangpo. Kintup, who could not read, had not been able to check the report or its translation, and it was obviously not read back to him for checking. For 30 years, the British had been looking for a phantom waterfall, a mirage created by an error in transcription—a typographic error turned into a topographic one.

Tibet's canyons are the deepest in the world—the ultimate challenge for kayakers, photographed on an expedition in the upper Drigung Chu gorge

While in Simla, Bailey arranged to have photographs taken of Kintup—rare portraits of the master spy. He is barefoot and dressed in robes that were similar to those he wore in Tibet, with large hands, a white goatee and white hair tucked into a cap. He has prayer-beads around his neck. He looks weary, has a forlorn expression in his eyes. In a word, he looks pissed-off. Then again, he had every cause to be very pissed-off. Here was a man who'd gone beyond the call of duty, done the mission he was asked to do—and a lot more besides—and had then been kicked in the teeth and abandoned on his return. Worse still, the Survey of India suggested that Kintup's version of things was not exactly reliable.

After his long talk to Kintup, Bailey pestered the Indian government to give the man a pension in recognition of his services to Tibetan exploration, but this was refused on the grounds of being 'an indefinite financial commitment' (meaning that Kintup, then around 64, might live to be 90). 'The best we can do is give the fellow a bonus of a thousand rupees, and leave it at that,' was the final assessment from officialdom, under pressure from Bailey. Kintup was presented with a parchment certificate of honour. Bailey writes:

> So Kintup went back to Darjeeling with a thousand rupees, which was far more than he would ever have received as a pension, as within a few months he was dead.

Bailey thought this was an end to the rumour of a great waterfall on the Tsangpo, but the river did not give away her secrets so easily. Read on to the next chapter for the continuing saga of the Tsangpo…

The riddle of whether the Tsangpo and the Brahmaputra are one and the same river was not conclusively solved until the 1924 expedition of British plant hunter Frank Kingdon Ward. But real credit for solving this riddle belongs to Kintup, who 40 years earlier had cast marked logs into the Tsangpo—which drifted unseen into the Bay of Bengal. Had those logs been spotted, as planned, it would have been proof of the link. Kintup would've been very proud to know that today's Western-created maps of the Tsangpo Gorge accord him a geographic honour. They name one feature 'Kintup Falls', at last giving the hardy explorer the measure of recognition he so richly deserves.

Incredible as it may sound, pundits continue to operate in Tibet. By 'pundit' is meant an undercover collector of information to be used by other agencies. Latter-day pundits are spying on what the Chinese are up to: the Chinese treat anything to do with Tibet as highly classified and sensitive information. Gadgets used by these pundits are far more sophisticated than a set of prayer-beads: GPS devices, tiny digital-photography devices, clandestine filming with mini-DV camcorders.

And who are the new spymasters? Well, you already know one. Activist and actor Richard Gere, heavily involved with the organisation International Campaign for Tibet. Banned from visiting China and Tibet since 1994, Richard Gere uses his own paid informer in the field to collect information on human rights abuses—which Gere himself presents at US Congress hearings.

A backpacker 'underground' collects material for human rights groups like Amnesty International, or for the TCHRD (a Tibetan human-rights investigation group, based in Dharamsala). Since no foreign news agencies are allowed to be stationed in Lhasa, the work of these 'pundits' replaces that of news correspondents. The news is passed to specialised agencies like Voice of Tibet (Tibetan-language radio broadcasts). News about religious persecution, about political prisoners—all comes from these informers. Information on environmental issues like plans for building mega-dams. Information on the extent of deforestation on the eastern side of the Tibetan plateau—which could result in massive erosion by rivers. Information on new villages that have sprung up—where nomads have been shunted off, forced to abandon their way of life of herding yaks.

In 1987, a young American backpacker, Blake Kerr, arrived in Lhasa. Fresh out of medical school, he could never have imagined he'd be putting his knowledge to use treating Tibetans with bullet wounds and severe burns. When pro-independence demonstrations erupted in Lhasa, Kerr was secretly conducted at night to safe-houses to treat wounded Tibetans, who refused to go to Chinese hospitals. Kerr turned from being innocent backpacker to involved activist—the same path that a number of backpackers visiting Tibet have taken. Kerr returned to Tibet a number of times to collect data on Chinese medical malpractices in Tibet, including forced abortions, and forced sterilization of Tibetan women. At considerable risk, he found his way into hospital wards to conduct his own investigation—which he writes about in his book *Sky Burial*.

Chinese mapping of Tibet is known to be highly detailed for military purposes, but little of this detail is released. Maps sold in Lhasa are printed in English and Chinese versions: curiously, the Chinese versions—intended for the large numbers of Chinese tourists—contain much more detail than the English versions (a case of selective information blocking). None of the maps show military camps or prisons.

Then there is the question of what Tibet is, cartographically speaking. In Tibetan eyes, the Land of Snows covers ethnic Tibet—all of the Tibetan plateau, including Kham and Amdo to the east and northeast. In Chinese eyes, Tibet is limited to an area roughly half that size, ludicrously designated the 'Tibet Autonomous Region'. Countering this travesty is a Tibetan-made map, *Tibet and Adjacent Areas under Chinese Communist Occupation*, issued by the Amnye Machen Institute in Dharamsala.

Surely one of the oddest maps ever produced is *On This Spot: Lhasa* (2001). Sponsored by the International Campaign for Tibet, this human rights map marks the places where Tibetans demonstrated, where killings took place. The map-booklet was released partly to redress the balance in guidebooks on Tibet, which often omit information on the human-rights situation. It identifies prisons and detention centres, gives background on Lhasa's tragic recent history, and includes subversive photos and an underground yellow pages.

Mounted in strategic spots around Lhasa are closed-circuit surveillance cameras. They are all around the Barkor, inside the Potala, up and down main thoroughfares. These sophisticated devices were purchased from the West for the purpose of monitoring traffic flow. But since Lhasa does not have a traffic-flow problem, the cameras are obviously intended for other uses. They are the Orwellian all-seeing eyes of the Chinese occupiers. In monasteries, faux monks turn informant on others within. Spies search for banned audiotapes or images of the Dalai Lama. Police come knocking in the middle of the night to arrest monks. In Lhasa, you can count half a dozen different types of military or para-military uniforms: the PLA, PSB, PAP, SSB.

In 1996, right under the noses of Chinese police, and under all-seeing gaze of closed-circuit surveillance cameras, American director Paul Wagner and his undercover film crew spent a week in Lhasa shooting material for a dramatic feature called *Windhorse*. They used small miniDV camcorders and pocket-sized DAT sound recorders. They posed as tourists. The director of photography recalls using his tiny camera to film panoramas of the Lhasa skyline from the roof of the Potala—and nearby he observed an American tourist in Bermuda shorts also shooting views of the city, using exactly the same camera. After clandestine filming in Lhasa, the crew moved on to Kathmandu and captured more scenes in Mustang, which is very Tibetan in landscape but lies on the Nepalese side. Here they could shoot openly, using an expensive digital camera—one nevertheless toted in a silver hard-case on the back of a Nepali porter wearing flip-flops. The movie *Windhorse* came out in 1998—probably the first dramatic feature movie ever shot entirely on digital cameras and subsequently transferred to 35mm for theatrical release.

The Chinese in Tibet closely monitor the activities of tourists since they've been known to act as messengers for Tibetans and the outside world—a message is thrust in the hands, a cry for Tibetan independence, an appeal to the UN. The Public Security Bureau occasionally swoops in to conduct hotel room searches if they have reason to suspect risqué behaviour. At military checkpoints on the Lhasa-to-Kathmandu route, there are searches of Landcruisers, looking for tapes and pictures of the Dalai Lama, the Tibetan flag, and other forbidden items. But also looking for outgoing messages or video.

Even on domestic flights, passengers are sometimes thoroughly searched. At pre-boarding procedure for a Lhasa-to-Kathmandu flight, a Westerner was asked to take apart his souvenir wooden Tibetan prayer-wheel to check the scroll of prayers within. Customs was evidently looking for concealed messages within the prayer wheel—in the form of human rights appeals being smuggled out. The old pundit concealment trick comes full circle.

On His Majesty's Secret Service: the elusive Eric Bailey appears
in full ceremonial regalia—with sword, chestful of medals and peculiar hat.
This somewhat-blurry photograph was taken in 1922 when Bailey
presented an official award to the Maharaja of Bhutan.
Bailey's real agenda more likely involved bagging
new butterfly and poppy species.

Eric Bailey
1882–1967

naturalist, frontiersman, consul, secret agent
& masterful player in The Great Game

Tibet with a Butterfly Net

Take two on the Tsangpo:
the Hatter finds himself in some
highly perilous situations

❖ ❖

Eric Bailey was a straight shooter: early in his career he shot
his way through the Tibetan highlands during the 1903 British
invasion of Tibet. Then he turned his attention to shooting rare
wildlife specimens for museum collections. He loved shooting
and fishing, but his greatest passion was netting butterflies.
Even when pursued by gunmen intent on killing him, Bailey
found occasion to indulge in some quick butterfly collecting
if a specimen caught his eye. Against all odds, on undercover
missions Bailey not only survived, he came out with flying
colours—and some new butterfly species. Along the way,
he discovered the Himalayan blue poppy
that today bears his name.

 CAPTAIN BAILEY was in a bit of a quandary. At the Consul-General of Chengtu, he received a cable from his father that bore the cryptic—and disturbing—message:

WARN BAILEY MASSACRE SADIYA

The four-word cable failed to explain who had massacred who or why—and Bailey could get no further news from the consul. Trouble was, Bailey was about to embark on a private expedition westward to pick up the pieces of the Tsangpo puzzle left by Kintup.

He decided to proceed anyway—with extreme caution. In May 1911, Bailey set off from Chengtu with his trusty young Tibetan servant Putamdu. The further he forged into the remote Mishmi Hills, the more he realised that the butterfly collecting was the best he'd ever come across: he netted some beautiful specimens, including some he was convinced belonged to entirely new species. This later proved correct—*Parnassius acco baileyi, Lethe baileyi* and *Ypthima baileyi* were later named after him, among others. Having their surname enshrined in scientific nomenclature was a powerful motive for many collectors, but Bailey must have become quite blasé about it—he racked up so many, so young.

Along the trail, Bailey had several close encounters with unruly tribesmen who were not fond of foreign incursions. Convinced that Bailey would be killed if he proceeded further, a Tibetan official refused him entry to his domain. Bailey and Putamdu were constantly drenched by heavy monsoons—this region being one of the wettest in Asia. These conditions competely rotted Bailey's boots, and he walked into India with feet wrapped in pieces of his canvas bath and a skin from game hunting. Thwarted in his main target of exploring the inner Tsangpo, Bailey nonetheless reconnoitred a large unknown swathe of territory between China and India. After four months of rough going, he and Putamdu finally made it through to the British outpost of Sadiya, in Assam, where he discovered what the cryptic cable was about. Noel Williamson, the Political Officer of Sadiya, along with his entire entourage of 38 men, had been hacked to death by fierce Abhor tribesmen. Williamson's party had been out on a reconnaissance mission. Bailey was lucky to be alive: he'd been in an area occupied by Mishmi tribesmen, who weren't so bloodthirsty—although they were not above raining down poisoned arrows if the mood took them. Another close shave for Bailey—who experienced many narrow escapes in his lifetime.

Eric Bailey was not normal—in the sense that normal people would be terrified of the things that Bailey did. Bailey *looked* quite normal— he was over six feet tall, lean and powerfully built. Perhaps the clue was in his brush moustache—under it all, he had a fascinating streak of eccentricity. He could be wildly unpredictable—a facet that had earned him a reputation for madness as well as a related nickname among fellow officers: 'the Hatter'.

The nickname derived from his mad-as-a-hatter interest in *shikar*— or shooting of wild game for sport. The nickname also is linked with Bailey's passion for catching butterflies—with a hat, presumably, if no net was at hand. Bailey was in the habit of stopping in the most life-threatening of situations to net a new species of butterfly or insect, or shoot a bird—or pluck a rare flower. He never travelled without his butterfly net and hunting rifles—he was addicted to hunting, fishing and netting butterflies. He was a fine horseman who loved playing polo. He indulged these addictions whenever chance presented itself—and if this should draw him away from an important mission, then Bailey was willing to be distracted, momentarily.

His penchant for hunting big game led him to some early adventures. As a subaltern in southern India, he shot his first tiger from a treetop perch. He and his accomplices descended to examine the prize. Bailey twisted the tiger's tail and made barrel-organ noises as the others danced and whooped around the kill. But this came to an abrupt end when the tiger returned from the dead and stood up growling.

The Hatter is a fitting nickname for a man who wore many hats— soldier, frontiersman, sportsman, naturalist, explorer, consul, spy. These roles were made possible by his unusual skills—by his mastery of colloquial Tibetan and other languages, by his marksmanship, and by his physical toughness. He was the ultimate survivor—miraculously escaping situations that others might not have. Sir Basil Gould, a colleague of Bailey's from service in Tibet, observed that when Bailey stood at gatherings he would invariably back himself into a corner— formed by the V of two solid walls—and would keep glancing this way and that, as if to make sure that nobody wanted to take a shot at him. But he had good reasons for this behaviour.

Eric Bailey first saw action in Tibet in 1903. Action means firing guns at full gallop, scouting enemy positions, fighting door-to-door in villages where Tibetan defenders were holed up. Bailey was a young subaltern who joined Francis Younghusband's controversial invasion of Tibet in 1903. After years of frustrating negotiations with the Tibetans, the British had had the biscuit, thrown down the gauntlet—and just decided to blast their way into Tibet to open up trade forcibly.

A force of 1,200 troops was dispatched into Tibet: the invasion was the last grand imperial fling of the British. Forcing their hand was shady Great Game manoeuvring: the Russians were thought to be gaining great influence in Lhasa. In particular, a Buddhist monk called Dorjieff had gained access to the Dalai Lama's inner circle. Dorjieff is not counted among the first explorers to reach Lhasa because of his ethnicity—he was a Buriat, a tribal group closely related to Mongolians. He arrived in Lhasa to study in 1880. But the fact that he acted as go-between for Tsar Nicholas II made him somewhat special. While Dorjieff and assorted Mongols and Russians were supposedly currying favour with the Dalai Lama, the British were getting nowhere. Letters sent by Lord Curzon, Viceroy of India, to the 13th Dalai Lama, were returned unopened—taken as a huge insult by the British, and in fact cited as reason enough to invade.

Frederick Marshman Bailey was just 21 at the time of British invasion of Tibet. He was born in Lahore on February 3, 1882, and educated in England at Wellington and Sandhurst, groomed for a military career to follow in the footsteps of his father, an officer in the Indian Army. Because his father had the same name and was in the same profession, Bailey junior acquired the name 'Eric' to sort out the difference. There were two sons in the family. At age 18, Eric Bailey returned to India. He transferred from the Bengal Lancers to the 32nd Sikh Pioneer Regiment, which was suddenly called up to Gangtok in Sikkim. En route, as they marched up the Tista Valley, Bailey was amazed by the magnificent butterflies. In Sikkim, he started learning colloquial Tibetan: his favourite phrases were threats in Tibetan, like: *Where does this road lead to? If you lie to me, I'll shoot you*, or: *Let go of my bridle or I'll shoot you dead.* Bailey's regiment was ordered to cut roads on the Sikkim border to facilitate access for a large number of mule caravans—which were carrying army rations and supplies toward the Tibetan border.

The British invasion of Tibet encountered many obstacles, but the most severe were the elements and the weather: pack animals died;

there were altitude problems. Guns became jammed from the cold (lubricant oil froze inside them), ink froze in pens, kerosene had to be thawed before it could be used for lamps. At Christmas 1903, Younghusband's officers complained that the champagne was not only chilled—it was frozen. When it came to fighting, the British invasion of Tibet was hardly a fair battle: it pitted the world's most powerful military force against the world's least powerful. Two pieces of heavy artillery and a thousand British rifles were ranged against the ancient matchlock rifles, swords and slingshots of the Tibetans. The British expedition included a regiment with two Maxim machine

Now a museum piece, the Maxim machine-gun was the most terrifying gun in the world in 1903, used to deadly effect by the British invading Tibet

guns—very recent addition to the British arsenal—and very deadly ones. Believing their amulets would protect them from British bullets, the Tibetans simply walked away from a battlefield near Guru: in less than four minutes, they were mowed down by the devastating Maxim guns, each capable of firing 2,000 rounds in three minutes. Over 600 Tibetans were killed; more than 200 were wounded. The amulet makers would later explain that their charms only worked against lead and copper bullets—and the British had obviously used another kind of metal (the Tibetan amulet designers promised to rectify this situation for future encounters).

British casualties in the same encounter amounted to a dozen—none of them fatal. These were inflicted by sword or slingshot: on the Tibetan side, three antiquated Russian guns were later found on the battlefield. Among the casualties was correspondent Edmund Candler of the Daily Mail, who spoke of 'temporary incapacity' in missing coverage of some battles. What he meant was that his left hand had been hacked off by a Tibetan sword, and his right hand was badly injured. At the British field hospital, he was baffled by how stoic the Tibetans were in accepting their fate—not seeming to notice the pain of severe wounds. And for their part, the Tibetans—who fully expected to be tortured to death—were astonished that the British would make attempts to save Tibetan wounded. Stiff-upper-lip Candler was an early instance of an embedded reporter—locked in heated competition with three other newspaper correspondents writing eyewitness reports about the Younghusband campaign. Due to his severe injuries, Candler had to go back to Darjeeling, but his replacement didn't show up, so Candler returned to Tibet—reaching Lhasa, but missing half the campaign. Some photos by Lieutenant Bailey were used to illustrate Candler's 1905 book about the invasion, *The Unveiling of Lhasa*.

When not busy shooting at the Tibetans, Bailey was heavily involved in *shikar*: he stalked gazelles, blue sheep and Argali sheep—the latter prized as a trophy for its long curling horns. And he indulged his passion for butterfly collecting. Indeed, at one point during the campaign he was invited by Younghusband to his tent so they could compare collections. Bailey smugly wrote: 'He hadn't any that I hadn't got.'

Eventually, the Tibetans bowed to the British goddess of war, Queen Victoria—whom they regarded as a reincarnate of Palden Lhamo (Lhasa's protector-goddess). There was a prophecy that while the Great White Queen was still alive, the British would not invade Tibet. This proved true in the end—the British invaded three years after Queen Victoria's death. Apart from Hannibal, in the entire history of warfare it would be hard to beat the range of riding and pack animals deployed on the Younghusband Mission: six camels, 138 buffaloes, 185 riding ponies, 1,372 pack ponies, 1,111 ekka (cart) ponies, 2,953 Nepalese yaks, 1,513 Tibetan yaks, 5,000 bullocks and over 7,000 mules. Keeping this motley circus fed and healthy at altitude proved a logistical nightmare. Sad to relate, most of the pack animals perished along the way—the Nepalese yaks were struck down by anthrax. Only the mules showed any stamina.

Here's the strange part: Kintup was also on this expedition, as humble assistant to Captain Waddell of the Indian Medical Service. But it is almost certain that Bailey and Kintup never crossed paths in the course of the 1903–04 British campaign. Which is odd, considering that there were only about 100 Englishmen involved, and Kintup was assistant to one of those Englishmen. The only explanation for not crossing paths is that Bailey and Waddell did not see eye to eye, and Bailey probably avoided him altogether. Bailey would, however, undoubtedly have come across Waddell's book about the Younghusband mission, *Lhasa and Its Mysteries*, published in 1905. On the

1903–04 mission, Waddell indeed grilled Kintup over his Tsangpo adventures—in particular about the fabled waterfall. Waddell claims he elicited from Kintup 'a vivid picture of this great Unknown Land'— so it's odd that the error of Kintup's falls of the Tsangpo is perpetuated here, but in a different version. Waddell writes about the Tsangpo:

> ...gathering its waters into a narrow torrent, it rushes down southwards in a series of rapids, precipitating itself over a cliff about 100 feet in depth, cutting and boring its way so deeply through the rocks that about 100 miles below these falls it is said to go quite out of sight...

Not only this, Waddell gives precise latitude and longitude of the falls and includes a drawing of them made by a Tibetan lama on pilgrimage to the area. This drawing clearly shows a demonic head carved on rock inside the falls, which meant it would match the sidestream that Kintup later talked to Bailey about —except that Kintup told Bailey the stream was 150 feet high, not 100 feet high. The only excuse for this comedy of errors is the fact that Kintup could not read, and had not checked any printed source—including Waddell's book—for accuracy. But another anomaly surfaces here: the same drawing of the mystery waterfall appeared in an article by Waddell in the *Geographical Journal* of 1895—only six years after the official publication of Kintup's report.

On August 4th, 1904, British officers in full-dress uniforms and with an escort of 300 men, marched through the west gate of Lhasa. They made all the noise they could—a Gurkha band of sorts played march music—and were met by crowds of cheering and clapping Tibetans, according to Younghusband. Taking this as a sign of welcome, the British officers doffed their hats and said thank you. They did not realise that Tibetans make clapping gestures to expel evil spirits, and they were chanting and shouting to bring down rain.

Another gesture easily misconstrued was the Tibetan custom of sticking out the tongue as far as it could extrude, downwards—not in rudeness but as a mark of respectful greeting. It was believed that constant repetition of black mantras by the ancient Bon sect and other heretical faiths turned the tongue a devilish black or brown. So a submissive party could demonstrate innocence by sticking out the tongue when meeting someone of high rank—and it had better be a pink tongue. And to bid farewell, two relatives or friends would often doff hats and rub foreheads.

Lhasa, noted Edmund Candler, was pretty much the same as Thomas Manning reported it ninety years before—lots of beggars, lots of filth, and the Potala Palace towering serenely above it all.

The British troops found their triumphal march into Lhasa impeded by piles of refuse, stagnant pools of water, open sewers, and various rabid animals foraging for putrid scraps of food. They did, however, note the gleaming roofs of the Jokhang Temple and the Potala somewhat restored the balance in favour of the majestic. Amid the squalor and drabness, occasional splashes of dazzling colour. Candler, who pronounced the Tibetans 'the strangest people on earth' after learning of their sky-burial customs, describes a noble's retinue passing through the bazaar:

> The crowd is parted by a Shapé riding past in gorgeous yellow silks and brocades, followed by a mounted retinue whose headgear would be the despair of an operatic hatter. They wear red lamp-shades, yellow motor-caps, exaggerated Gainsboroughs, inverted cooking-pots, coal-scuttles, and medieval helmets.

An extra operatic touch: nobles commonly carried a scented handkerchief to ward off the foul smells as they rode through the streets of Lhasa. Most of his adult life, Bailey kept a diary—albeit in very brief form, with only a line or two was devoted to each day, indicating location and activities. At other times he might include a list of what he had shot that day. His diary for late August 1904 records life in occupied Lhasa with in laconic notes:

> Thur 18. Went to Drepung [Monastery] with White & Wilton. Lama ran amok. Gymkhana. Fri 19. Hung Lama. Football...
> Sat 27. Races. Sun 28. Auction of silks. Football. Out fishing.

Bailey shows considerable detachment in his diary entries—not seeming to distinguish between football or executions. And giving no background context. The unfortunate lama who ran amok was a Sera monk out to revenge the death of his brother: the lama had broken into the British camp and slashed two officers with a sword. For this transgression, a fine of 5,000 rupees had been levied on the Tibetan government, which was paid in kind—in the form of fine Chinese silk—auctioned off among the British troops. Football was one of the sporting events

organised to keep the troops happy—at this altitude, the game was
similar to one played at sea-level but a player had the sensation of feeling as if he were carrying an 80-pound backpack when running down
the field. 'Out fishing' sounds rather mundane, but for Tibetans it was
extraordinary to watch Bailey in action, because the taking of any life
in or near the Sacred City was forbidden.

The invasion of Tibet was imperialism at its worst: the British
had received no military provocation from the Tibetans, who simply
wanted to be left alone. But there was another agenda for the invasion—the intense colonial rivalry between the powers of England and
Russia. The players in this complex chess match (the Great Game)
were spies, explorers and diplomats—and the 'board' was the vast ex-
panse of Central Asia. Rumours of Russian influence over Tibet raised
British hackles: they wanted Tibet as a neutral buffer zone between
the powers of China and British India. By the time the British troops
reached Lhasa, the Dalai Lama had fled to sanctuary in Mongolia, and
the British were left in the embarrassing position of having no high
official to negotiate with or sign a contract. Neither could they find
any Russians in the woodwork. Reports of Russian military assistance
to the Tibetans had been greatly exaggerated—during the entire invasion, the British uncovered only a few dozen Russian-made rifles.
The Brits drank a lot of tea with minor Tibetan officials, negotiated
a useless treaty, and withdrew, leaving behind a telegraph line—and
Eric Bailey.

Bailey switched from soldier to explorer in the blink of an eye. The
British realised that the invasion of Tibet was their great chance to fill
in the blanks on the map, augmenting the Survey of India. Younghusband wanted to send a party of men with 100 Gurkhas eastward along
the Tsangpo and follow it all the way into India—but this plan was
scotched when a report came in of a mail convoy ambushed by what
appeared to be Tibetan bandits. A new mission was devised to recon-
noitre the region near the source of the Tsangpo in far west Tibet.
Although the bulk of the British force had withdrawn by late 1904,
some Indian troops remained. As part of their treaty with the Tibetans,
the British were permitted to operate a handful of trade agencies in
Tibet: at Yatung (south Tibet), Gyantse (central Tibet) and Gartok (far
west Tibet).

On the 1904 mission to west Tibet, Bailey was the junior officer. Leaders of the group were officers Ryder, Rawling and Wood.

Bailey was excited by the trip. He wrote in a letter: 'There ought to be very good shooting on the way.' Younghusband wanted him to be the Trade Agent at Gartok, but Bailey reported that the place was isolated and unimportant. In the end, the mission only stayed for one day at Gartok, as they were in a hurry to get across the passes into India in case they got stuck for the winter. They did investigate Thok Jalung goldmines—but decided there was no basis for a commercial operation. Bailey got his first taste of exploring and took easily to it: he acclimatised to altitudes exceeding 18,000 feet and was inured to temperatures of well below zero. In the end, the Government of India decided it was far cheaper to use a local employee from the Punjab Hill States as the Gartok Trade Agent, and Bailey instead became Trade Agent at Gyantse.

Although it was not the primary aim, Bailey and crew mapped the route along the Tsangpo—the river that came to obsess him for the next decade. They ended up following the Tsangpo from Shigatse for 400 miles to the source—a glacier near Mount Kailash. It's debatable who discovered the source of the Tsangpo. Oddball English adventurer Henry Savage Landor claimed to have found the source in 1897 but his heroic account was dismissed by Sven Hedin as a 'Munchausen romance'.

By December 1904, Bailey's party crossed Shipki pass back into India and down to Simla, where Bailey rejoined his regiment. In May 1905, tired of everyday military routines, Bailey decided to apply for transfer to the Indian Political Department, an élite body that basically indulged in spy activities in the setting of the Great Game. Bailey wanted to put his language skills to good use.

In August 1905, Bailey missed out on another prime chance to hook up with Kintup, the pioneer of the Tsangpo. When Bailey took his final Tibetan language test in Darjeeling, his examiners were the pundits Sarat Chandra Das and Ugyen Gyatso. Ugyen Gyatso was the man who transcribed Kintup's tale some 20 years previously—and he must've known where to find him in Darjeeling bazaar.

In December 1905, Bailey took up residence in Gyantse as British Trade Agent—little more than a cover for intelligence work. Gyantse was the closest to Lhasa that the Tibetans would allow the British. Bailey spent almost three years in Gyantse and Yatung (another trade agency near the Sikkim border). Where other British officers found the remote outpost of Gyantse a total bore, Eric Bailey found endless fascination in his environment. He improved his command of Tibetan, played football and polo, and chatted with those passing through Gyantse en route to Lhasa. And he shot things. 'Bailey Sahib'—as he was known to the locals—shot lots of things. He wrote in an article for Blackwood's Magazine: 'What is to be done today?...the obvious answer to this question has just presented itself—*Let us kill something*.'

Bailey took no notice of a ban by the Dalai Lama on hunting wildlife. He sent skins and specimens to museums in India and England to supplement his income. One of these specimens—a snake captured at 14,000 feet—was a new species, later christened *Thermophis baileyi* (also known as 'Bailey's snake' or the 'hotspring keelback'). Endemic to Tibet, it survives by squatting hotspring locations. The world's only high-altitude snake, this black snake is today found in hotspring locations like Tidrom Nunnery, where nuns and snakes have coexisted for centuries (the snakes do like to swim around the hotspring enclosures where Tibetans bathe). This was the first in a long line of fauna—and flora—named in honour of Bailey.

The first stuffed Tibetan mammals and birds to arrive in British museums were dispatched by naturalist Brian Houghton Hodgson, based in Kathmandu from 1824 to 1843. For political reasons, Hodgson was confined by the Nepalese to the Kathmandu Valley. He chafed at these restrictions but to no avail. So he did next best thing: he devised a way of sending his own 'pundits' into Tibet to hunt for new species. They would bring back skins and describe the animal to Hodgson, and artists would draw it all up. Hodgson kept a staff of over 20 busy with his collecting of flora and fauna, and compiling of Sanskrit manuscripts. Half a dozen species bear his name. He was the first to identify the Tibetan antelope and the takin. He recognised Tibet as a place apart, with hardy species that adapted to the elevation and harsh climate.

What Hodgson saw only as skins, Bailey observed in person— and then bagged or shot. He started a menagerie in Gyantse for the orphaned young of species he shot. He experimented with the wildlife, trying to domesticate and breed animals. In 1907, he kept a couple of Tibetan wolves and a monkey. The monkey died when he was away on tour—Bailey had been in the habit of tying it up by the fire at night, but his servants probably forgot this custom and the monkey probably died from cold. One of his wolves escaped, but several nights later it came back—Bailey found it sitting on top of its kennel. The wolves got into the habit of going all over the place and only turning up for meals, but still they were not tame—one of them bit him. Unfortunately, Bailey wrote, in letters to his parents, by December 1907, the wolves, his spaniels and his gazelle had all died of distemper. Bailey got a badger, but it died too.

In July 1908, he took in three snow leopard cubs. The mature snow leopard, with its mottled white coat, is about the size of a large dog, but with a huge tail that is used as a kind of stabiliser for balancing. It ranges over the Tibetan plateau and beyond—into Central Asia—but

is so well-camouflaged and so stealthy it is seen only rarely by herdsmen—who would rather not see it, as it would probably be encountered when preying on their livestock. The snow leopard is a non-roaring cat—its set of throat bones is fixed—like that of the cheetah—rather than flexible like the tiger's. It was such a stealthy beast that even Hodgson completely missed it, though he wrote lots about its prey—blue sheep and wild goats. Bailey himself didn't get much of a chance to study his snow leopard charges—unfortunately, all three died within weeks. Bailey's early publications derive from his Gyantse sojourn: papers were published in the Journal of the Bombay Natural History Society on the bar-headed goose, the Tibetan wild ass, the serow and the takin.

Transport around Gyantse was mainly by horse—the Trade Agency had its own stables. British attempts to introduce wheeled vehicles were a failure. In November 1906, Captain Frank O'Connor arrived in grand style in Gyantse with two motor cars, brought in piece-by-piece and reassembled. One was a Clement, intended as a gift for the Panchen Lama of Shigatse; the other was a Peugeot for the agency. However, with no roads—and, more to the point—no gasoline supply, the British soon went back to riding horses. These motorised vehicles, the first to be brought into Tibet, ended up gathering dust.

During his time in Gyantse and Yatung, Bailey greatly improved his command of Tibetan by speaking with Tibetans from all walks—from farmers to the Panchen Lama. And the 13th Dalai Lama. In 1910, when several thousand Chinese troops marched on Lhasa to assert

Gyantse Dzong, a major fort on the route from India to Tibet

their authority, Bailey came up with the idea of disguising the 13th Dalai Lama as a postal runner, complete with an official mailbag to get by Chinese frontier posts. As Lord Cawdor later described it, this was 'the only time on record when Her Majesty's mails were carried by an Incarnate God.' The ruse worked. The Dalai Lama slipped over the border, south into Kalimpong, India, where he spent several years as guests of the British—before returning to resume control in Lhasa and declaring Tibetan independence from the Chinese.

After his long service in Tibet, Bailey had accumulated two years' furlough. At the end of August 1909, Captain Bailey (recently promoted to this rank) boarded a ship in Bombay, bound for England. In Edinburgh, he abandoned himself to a life of leisure: he hunted and fished, hobnobbed at his club, went to the opera and to concerts. In London, he took women to dine at the Ritz or the Trocadero—in his diary, the name of a woman would occupy his attention for a month or so, then disappear—to be replaced by another name. Refreshed by 20 months of amusement and distraction in England, Bailey set off in January 1911 for Paris, and then by rail to Peking—intent on solving the riddle of the Tsangpo, and collect flora and fauna specimens. However, as already related, Bailey's object of trying to trace the Tsangpo was derailed by the murder of British officer Williamson and his party by Abhor tribesmen.

The Abhors, known to the Tibetans as the Lopas, derived from the most savage of Assamese jungle tribes. Passing through much later, Frank Kingdon Ward described an encounter with three Abhors on the trail in the Tsangpo Gorges:

> These dwarfs had small animal eyes, bulging foreheads, and projecting muzzles which called to mind the Neanderthal man... They were unfriendly, spoke no Tibetan, and wore next to no clothes; but they carried 80-pound loads over tracks that would kill a white man, and crossed the Dashong La almost naked in deep snow, and in the teeth of the awful interstellar wind which eternally scours the Tibetan uplands.

After the murder of Williamson and his party, the Abhors, who evidently enjoyed blood sports and who obviously felt they were invincible on home turf, even went so far as to send an envoy to mock the British and invite them back for another thrashing. The cheeky Abhors did not realise they were up against the most powerful imperial force on earth. The British, not amused, took them up on the offer—sending in an army of 725 jungle-trained Gurkhas and 3,500 headhunting Nagas, who advanced making a terrific chanting noise as they brandished their spears.

The fierce Nagas, long-standing enemies of the Abhors, had some personal scores to settle—making them an ideal force. As the British commander put it: one group of savages was pitted against another. The Nagas were traditional headhunters until the British set about outlawing the practice in the 1890s. But on this expedition, it seemed the British were actually encouraging the headhunting aspect. Naga men were in the custom of presenting a human head to females with whom they wished to mate—and this expedition was the perfect opportunity to get a head (pardon the awful pun here).

Due to his invaluable knowledge of the region, Bailey asked to be posted back to Sadiya to join the Abhor punitive expedition. He was not well received: General Bower in Assam regarded Bailey as 'that damn fellow from Simla'. To get rid of him, the general sent him to Chulikatta Mishmi country to determine if they were going to rebel as well. Bailey was assigned a detail of 25 military police and 90 Nagas to act as porters. When he reached Mishmi country, he determined that they had no intention of rebelling, but were delighted when told about the punitive expedition against the Abhors—and expressed their fond hopes that the entire tribe would be annihilated.

The Abhors were duly crushed by the Naga-Gurkha-British forces: their villages were burned to the ground. This pith-helmet Gunga-Din fighting epic of spears and rifles paved the way for Eric Bailey to finally explore the Tsangpo and carry on with butterfly collecting. Year of the Water Bull: Captain Bailey was back in the Tsangpo region in May 1913, again on leave. He received sad news of his father's death. This was a great shock, but Bailey was adamant about carrying on with his mission. To tackle the Tsangpo properly he realised he would need to engage a first-class surveyor. He put the idea to Captain Henry Morshead of the Royal Engineers, who had worked for six years with the Survey of India. Morshead leaped at the opportunity. The idea was to map the unknown terrain between Tibet and Assam, collect rare flora and fauna. But the main object was to solve the riddle of the Tsangpo and to look for huge waterfalls. There was no official sanction for this trip from the British—the two decided to sneak in.

Bailey would invariably lead, scouting ahead—keeping an eye out for butterflies. Trailing behind was Morshead, diligently mapping and surveying—lugging a theodolite up mountain peaks to take readings. Following them were porters and a caravan of mules laden with expedition and surveying equipment. The two explorers would meet briefly in the evenings, or might pass several days apart. They worked very well together, considering they had teamed up by chance. Bailey needed Morshead's surveying skills and Morshead depended on Bailey's language skills to forge through this hostile territory.

The Abhor threat had largely been extinguished by British and Naga action of 1911, but there were other tribes to contend with. There were the Monbas (from eastern Bhutan), the Pobas and Kongpopas from Pomi, and fierce Khampa immigrants from east Tibet. These tribal groups fought among each other tooth-and-nail and clashed with Chinese troops. They were treacherous and riddled with suspicion. Bailey wrote:

> They regarded strangers as welcome only as possible victims of extortion by pacific or violent means, or as allies from whom they might extort weapons with which they could massacre their

neighbours more efficiently than with their simple implements of death.

In other words, not a good idea to have them swap their spears and arrows for Maxim machine guns. Rumours abounded about other bloodthirsty groups. The Mishmis were known to conduct raids into Assam to kidnap children, who were sold in Tibet as slaves. Captain Waddell refers to the Glaklo Nagpo or Black Savages, who indulged in random cannibalism. They were said to eat their prisoners-of-war, and at marriage festivals, were said to kill and eat the mother of the bride if no other person was forthcoming. Another pleasant group rumoured to live in the southern jungles were the Dugmas—female practitioners of an ancient cult versed in the art of concealing snake venom and toxic mushrooms under their fingernails. They used this mixture to poison the food of victims, or to scratch them while sleeping.

Fortunately for Bailey and Morshead, the Glaklo Nagpo and the Dugmas never materialised. They managed to avoid nasty encounters with the tribes of the Tsangpo. That left the battle with the terrain—the Tsangpo river flowed through some of the most mountainous, difficult and inhospitable country on earth. Venturing deeper into the Tsangpo valley—never before seen by Western eyes—proved a windfall for the collection of rare species. In the course of the six-month journey, Bailey collected over 2,000 butterflies belonging to nearly 200 species—a few of them new to science. Bailey had seen a number of blue poppies in Tibet, but none as beautiful as those of the valley near Lunang. He plucked one and pressed it into his notebook and didn't think about it much further. He recorded the find in his diary (July 10th, 1913) as nothing special:

> I rode a pony on a rather uncomfortable Tibetan saddle for the first time today. Among the flowers were blue poppies I had not seen before and purple iris and primulas. There was also a good deal of aconite.

The tall Himalayan blue poppy he plucked didn't even rate a single sentence to itself, he later remarked. But these particular poppies were very special because of their garden-cultivation potential. Growing wild blue poppies in England was extremely tricky because they did not readily adapt to conditions there. These hardy plants were well acclimated to the Tibetan plateau—where they had even been observed flowering with every hair on every petal encased in a coating of ice. Transferred to England, they did not fare so well, but later thrived in climates like that of California.

It was not until a decade later that plant hunter Frank Kingdon Ward, alerted by Bailey to the exact location of the poppies, managed to bring back the seeds of these turquoise beauties so they could be propagated in the West. Kingdon Ward's description of the same blue poppy is far more rapturous than Bailey's—oddly, the flowers reminded him of butterflies:

Just add deep blue: this stamp shows one of the dozen poppy species found in Bhutan—this particular species is collected for use in Bhutanese traditional medicine.

> This fine plant grows in clumps, half a dozen leafy stems rising from the perennial rootstock to a height of 4 feet. The flowers flutter out from amongst the sea-green leaves like blue-and-gold butterflies; each is borne singly on a pedicel, the plant carrying half a dozen nodding, incredibly blue 4-petalled flowers, with a wad of golden anthers in the centre... Never have I seen a blue poppy which held out such high hopes of being hardy, and of easy cultivation in Britain.

Kingdon Ward's hunch proved correct: being a woodland plant, this blue poppy was able to adapt to British gardens, and is today widely cultivated in cooler climes such as Scotland. Kingdon Ward immortalised Bailey by naming this blue poppy *Meconopsis baileyi*, but the plant is also known as *Meconopsis betonicifolia* after an earlier Chinese specimen, collected in the 1880s. Unsure which to use, some botanists merge the two names: *Meconopsis betonicifolia baileyi*. Bailey would've been very surprised to find this species today flourishing in the extensive gardens of Samye Ling Monastery—in Dumfriesshire in the Scottish lowlands. The Tibetan Buddhist retreat centre, started in 1967, is located in a region with Tsangpo-like conditions—meaning lots of rain. A small area of the monastery is dedicated to Tibetan medicinal plants.

Instead of going out and hunting the fauna, Bailey found that sometimes it just came to him. Setting up in a cave in May 1913, he writes:

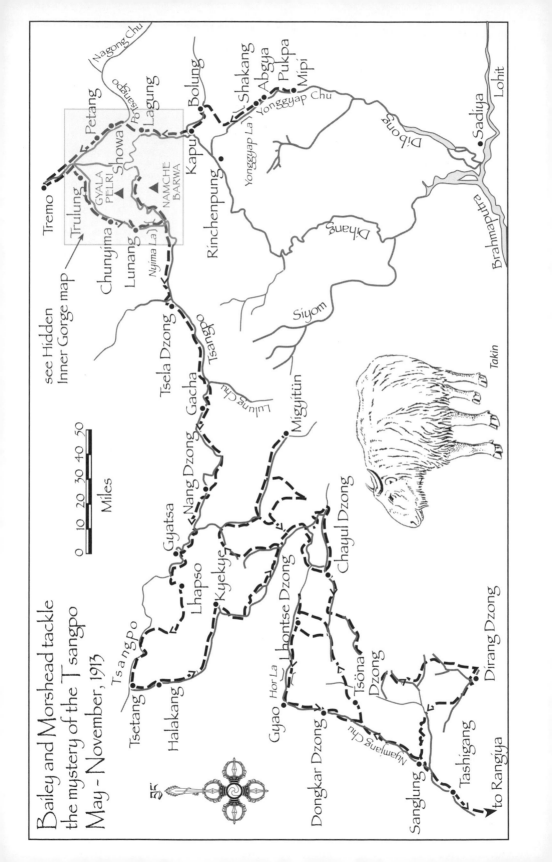

Bailey and Morshead tackle
the mystery of the Tsangpo
May – November, 1913

Miles
0 10 20 30 40 50

Nagong Chu
Po Tsangpo
Petang
Lagung
Showa
Bolung
Shakang
Abgya
Pukpa
Mipi
Yonggyap Chu
Yonggyap La
Sadiya
Lohit
Dibong
Tremo
Trulung
GYALA PELRI
NAMCHE BARWA
Kapu
Rinchenpung
Brahmaputra
Chunyima
Lunang
Nyima La
Dihang
see Hidden
Inner Gorge map
Siyom
Tsela Dzong
Gacha
Tsangpo
Takin
Lilung Chu
Migyitün
Nang Dzong
Gyatsa
Chayul Dzong
Lhapso
Kyekye
Tsangpo
Lhontse Dzong
Gyao Hor La
Tsöna Dzong
Dirang Dzong
Tsetang
Halakang
Dongkar Dzong
Nyamjang Chu
Sanglung
Tashigang
to Rangiya

N

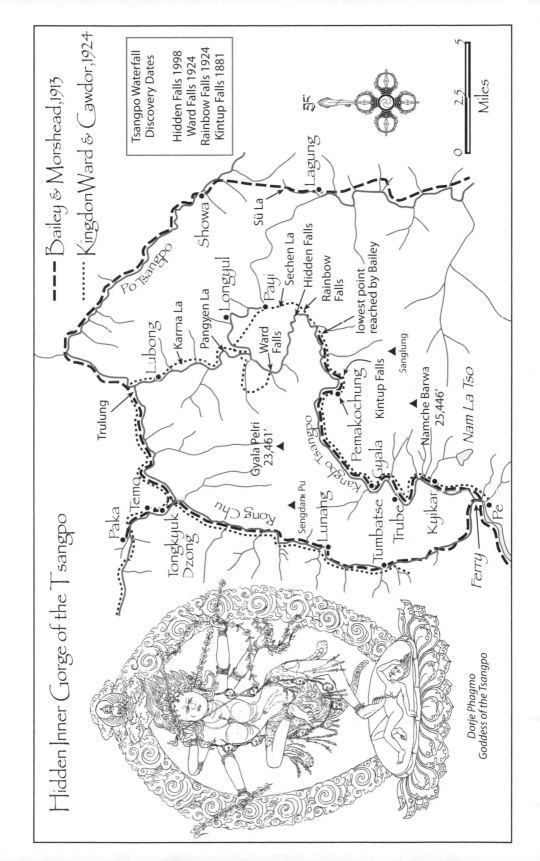

Hidden Inner Gorge of the Tsangpo

- - - Bailey & Morshead, 1913
.... Kingdon Ward & Cawdor, 1924

Tsangpo Waterfall
Discovery Dates

Hidden Falls 1998
Ward Falls 1924
Rainbow Falls 1924
Kintup Falls 1881

0   2.5   5
Miles

Po Tsangpo

Showa

Lagung

Sü La

Paji

Sechen La

Hidden Falls

Rainbow Falls

lowest point
reached by Bailey

Longyul

Pangyen La

Ward Falls

Karma La

Lubong

Sanglung

Trulung

Kangbo Tsangpo

Pemakochung

Kintup Falls

Gyala Pelri
23,461'

Namche Barwa
25,446'

Nam La Tso

Sengdam Pu

Rong Chu

Lunang

Gyala

Tumbatse

Trube

Kyikar

Paka

Temo

Tongkyuk
Dzong

Ferry

Pe

Dorje Phagmo
Goddess of the Tsangpo

The takin, a large mammal found in the Tsangpo region and other parts of the Tibetan plateau. Bailey shot a few of these.

My friendliest visitor was a shrew, which came to my table as I was working. I grew fond of it as a companion, and yet the more I looked at it the more I felt that it might be a new species which had never been seen or heard of before. As a man I wished it a long and happy life; but as an amateur naturalist I felt that the interests of science came first, so just before I left I converted my friend into a collector's specimen. It proved to be a new species and was named *Soriculus baileyi*.

Bailey was torn between preserving the beauty of the fauna and bagging it for science—or food. Gastronomy or taxidermy? That was the question. Another mammal specimen that Bailey brought back was a new species of goral (wild goat), later christened *Nemorhaedus baileyi*—adding to the list of things named after Bailey. But his most spectacular wildlife encounter was with the takin—at the time the most rare of game animals. This buffalo-sized beast resembles a strange cross between moose, musk-ox and deer—a herbivore with a bulbous nose and a short thick neck. A bull takin can easily weigh 700 pounds, and though it is a vegetarian and may appear docile, if you catch it in the wrong mood, an encounter with this beast can be life-threatening. Bailey shot several takins—he gave the meat to his guides for food and kept the heads as trophies. The takin was actually important to their quest. At certain stages, Bailey and Morshead proceeded along 'takin trails'—created by these hardy animals as they barrelled through dense thickets of rhododendron and stinging nettles.

There were some species that the explorers would rather not have come across: at lower elevations, there were leeches and ticks to deal with. In an earlier foray to this region, Bailey recalled a halt where he plucked 150 leeches from himself and his clothing. But the leeches did not seem to faze Morshead: all he cared about was surveying:

Morshead appeared indifferent to them [the leeches]. I thought at the beginning that this indifference might be a residue of his fever. But later I found this was not the case. When his temperature was indubitably normal, he would stand there covered in leeches and with blood oozing out of his boots as oblivious as a small child whose face is smeared with jam.

Bailey was alarmed by Morshead's apathy about leeches—if he lost too many pints of blood to the leeches, his health might suffer. So Bailey was relieved when they gained higher ground and the leeches disappeared—or, in Morshead's case, dropped off. Morshead's other worrisome habit was eating any fruit he found, even when informed it could be detrimental to his health. Bailey described camping in a cave near a clearing with:

> ...wild white strawberries, raspberries and gooseberries in the clearing. There were also red currants, which we were told were uneatable. But Morshead ate them all the same. His digestion seemed to be as insensitive to food as his body was to leeches. He ate any fruit he found.

Meanwhile, Bailey was having his own difficulties, navigating higher ground. Up ahead one day, Bailey and his guide had a spot of trouble on a steep snowbank:

> As we went down, we started slides and avalanches of our own. I had a dangerous fall which I thought was going to be my last, but I saved myself with the handle of my butterfly net. Then Sonam Chumbi started one. It was a very steep slope and as he went down he cried out, calling on Ugyen Rinpoche [the Saint Padmasambhava] to save him. Suddenly the mists parted and there was a gasp of horror as we saw that the slope ended in a sheer drop.

Using the handle of the butterfly net like an ice-axe to arrest his slide down the snowbank, Bailey had saved his life. For Sonam, salvation came in the form of some bushes at the edge of the drop.

After many trials and tribulations, Bailey and Morshead finally reached a bend in the river where they entered the Tsangpo gorge. They were in Kintup country now. Near Gyala, Bailey found the waterfall of Sinji-Chogyal that Kintup referred to, but it was not on the

Tsangpo—it was on a sidestream. The deity carved in rock behind the falls, he was disappointed to learn, was only visible through the water when the stream was low, in February and March.

Carrying on into the gorge, Bailey and Morshead got a magnificent view of Gyala Pelri, an unmapped colossus of 23,461 feet. The peak was only 13 miles distant from Namche Barwa, standing 25,445 feet high: between the two peaks crashed the mighty Tsangpo. Bailey described the scene: 'It was a fantastic landscape, with its different glaciers, some covered in rock and earth and others just masses of dirty ice.' The going got rougher here, with overgrown trails to hack through. They passed the small monastery at Pemakochung, which Kintup had visited. A few miles further, Bailey came across a surging 30-foot waterfall that sent up a huge cloud of spray—he took photographs of it.

One of the early signs they were breaking new ground was when Bailey rounded a corner and a woman looked up and fled screaming into her house, thinking he was Chinese. Morshead and Bailey forged on, crossing Sanglung Glacier. At this point, Bailey wrote:

> We were both excited, because until this moment we had largely been following in Kintup's footsteps down the Tsangpo, confirming his information, correcting it in places, adding what information our instruments gave us and, what was the most important of all, making a map. But from the Sanglung Glacier downwards, we, as far as the western world was concerned, were exploring country of which nothing was known, but much was speculated; one of the last remaining secret places on earth, which might perhaps conceal a fall rivalling the Niagara or Victoria Falls in grandeur.

The obstacles mounted—the forest on this side of the glacier was thick; it rained continuously, making the going very slippery. Both men had raw and blistered hands; Bailey's knees were swollen and throbbing from poisoned cuts caused by rhododendron twigs. His boots were falling apart. Bailey sighted some tantalising spray further along the Tsangpo—perhaps another great waterfall, but he couldn't be sure because of cloud and mist. The party was lacking food and water, and was poorly equipped to deal with the steep terrain: 'Reluctantly, we had to admit ourselves beaten.'

But not quite. Remarkably, Bailey and Morshead encountered a group of Monbas who had travelled some secret path along the inner Tsangpo to escort a lama toward Lhasa, and were now making their way back home—to the northeast, along the impossible-to-negotiate gorge. After some consultation, it was decided Bailey would try and attach himself to the Monba group and Morshead would turn back toward Gyala, slowly mapping. Bailey and his Monba porter Anay caught up with 18 surly Monbas, heading home northward. If that were true, they were heading right through the impenetrable part of the gorge. Bailey offered the Monbas a sum of money to guide them through.

At this point, Bailey noticed his precious camera was missing—and so was his Monba porter. He went back to search for the camera—and retracing his steps, found Anay with the Monbas. He suspected that either Anay or the Monbas had stolen his camera, but could not be sure: he knew he had to be on his guard with this shifty looking mob. At the crack of dawn, the Monbas started to make off stealthily: Bailey caught up with them and followed for four miles through rough jungle, then a steep climb of 800 feet, and a drop to the river-bed again. But the Monbas were growing increasingly agitated. Finally, they gave Bailey and Anay the slip— abandoning them below unscalable cliffs and retracting a rope ladder they'd used to aid their climb. Bailey and Anay had to turn back to Pemakochung. Here, it became apparent why the Monbas were eager to give Bailey the slip—they'd stolen pot and pans from houses, and had stolen supplies from Bailey's own party, including a pair of boots. They most likely made off with Bailey's Kodak camera, too—though it would have been of little use to them. Bailey had come within a hair's breadth of finding a way through the gorge and unlocking the secrets of the Tsangpo.

Time for afternoon tea. At Gacha, much further west along the Tsangpo, Morshead and Bailey were greeted by the Depa, or local head honcho. The Depa was obviously a man of some refinement: he offered some them some biscuits. In the background came a strange vocalisation: 'Drink some tea'. It was the Depa's parrot. Bailey notes:

> The Gacha Depa possessed a tin which had contained Hunt-
> ley & Palmer's biscuits (on sale in Lhasa, he said, at 3 trangkas a
> tin); also a parrot which said "Om Mani Padme Hum", and "Drink
> some tea" and "Give a walnut to the parrot", but nothing else. It

was a limited parrot but rather pathetic as it had no feathers, only down. The Depa had absentmindedly left a light beneath the bird and burnt its feathers off.

Still, a parrot that could recite the religious mantra *Om Mani Padme Hum* must have been regarded as something special in these parts.

Further towards the Assam frontier, Bailey and Morshead encountered some wild-looking Lopas clothed in serow skins: 'They wore very large earrings and cane hats, and across the front of their foreheads their hair was fastened with long brass pins like chopsticks.' They passed through thicker jungle, with abundant wildlife: Bailey shot a rare Sikkim stag. Coming out of the steamy jungle of Assam, nearing the British railhead of Rangiya, Bailey said they both looked ragged and filthy. For the first time, they started to think about how they smelled. They were flat broke because their native guides had absconded with the last of their funds. Further down the line, Bailey made a Freemason sign to an Anglo-Indian guard, who recognised it immediately and offered to lend them funds for the journey to Calcutta. They had to settle for second-class on the train—something that no self-respecting Brit would do in India, but they had little choice. Bailey says he enjoyed 'the look of horror on the faces of the European ladies in first class, who shrank to avoid contamination with us tramps.'

In the course of six months, Bailey and Morshead had charted some 380 miles of the Tsangpo, including the previously undocumented Namche Barwa and Gyala Pelri—two giant snowcaps that the Tsangpo gushed between. Bailey and Morshead definitively solved the Tsangpo-Brahmaputra connection—they were one and the same, emptying into the Dihang. They had accounted for all but 50 miles of the river. Bailey maintained there were no big falls were likely to be found—just a series of rapids dropping through the gorge.

On the naturalist score, considerable success: Bailey brought back 37 specimens of rare birds, including Harman's pheasant. A single birdskin had been discovered by Captain Harman of the Survey of India (Kintup's boss) but the specimen had not been properly preserved—and the sole evidence was a bunch of feathers that Bailey had seen at the Natural History Museum in London. Bailey bagged two magnificent specimens of Harman's pheasant. And Bailey's 1911 and 1913 expeditions established him as the recognised authority on butterflies of the region.

In November 1913, Bailey was summoned to take part in the Simla Conference, convened to demarcate borders between India, Tibet and China. Since negotiations with the Chinese were going nowhere, Bailey decided to try and find Kintup. The two met in May 1914 and Bailey was able to clear Kintup's name. Bailey returned to London on leave and read a full account of his expedition to the Royal Geographical Society on June 22, 1914, with Morshead in the audience. In 1916, the RGS awarded Bailey the Patron's Gold Medal, while Morshead received the Macgregor Medal. Bailey had meanwhile picked up another significant award, Companion of the Indian Empire, bestowed on him by King George V in January 1915; in 1920, he received the Livingstone Gold Medal of the Royal Scottish Geographical Society. Bailey would undoubtedly have gone back to the Tsangpo region a third time to explore the missing stretch of the river, but World War I got in the way.

Both Bailey and Morshead went on to distinguish themselves in the war. Bailey was wounded in the arm at Flanders, recovered and returned to duty—only to be wounded in both legs at Gallipoli. He was posted to Persia, where an undercover struggle was going on between the British and the Germans for the hearts and minds of the (neutral) Persians. In March 1918, Bailey was having a spot of trouble: posted to the town of Shushtar, he'd taken over a kind of blood feud from his predecessor and he learned that a three-man hit squad had entered town, intent on killing him. As he was the only European in the place, and the streets were narrow, he had every reason to be nervous. Around the same time, a telegram arrived asking if he was medically fit for an arduous journey in Central Asia, starting in Kashgar, in far west China. Bailey jumped at the chance—he took a steamer to Karachi and proceeded overland to Simla.

What really set Bailey aside from the rest of the pack was his uncanny knack for picking up languages. He'd earlier acquired Urdu and Tibetan, and now picked up Persian and Russian—as well as dusting off his school-learned French. He made full use of this linguistic advantage to blend in for undercover work. In India, Bailey learned he was to take command of a small secret mission bound for Central Asia to find out what was going on there after the Bolshevik seizure of power, and to find out what the Germans were up to with the Bolsheviks. The Great Game, which had pitted Britain against arch-enemy Tsarist Russia, had metamorphosed into an early version of the Cold War, taking on the Bolsheviks.

On the trip from Srinagar to Kashgar, Bailey had time to indulge in his passions—he collected a number of butterfly specimens. Riding on into Central Asia, Bailey even picked up a new butterfly net from Tashkent Natural History Museum. But there the pleasant distractions ended. Tashkent was the headquarters of the Bolsheviks in Central Asia, and fighting had just broken out between the Bolsheviks and British troops from Meshed. Bailey found himself out on a limb in Tashkent. His cohort Major Blacker, not in good health, had departed—deciding to accompany British diplomat Sir George Macartney back to India. While Bailey was having lunch with the American Consul one day, an ominous message was received—written in English, it announced that they would all be arrested and concluded: *For Bailey the position is especially dangerous and shooting is not out of the question.* That evening, Bailey disappeared.

For sixteen months, he played a deadly cat-and-mouse game with the Bolshevik secret police, the Cheka. Using a false identity as an Albanian deserter, at one point he actually joined the ranks of the dreaded Cheka, who sent him to Bukhara to track down a British agent called.... Bailey. Bailey finally escaped through Meshed in northeast Persia—on his way out, he bagged a specimen of a rare gazelle species. He reached Delhi in January 1920.

Bailey's miraculous return made front-page news in England. He was given a special reception by King George V in London, and was the talk of England. His daring double-agent exploits on this mission are worthy of a separate book—and indeed, Bailey wrote one—*Mission to Tashkent*. He drafted the manuscript as early as 1924, but could not clear the contents past his secrecy-obsessed superiors. Even as late as 1946, when the book was finally published, Bailey was forced to exclude some details and disguise identities because the information was still classified. He could not draw on the original 17-page report he'd written for officialdom. Major Blacker, his comrade, failed to even mention Bailey's name—even though Bailey was the expedition leader.

There was a lot more to Bailey than he ever let on himself. Witness this footnote in Swinson's biography about Bailey's activities in Persia in 1917: 'During this period he founded a Masonic lodge in Basra.' Secret mission, secret agent, secret society: Bailey was a Freemason, a member of a secret brotherhood. It was, however, not uncommon for those in the upper echelons of the British administration of India to become Freemasons. Contemporary with Bailey—among the illustrious Freemasons in Britain—were Antarctic explorers Robert Falcon Scott and Ernest Shackleton, and authors Rudyard Kipling and Arthur Conan Doyle. Winston Churchill was apparently a Freemason for a few years, before having a change of heart and being initiated into the Order of Druids. Since Freemason members are sworn to secrecy, it's hard to know what Bailey was into here, but the Freemasons are an all-male brotherhood dedicated to upholding moral ethics and encouraging charitable work. The Freemasons date back to 18th-century guilds of British stone masons; some hold that the society owes its origins to survivors of the order of the Knights Templar, a powerful group persecuted in Europe in the 13th century. The Knights Templar claim to be guardians of the Holy Grail.

On home leave in Britain in 1921, Bailey won the hand of Irma Hepburn, the only daughter of Lord and Lady Cozens Hardy, upper-crust British aristocracy. Eric and Irma left together by ship to take up Bailey's plum new position as Political Officer of Sikkim, starting in June 1921—a real adventure for Irma, who had never been east before. The Political Officer of Sikkim was directly responsible for British relations with Tibet, Sikkim and Bhutan. By the late 1920s, the Political Officer could grant permits for travel up the Chumbi Valley to the British Trade Agency at Gyantse—and was thus effectively the gatekeeper for Tibet.

Major Bailey (now promoted in rank) found the British Residency of Gangtok a charming place. The Residency was a two-storey mansion, modelled after an English country house: it faced the royal palace and temple of the Maharaja of Sikkim, but on higher ground, discreetly hidden behind ferns and trees, and boasting extensive gardens. From this base, Bailey could indulge in his passions of hunting and fishing: he succeeded in introducing trout into Sikkim (notably at Lake Changu) and later in Bhutan.

Although he welcomed guests and posed with them for photos, Bailey had a knack of somehow eluding the camera. He ends up either blurred, partially hidden behind an umbrella, hidden behind someone else in the foreground, or standing at the edge of the frame—glancing sideways, not directly at the camera. Freeze-frame: a picture taken at the residency shows Bailey holding a Lhasa Apso, Irma Bailey seated with a terrier, and intelligence officer Frank O'Connor holding another terrier. Lhasa Apsos were the royal Corgis of Tibet—fluffy lap-dogs that Tibetan nobles favoured. The Baileys had plans to make it big on breeding these dogs, along with Tibetan mastiffs, and introducing various Tibetan breeds to England.

Eric Bailey, the animal lover, was amazed by the endurance and loyalty of hunting dog breeds in Tibet. He had acquired a Tibetan spaniel during the invasion of Tibet in 1904, and said the dog accompanied him on a journey of more than a thousand miles, over snowy passes, from Tibet to Simla. Dogs are well-treated in Tibet: they find sanctuary close to monasteries, where Buddhist compassion encourages kindness to all animals. From nomads to nobles, many Tibetans were fond of dogs. The 13th Dalai Lama was very fond of dogs—he kept a number of Tibetan mastiffs, as well as other dogs of rare breeds, including foreign dogs like English greyhounds. Bailey took a photograph of one special dog of the 13th Dalai Lama, said to be a cross between a Tibet mastiff and a breed called 'the large Apso'. It was the only one that he ever saw of this cross-breed.

The most loyal breed is the Tibetan mastiff—a huge guard dog that rivals the St. Bernard in size, and somewhat resembles it in appearance. Tibetan mastiffs have been used by Tibetan nomads for some 5,000 years—perhaps the oldest, fiercest and biggest guard dogs known. Nomads leave them chained up to guard their tents during the day while they follow their flocks of yaks, sheep and goats. Along with a small menagerie of exotic Tibetan species, several Tibetan mastiffs were brought back to England from Lhasa after the Younghusband expedition in 1904. One of them ended up in a glass case at the Natural History Museum in London. In 1928, Irma Bailey arranged for five Tibetan mastiffs to be imported to the UK for breeding purposes. They are impervious to cold weather. Irma Bailey noted that on a freezing winter's day in England, with high wind, that the mastiffs will 'elect to lie out on a patch of snow, if they can find one.' Some of these dogs ended up living in zoos, and the breed never really caught on in England. The Baileys were ahead of their time. Tibetan mastiffs today command high prices in Europe and North America, and they have become a status symbol among China's elite. A Tibetan mastiff with a pure bloodline can fetch up to $400,000.

The Baileys met all guests headed for Tibet, since they had to hand over passports for entering the Land of Snows. Eric Bailey kept dinner guests spellbound with fund of amusing anecdotes—but became easily distracted, and would switch abruptly from Tibet to China to Assam and back again. Among guests passing by in 1921 and 1922 was Bailey's fellow-explorer of the Tsangpo, Captain Morshead, who joined the British Everest expeditions as surveyor. On the second expedition, climbing with Mallory to 25,000 feet, he fell seriously sick and had to be evacuated—losing several toes and fingers to frostbite in the process. Bailey was convinced that Morshead would be killed from his reckless disregard for personal safety, but having survived all the hair-raising expeditions, Morshead was murdered in Maymyo, Burma, while out for a ride in the jungle one morning, in May 1931. Bailey named a new species of butterfly after him: *Lycaenopsis morsheadi*, collected from the Tsangpo valley.

In the 1920s, Bailey developed a special interest in Bhutan. In June 1922, Bailey, his wife and Constance (mother of his wife) and David MacDonald off to present the Great Commander of the Order of the Indian Empire to the Maharaja of Bhutan, III I 3lr Ugyen Wangchuk. Following the invasion of Tibet, in 1907, the British helped engineer a sort of coup in Bhutan—installing the Wangchuk dynasty—and they aimed to monitor that connection. Despite his string of regal titles, Sir Ugyen Wangchuk still padded around barefoot—and wearing simple Bhutanese robes—while Bailey strutted around in imperial splendour with full uniform, a sword, a chestful of medals and a cocky hat. Later, perhaps to make the Maharaja feel more at ease, Bailey and his wife put on Bhutanese striped robes for group photos. But with their pale legs, the Baileys look like they're wearing bathrobes.

On the Ha La, on his way to Bhutan in 1922, Bailey rediscovered a beautiful white poppy, *Meconopsis superba*, which had been lost to science since 1881. His wife wrote:

> My husband was riding well ahead of the cavalcade, as was his usual practice, so as not to disturb the butterflies, when he saw this beautiful white Meconopsis as large as a saucer with a gold centre. He left a piece of paper stuck into the middle of the road telling me to look up on the left and collect some which I did, and a pressed specimen was sent to Edinburgh Botanical Gardens. It was a really thrilling moment for me...

As gatekeeper to Tibet, Bailey had to deal with those bent on sneaking into Lhasa—and those thrown out of Tibet. Among the more colourful gatecrashers was William McGovern, an American student of Buddhism. When a British Buddhist Mission passed through Sikkim, Bailey gave its six members permission to proceed as far as Gyantse, but no further. McGovern did this, then turned around and headed back into Tibet, disguised as a Sikkimese coolie—staining his skin with iodine and walnut juice, and wearing snow goggles to hide his eyes. Close to Lhasa, McGovern almost pissed his chance away: he made the supreme mistake of standing up when he paused for a roadside pee stop. A Tibetan official riding by stopped and asked about him. Tibetans are rough and ready when it comes to performing bodily functions, but there is still etiquette to follow. No twirling of prayer-beads at this time, and for both Tibetan men and women, squatting is *de rigueur*. McGovern succeeded in getting to Lhasa but encountered hostile mobs: he turned himself in and was expelled. Back in Gangtok, Bailey reprimanded McGovern for embarrassing the Indian Government—and then as the night proceeded, amused the party with tales of his own illicit adventures.

Response to gatecrashers varied: in 1924, when Alexandra David-Néel reached Gangtok after her extraordinary travels, the Baileys congratulated her and welcomed her to the Residency. Given a much curter reception—and an onward kick—was another Theosophist seeker of enlightenment, Mr Carpenter, a wealthy retired engineer who was determined to get to Shigatse, where he would study under his 'master'. Believing that a man had followed him from America, Carpenter always carried a loaded pistol in his pocket in case of an attack. He made it to Gyantse in 1926, but was prevented from proceeding to

Shigatse. That same year, Nicholas Roerich, a Russian mystic bent on finding the lost kingdoms of Shambhala and Agharti, was detained in northern Tibet and expelled by the British. Roerich's party ended up in Gangtok, where the Baileys entertained them—but Roerich was quite unaware that Bailey was instrumental in stopping him.

In the Year of the Wood-Mouse, July 1924, Bailey rode up from Sikkim to Lhasa to discuss pressing problems with the 13th Dalai Lama. Having delivered some Shetland ponies as gifts, Bailey started on the agenda: rumours of Bolshevik influence in Tibet, trouble over Everest expedition behaviour. Bailey was the only British officer around who could talk freely to the Dalai Lama without an interpreter. The Dalai Lama was upset over reports about the Everest expedition removing gem-stones from Tibet, filming monks and exporting monks to England for live performances. With the recent deaths of Mallory and Irvine clouding the issue, the Dalai Lama shut down the Everest expeditions for the rest of 1920s and imposed a ban on filming in Tibet. But Political Officers seemed to be exempt: Bailey shot movie-film of monks dancing (at Gyantse in 1925, and again in 1928). And Bailey also indulged in hunting and fishing in Tibet—which the Dalai Lama had specifically forbidden.

While Bailey and the Dalai Lama were discussing these delicate matters over tea, strange politicking was going on outside the Potala Palace. It centred around a Sikkimese Police Inspector from Darjeeling called Laden La, who was nephew to the pundit Ugyen Gyatso and loyal to Bailey. Laden La had been involved in a number of important missions, including providing security for the Dalai Lama in India (1910 to 1912). Laden La had reached Lhasa the previous year, in September 1923, intent on establishing a modern police force in Lhasa. Security in Lhasa was mostly provided by *dob-dobs*—oversized monk-police with whips and sticks. Laden La recruited 200 policemen and developed strong ties with Tsarong, commander of the Tibetan Army.

In May 1924, a fight broke out between the new police force and some drunken Tibetan soldiers. A policeman was fatally stabbed. Tsarong had two soldiers punished by mutilation. The incident brought the modernising and conservative elements in Tibet head-to-head. Tsarong was a firm supporter of modernisation and had long petitioned for a stronger armed force, with more modern weapons. However, the

High Lamas at monasteries in Lhasa saw this as giving more power to the army, which represented a threat to the power of the monks. Bailey arrived in Lhasa in the middle of all this and noted in his diary that he asked Tsarong what would happen if the Dalai Lama died. Tsarong and Laden La may have been behind a plot to take over secular power from the Dalai Lama, backed by British support.

Bailey departed Lhasa in August 1924. When Laden La left six weeks later, his new police force went into quick decline. Tsarong, who was travelling in the south, returned to find he had been dismissed as Army Commander and demoted in rank; his main supporters had also been dismissed from their posts or sent to outlying provinces. In his book *Tibet and the British Raj* (1997), British scholar Alex McKay suggests that the weight of circumstantial evidence points to a coup planned under Bailey's direction. McKay concluded that if the Dalai Lama were unwilling or unable to follow British advice, then from Bailey's perspective, Tsarong would have been a better leader. Keeping his distance, Bailey never wrote anything about the incidents of 1924—not even in his diary. As far as he was concerned, he was just having afternoon tea with the Dalai Lama and nothing more. The Indian National Archives kept the relevant files sealed, and Swinson, Bailey's biographer, says absolutely nothing about it.

In August 1924, the 13th Dalai Lama granted Bailey permission to travel down the Tsangpo from Lhasa to Tsetang. This four-day journey would allow Bailey to claim: 'I may say that I have seen this great river over all its length in Tibet except for a few small sections.' One of those 'small sections' was the Tsangpo gorges. At the same time that Bailey was following the Tsangpo, two other British explorers were in the thick of things, attempting to unravel the secrets of the gorges.

In March 1924, at the Residency in Gangtok, the Baileys had hosted botanist Frank Kingdon Ward and his colleague, Lord Cawdor. Bailey was passing the baton to Frank Kingdon Ward, bent on doing thorough exploration of the Tsangpo—especially the inner gorges. Bailey told him where to look for the blue poppy, and to keep an eye out for waterfalls. Kingdon Ward was a plant hunter who mounted a number of expeditions to the Tibet-China borderlands between 1911 and 1935. His eagerness to collect plant specimens had to overcome his great fear of heights: he would turn white as chalk when faced with a cliff-drop.

Kingdon Ward's expedition to the Tsangpo took place the same year as ill-fated Everest expedition with Mallory—indeed the two expeditions crossed paths in Lhasa. In the course of ten harrowing months, Kingdon Ward collected blue poppy samples (named after Bailey) and a staggering amount of flora (a number of species named after himself—like *Rosa wardii*, a species of wild rose). He sent home seed of about 250 species—many to the Royal Botanic Gardens at Kew, while others were planted in New Zealand, South Africa, South America and North America.

On this expedition, Kingdon Ward and Lord Cawdor were also to turn into waterfall hunters. Kingdon Ward described the sidestream falls of Sinji-Chogyal as 'a collection of poor little temples clapped against the face of a cliff over which a glacier torrent leaps 200 feet into the Tsangpo.' That made it three versions for the height of these falls (Kintup estimated 150 feet, Waddell said 100 feet, and now Kingdon Ward claimed 200 feet). In any case, Kingdon Ward was more concerned with attack of fleas at the rooms they lodged in. Lord Cawdor came across Bailey's 30-foot fall on the Tsangpo—but described it as unimpressive, more of a rapid. Bailey had seen it in high water, while Cawdor saw it in low water. More impressive was a drop christened Rainbow Falls, which Kingdon Ward estimated at 20 to 40 feet high. And he found another thundering waterfall of about 30 feet, today christened Ward Falls. Yet to be explained was the great drop in elevation between the Tibetan and Indian parts of the river. A long, descending chain of rapids? Or was there some sort of Niagara hidden in a bend of the Tsangpo? Kingdon Ward speculated:

> Our excitement may be imagined; and the fact that the river between Rainbow Fall and the confluence dropped 1,851 feet was favourable to the theory of a 100-foot waterfall somewhere.

While Kintup had reduced the unexplored part of the inner Tsangpo Gorge to about 100 miles, and Bailey had trimmed the unknown gap to 50 miles, Kingdon Ward figured he'd seen all but a five-to-ten mile gap of the mysterious river gorges. In his book *The Riddle of the Tsangpo Gorges*, published in 1926, he gave a detailed account of the expedition's achievements. And there the riddle rested—until 70-odd years later, when interest resumed in the unexplored miles of the river.

In 1927, Lieutenant-Colonel Bailey was back as Political Officer of Sikkim. He stayed on a few years. On October 16th, 1928, the Baileys left Sikkim—and Tibet—never to return to the Tibetan world. Bailey had accumulated a two-year leave: details about what he did during this time are sketchy. The Baileys had no children, and were thus free to travel at will—their favourite indulgence. In the summer of 1929, the Baileys were in San Francisco. In October 1929, Francis Younghusband met Bailey on the street in London and invited him to lunch. Younghusband said Bailey was most amusing—he'd brought home 13 Tibetan dogs, and said was going to make his fortune from them. They were Lhasa Apsos—and Bailey's connections with the upper class, through his wife, led to the introduction of the dogs in British society. In 1930, the Baileys had planned a ten-month round-the-world tour, starting out in Europe. But this was cut short: they were travelling in Switzerland when word came through that Bailey was to report for duty as Political Officer in central India.

Although Bailey was to serve for another dozen years in His Majesty's Service, he led a lacklustre later career. This was likely due to fallout from the events of 1924, when Bailey trod on a lot of toes in Tibet and elsewhere. Bailey was falling into obscurity and he knew it: he was passed over for higher postings that might have carried a knighthood. He was offered obscure residencies in India. The first, in October 1930, was as Political Officer in Baghelkhand, central India. After 15 months, he transferred to the position of Resident at Baroda. From 1932–33, he was the Resident in Kashmir, which was most prestigious—but there were troubled times here. In February 1935, he was appointed as His Majesty's Envoy Extraordinary to the Court of Nepal—a position he held for three years.

On April 23rd, 1938, Bailey retired at the age of 56. He set sail for Italy to meet his wife, who'd been touring Europe for most of the time Bailey was in Nepal. From Nepal, Bailey took with him 2,306 bird specimens, which he later presented to the British Museum of Natural History. A letter sent to Bailey in 1938 bore many directional marks on the cover—the postmarks of Gangtok, Calcutta, Nepal, London and Scotland. Eric Bailey—of no fixed address—was away on a fishing trip.

When WWII broke out, Bailey joined the Home Guard in 1940, helping to organise guerrilla units. He enrolled as a King's Messenger in 1942, back in diplomatic service again. For two years, he was based in Miami and Washington, DC—flying around central and south America, delivering diplomatic dispatches. In 1943, he was back in Norfolk, England, working on his butterfly collection and on book projects.

His first book, *China-Tibet-Assam*, appeared in 1945, followed a year later by *Mission to Tashkent*. The books were disjointed in narrative and disappointingly devoid of emotion—almost never attempting to convey the beauty of the majestic surroundings. But the very publication of the books was a revelation to many because the astonishing nature of Bailey's adventures was not generally known. To others, it was a revelation that Bailey was still alive. Back in 1924, Bailey's mother had approached the War Graves Commission to have his name taken off a memorial. After checking the records carefully, Lord Stopford asked Mrs Bailey where her son might be now. She replied that he was alive and well and staying in Lhasa as a guest of the Dalai Lama. Upon hearing this, the commissioner showed the woman the door, presuming her to be demented.

As a rare expert on Tibet, Bailey advised many—and maintained contact with learned societies. For some years, he was honorary librarian of the Royal Central Asian Library in London. He was a great speaker too, but his fund of anecdotes belonged more to the dinner table. A number of attempts were made to record his story, but he didn't seem to work well with a microphone. Historian Alastair Lamb offers a few clues as to why. When he went to interview Bailey in the early 1950s, Alastair Lamb recalls that at his country estate, the drawing-room window was open—and without breaking sentence, Bailey would take up a pearl-handled revolver and shoot at any bird that happened to alight on the trees outside. Here was a man obsessed with shooting right to the end. In his youth, he'd shot his way into Lhasa, he'd shot wildlife for museum collections—and he wasn't about to lose his touch.

The country estate Lamb talks about was a rambling mansion the Baileys bought in 1952. It was located in Stiffkey, a small isolated village on the Norfolk coast. The mansion was chosen because it was big enough to hold Bailey's butterfly and stuffed animal collections. Stuffed Tibetan pheasants sat in glass cabinets, while on the walls were preserved heads of Tibetan wildlife specimens from his hunting trips. In Norfolk, Bailey finished a third book, *No Passport to Tibet*, about his 1913 adventures on the Tsangpo—it was published in 1957. The book was somewhat out of

Bailey finally got round to publishing his Tsangpo adventures four decades later. *No Passport to Tibet* was published in 1957. The cover art shows Bailey (left) and Morshead (right) surveying the Tsangpo from a viewpoint, with big snowcaps in the background.

synch with times: after WWII, the global power of Britain had dwindled, but Bailey wrote in the old colonial vein. He assessed the Lepchas of Sikkim, for instance, as 'a most charming people...They make excellent servants, as much at home in the drawing room as in the forest.'

Bailey was known to be working on a full autobiography, but it was never completed. After all his close brushes with death, Bailey passed away from natural causes at the age of 85, on 17 April, 1967. Irma Bailey, his wife, burned a lot of his papers after his death—apparently bent on sanitising his reputation. Whether drafts of Bailey's autobiography went into the fire is unknown: at any rate, Irma co-operated with biographer Arthur Swinson on a more sanitised version of Bailey's life. Bailey's butterfly collection went to Metropolitan Museum in New York—although the 'types' collection had been given to the British Museum a few years before he died.

And the mystery of the Tsangpo lived on, with still-unseen sections of the river. Kintup had reduced the unexplored section of the Tsangpo to a 100-mile stretch, which Bailey later reduced to 50 miles; Kingdon Ward had whittled that down to an estimated five-to-ten miles left unexplored.

After Kingdon Ward's foray, the Tsangpo Gorges were more or less locked off for the next 50 years. The area became particularly sensitive from the 1960s onward as Chinese PLA troops conducted periodic border warfare designed to test the patience of rival power India. When the Chinese finally allowed foreign expeditions back into the Tsangpo area, around 1985, there was a steep price to pay. There were two great firsts on offer here: river deep, mountain high. There was the first descent of the Tsangpo, the world's highest river, and the first ascent of 24,436-foot Namche Barwa, at the time the world's highest unclimbed peak. When British explorer John Blashford-Snell inquired about running a section of the Tsangpo from its source in western Tibet, he was quoted an expedition price-tag of a million dollars. Bashford-Snell retorted: 'We don't want to *buy* the bloody river—we just want to *run* it.'

Bargaining to enter the region only became possible after a successful 1992 summit climb of Namche Barwa by a joint Sino-Japanese team. After losing her virginity, the peak was no longer so special and the turf around her came with a more reasonable tariff. China lifted the travel ban in southeast Tibet. A trickle of high-paying foreign expeditions gained access. Supported by the deep pockets of the National Geographic Society, Ian Baker and Kenneth Storm wrangled permits to enter the area.

In 1994, a wilderness guide from Arizona called Richard Fisher claimed an entry in the *Guinness Book of World Records*: his altitude readings placed the Tsangpo Gorge at over three miles deep. Which was a mile deeper than Rio Colca in the Peruvian Andes, and three times deeper than the Grand Canyon. There was some dickering over semantics—did the Tsangpo qualify as a proper canyon or was it just a valley? But even as a valley, it was still 1,200 feet deeper than the 14,400-foot Kali Gandaki Valley in Nepal. At around the same time, the Chinese Academy of Sciences announced similar findings. While Kintup, Bailey, Morshead and Kingdon Ward had all been looking for a mammoth waterfall, they had entirely missed something right under their noses—a world record-setting deepness. They knew the gorge was very deep: what these explorers did not know was comparative data about other canyons worldwide. In places, the Tsangpo gorge is over 16,000 feet deep. Apart from carving out the world's deepest gorges, the Tsangpo is the longest river on the Tibetan plateau and the highest on earth: it runs over 1,800 miles through Tibet, India and Bangladesh.

After several expedition probes into the gorges, in 1997, Baker and Storm got a glimpse of Rainbow Falls. And they noticed, some distance off, spray from what appeared to be a large cascade. But they couldn't get in closer to investigate. These falls had also been spotted from a great distance by others, but no-one had found a way to see them up close and accurately measure them.

In 1998, Baker and Storm returned with climbing equipment. They reached Rainbow Falls, and using a clinometer, calculated its height at 70 feet—almost double the estimate of Frank Kingdon Ward. Baker and Storm were thrilled by this discovery, but there was more. When pressed, Baker's guide—a local Monba hunter—revealed that there was a way to get in closer to the second set of mystery falls further on—by following takin tracks, or to be more precise, 'takin tunnels'. The takin has created its own tunnels through dense undergrowth, rather like trails for dwarfs. Just make sure you don't meet a takin coming the other way (actually, the guide shot some takins, which provided good meat). By crawling through these takin tunnels, Baker and Storm were able to get through—and came face-to-face with a crashing torrent that pooled in a boiling cauldron at its base.

Baker and Storm rappelled down to the bottom of the falls over mossy rocks, buffeted by spray and deafened by the thundering noise. Using a clinometer the pair were able to gauge the exact height of the falls. They calculated it at just over 100 feet, but somehow this got adjusted—auspiciously but suspiciously—to 108 feet, a sacred number in Tibetan Buddhism. Says Baker: 'It was the convergence of a Western dream with the Tibetans' own vision of a sacred realm. We all had a great sense of shared discovery.' They christened the cascade 'Hidden Falls'.

These falls lie just upstream from Rainbow Falls: Frank Kingdon Ward missed the grand waterfall prize by a quarter-mile. The legendary falls that had kept geographers excited since Kintup's time were now, strangely enough, a reality—a waterfall of over 100 feet and another of 70 feet. The fabled 100-foot waterfall that Kingdon Ward had speculated about in 1924 was indeed there.

The thundering waterfall is the highest yet discovered on a major Himalayan river.

Baker and Storm never claimed to have discovered these falls. They acknowledged others who'd explored at the same time had seen them. But they did lay claim to being the first to get in close and measure Hidden Falls accurately. 'Discovery' is a slippery word because it discounts what the locals may have known for aeons. As is the case here, it seems. The Tibetans had known about the hidden falls all along, probably for centuries. It was Tibetan hunters who finally showed Baker and Storm the way through 'takin tunnels' to the lip of the falls. Back in 1913, Eric Bailey met a group of Monbas returning home along a portion of the Tsangpo—they had given him the slip when he tried to follow them.

Tibetan extreme reluctance to reveal these areas to outsiders evidently comes from their reverence of the zone as the home of goddess Dorje Phagmo, the protector deity of Tibet. The area of the Great Bend of the Tsangpo is known in Tibetan as Pemako, a sacred realm referred to in Tibetan scriptures. It was one of the 'hidden treasures'—one of a number of places consecrated by the great sage Padmasambhava as a hidden refuge to be sought in times of turmoil. So it would be the job of the Tibetans to keep it hidden from outsiders. Tibetans visualise

Whitewater explorer Chris Jones on a first descent of the
upper Parlung Tsangpo

the Tsangpo gorges as suffused by the energy of tantric goddess Dorje
Phagmo. They visualise her anatomical features in reclining posture
correlating to physical features of the gorges—with the Tsangpo river
as her spinal cord, the soaring peaks of Namche Barwa and Gyala Pelri
as her breasts, and the secret valleys beyond Tibet's southern frontier
as her womb. Anyone discovering these hidden valleys, legend has it,
will find redemption and be reborn.

In 1999, the Chinese jumped in to stake their claim. They said the
Chinese military had discovered Hidden Falls much earlier, whirring
along the Tsangpo in a helicopter in 1987 on a mapping reconnaissance mission. Baker calls this 'backwards discovery'—because the

Portable boats: at left, a boatman carries his Tibetan craft like a turtle—the boat is ingeniously made from yak-hide stretched over a simple frame, and used for river crossings today. At right, adventurous paddlers portaging their kayaks near Rong Chu, Everest region. If only Bailey had one of these.

Chinese did not make their announcement until after Baker made his. From the air, it is hard to determine the height of any falls: even satellite imagery could not probe this section because the gorge is deep and twisted, with overhanging vegetation. Sour grapes: shortly after Baker's big discovery, the Chinese closed the area to foreign visitors for some time. Hidden Falls, as named by Baker and crew, will never appear under that name on any Chinese map. And nor, probably, will Ward Falls or Kintup Falls.

The ultimate quest on the Tsangpo—the final frontier—is exploration inside the gorges, along the river itself. In the days of Kintup and Bailey, there was no watercraft capable of handling such wild waters. But with the emergence of sophisticated whitewater kayaks and rafts, that changed. Among kayakers and rafters, the Tsangpo came to be regarded as the Everest of whitewater. The trouble is, once inside the steep canyons of the gorges, there is no way out. The first whitewater kayakers to venture into the gorge were killed—Japanese kayaker Yoshitaka Takei vanished in 1993, and American kayaker Doug Gordon was lost in a massive rapid on an expedition in 1998. After Gordon's death, white-water experts wrote the Tsangpo off as unrunnable.

In February 2002, however, a team of explorers and kayakers from seven nations began a two-month expedition through the Upper Tsangpo Gorge. Their goal was twofold: to chart some of the unseen parts of the gorge, and to complete its first white-water descent. Expedition leader Scott Lindgren, from California, had his eyes on the gorge for more than a decade, after pioneering kayak descents of other Himalayan rivers. After scouting the Tsangpo several times, he concluded that the flow of water was suicidally high in the spring, but that late winter might work because of the lower flow.

Seven of the world's top kayakers launched into the wild water of the Upper Tsangpo Gorge—the most fearsome they'd ever seen—and went where nobody had ever been before. They survived Class V+ rapids, thundering past boiling eddies, great vertical drops, massive lateral waves and huge boulders. Alternately paddling and portaging—and seal-launching from boulders—the team paddled about 90 percent of the Upper Gorge. Then they started an epic winter portage over Sechen La to by-pass the unrunnable Rainbow Falls and Hidden Falls. Threading their way up treacherous couloirs and steep snow-slopes must have looked a strange spectacle with kayaks in tow. Finally, they rejoined the river, but found that a flash flood had scoured the banks of the Tsangpo to near-vertical rock. At this point, they prudently decided to pack it in. The team had covered 45 river miles—the first-ever descent of the Upper Tsangpo Gorge—and lived to tell the tale.

The Tsangpo has never been run in its entirety. One rather large obstacle to achieving this feat looms on the horizon: a Chinese proposal to build a mega-dam at the Great Bend of the Tsangpo. First reported in 1996, the Chinese plan is to drill a 9.3-mile tunnel through the Himalayas to divert the water before it reaches the Great Bend—and direct it to the other side of the bend. In effect, instead of dropping 9,800 feet over a distance of 125 miles, the powerful waters of the Tsangpo would hurtle through a tunnel of just 9.3 miles in length. Creating a tunnel at the Great Bend of the Tsangpo with conventional methods would be impossible, but engineers at the Chinese Academy of Engineering Physics in Beijing stated that the project could 'certainly be accomplished with nuclear explosives.' The Chinese plan would be in breach of the CTBT, the international nuclear test-ban treaty of 1996.

If the Tsangpo project were to go ahead, it would be the largest dam in the world, generating 40,000 megawatts— more than twice the electricity produced by Three Gorges Dam on the Yangtse. A project involving an experimental nuclear explosion could cause devastating results in a zone that is known to be earthquake-prone and mudslide-prone. But the news gets worse. The Chinese plan envisages harnessing the colossal hydropower potential of the Tsangpo Dam to pump water *northward* to the Gobi Desert, over 500 miles away.

Northern China in the north faces two grave problems: acute shortages of power and water. As China's economy soars ahead with rapid growth, the country cannot keep pace with skyrocketing demands for electricity, despite massive investment in power plants and nuclear stations. This has resulted in brownouts, power cuts and power conservation measures in many urban centres. A large-capacity dam on the Tsangpo could alleviate the acute demand for electricity.

Water is becoming an increasingly rare commodity in the north, where agriculture depends on water to sustain food production. China's new 'emperors' are not quite sure what to do about this, but if they want to avoid mobs of starving pitchfork-throwing peasants, they have to do something. And do it soon. The regions of northern China are particularly hard-up for water because of intensified desertification and industrial pollution. On the drawing-board is a solution to divert river water from the south to the north. There are three diversion sectors: eastern, central and western. The western sector eyes the Tibetan plateau as a water-diversion target. Tibet is the principal watershed of Asia and the source of its ten major rivers: about 90 percent of Tibetan rivers' runoff flows downstream into China, India, Bangladesh, Nepal, Pakistan, Thailand, Myanmar, Laos, Cambodia and Vietnam.

In Imperial China, people traditionally respected their emperor when he undertook grandiose projects that no sane human would ever contemplate. One of them is the 1,500-mile Great Wall—which never worked for its intended function—to keep the Mongol hordes out—but that's besides the point. It looked good. Another huge undertaking was the digging of the Grand Canal which, due to silting and pollution, has today lapsed into a mere tourist attraction. Recent times have witnessed a renewed interest in gargantuan-but-dubious projects, hosted by China's new 'emperors'. China's first manned spaceflight in 2003 was undoubtedly one of these. And the highly controversial

Three Gorges Dam definitely qualifies. But the proposed Tsangpo Dam would take it to a higher level.

While peaceful nuclear explosions might work for the Chinese, going ahead with this insane project would be a virtual declaration of war on India and Bangladesh—sitting at the tail-end of the river. Millions of Indians and Bangladeshis rely on the Brahmaputra to irrigate their crops: with the Tsangpo Dam in place, they would be at the mercy of China for adequate release of water during the dry season and for protection from floods during the rainy season. Nutrient-rich sediments could be held back in a reservoir in Tibet instead of reaching India and the river's delta in Bangladesh.

If you were to interview Eric Bailey about the fate of the Tsangpo— the river he was largely responsible for exploring—what would he have to say? He'd probably let loose a few expletives: *Blasted Chinese! Damn hidden waterfall!* And he'd curse a dam on the Tsangpo because it would ruin all the fishing. The Indians and Bangladeshis would not appreciate the theft of a river. And the Tibetans would definitely not appreciate a nuclear-blasted tunnel, boring through the heart of the sacred realm of Pemako—home of Tibet's protector goddess, Dorje Phagmo.

Man in a hurry to get to Everest: Maurice Wilson strikes a cocky pose next his Gipsy Moth, the incredible flying machine he christened *Ever-Wrest*. This picture was snapped at an airfield close to London, circa 1932—before he took off for India.

 # Maurice Wilson
1898–1934
daredevil aviator & lunatic adventurer

Everest on Faith & Figs

Quest for the Holy Grail
of mountaineering

❖ ❖

*You can't fault Maurice Wilson for sheer audacity. He came
out of nowhere, aiming to bag mountaineering's greatest prize.
Wilson had never been on a mountain in his life, but why not
start at the top? And go for Mount Everest? Wilson's grand
plan was to fly a small aircraft from England to Tibet, crash-
land on the slopes of Everest—and hike up from there to plant
the Union Jack on the top. The loneliness of the long-distance
aviator: in 1933, Maurice Wilson set forth on a quixotic quest
to do battle with the Goddess of the Snows—a nasty piece of
work, by any reckoning. It was the ultimate adventure.*

 How WOULD YOU define the word 'adventure', exactly? Some 70 years after Wilson's escapade, a group of American magazine editors were locked in furious debate over The Adventure Issue. They finally settled on the following definition: Adventure is when an individual (or a group) encounters and combats physical dangers, usually involving one or more of the elements (earth, air, fire, water); it can, but doesn't have to, include at least one of the following items: avalanches, pirates, brutal desert landscapes, improperly equipped flying machines, hot-air balloons, castaways, buried treasure, swords, wolves, tigers, bears, birds of prey, frozen tundra. On his Tibetan foray, Maurice Wilson encompassed practically *all* of those items, plus a whole raft of others. His story starts out with the improperly equipped flying machines—and ends with the frozen tundra. And the birds of prey.

The 'Mad Yorkshireman' (as the press had dubbed him) apparently derived his crazy notions from reading about the 1924 British Everest expedition. The fact that the ace mountaineer of the day, George Mallory, had perished in the 1924 attempt on the peak did not seem to faze Wilson. Wilson certainly had balls, but did he have the brains to go with them? There were a few hitches to his plans. For starters, he had absolutely no flying experience. These were pioneering days in aviation: Wilson simply bought himself a second-hand biplane and set about learning how to fly it. And then he indulged in some hill-walking in the Lake District and the Welsh mountains as preparation for the ascent of the peak.

Wilson's motivation for all this appears to be a combination of divine faith and megalomania. He wanted to be a celebrity, and he figured being first on top of Everest would definitely get him onto the front pages of newspapers—and into the history books. Actually, he'd been in the news once before—in World War I when he won a Military Cross for single-handedly withholding a German attack. In this action, everybody around Wilson was killed, but he miraculously survived. A short time after, he was sprayed with machine-gun fire—he hovered close to death, but managed to recover. His left arm was rendered practically useless.

Born in Yorkshire on April 21st, 1898, Wilson had enlisted the day after he turned 18. He was physically imposing—six-foot-one and brawny, with a determined jaw. He was the third-born of four brothers in a middle-class family involved in the textile industry in Bradford, an industrial city in the north of England. Wilson was demobilised in July 1919, but his war experiences—his miraculous escapes from death—seem to have had a profound effect on him. He found it impossible to settle down in the family textile business. Except for his mother, Wilson did not develop a lengthy emotional attachment to a woman. He married briefly in Britain, then divorced. He drifted from job to job—and drifted from country to country, travelling across America. He stayed for several years in New Zealand, where he married a Maori woman, then divorced. He took on a job as a shiller of snake-oil—a tincture of opium and alcohol that he bottled himself and sold from his car. He tried his hand at farming. Then he bought a ladies' dress shop—which turned into a prosperous business. But suddenly he pulled up stakes and boarded a ship back to England. He was back home, but he was more restless than ever.

Intense interest in Mount Everest started up in March 1856, when Andrew Waugh, the Surveyor-General of India, wrote a short report citing 'Peak XV' as probably the highest in the world. As the peak lay in a remote area of off-limits Nepal and Tibet, Waugh could not identify any native name: in the same report, he christened it 'Mont Everest' in honour of the former head of the Great Trigonometrical Survey of India, Sir George Everest. It was a fitting honour for Everest, who earned his nickname 'compass-wallah' from having spent half his life surveying India (his other chief pursuit was chasing nubile young women—as in collecting Indian mistresses).

Peak XV was officially designated a height of 29,002 feet. The height of Everest has since been adjusted a number of times, but all measurements rank Everest above 29,000 feet—which puts the peak in a class of its own. Other candidates for the world's highest peak—Nanda Devi, Kangchenjunga, Nanga Parbat—paled in comparison. No other peak has broken the 29,000-foot barrier. As the highest known peak, Everest quickly excited the interest of the British, the Swiss, the

Austrians, the Italians, the Germans and the French who were caught up in the new-fangled sport of alpinism and peak-bagging. But everything about the Himalayas was daunting: the highest summit in the Swiss Alps was the elevation where climbs on Everest *began*. This begged the question: Could Everest be climbed?

Everest was a British discovery—and reaching its peak rapidly became a very British obsession. After the British invaded Tibet in 1903–04 and 100 Englishmen reached Lhasa, the Sacred City had somewhat lost its lustre on the explorer's check-list. The explorer's race to reach Lhasa was never quite the same after that mass onslaught. The leader of the British invasion of Tibet, Sir Francis Younghusband, later became instrumental in getting a brand-new race off the ground: a military-style assault on Everest. Some time after retiring from the army, Sir Francis Younghusband had become the president of the Royal Geographical Society, which, along with the Alpine Club, backed the early expeditions to Everest. The thinking was that scaling Everest would require a military-type assault, requiring porters, strategy, and so on. Personifying Everest as some sort of virginal Amazonian warrior, Younghusband wrote:

> The doom of Everest is sealed, for the simple and obvious reason that Man grows in wisdom and stature, but the span of mountains is fixed. Everest fights stoutly with her many terrible weapons. She is surrounded by unscalable rocks, which are her armour, but she fights blindly beneath her armour. She cannot learn from experience. She cannot rise to occasions…for man's full cunning will find a way to outwit the mountain's allies… Man is relentlessly overtaking her.

One thing explorers and public alike really enjoy is a good race. People were enthralled by the 1911 race for the South Pole between the British and the Norwegians. By 1920, with both the South Pole and the North Pole races long gone, the attention of explorers shifted to another frontier: the conquest of Everest. Unlike the race for the poles, which could be justified on scientific grounds, an Everest expedition would contribute little to scientific or geographic knowledge. The contestants were largely in it for the sport, for the national glory: it was something that just had to be done. All eyes were on the Holy Grail of mountaineering: a piece of shattered limestone about the size of a billiard table, coated in snow and ice—the summit of Everest.

In 1905, Lord Curzon, Viceroy of India, wrote in a letter to Douglas Freshfield, then the president of the Royal Geographical Society:

It has always seemed to me a reproach that with the second highest mountain in the world for the most part within British territory [K2 in Kashmir] and with the highest in a neighbouring and friendly state [Everest in Tibet], we, the mountaineers and pioneers par excellence of the universe, make no sustained and scientific attempt to climb to the top of either of them.

To put that in plain English, he was saying British mountaineers should be the first to plant the British flag on top of Everest or K2—or both. He detailed plans for an expedition escorted by Swiss guides and 'coolies' that might establish higher and higher camps 'until one day the advance camp would be placed on a spot from which a dash could be made for the summit…Ought we not be able to do this?'

Practically, the answer was yes, but plans were stymied due to political manoeuvring with Nepal, Tibet, Russia and India. Routes to Everest from Nepal were firmly closed, but access from Tibet looked promising. Since invading Tibet in 1903–04, and establishing trade relations, the British enjoyed a virtual monopoly on access to Tibet—they could (and did) exclude European rivals.

But first the Brits had to find the colossal peak. Surveying of Everest had been done from the Nepalese side, not the Tibetan side. Even the masters of the universe had trouble getting to the north face of Everest. Several of the pundits managed limited reconnaissance, including the first reports of the mysterious Lamasery of the Snows. The 13th Dalai Lama was reluctant to grant permission to even visit the area, let alone climb. In 1913, off-duty British officer Captain John Noel sneaked overland in disguise to get a view of the mountain. When fired upon by a Tibetan rider with a matchlock rifle, Captain Noel returned fire with his American rifle, which sent the Khampa off at a gallop. Noel's frightened escort said that they must now retreat in full haste, convinced that the whole of Tibet would return to get them. Noel gave up his scouting mission, but he got a glimpse of the mountain closer than any European had ever seen it—about 40 miles away from the colossus.

The outbreak of WWI delayed any efforts to reach Everest again. In March 1919, John Noel delivered a lecture at the RGS about his 1913 incursion in Tibet: in the discussion that followed, the president of the

Alpine Club proposed climbing the summit of Everest. In 1920, permission was finally granted to approach Everest by the 13th Dalai Lama, under the influence of Sir Charles Bell, and the first British expedition got under way. Here, another obstacle arose: how to get several tons of equipment and supplies through to the base of Everest, and how to portage those supplies to advance camps on the flanks of the peak. Without this pyramid of logistical support, the assault might falter.

The British came up with an answer for the supply system—for the 1921 reconnaissance, they forged through to the base of the mountain with a caravan of porters, yaks and mules. The 1922 expedition had a caravan of over 300 yaks, all with cow-bells round their necks and small bells tied to their tails. The expedition was the size of a small army. Colonel Howard-Bury favoured using Sherpa porters from Nepal, and General Bruce favoured the Gurkhas. The Gurkhas excelled at the sport of *khud*, which was racing up and down steep mountains— generally before breakfast. But in the end, Sherpas prevailed because they performed outstanding feats at altitude. The British also recruited Tibetan porters, but they did not get along with the Sherpas, who looked down on them. And Tibetan porters refused to climb high on Everest, terrified of the resident spirits said to live there.

On a lecture-tour of America in 1923, George Mallory was spotted by a photographer in the act of scaling the exterior of his skyscraper hotel in New York—on the underside of the fire-escape. A spot of light training, you might say. Mallory was very impatient with reporters. Earlier, when one asked for the umpteenth time why he wanted to climb Everest, he turned and snapped: 'Because it is there.'

The Tibetans all had exactly the same question: Why? Why on earth would anyone want to do this? Getting into the record books meant nothing to the Tibetans. The only sports they understood were polo and archery. They couldn't understand why anyone would want to climb Everest, but they indulged the whims of the British. One of those whims was a box 40 feet long, which held cine-camera equipment that John Noel wanted to bring along on the third British expedition to Everest in 1924. Hard to find mules for that load. John Noel pioneered the developing of cine-film on the spot, under primitive conditions, in a special lightproof tent. He developed and washed thousands of feet of 35mm film, drying it over a yak-dung fire—a technique later adopted by Joseph Rock.

After the death of Mallory and Irvine on Everest in 1924, the curtain fell on summit attempts: permission to mount new expeditions was refused by the Dalai Lama. The inauspicious deaths of the climbers had something to do with it, but the biggest problem was John Noel's cine-film extravaganza. Noel had filmed sacred masked dance in Tibet—which ended up being shown to huge audiences in London. This was the silent-movie era: sound effects for this film were provided by seven Tibetan monks who had been spirited out of Tibet and shipped to England by Noel. Getting them out was quite a coup—and it was done by telling lies to the India Office about the monks' travel documents. At the Scala Theatre in London, a scene painter had built and painted an exotic Himalayan set, with temple doors and monastery courtyard in the foreground and snowpeaks in the background. The Tibetan monks played horns, drums and cymbals in the foreground while lighting illuminated the mountain peaks behind. Then the lights dimmed, and temple doors swung slowly open to reveal a movie screen—and *The Ascent of Everest* started to roll.

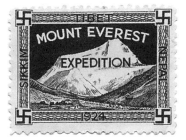

Special souvenir stamp commissioned for 1924 Everest expedition postcards. The motif at the corners of the stamp is the ancient Tibetan symbol for peace and longevity—called *yungtrung* in Tibetan and *svas-tika* in Sanskrit. By the 1930s, the symbol was hijacked by the Third Reich as its logo—definitely not a symbol of peace. The 1924 Everest postcards, some 40,000 of them, were dispatched from basecamp by postal runners to India, where they entered the international postal system.

And all this ran counter to agreements made with the 13th Dalai Lama about conduct rules for the expedition. It offended Tibetan religious sensibilities to have sacred religious ceremonies shown to all and sundry in a foreign land, especially with Noel's often-frivolous and disrespectful captioning. Even more upsetting to the Tibetans was the mystery of how Noel had smuggled out seven lamas for a live performance in London. Noel went on lecture-tour with his film, working through Britain, Europe and the US. Back in Tibet, Eric Bailey stepped into the fray—supporting the Tibetan side—and a furious row erupted between the Tibetan government and the Everest backers, with Bailey in the middle. Which put Bailey at loggerheads with the Royal Geographical Society and the Alpine Club.

Captain Noel's book *Through Tibet to Everest*, published 1927, may well have inspired Wilson's bizarre aerial plan. Noel talked about air-dropping someone on the top of Everest and hiking down. This was dismissed in climbing circles as 'unsporting', but it might have got Wilson thinking: here was a way of dispensing with all those loads of porters and caravans of sluggish yaks. An aerial approach would cut a month of arduous overlanding to a few hours.

It was typical of Maurice Wilson's approach that he bought a plane before he learned to fly. There was never any question in his mind that he would get his certification. He purchased a secondhand 1930 de Havilland Gipsy Moth, a biplane with a 55–100 horsepower engine and a single propeller up front. The Gipsy Moth was a workhorse of the skies—a reliable aircraft that had been used by famous loners like Amy Johnson and Alan Cobham. On the nose of the aircraft, Wilson painted the words EVER-WREST. And then he joined the London Aero Club to learn how to fly. When asked by other pilots about *Ever-Wrest*, he would reply:

> I intend to fly to the lower slopes of Everest and land there, prob-
> ably at around 14,000 feet, and then continue on foot. I know I
> shall be taking a big chance, but I shall pray for a safe landing.

Wearing hobnailed boots, fawn-coloured breeches and a large leather jerkin, Wilson showed up for flying lessons. He proved to be an erratic and nerve-wracking charge for the instructors, with his rodeo-style handling of a biplane, but he eventually got his pilot's licence, and started clocking up solo flight time. As for mountaineering, his training consisted of long rambles. In early 1933 he went to the Lake District and the Welsh mountains to have a hack at the mountains, but he spent most of his time on hikes, with little attempt to master snow climbing techniques like step-cutting or the use of crampons. He did some rock climbing and a little rope work, and that was it—apart from marching around the airfield in his hobnailed boots.

But he did hone up on parachute jumping. By chance, two reporters in London ran into Wilson coming out of Piccadilly underground: detecting a slight limp, they asked what he'd been up to. Wilson replied that he got it from a parachute jump. When was that? Wilson glanced at his watch: about 20 minutes ago, he said. And why, asked one reporter, had he jumped? 'Just to test my nerves,' came the reply.

A few days later, he was warned by the Air Ministry against making unauthorised jumps over London.

The *Ever-Wrest* was overhauled at the De Havilland hangars and the passenger's cockpit was fitted with a special long-range fuel tank. Wilson set a departure date for late April, 1933. Close to his intended departure date, disaster struck. On a routine solo flight, the *Ever-Wrest* stalled in mid-air: Wilson desperately looked for a place to land. He spotted a suitable field but miscalculated on the approach: the wheels of *Ever-Wrest* hit a hedge and the plane cartwheeled. When the plane came to rest, Wilson was left dangling upside-down from the safety harness—he was helped out by a passing boy. Miraculously, Wilson survived unscathed, but the Gipsy Moth was a wreck. It took a month to render the plane airworthy again.

In the meantime, Wilson anxiously monitored two expeditions that were tackling Everest in early 1933—one by land, the other by air. After a hiatus of nine years, the British Everest expeditions were again allowed to proceed. To arm themselves with more accurate information on approach routes to the summit, an aerial reconnaissance was planned. The overflight took place on April 3, 1933. This stole some of Wilson's thunder because the first aviation approach to Everest had been nabbed. To get to the starting point, three pilots had flown from England to India in a Fox Moth, a Gipsy Moth and a Puss Moth.

In the early 1930s, with both poles flown over, pilots started looking at an overflight of the Himalayas. At the time, it was rare for an aircraft to fly much above 10,000 feet, though the altitude flying record was around 40,000 feet. Everest would require clearance of over 30,000 feet, but dealing with severe winds. They had flying suits that were electrically heated, and carried oxygen masks and goggles. There were a number of technical problems to solve—engine coolants, lubricants, fuel additives, and a liquid oxygen system to operate at high altitudes.

The success of the aerial reconnaissance relied on a prototype Westland PV3, powered by a supercharged Pegasus engine. There was only one of these biplanes in existence: a companion biplane added was a Westland Wallace. The two biplanes took off from Lalbalu airfield near Purnea in India, 150 miles south of Everest—and headed north into the Himalayan massif. Ferocious winds and unpredictable down-currents waylaid them: one pilot was caught in downdrafts. And then the glorious summit of Everest was glimpsed for the first time—from a few hundred feet away—by a stills photographer named Blacker, who wondered if that wasn't a bit too close to be filming. He was looking down a hatch in the back-seat floor of the biplane. Wilson's absurd crash-land approach to Everest almost become fact: imagine climbers getting to the top and finding a biplane rammed upside-down in the summit. The pilot pulled the biplane out at the last minute—and then had to deal with a plume rising up from the Himalayan peaks. The plume turned out to be full of ice crystals that rattled violently into the cockpit.

Each biplane had two seats—the forward one with the pilot, the rear one with the observer. As for the other plane—it cleared the summit of Everest by a slim margin: on a second circuit of the peak, McIntyre, the pilot, noticed that his observer, the cine-cameraman Bonnett, was no longer visible. His oxygen apparatus was malfunctioning: he'd blacked out and slumped to the floor. On the trip back to India, dropping to lower elevations, the unconscious photographer revived and struggled to rip off his oxygen mask: his face, according to the pilot, was 'a nasty dark green shade'—but he survived. And the planes came back with the first aerial pictures of the virgin summit of Everest.

Wilson had tried to get in on that aerial reconnaissance—his plan was to hitch a wing-lift with the Westland, and then bail out—parachuting onto the lower slopes of Everest. This plan was wisely ignored by the pilots.

Meanwhile, on land, Hugh Ruttledge's 1933 Everest climbing expedition encountered heavy monsoon weather and failed. Since 1924, climbing equipment had improved considerably—superior tents, boots and clothing. However, it's dubious whether Wilson was able to take advantage of this new technology—or of the new aerial reconnaissance information (revealing the likely routes to the summit). The problem of altitude was completely overlooked in Wilson's crash-landing plan. With sudden aerial rise to high elevation, there is no chance to acclimatise. If a hot-air balloon were to land on top of Everest, the balloonist—warmly wrapped but without oxygen supply—would last less than an hour before succumbing to an altitude-induced death. Probably more like ten minutes before collapsing. Mallory thought the use of supplemental oxygen was unnecessary and unsporting, but on the 1922 expedition, when George Finch performed much better at altitude, a tradition was established.

VÉRITABLE EXTRAIT DE VIANDE LIEBIG.

RACES BOVINES : Yack, Thibet.

Voir au verso.

Produced from the 1880s onward in Belgium, Liebig cards were designed to encourage travellers to go to exotic places. And to take Liebig Meat Extract along with them for sustenance and to bolster their health—the Vegemite or Marmite of the day. This card shows a yak caravan—a transport method used for carrying supplies for early British expeditions to Everest.

The Sherpas called it 'English air': the oxygen canisters that they had to lug up to high basecamps. At the time, it was unknown if a climber could survive at these elevations without oxygen. At first, the Sherpas laughed at the Englishmen for bringing oxygen all the way from England when the air of the Himalayas was quite fresh. But when they got a taste of what the English air did for the constitution, they would periodically approach the climbing Sahibs, complain of feeling sick, and ask for a shot of oxygen to revive themselves. The equipment was in its experimental stages, and was often faulty. Many of the canisters transported to Everest by yak turned out to be empty—the gas had leaked out en route.

Apart from oxygen supply, Wilson had another pressing technical problem: in the event that he made it to the top of Everest, how could he prove it? With a solo attempt, the only proof would be photos taken from the summit—which could be of the expansive views (thus confirming the high position of the photo-taker), or of the climber on the summit. Wilson thoughtfully packed a camera with a self-timer feature so he could pose and take his own picture.

On May 21st, 1933, Maurice Wilson joked with dozens of reporters before firing up his Gipsy Moth—and taking off from London. Heading due east across the English Channel. Destination: Mount Everest.

The decade 1925 to 1935 was the golden age of aviation, with lone daredevil adventurers blazing new routes across the globe—among which a number crashed in distant desert or jungle, or worse, ocean.

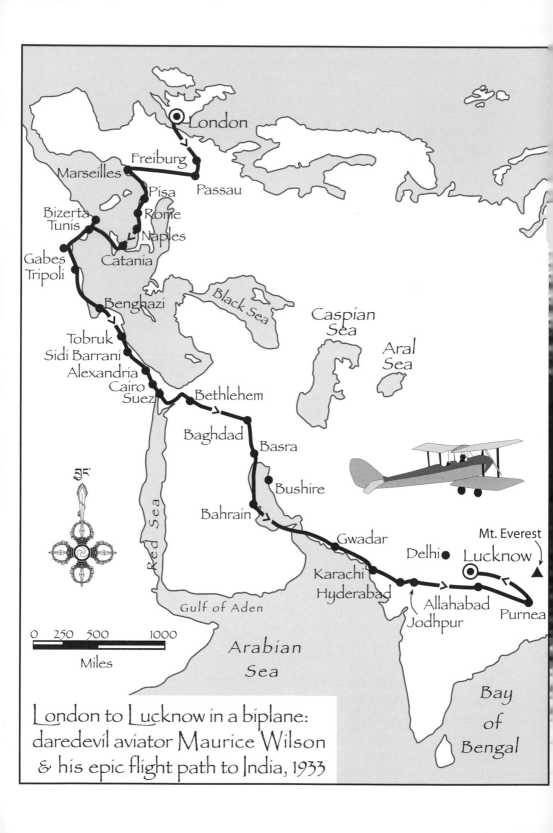

London
Freiburg
Passau
Marseilles
Pisa
Rome
Bizerta
Tunis
Naples
Catania
Gabes
Tripoli
Benghazi
Tobruk
Sidi Barrani
Alexandria
Cairo
Suez
Bethlehem
Baghdad
Basra
Bushire
Bahrain
Gwadar
Delhi
Lucknow
Mt. Everest
Karachi
Hyderabad
Allahabad
Jodhpur
Purnea

Black Sea
Caspian Sea
Aral Sea
Red Sea
Gulf of Aden
Arabian Sea
Bay of Bengal

0   250   500   1000
Miles

London to Lucknow in a biplane:
daredevil aviator Maurice Wilson
& his epic flight path to India, 1933

The DH-60 Gipsy Moth was the airship of choice—it was inexpensive, easy to fly, and dependable. In 1930, Francis Chichester piloted a Gipsy Moth solo from England to Australia—a record feat matched in the early 1930s by solo aviatrixes Amy Johnson and Lores Bonney. The popular Moth was produced in different versions in the 1930s: it metamorphosed into the DH-80 Puss Moth, the DH-61 Giant Moth, and just prior to WWII, was modified as a military training plane, the Tiger Moth.

Wilson was right up there in the ranks of the daredevil aviators: by air, India was some 5,000 miles away from England. Wilson had none of the controls that modern pilots take for granted such as radio contact or navigational aids. And in his case, the route was mostly illegal—he was stymied by British officials who didn't want this crazy Brit making a fool of himself in strange lands.

By adding a 20-gallon petrol tank to the passenger's cockpit, Wilson extended the range of his Gipsy Moth to possibly 750 miles, or a bit over eight hours aloft. Wilson sat in the open pilot's cockpit. He hopped from aerodrome to aerodrome, making his way across France and Italy to Tripoli and Cairo. In Cairo, he was refused a permit to fly over Persian territory—something to do with the British Legation. He decided to press on to Baghdad to see if he could arrange a permit there. He covered the thousand-odd miles from Cairo to Baghdad in a single day, with several refuelling stops on the way. Landing in Baghdad, he soon discovered there were no decent maps of Persia available, but he managed to unearth a child's school atlas that showed part of the coastline. He took off for Bahrain, a British protectorate in the Persian Gulf. He had learned that the airfield as Basra was closed, so he would have to fly a distance of 700 miles to reach Bahrain. This was within the maximum range of his aircraft—but for the last 200 miles he had no maps. There was no margin for error—if he got lost, there was only desert below. After eight-and-a-half hours aloft, with darkness closing in, Wilson spotted Bahrain airstrip.

The next morning, Wilson was refused petrol on the instructions of the British Consul. Infuriated, Wilson called on the British Consulate, where an official explained that he had no permit to fly across Persian territory. Over tea, the official suggested that he fly across to Bushire, which was the nearest Persian aerodrome, and ask for permission there. Wilson knew this was a trap—once he landed in Bushire, his plane would be impounded and he would be likely be imprisoned.

Meanwhile, on large-scale wall-map of the Persian Gulf behind the official, he noticed a newly built airstrip at Gwadar—a small Baluchistan town lying just beyond the Persian frontier. Wilson wandered over to study the map in more detail. From the scale, he worked out that Gwadar was just less than 800 miles away. He jotted down map details on the cuff of his shirt.

The British official gave Wilson a chit to refuel and fly to Bushire. While the plane was being refuelled, Wilson talked a native mechanic into filling up his extra tank and supplying a small extra drum of petrol—which he stashed in the front storage locker of the plane. Waving goodbye to the British official, Wilson became airborne—and then turned the nose of the plane not northward for Bushire, but due east for Baluchistan. Wilson said he wished he could've seen the official's face when he did that.

The exact range from Bahrain to Gwadar was actually 775 miles, over very remote terrain. It was an incredible gamble—if he ran out of petrol and crashed, there was zero chance of survival. Fortunately, the Gipsy Moth was in fine condition and up to the task. But after eight hours aloft, Wilson—not a small man—was fighting cramps and drowsiness. Once, he nodded off at the controls and woke up to find himself going into a screaming dive—which he corrected at the last minute. He prayed that the plane would make it. After close on nine-and-a-half hours in the air, with darkness closing in, Wilson spotted the white buildings of Gwadar airstrip. His prayers had been answered. And as he headed in for a landing, the engine began to splutter. His fuel was completely spent.

Wilson's great achievement was not in climbing Everest but in getting there. Nobody had attempted a solo flight like this. The Mad Yorkshireman had made it to India in under two weeks. Not only that: despite several more petrol refuelling obstacles, he made it to Lalbalu, a military airfield nine miles from Purnea and only 150 miles away from Everest. The British press started to take him more seriously. Stringers interviewing him in India were startled when Wilson challenged Mahatma Gandhi to a fast. Wilson claimed that he mastered the art of starving himself by locking himself up in an airtight container 'to learn the effects of low oxygen levels'. He might obliquely have been referring to being trapped inside the cockpit of his biplane for long stretches.

Wilson's dream of winging it to Everest was dashed when the Nep-

Crossing a high pass in the Himalayas—a hard slog through snow

alese flatly refused him permission to fly over their country. Wilson never got around to asking the Tibetans about dropping in by plane, probably for the very good reason that he already knew the response: no aircraft had flown into Tibetan airspace, apart from the brief incursion by the 1933 Everest aerial survey. Tibetan monks were adamant that they would never allow aircraft to fly over Tibet because these machines might disturb the spirits that dwelt in the upper air.

Wilson was down to his last £20. He toyed with the idea of just taking off and flying over Nepal anyway, but the weather was uncertain for Himalayan flying, and his plane was under constant surveillance. He realised his only wealth consisted of his beloved Moth. Reluctantly, he decided to sell the plane. He flew to Lucknow in July and sold the plane for £500 to a planter named Cassells at Lucknow Flying Club. Then he set off for Darjeeling. The climbing season had passed—he would wait it out till the following spring.

In March 1934, Wilson paid the rent for his Darjeeling rooms six months in advance, and slipped out one night for a rendezvous with three Sherpas. Tsering, Tewang and Rinzing had been hired as porters on the 1933 British expedition to Everest, and Wilson was lucky to

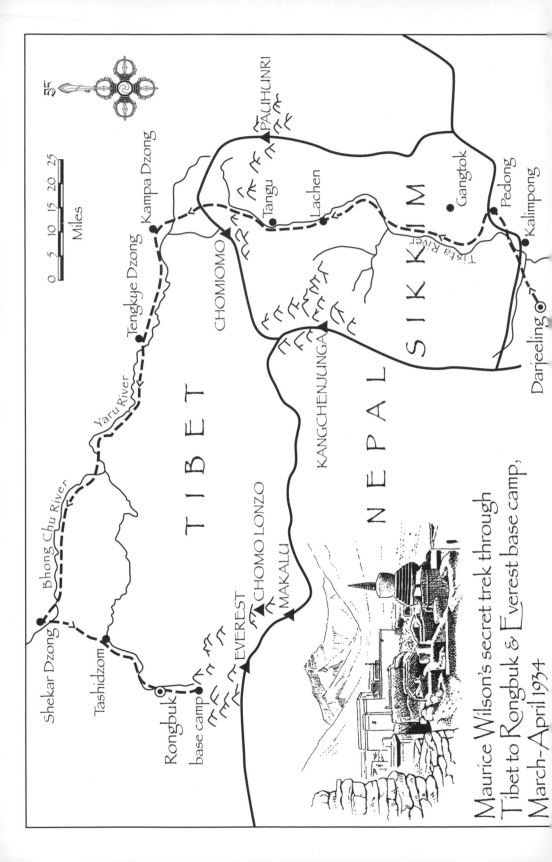

Maurice Wilson's secret trek through
Tibet to Rongbuk & Everest base camp,
March–April 1934

Miles
0 5 10 15 20 25

TIBET

NEPAL

SIKKIM

Shekar Dzong
Bhong Chu River
Tashidzom
Yaru River
Tengkye Dzong
Kampa Dzong
Rongbuk
base camp
EVEREST
CHOMO LONZO
MAKALU
CHOMIOMO
Tangu
Lachen
PAUHUNRI
KANGCHENJUNGA
Tista River
Gangtok
Pedong
Kalimpong
Darjeeling

A monk from Shegar Gompa holds a photograph of the former High Lama of Rongbuk, from the days of the 1920s expedition. The High Lama had the luxury of a glassed-in aerie. The photo was sent back from England to Shegar.

engage them as guides for his trek into Tibet—especially as he envisaged travelling by night to evade border patrols and checkposts.

Wilson disguised himself as a deaf-and-dumb monk. He wore, from top to bottom: a fur-lined Bhutia cap with huge earflaps, a great waistcoat with brass buttons and gold brocade, dark-blue cotton trousers, a twelve-foot sash of red silk wrapped around his stomach, and enveloping all this, a heavy woollen cloak—hanging down to his feet. Wilson wore his hobnailed cork-insulated boots—he couldn't part with those. To hide his blue-grey eyes, he wore dark glasses, and shielded his face further with an umbrella if the occasion called for it—like close proximity to a policeman or official. And because he was six-foot-one, he shuffled along on half-bent knees if any official was within range. His kitbags with his climbing supplies were disguised as sacks of wheat. He had purchased one pack-pony to carry supplies.

Remarkably, the small team made it over very rough terrain to Rongbuk in record time: by a little-used route, they covered the 300-odd miles from Darjeeling to Everest in 25 days—which was ten days less than the time taken by the Ruttledge expedition of 1933. Wilson had so far overcome every obstacle that had faced him. He appeared unstoppable.

Wilson and the three Sherpas arrived at Rongbuk Monastery on April 14th, 1934. The monastery, nestled at 16,500 feet, is reckoned to be the highest in the world—it lies about seven miles from the base of Everest, and affords a magnificent view of the peak. Wilson and the Sherpas managed to get an immediate audience with the High Lama, a dignified yet jovial man of around 70. The High Lama lived in an aerie at the top of the monastery. Reached by rickety ladder, the small wooden room had windows of real glass—a rarity in these parts as it had to be carried over the Himalayas from India on mules. A couple of senior monks were present for the audience, as well as an interpreter.

Language was a problem, but Wilson somehow got along very well with the lama. The two exchanged gifts: the High Lama offered Wilson half a cooked goat. Then he blessed Wilson and the Sherpas by passing his sceptre over their heads and chanting a mantra. This was the sacred blessing sought by climbers—especially Sherpas—before proceeding further on Everest. The lama told Wilson about religious life at Rongbuk, which he began to take an interest in. Life at the monastery, Wilson found, was 'a mixture of piety, gentleness, laughter and dirt'—a life of contemplation, albeit with much chanting and drum-beating.

Further out, near the base of Everest, was a small nunnery and Chamalung—the Sacred Valley of the Birds—where hermits lived, walled into cells cut into glacial moraines. They spent years in meditation, relying on a meagre daily handout of water and *tsampa* from the Rongbuk monks. One of the conditions of the Dalai Lama's passport issued to the British expeditions of the 1920s was that they would not kill any birds or animals of the valley of Chomolungma. Tibetans regard wildlife as reincarnate spirits—previously human. So in this sense, the Rongbuk area was like a great wildlife sanctuary: bharal (wild blue sheep) and Himalayan tahr (a species of wild goat) used to come to Rongbuk to be hand-fed by the monks.

At Rongbuk, Wilson was delighted to discover supplies left behind by previous British expeditions. He convinced the monks that these stores belonged to him, and tucked into them with childish glee— he helped himself to a seven-pound tin of bull's-eyes (sweets). These rations supplemented those he had brought along—large quantities of dates and special biscuits that he had baked himself.

'Only another 13,000 feet to go!' Wilson told the Sherpas, beaming. Wilson's solo attempt on the summit was a folly beyond imagination at the time, given his lack of climbing experience and his poor equipment—these were the days of climbing in tweed trousers and hobnailed boots, and using hemp ropes. But Wilson's steadfast belief in his own particular brand of divine faith and fasting was what drove him on. He believed this force would propel him safely to the top and back.

An inkling of the origins of Wilson's self-created faith is provided by biographer Dennis Roberts, who says that in 1932, when Wilson returned from travels to New Zealand, his health suddenly began to deteriorate. He dramatically lost weight and developed a racking cough. He took his problem not to a doctor but to a wealthy man in Mayfair credited with miracle cures. The man remains unnamed in all of Wilson's papers, but this mystery person had been given three months to live by every doctor he consulted. Refusing to accept their opinion, however, he subjected himself to his own unorthodox treatment—and not only recovered, he was still alive 17 years later. In the interim, having escaped the clutches of death, he decided to devote his life and his considerable fortune to propagating his treatment method, affecting complete cures in over 100 men and women suffering from diseases such as cancer, arthritis, TB and syphilis. In a number of cases, doctors had diagnosed the patient as incurable.

The treatment consisted of two things: faith and fasting. It would be easy to call this man a crank and a quack were it not for the fact that he never accepted money—and his miraculous cures actually seemed to work. Wilson followed the man's advice to the letter: he fasted for 35 days, drinking only small quantities of water—thus purging himself physically and mentally. While lying close to death under the effects of this severe fasting regimen, he prayed to God that he might, in the words of the Bible, 'be born again of water and of the Spirit.' And it seems his prayers were answered: a complete recovery was made.

Taking some time out to recuperate in the Black Forest, Wilson was sitting in a Freiburg café when he spotted an old newspaper story about the 1924 Everest Expedition. This may have been the Divine Call—the ultimate catalyst. Wilson decided to apply his fasting-and-faith technique to the challenge of conquering Everest. As he explained to Enid and Leonard Evans, his trusted friends back in England, fasting was the key. Wilson insisted that faith could move mountains—that a man with sufficient faith could accomplish *anything*. He said that when a man fasted and was severely drained—and committed his soul to God—then his body and soul were ready to be born again. A dubious Leonard Evans responded by knocking the ashes from his pipe, telling Wilson it all sounded rather far-fetched, and ordering Enid to make some more tea.

When it came to Everest, Wilson believed in miracles, too. Just as Simon Peter could walk the waters of Galilee, so God would guide him up the glaciers and icy slopes of Everest—a divine presence would be with him for the climb. He also believed that ice-steps cut during the

1933 British expedition would still be intact, making his ascent easy. Wilson thought that the notion of fasting was the remedy to all mankind's problems and that he would fast his way to the top. He had been fasting for some time on a diet of cereal, dates and figs. The figs provided an instant energy booster. It was an attempt to 'climb Everest on faith and figs', as one critic phrased it. Add porridge to that mix—he was fond of that too.

Two days after arriving at Rongbuk, Wilson set off on his solo climb on Everest, leaving his Sherpas at the monastery. Wilson had a 45-pound kit load that included an ice-axe and a single length of rope—neither of which he had any idea how to use. Nevertheless, he made good progress on the slopes—a tribute to his remarkable fitness. Miraculously avoiding crevasses and other potential hazards, he reached Ruttledge's Camp II, where he foraged for food. But all he could find was a pair of crampons. Ignorant in technical climbing skills, Wilson did not realise the lifesaving value of crampons on snow and ice: he tossed the crampons aside in disappointment. And carried on.

He was entranced by the beauty of the upper Rongbuk glacier, but was caught in a blizzard high on the mountain. His food supplies dwindled. He realised he would have to turn back and wait for more favourable weather. Battered, dazed, half snowblind—and with swollen eyes and sore throat—he staggered back into Rongbuk. The Sherpas revived him with vegetable soup, a bowl of fried meat and rice, and a mug of tea. He collapsed into a deep sleep for 38 hours.

At this point, if Wilson had pulled out and called it quits, he would've had an astounding story to tell—and would surely have been the toast of England for his audacity. Everybody loves the underdog: Wilson certainly qualified. But Wilson was a man obsessed—he simply would not give up on his quest. He was so sick that he barely moved for four days after getting back to Rongbuk. In the meantime, his Sherpas had succumbed to various ailments and were off-colour too. Tsering never really acclimatised, and was given leave to head down to a village at lower elevation.

Wilson spent several weeks recuperating at Rongbuk, spending pleasant time with the High Lama. When the weather looked better, he rallied for a second assault on the summit. He modified the solo approach in favour of a semi-assisted attack on the peak. He persuaded Rinzing and Tewang to go with him as far as Camp III, from where he would launch his solo bid. He was so pleased that the Sher-

Everest herself: the imposing north face of Everest, seen from basecamp

pas agreed to accompany him that he even shared a slab of precious Kendal Mint Cake with them. This sugar-laden bar was his emergency energy booster.

At Camp III, more good news on the energy front: Rinzing found Ruttledge's supply dump. He staggered back into camp with a forty-pound box. Wilson's eyes widened as he forced open the wooden crate: inside was a treasure-trove of honey, butter, cheese, anchovy paste, chocolate biscuits, Huntley & Palmer ginger-nut biscuits, Ovaltine, tins of soup and meat, and sardines from Sainsbury's. Although the stash buoyed his spirits, Wilson was sadly out of touch with reality: he also expected Ruttledge's step-cutting in the ice to be left intact—from a year ago—and for climbing ropes to be left in convenient positions.

From Camp III, Wilson headed higher solo—except that he was convinced someone was there with him, and that if he were to slip, this 'companion' would come to his rescue. Unbeknown to Wilson, he was entering the 'Death Zone'. This is the region above 23,000 feet where acclimatisation to altitude is no longer possible. Climbers entering the Death Zone must work quickly—head for the top and retreat before their strength is sapped by dehydration, cold and high altitude. The only way around this is by use of bottled oxygen. Altitude sickness is a mysterious phenomenon that physiologists still do not fully understand—in mild cases, it causes dizziness and blinding headaches; in more serious cases, it can rapidly lead to death from fluid leakage in the brain or the lungs.

Wilson got to a chimney at around 23,000 feet but gave up trying to climb it, and retreated—slithering back down 1,500 feet of sheer ice. He collapsed into the arms of the Sherpas, had a bowl of hot soup, and fell asleep in the tent—for the next 30 hours.

He awoke at 11 pm on Saturday, May 26th, more determined than ever to make it to the top. This would be the final push, he said. He could not persuade the Sherpas to go anywhere higher than Camp III, so he told them to wait for him at basecamp for ten days. Then he resumed climbing. When Tewang and Rinzing last saw him (according to the *Daily Press* correspondent in Calcutta), Wilson was setting off toward the summit, plodding crossing a glacier carrying a rucksack with a light tent, three loaves of bread, two tins of porridge, a camera— and his Union Jack.

And then Wilson vanished.

The monks of Rongbuk could have told you exactly what happened to Wilson. He had tangled with the goddess. By this, they meant Jolmo Langma, the Goddess of the Snows. The monks harboured very different viewpoints from Wilson on the religious aspects of his mission. The monks were upset with British climbers for disturbing the spirits of the upper air, in particular the goddess Jolmo Langma. Everest is a sacred peak, with a monastery for the contemplation—Dza Rongphu or Rongbuk—named after the cave of the great ascetic Padmasambhava, who spent many years there in meditation.

On the 1921 reconnaissance, British expedition leaders managed to convince the clergy at Rongbuk that the British were on a pilgrimage to the sacred peak. Twisting this story for the 1922 assault on the peak, Captain Noel says that expedition leader General Bruce told the Tibetans that it was the religion of the white men—the tribe called mountaineers—to climb to the tops of high mountains in order to reach near heaven. On Everest, they would reach nearer to heaven than any man on earth. But by 1922, the High Lama of Rongbuk had wised up, saying that the goddess of Rongbuk would cast down anybody who dared to climb her flanks. He claimed the goddess had great powers: she could open fissures at her side at will—against which powers men had no strength. A stark demonstration of these powers came when seven Sherpas perished in an avalanche on Everest in the course of the 1922 British expedition.

Jolmo Langma,
Goddess of
the Snows:
the wrathful
deity on Mount
Everest

Ruins of Rongbuk Monastery, with Mount Everest looming in the background

Before the climbers set off for the summit in the disastrous climb of 1924, the lamas of Rongbuk performed a 'devil-dance', described by John Noel in his 1927 book *Through Tibet to Everest*. The orchestra was spectacular: monks blowing eight-foot-long horns made of copper and silver, whose doleful sound reverberated across the valley; others with trumpets fashioned from human thigh-bones, and drums made of human skulls. The dance was a kind of medieval passion play, with a human protagonist fighting with grotesque monsters. The monsters won, the human lost. A dance of ghouls followed, with monks dressed in skeleton costumes and hideous masks dancing over the dead body, fighting good spirits for possession of the corpse. John Noel describes the extraordinary drama:

> Out of the monastery windows leaped a troop of demons, fantastically clad, flinging themselves into the struggle for possession of the poor little white soul about to be reincarnated and embark on a new weary life in the world... A long procession of gowned monks preceded by cymbal-players and drummers and thigh-bone trumpeters paraded around the monastery courtyard carrying grotesque idols.

More to the point, it could well have been a passion-play about the mountaineers and their struggles with the demons of Everest. Noel wrote that the monks scattered rice grains over the pilgrims who had come to pay homage, and extended half-hearted blessings to the Everest expedition members and porters. But there was a chilling rejoinder. The monks mumbled something that Noel asked to have translated. It came out like this: 'Chomolungma, the awful and mighty Goddess Mother, will never allow any white man to climb her sacred heights. The demons of the snows will destroy you utterly.'

Not a very cheery send-off, Noel noted dryly. And just in case the British had missed the point of the devil-dance, a wizened lama with only two teeth in his head took Noel aside and led him to the temple entrance—where he pointed out a fresco painted on a wall. Noel had seen the fresco before, in 1922—it had been given a fresh coat of paint:

> This extraordinary picture shows the angered Deity of the Mountain surrounded by weird, wildly dancing Demons, White Lions, Barking Dogs and Hairy Men [yetis], and at the foot, speared through and through, lies the naked body of the white man who dared to violate the ice-bound tempest-guarded sanctuary of Chomolungma—Goddess Mother of the World.

According to the Tibetans, a whole host of high-altitude demons and ghosts were arrayed against the British mountaineers. Tibetan belief held that high peaks were the abodes of the gods, goddesses, demons, ghosts and Sukpas. Sukpas were Snow Men—also known to the Sherpas as Yetis. Sherpas live in fear of this huge, hairy bad-smelling ape-man—a combination of Bigfoot and King Kong. In Tibetan lore, the abominable snowman would sometimes abduct chaste young women for sexual purposes, and sometimes leave a yak half-eaten. It was said that the King of the Snow Men lived on top of Everest—from this perch, he could gaze down on the world below and choose which yak-herd he would dine on next. According to Noel, the yak-herders said that:

THE ABOMINABLE SNOWMAN

> ...the Sukpa can jump by huge bounds at a time, that he is much taller than the tallest man, and that he has a hard tail upon which he can sit. The men he kills he will not eat. He just bites off the tips of their fingers, toes and noses, and leaves them.

The yeti would seem to be quite a large and hairy monster on this stamp from Bhutan, where a special nature reserve has been set aside for yetis to roam

This description would provide the Tibetan explanation for frostbite, affecting the body of a yak-herder who died at these altitudes. Noel neglected to mention another alarming fact: the Sukpa also dines on testicles.

In the eyes of the Tibetans, the summit of Everest was where otherworldly figures dwelled. And quite a crowd of them. Apart from being the abode of the King of the Yetis and Jolmo Langma, the summit of Everest was thought to be the site of the magical Sacred Chair of Padmasambhava—a great tantric master given to flying around on tigers. Another legend held that the mythical White Lion lived there. Snow Lions are dog-like white-bodied creatures with turquoise manes, capable of bounding from snowpeak to snowpeak, and the special guardians of the Dalai Lama and Tibetan Buddhism. The Tibetans came to the conclusion that the British were either after the magical Sacred Chair or the milk of the White Lion.

Despite all the legends, the Tibetans had no name for the peak that Rongbuk (aka Rongphu) monastery faced: it was simply known as 'the snowpeak of Rongphu'. Pilgrims would come here from great distances to pay their respects to the monastery and to make offerings of barley to the revered abbot. The abbot would give a *khata* (sacred scarf) back. The Tibetans had long identified the massif by its resident goddess, called Miyo Langsangma—or in shorter form, Jolmo Langma.

Over time, this has been adopted as the official Tibetan and Chinese name for Everest in variants like 'Chomolungma'—to counter the British name.

Chomolungma has been prosaically rendered as 'Goddess Mother of the World' but the title translates literally to 'Immovable Goddess Mother of Good Bulls', as *Jolmo* (queen or goddess) is often shown riding a *glangma* (an ox), though sometimes she is shown astride a tiger. Wall paintings at Rongbuk show her holding a bowl of roasted barley flour in one hand, and a mongoose spitting jewels in the other. These are meant to show that she bestows food and wealth on those who show devotion to her. But to those who have no respect, she gives no quarter, turning into a wrathful Ice Queen.

Jolmo Langma was originally a demoness—the second of five long-life sisters said to dwell on certain Himalayan peaks on the southern Tibet border. One sister goddess lives on Gauri Shankar, another at the summit of Mount Chomolhari. Legend has it that in the 8th century, the great sage Padmasambhava subdued the sisters. He flew to the top of Everest and converted Jolmo Langma to Buddhism. But she retained residual demonic habits—one of which is pushing mountaineers into crevasses, or hurling them off the slopes when she gets the urge. Although she may look angelic on a *tanka*, the goddess is offended by pollution, lack of respect, and by sexual activity. And when push comes to shove, according to the Sherpas, she can respond by triggering avalanches, whipping up the wind, causing the weather to change rapidly and other dire phenomena.

On the Nepalese side, the peak is known as Sagarmartha, a Nepalese word roughly translated as 'Forehead of the Sky'. The Nepalese believe Everest to be the abode of the Hindu god Shiva (the Destroyer) and Parvati (his female consort). But for the Sherpas—ethnic Tibetans who migrated to Nepal around the 1500s—the goddess on top is the same, Jolmo Langma. The Sherpas are in awe of the goddess as much as the Tibetans, but they also realised that supporting Sahibs to climb Himalayan peaks was a very good way to earn a living. So they worked out a compromise. The Sherpa tack is that if you propitiate the goddess and make the right offerings, she might turn a blind eye long enough to make the ascent and descent. Thus the Sherpas engage in elaborate rituals. Everything must be blessed: the climbers are blessed by a lama, the ice-axes are blessed, all the gear is blessed. And then offerings are made directly to the goddess in fire puja ceremonies. It seems that the British tried to get the Rongbuk monks onside by asking them to perform such propitiation ceremonies before setting out for Everest. But no amount of enticement could lure Tibetan porters to the upper slopes—that was the domain of the Sherpas. The history of climbing in the Himalayas is inconceivable without them.

Wilson's two Sherpa companions were sighted by Tenzing Norgay in Darjeeling, displaying visible wealth that could only have come from Wilson. They were thoroughly grilled about Wilson, but since they had no details about his solo forays, crucial parts of his story were still missing.

In 1935, a small British reconnaissance team was put together at short notice, led by Eric Shipton. The party explored and surveyed the country to the north and west of Everest. It was in the course of this lightweight venture, on July 9th, that Eric Shipton found the body of Wilson. Soul on ice: Wilson was dressed in his windproof clothing, with his rucksack at his side. He was frozen in the act of taking a boot off. It is most likely that after leaving the two Sherpas, Wilson had battled his way through the seracs and crevasses of the ice-fall, and had pitched his tent a few hundred feet above Camp III, at around 21,000 feet. The tent had been swept away by strong winds, raking monsoon and storms—all that remained of it were the guy lines, held down by boulders. Retrieved from Wilson's pocket was a small diary. Shipton later wrote:

> I still have a vivid recollection of sitting with my companions under a rock at 21,000 feet in the upper basin of the East Rong-buk Glacier, while Kempson read aloud from the diary of the man whose body we had just found on the moraine a few yards away. It had been lying there for more than a year, and now it was as if the man himself was speaking to us, revealing his secret thoughts. Outside our shelter there was complete silence as the snow fell in large fluffy flakes. As I listened to the strange, intimate story, I soon had little doubt of the writer's sincerity. The motive behind his wild venture was unusual.

It was a battered pocket-book, palm-sized with coarse-grained pages, made in Japan: Wilson had purchased it in Darjeeling before he set off overland. Unfortunately, in the diary Wilson rarely waxes lyrical about the ideals that brought him to Everest or about his divine faith: most entries are mundane daily logs. The last entries are pencilled in a spidery hand that grows fainter as Wilson slips into high-altitude torpor and delirium (the following entry for 24th May has been shortened):

20th Sun. These violet rays are terrible: have thick blanket over but yet I can feel them thru my balaclava helmet. When I've had my Irish Stew shall have to get another helmet.
21st Mon. We start again. R. brought me about ½ way to Camp IV but there was no rope guide & every step up the last grade had to be cut. I parked soon after and he left me as the sun was sinking low.
23rd Wed. Just going to have another shut eye.
24th Thurs. Most perfect day in the show & I spent it all in bed. Had a terrible job yesterday & whoever selected that route ought to be poleaxed. Am parked at an angle of 35°, but have shaped the snow to my carcass. Had 5 dry biscuits yesterday a.m. & nothing since, as there is nothing to have. Camp IV is somewhere within ½ mile radius so should be on the eats again by mid-day tomorrow....
25th Fri. Only one thing to do—no food no water—get back. Rintsi came to meet me & wasn't I glad. Did 2 sheer drop-rolls down the face of the ice, but fortunately without any effect. Ribs sore a bit but not much. They said that I could get to Camp IV and help but of course were thinking of help days when all steps were cut.
26th Sat. Stayed in bed
27th Sun.   "   "   "
28th Mon. Te Whang wanted to go back, but persuaded them to go with me to Camp V. This will be last effort & I feel successful. From Camp V it is less than 1 mile to top. Have just pulled out my flag of friendship & it feels quite cheering. Strange, but I feel that there is somebody with me in tent all the time.
29th Tues. S. of ½ mile up to Camp IV had turn back. N. wind nearly ate thru my nights.
30th Wed. Stayed in bed
31st Thurs. Off again, gorgeous day

That was the last entry: *Off again, gorgeous day.* The flag of friendship he talked about was a silk pennant on which his closest friends had signed their names before he left London—just over a year before.

Despite what the diary says, Wilson could not persuade the Sherpas to go beyond Camp III: Wilson set off by himself for the summit from there—he reckoned he was only a few miles away from his goal. But those miles were vertical—and he never made it to Camp IV. What is engrossing is the entry for May 28th: *Strange, but I feel that there is some-body with me in tent all the time.* Was this the Divine Presence that Wilson hoped would guide him to the summit? Or a malevolent spirit, out to get him?

Shipton held a simple funeral service, and then gave Wilson a 'mountain burial'. As opposed to sky burial (used for Tibetan porters who die in expedition attempts), mountain burial is when the body is simply pushed into a crevasse. The climbers pushed Wilson's body down a ten-foot snow-crevasse and raised a cairn over the spot. His diary was later handed over to the Alpine Club in London, where it remains in the archives. The great mountaineer Frank Smythe later wrote:

> It was not mountaineering, yet it was magnificent. Call it mad-ness, call it anything you like, but is there not an element of gran-deur in the thought of this young man actuated, perhaps by a flame of idealism…setting out alone to scale the world's high-est mountain, which four elaborate expeditions of experienced mountaineers have already failed to climb?

Wilson had done amazing things: against all odds, he'd flown solo from England to India, slipped past Tibetan authorities at night, trekked over a very rough route in record time to Everest basecamp—with only three porters in support—and then mounted the first-ever solo attack on Everest. The High Lama of Rongbuk told members of the Shipton expedition how impressed he had been with Wilson's courage and determination—and how his death had caused him deep personal grief. But the newspapers in England did not see it this way: they called Wilson's attempt an elaborate form of suicide.

Given the Tibetan fear of resident goddess, demons, roving ghosts and vicious Snow Men on Everest—and given the Tibetan reverence of sacred peaks and their deference to climbing them or even tram-melling their slopes—the most astonishing part of the triumphant first ascent of Everest in 1953 was that a Tibetan climber would reach the summit. In May 1953, Tenzing Norgay dispatched this news to his family: 'Myself along with one Sahib reached summit Everest on 29th May. Hope you will feel happy.'

The Sahib was Edmund Hillary. And although known as Tenzing Norgay Sherpa, Norgay is not of Sherpa descent—he is Tibetan. He was born in the Kharta valley, in the shadow of Everest's north face. Norgay was the eleventh of 13 children in a humble yak-herding family that left Tibet in search of a better life on the other side of the border, in Nepal. As a young man, Norgay eloped with a Sherpani woman and settled in Darjeeling, the base for early British attempts on Everest. He never revealed his true identity because he needed work as a Sherpa.

Norgay later wrote: 'Always as a child, a boy, a man, I have wanted to travel, to move, to go and see, to go and find.' And along the way, in Tibet and Nepal and India, he met with many luminaries. He met the 14th Dalai Lama on several occasions—the first when he was sirdar of Giuseppe Tucci's 1948 expedition to central Tibet. He met Peter Aufschnaiter and Heinrich Harrer in Lhasa. He may even have met George Mallory: when he was a boy, Mallory's team passed through Norgay's village of Moyun.

Norgay's tale is one of extraordinary courage and drive and determination, overcoming Tibetan taboos. Norgay shifted gears from being a porter on the 1935 Shipton expedition to an ace climber—definitely an innovative move when climbing was considered exclusively a 'Sahib's game'. Everest quickly became an obsession for Norgay—he earned the grudging respect of the goddess at the top. He took part in four more expeditions to Everest. His seventh time on Everest, he signed on as sirdar and climber for the military-style 1953 British assault on Everest that 'knocked the bastard off'—as Hillary phrased it. There were 12 climbers on that expedition, and 350 porters handling some 10,000 pounds of equipment. By this time, Norgay had spent more time on the mountain than any other climber.

Norgay took great care to stay on good terms with the goddess Jolmo Langma: Norgay's son revealed that his father used to pray in his private chapel before a *tanka* scroll painting depicting the goddess. But Hillary was obviously not versed in goddess etiquette: he emptied his bladder on the summit of Everest before descending. That act was bound to have offended the goddess, but it did set a new record for the highest terrestrial bathroom in the world.

On the early Everest expeditions, Captain John Noel noted that Tibetans were superbly adapted to altitude and very strong: they would make fine porters and climbers. Some were employed for high-altitude portering and yak-handling, but the Tibetan potential was never realised. However, Chinese expeditions to claim the first ascent of Everest from the north face used Tibetan crews as well as Chinese soldiers, and included Tibetan climbers—although they are credited as 'Chinese nationality'.

By 1950 Tibet was closed off by the invading Chinese, bent on saving the north face for a communist flag—their object was to place a bust of Mao Zedong on the summit. After a rumoured catastrophic Chinese-Russian attempt in 1952, and another climb in 1960 that could not be confirmed since it took place at night, the Chinese finally staked their claim in 1975 when a team of nine summited—one Chinese climber and eight Tibetan climbers. Among the Tibetans was a female climber called Phantog—the first woman ever to summit the north face.

It was during this expedition that Maurice Wilson surfaced again. Eric Shipton had disposed of Wilson's body in a snow crevasse in 1935, but it had evidently been thrown up by the advancing East Rongbuk glacier. The 1975 expedition climbers found Wilson's body and dropped it back into another crevasse.

In 1979, on a joint Sino-Japanese expedition to Everest, Chinese climber Wang Hongbao told an incredible story to Japanese climber Ryoten Hasegawa. He said that on the 1975 expedition said he saw two 'English dead'—one lower down, one higher up. The lower body was definitely that of Wilson, and the body on the upper slopes had to be either Mallory or Irvine. Because there had been few climbers on the north side at this point in time, there could be little mistake about the identity of a body. If the body had European features and was pre-WWII, it had to be English. The Chinese climber insisted the bodies were both pre-WWII due to their distinctive clothing. The following day, Wang Hongbao died in an avalanche, taking his tale with him.

Pre-1940, there were only a dozen bodies on the slopes of Everest—all on the north side of the peak. Seven Sherpa porters were swept away by an avalanche in 1922, and two Gurkhas perished in a storm in 1924. The 10th and 11th casualties chalked up on Everest were George Mallory and Sandy Irvine, in 1924. Following up on the sighting by the Chinese climber many years later (in 1999), an American expedition launched by Eric Simonson discovered Mallory's body, planted face-down in rocks, bleached white from the sun—like an alabaster statue. Expedition climbers retrieved Mallory's snow-goggles, altimeter, letters and other personal effects—but could not find any pocket camera.

As mad as Wilson's solo ascent of the world's highest mountain might have sounded in 1935, this very feat was accomplished on August 20, 1980 by Austrian mountaineer Reinhold Messner—from the north face of Everest, without oxygen. With their first North Face summit claim secure in 1975, the Chinese opened up to foreign climbers again in 1979. Messner arrived with no support crew—just his girlfriend, waiting at basecamp in a tent. To put this in perspective: Messner is a master climber—in a class of his own—and he pushed the boundaries of mountaineering with this feat. He was using climbing techniques far advanced from Wilson's day, and he was using far superior climbing hardware.

Early on during the attempt, Messner nearly died: he fell into a deep crevasse but landed on a ledge. He promised himself that if he ever escaped this icy prison, he would give up on the summit attempt. As soon as he managed to extricate himself, he promptly broke his word to himself and continued upward. He made it to the top, without oxygen, and he took photographs with a self-timer on his camera, just as Wilson intended to do. Messner's feat has never been repeated: it is the first and only pure solo ascent of Everest.

This was Messner's second time at the top: in 1978, when he set out to climb Everest from the Nepalese side with partner Peter Habeler, the peak had never been summited without use of oxygen. Experts had bluntly told the climbers that they would come back raving madmen—or at the very least, brain-damaged automatons—if they attempted the peak without oxygen. But they got their timing right and made it to the top and back. Then, to confound the skeptics, Messner went on to bag all 14 of the world's highest peaks—without oxygen.

History would brand Maurice Wilson as an eccentric and a failure. His Everest attempt infuriated the Indians and the Tibetans because he slipped through their net and endangered the lives of porters. But over the years, many others have been drawn to risking all in the hope of reaching the highest point on earth. Some are driven by national pride, others by love of climbing, others in quest of records: the oldest climber, the youngest, the first climbing couple to reach the top. Everest continues to lure crazy dreamers. And like Wilson, some of the contenders have very little climbing experience. Among the 'clients' are high-powered business folk looking for the ultimate challenge—and willing to pay $70,000 for someone to guide them to the top.

Captain John Noel outlived all the early British Everest pioneers: he exalted in each new conquest of the mountain as it fell to the record books—the first successful ascent in 1953, the first ascent by a female climber in 1975, the first solo climb in 1980. With the major ascent routes on Everest claimed in the record books, attention turned to the descents: the first ski descent, the first snowboard descent. And here's a dream that Wilson could identify with: the man who flew down Everest. In September 1988, French climber Jean Marc Boivin paraglided off the summit of Everest, taking eleven minutes to float back to basecamp on the Nepalese side.

But Captain Noel, who died in 1989 at the age of 99, did not live to see the realisation of his wildest prediction, made back in 1927: an airborne landing on the summit of Everest. It is the same outrageous idea that most likely inspired Maurice Wilson's quest. Balloonists had come closest to the idea, with the crashlanding of Japanese balloon team near the north face in 1990, followed by a successful British flyover of Everest—well, barely. A hot-air balloon is entirely at the mercy of the prevailing winds—and both British balloons ran into big trouble. In one balloon the burners suddenly failed, causing the balloon to plummet. The pilot managed to relight the burners, but the angle of relighting was not auspicious and molten nylon swirled around the heads of the two balloonists. Suddenly there was a series of ominous loud twangs as steel wires snapped from excess heat—seven of the 28 steel wires anchoring basket to balloon had snapped. With the basket swinging at a precarious angle, the balloon managed to gained height, clearing Everest by barely 2,000 feet. The second balloon experienced a rough landing, hitting a moraine ridge—with balloon and basket dragged across boulders.

On May 14, 2005, French test pilot Didier Delsalle made aviation history when he touched down on the summit of Everest in his turbo-engine AS350-B3 helicopter for a few minutes. This broke the record for the highest helicopter landing—a record that actually cannot be bettered. By doing this, Didier Delsalle improved the possibility of alpine rescues in future. In fact, he mounted a helicopter rescue of two Japanese climbers on the way out. And here's a scenario very close to what Wilson envisaged: in 2008, a British tour company called High & Wild arranged to take adventurers in a plane over Everest and have them step out the door close to the peak—in a freefall skydiving mission to land on Nepalese soil. No experience required, just nerves of steel--and a wallet with $36,000 in it—clients jump in tandem with a skydiving pro. Or jump solo, which is about $9,000 cheaper.

The goddess of Everest doesn't let climbers off easily. There are many deaths on the way down from the summit—in a state of extreme exhilaration, climbers lose their focus—and lose their footing. Lack of experience was cited as a key factor in the deaths of a dozen climbers in two expeditions on the mountain in 1996, trapped by a sudden storm. Swedish climber Goran Kropp offers another take on the disaster— too much *taki-taki*. In *Ultimate High*, the book chronicling his Everest adventures, Kropp divulges that the Sherpas on the mountain were very upset by *taki-taki* going on in the tents of climbers on the Scott Fischer expedition on the upper slopes. They said these sex acts would greatly anger the goddess and stir up bad spirits, causing adverse weather conditions.

Anatoli Boukreev, a Russian guide with Fischer's expedition, was involved with a woman who'd come to mourn the loss of her climber husband. And a wealthy client, 46-year-old New York socialite Sandy Pittman, had hooked up with 26-year-old Californian snowboarder Stephen Koch. Very bad karma for the expedition. No *taki-taki* on the mountain: the Sherpas have a taboo against 'making sauce' and aren't shy about rattling the tent of a climber indulging in an amorous escapade and shouting, *You make sauce! Bring bad weather. No sauce-making!* Other behaviour considered offensive to the goddess of Everest includes drinking to excess, burning trash, slaughtering animals, immorality, running around naked, or sleeping with feet toward the mountain. Tibetans talk about an essential attitude of reverence and purity on a sacred peak. The resident goddess is bound to be disturbed by any activity on her flanks—skiing or climbing, for instance.

Swedish climber Goran Kropp devised a long-range transport approach to Everest that eclipsed even Wilson's for eccentricity. He decided to do everything under his own steam—no airplanes, no porters, no help. He set off on a bicycle from his hometown in Sweden with a couple of hundred pounds of gear on board—bound all the way overland to Nepal. Which took about four months. And then, disdaining any porters or Sherpa assistance, Kropp not only lugged his own loads up to Everest, he decided he could not follow in the footsteps of others. So he forged a new route through the Khumbu Icefall and a climbing-route variation to the summit—all accomplished without oxygen. Agonisingly close to the top, he encountered high winds and had to turn back.

Despite this, Kropp had not given up: for his second and third attempts, he realised he would have to accept assistance—and teamed up with Jesus. That was Spanish climber by the reassuring name of Jésus Martinez. On the third summit bid, along with several other climbers, Kropp hiked past the frozen bodies of guides Rob Hall and Scott Fischer. That speeded him on his way: he says he spent four minutes on top, scared to death, and then descended. Back to his bicycle again.

Kropp was later responsible for another unusual climb on Everest. His girlfriend, Renata Chlumska, a former model, developed a strong interest in climbing, so Kropp took her back to Everest for a summit bid. She became the first blonde Swedish model to summit Everest. Kropp joked that Renata was the only girlfriend he'd ever had who didn't make him choose between her and the mountain. Kropp laced his post-Everest public presentations with dark humour, making wisecracks at the expense of his sponsors. While Swedish newspapers referred to him as the 'national hero', Kropp said that he was more like 'the national idiot.' He had a great gift for one-liners. In an interview, Kropp admitted that he sometimes took elevators. Why? 'Because they are there,' he quipped. After surviving all the hazards of Everest, on September 30, 2002, Kropp slipped during a roadside climb in Washington, struck his head on a rocky ledge, and died of his injuries.

May 29, 2003 marked the Golden Jubilee of the first summit climb of Everest, with big celebrations in Nepal. Part of this—not so widely reported—was a clean-up of the mountain itself. Between 1921 and 1960 there were around 20 expeditions to Everest; from 1960 to 2000, there were over 400 expeditions. Over 1,500 climbers have summited

Everest, and a further 200 climbers have perished in the attempt. Today, scores of teams vie for permits in a single climbing season: as many as forty climbers have been known to reach the top in a single day, creating a traffic jam at the summit.

And all this has left Everest with ton upon ton of discarded gear on the upper slopes—tents, cans of food, oxygen canisters—all well-preserved by the extremely dry air at altitude and susceptible to slow decay. A cleanup effort on the Nepalese side between 1994 and 1996 removed over 750 oxygen canisters. But they didn't get round to the bodies. Among the macabre landmarks high on Everest are frozen bodies or partial cadavers. Climbers on Everest are killed by avalanches, but most who perish simply run out of gas—for various reasons—and remain frozen in place, particularly visible in seasons of light snowfall. At this altitude, great exertion is required to carry a body down: the dead are either left where they fell, or given a 'mountain burial', or provided with a cremation ceremony if lower on the slopes. Sherpas don't like to mess with dead bodies, believing that a climber's ghost may reside close to the body.

And you might ask: what of the goddess? Well, she's probably hopping mad with all the frozen oxygen canisters on her flanks—not to mention other fallout, like frozen human excrement. She's got her work cut out for her as garbage and detritus pile up, threatening ecological disaster. In his book *Touching My Father's Soul*, Jamling Norgay relates a feeling of being shadowed by some mysterious presence on the upper slopes when he summited Everest in 1996. And on that expedition, he saw the full wrath of the goddess unleashed, decimating two expeditions. Jamling Norgay is the son of Tenzing Norgay, who passed away in 1986 at age 72.

Jamling related a few other stories about ghosts and goddesses on Everest. In 1997, an American climber went to retrieve the wedding ring of Scott Fischer, who perished near the summit the previous year. After removing the ring, the climber took a few steps and fell 400 feet down the mountain. He wasn't badly injured, but he felt he'd been pushed. The Sherpas claimed it was Fischer's ghost that pushed him. But the climber consulted a Navajo shaman who said it was a female deity—a goddess. In 1998, another American climber, Jeff Rhoads, reported seeing two climbers ahead of him, going for the summit—one a woman. But she climbed so fast that she disappeared, and Rhoads never saw her again, even though she was ahead of him. Later he learned than no female climber was attempting the summit that day.

Encountering a goddess or other ghostly figure could possibly be explained as some kind of hallucination. Mirages are known to materialise at extreme altitude as the brain slows down and becomes clouded and confused. Mountaineers have found that rising to altitude causes memory loss, befuddlement, erratic behaviour and delirium. Not to mention hallucinations like the arrival of a hovering aircraft with squat wings and a beak, ringed with a pulsating aura (this 'sighting' by a British mountaineer high on the slopes of Everest).

Reinhold Messner, a purist who mostly climbs without oxygen, recalls not only talking to his ice-axe high on Everest, but also having conversations with George Mallory—or the ghost of George. And who knows—as well as meeting George and Jolmo Langma, a future climber may even encounter the hungry ghost of Maurice Wilson, taking a breather on the upper slopes of Everest, with a handful of figs. A hungry ghost with fiery eyes, more determined than ever to make it to the top.

Joseph Rock hams it up in full Tibetan costume (sheepwool cloak, felt boots, foxfur hat) in this image, taken in the courtyard of his villa near Lijiang. Self-portraits like this were Rock's favourite way to impress his National Geographic readership.

Joseph Rock
1884–1962

*pioneering photographer, botanist & ethnographer—
a man with a short fuse, given to exaggeration & vanity*

Horsing Around in Shangri-La

Paradise for a plant hunter—
tainted by fear & loathing in Lijiang

❖   ❖

Joseph Rock was a cranky explorer—caught in a web of contradictions. From 1922 to 1935, the Austrian-American botanist roamed the remote Sino-Tibetan borderlands, collecting plants and animals, and ethnographic data. Rock was prepared to shoot his way past bandits, but travelled with a gramophone that played opera in Italian or German to incredulous villagers. Though considered the world expert on the flora of southwest China, he never wrote a single academic paper on the subject. He argued bitterly with editors at National Geographic, his main expedition sponsors. And he detested the Chinese communists—who today use Rock's story as centre-piece for a major campaign to attract tourism to southwest China.

❖

 EARLY IN 1930, an astonishing cablegram arrived at the offices of National Geographic in Washington. It read:

MINYAKONKA HIGHEST PEAK
ON GLOBE 30250 FEET ROCK

That wasn't 30,250 feet of rock—it was 30,250 feet as calculated by Joseph Rock. The mountain was located in western Sichuan: if Rock's arithmetic were correct, the peak would eclipse Everest, and Rock would be world-famous as the man who discovered it. Erring on the side of caution, National Geographic knocked almost a mile off Rock's calculation, rendering the height as 25,600 feet when the article appeared in the October 1930 issue under the title 'The Glories of Minya Konka'—a mammoth 53-page article that included 16 pages of colour pictures.

Just eight months earlier, in the February 1930 issue of National Geographic, Rock had staked the claim that an unnamed peak in the Amnye Machen range rivalled Everest, so editors had every reason to be cautious. As it later turned out (the mysteries were not unravelled till some 30 years later) the Amnye Machen peak is 20,610 feet, while Minya Konka is now pegged at 24,790 feet. Other times, Rock's chest-thumping prose and inflated claims slipped past the editors—as in the 1926 issue, when he stated that mighty gorges at the edge of the Tibetan plateau had canyon walls that towered to a height of more than two miles.

The gargantuan peaks and gorges in question lay in bandit-infested country in Tibetan-Chinese borderlands. Rock rode into these regions at the head of what could be best described as a National Geographic army. Just as the Alpine Club and the Royal Geographical Society in England had created an army of porters and climbers for a military-style assault on Everest, so Rock forged through to remote areas with a posse of loyal bodyguards, all armed to the hilt. Rock himself carried two Colt .45 pistols on his belt, plus a rifle. He was ready to shoot bullets in order to shoot pictures.

Surveying was not Rock's forte: photography was. Rock managed to get the first photographs of Minya Konka—and in colour, to boot. This was no mean feat: Rock was a pioneer in the use of colour photography. In the late 1920s, he began experimenting with five-by-seven-inch glass plates of the Autochrome colour process, which originated in France in 1907—the first practical colour process commercially available. Previously, colour in the magazine had been achieved by National Geographic artists—in Rock's case, artificially tinting black-and-white images from information furnished by Rock himself.

Rock had to expose the colour plates for a full second, allowing the image to pass through a coating of potato-starch grains which were dyed orange, green and violet. The plates had to be developed promptly under primitive conditions: Rock employed a tent for the purpose, with dung fires used to warm chemical baths, and with a helper fanning flies away from the sticky emulsion. If the film did not dry quickly, the plate would burst out in green spots. And finally, the plates had to be packed and shipped from China back to the US. Some arrived in pieces, but nearly 600 made it to the magazine's headquarters intact. The plates depicted snowcapped peaks, tribal princes and potentates, Tibetan masked dance, pictures of oracles and shamans. That was in addition to a booty of 3,000 black-and-white prints and 100 sepia prints, now held in the National Geographic archives.

Between 1922 and 1935, Rock was National Geographic's man in the Tibet-China borderlands, bringing the wild and the remote into the living rooms of Americans. It was an era when the organisation was expanding and experimenting—and had taken to funding the daring exploits of explorers in the field, like Richard Byrd's flight over the South Pole in 1929. Rock was a high-flier, too—and eagle-eyed editors had to watch out for exaggeration. They had to deal with his temper tantrums: the more generous editors described him as 'cantankerous.' To make sense of his long-winded convoluted writing, editors had to cut out rambling digressions—sometimes eliminating entire introductory sections and sizeable scholarly segments. Rock was incensed when editors altered his bombastic prose into National Geographic-ese: he acquired a reputation of being very difficult to deal with. But he was exploring where few had gone before, and he took good photographs. He once demanded an entire issue be devoted to his adventures, and suggested that editors publish two or more of his stories a year. In the end, ten of his stories were published for National Geographic over the course of 13 years. Nine of those articles involved Tibetan borderland areas in Kham and Amdo.

❖

How did Rock end up at the edge of the Tibetan plateau anyway? Luck, it seems—but luck propelled by childhood dreams. Josef Franz Rock was born in Vienna, Austria, on January 13, 1884. Growing up in Vienna, he dreamed of someday going to China—in fact, he taught himself rudimentary Chinese to prepare for that day. Rock was self-taught because his father was poor as a church mouse. His mother died when he was six. His older sister, Lina, became his surrogate mother. Rock's father had decided that young Joseph would become a priest, since he was good at singing Gregorian chants. Joseph hated the idea—he fantasised about exploring and having great adventures; his attempts to learn Chinese grated on his father's nerves. Older sister Lina surreptitiously supported Joseph Rock's early adventures by sending him household funds when she could. In 1902, after graduating from high school, young Rock took off travelling in Europe and North Africa. His father died in 1904 and he returned for the funeral, but quickly departed again on the road, taking odd jobs as a tourist guide or paying his passage on ships by working as a seaman.

That was how he found his way to New York City. After more wanderings around the Mediterranean, Rock happened to miss a train in France—and set sail instead on a ship bound for the US. He worked his passage as a steward. When he got off the boat, he had only his steward's suit, which he pawned for 50 cents. He found a job as a dishwasher and started to learn English. Several times already, Rock had been hospitalised with bouts of tuberculosis. When a doctor advised him against the climate in New York, he boarded a steamer south and dallied in Mexico. He cruised back to Texas, but again had lung problems and decided to go to Hawaii. He arrived by ship in 1907. He took a job teaching Latin, but determined for health reasons he must work outdoors. He quickly gravitated to another profession—collecting seeds and herbarium specimens of rare Hawaiian trees and shrubs for the Division of Forestry.

How on earth he landed this position is unclear—but he excelled at it, indulging in vigorous fieldwork. In 1911, he talked the Division of Forestry into transferring his vast herbarium to the College of Hawaii, where he joined the faculty as botanist. Edwin Bryan, the man who helped Rock catalogue his entire herbarium collection, recalled that his mentor was as temperamental as a prima donna. If, in the morning, the bespectacled Rock walked in singing snatches of opera in French, German or Italian, the day would be a good one. If, on the other hand, he was silent, this indicated a day filled with sulkiness, foul temper, unreasonable demands and stinging barbs. The amazing part of all this was that Rock was entirely self-taught: he fabricated a doctorate from the University of Vienna to save face among his colleagues—who, in light of his considerable knowledge, never thought to question it. Rock became an American citizen in 1913.

Rock went on to publish three classic books on the botany and forestry of Hawaii over a nine-year period—establishing him as the leading authority on the subject. In this period, he also took long leaves of absence, indulging his wanderlust. He cruised to the East, stopping at various ports. In Hong Kong and Canton, Rock got his first taste of China—his childhood dream. The rest of the trip was a blur—he dreamed of returning to China. In 1919, Rock was promoted to the rank of Professor of Systematic Botany, which must have pleased him. But in November that year, a dispute broke out over the future of his pet project, the herbarium. As the college was being upgraded to university level courses, it was decided to move Rock's herbarium—by then comprising some 28,000 specimens—to the Bishop Museum. Rock was powerless to prevent the move. In May 1920, he left Hawaii in a huff and headed for the mainland.

Rock approached Harvard University looking for a job, and then the New York Botanical Garden. Nothing. But the third door he knocked on, he got lucky: he found a job with the US Department of Agriculture, searching for seeds of the chaulmoogra tree. An extract from chaulmoogra oil was believed efficacious in treating leprosy and the department wanted to grow the tree in the US. The department sent Rock for a year to Siam (Thailand), Burma and India to search for the seeds. Rock brought back a cache of chaulmoogra seeds, but oil extracted unfortunately proved of very limited value against leprosy. By the time that was determined, Rock had moved onto better things. He picked up another sponsor—National Geographic—to write a story about the search. They offered him $400 for the story and 40 photographs—a princely sum at the time.

Exhilarated by his adventures in the wilds of Asia, Rock determined to go back. In 1922, he set off on another mission—this time a much longer one, backed by both the USDA and National Geographic. After travelling through Thailand and Laos, he slipped across the Chinese frontier through the back door—into remote Yunnan province. Rock's caravan reached the ancient trading town of Lijiang (then known as

Likiang), centre of the Naxi culture—a splendid labyrinth of weathered wooden shophouses and dwellings with tiled roofs. Twisting through it are cobblestone alleys, stone bridges and scores of canals. The Naxi believe that water is a god that must be propitiated through rituals. Lijiang has been the heartland of the Naxi ethnic group since the 14th century—an ancient market town that grew to prominence as a staging point on the Tea-Horse Road—on the long overland haul from India through Tibet to southwest China. Tea went west from China; in the other direction went hardy horses from Tibet, which were highly prized by Chinese traders.

Although the Chinese sold them the worst-grade tea-leaves, the Tibetans could never seem to get enough of the stuff. At times, caravans of up to 500 yaks would converge on the town of Tachienlu, at the frontier of Tibet, waiting for tea to be loaded. This low-grade tea became such an addiction for the Tibetans that the tea-bricks—stamped with Chinese characters for the weight—were used as actual currency in the Land of Snows.

The attraction for Rock in Lijiang was the abundant plant life found in the vicinity. A few miles north of Lijiang lies Jade Dragon Snow Mountain, a snowcap of 18,360 feet—a prime area for plant hunting. The mountain's micro-climate hosts a huge range of flora, depending on altitude. There are 50 species of azalea, 60 kinds of primrose, five species of camellia—the list goes on. Many ornamental plants in the West today derive from southwest China. There are estimated to be over 600 medicinal herbs in the Lijiang region. The local remedy for high blood pressure, for instance, is wild snow tea, a rare kind grown on mountain slopes, while leaves from the Yunnan rhodiola plant are used to make a tea for altitude sickness.

Tibetan medicinal cures are based on a combination of faith, astrology and a pharmacopoeia of herbal medicines developed over a millennium. Diagnosis is mainly done by checking urine samples and reading the pulse to determine which humour-flow (bile, wind or phlegm) has been blocked or is excessive, so that herbal remedies can be prescribed to set the system in harmony. No surgery is performed by Tibetan doctors—this prohibition dates back to the death of a Tibetan king in the 9th century during surgery. Medicinal plants from the high-altitude regions of the Tibetan plateau were sought by Western botanists: one was a species of giant rhubarb, another was the snow lotus. In the early 20th century, Zhamsaran Badmaev—a Buriat

By late spring, the Himalayas are ablaze with rhododendrons of many kinds—which Rock went chasing. This photo is from Laya in Bhutan.

attached to the court of St Petersburg—became popular with the upper classes through his 'Tibetan medicinal cures', advertising elixirs like 'black lotus essence' and 'infusion of asoka flowers.' It is odd that Doctor Rock did not follow up on Tibetan herbal cures, given his initial quest in Burma to find a leprosy cure based on the chaulmoogra tree. Tibetan herbal cures could potentially have yielded valuable finds for Western medicine.

Rock somehow overlooked Tibetan herbal medicines right under his nose. One of these is Chinese caterpillar fungus (*Cordyceps sinensis*), endemic to the Tibetan plateau. Scientists are baffled about where to place this worm-like fungus—it lies in limbo between insect and plant. Like something out of *The X-Files*, *cordyceps* is a parasitic fungus that grows on the larva (caterpillar) of the ghost moth in surface soil over the winter season, and takes it over, killing it in the process. Tibetans medical texts list the remarkable properties of *cordyceps* as far back as the 15th century, claiming it to be highly efficacious against kidney, lung and heart problems. In the early 18th century, when *cordyceps* crossed over into the pharmacopoeia of Chinese medicinal cures, its profile jumped. It was claimed to have anti-aging and energy-boosting properties that stimulate the circulation and the immune system—in fact, acting as an aphrodisiac (today the list is even longer—embracing

Naxi assistants at Rock's villa in Lijiang pressing and preserving plant specimens, ready for export

a whole raft of anti-cancer, anti-tumour, anti-oxidant and anti-viral properties). Ageing Chinese with money to burn can enhance their lives with fungus-filled days. Top-grade *cordyceps* specimens from Tibet are worth their weight in gold—the worms are added to medicinal dishes in deluxe restaurants, and are convenient for bribery. Research into this mysterious medicine is on-going.

Rock was more interested in collecting ornamental plants for gardens in the US and Europe. In the 1920s, Lijiang was a remote backwater—but a magnet for plant hunters. Southwest China was rec-ognised as one of the richest botanical fields in the world. In the 1880s, an avid French collector, Père Jean Marie Delavay, had gathered over 200,000 plant specimens in northwest Yunnan, which were sent to Paris. In the 1880s and 1890s, Augustine Henry collected dried plants and sent them to the Royal Botanic Gardens at Kew. This sparked a rage for rare Chinese plants among horticulturalists in England—a fad that later spread to the United States.

In the early 1900s, plant hunters were dispatched to Yunnan by horticultural bodies from both the UK and the US: they included Ernest Wilson, George Forrest and Frank Kingdon Ward. Plant hunters are territorial: Rock was imposing on the 'territory' of British collectors Forrest and Kingdon Ward. Rock learned to be wary of them—indeed to dodge them altogether. Kingdon Ward accused Rock of stealing

As well as plants, Rock collected birds—sometimes big birds like this unfortunate Lammergeier, Eurasia's largest raptor. The men shoulder matchlock rifles, with antelope-horn prongs used to steady them.

his native assistants (Rock apparently lured them away with higher pay). Rock played a game of hide-and-seek with George Forrest: once, when he heard the rival plant hunter was on his way to Lijiang, Rock immediately left town for ten days on an expedition. The plant hunters snooped on each other, trying to work out where a beautiful new primula had been collected so they could get in on the action.

Rock's major collecting was for the Smithsonian Museum of Natural History and Harvard's Arnold Arboretum. By 1924 alone, he had collected over 80,000 plant samples plus seeds for the Smithsonian. Two plants are even named after him. Rock also sent back numerous animal specimens and 1,600 bird specimens. J. H. Riley, the ornithologist who studied the bird skins, identified three new species from western China and named several of them in honour of Rock—one being *Ithaginis rocki*. But despite being recognised as an expert in the field, Rock never wrote anything about Chinese botany—not even a simple paper for a journal.

Rock's plant collecting has assumed a whole new level of importance today because of the sad slide into extinction of many plant species. Due to habitat destruction by humans on an unprecedented scale, an estimated 25 percent of the world's plants are set to vanish within the next 50 years. The implications of this loss are enormous: plants provide staple food crops, and a source of many medicines, of fuel and

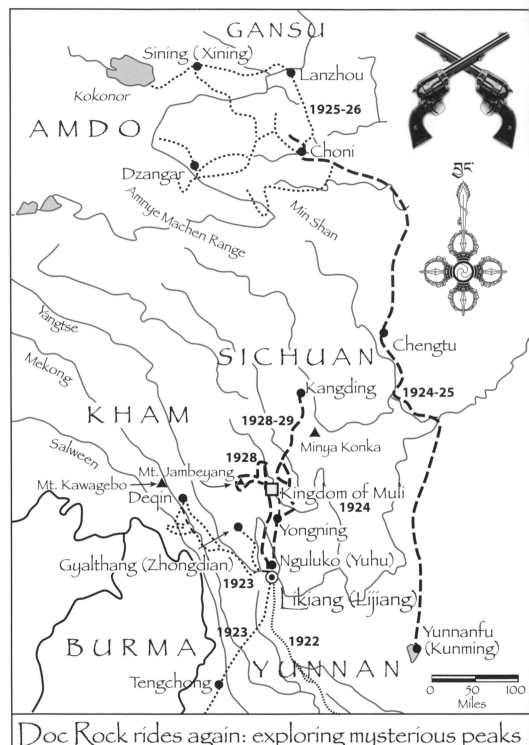

GANSU

Sining (Xining)

Kokonor

Lanzhou

1925-26

AMDO

Choni

Dzangar

Amnye Machen Range

Min Shan

Yangtse

Mekong

SICHUAN

Chengtu

1924-25

Kangding

KHAM

1928-29

Salween

Minya Konka

1928

Mt. Jambeyang

Mt. Kawagebo

Deqin

Kingdom of Muli

1924

Yongning

Gyalthang (Zhongdian)

Nguluko (Yuhu)

1923

Likiang (Lijiang)

BURMA

1923

1922

Yunnanfu (Kunming)

YUNNAN

Tengchong

0   50   100
Miles

Doc Rock rides again: exploring mysterious peaks
of the Kham and Amdo regions, 1922-1929

building materials, and they help regulate the climate and protect soil from erosion.

Sir Joseph Banks, the first director of the Royal Botanic Gardens at Kew, travelled with Captain James Cook near the end of the 18th century to indulge in exotic plant collecting. He was so driven to expand his collections that he sent botanists around the world at his own expense. But neither Banks—nor Rock—could have foreseen the day when seed hunters would be dispatched to the four corners of the globe to collect rare plant species that are being driven to extinction before their benefits are discovered. The Royal Botanic Gardens at Kew oversees the world's largest wild-plant depository—the Millennium Seed Bank in West Sussex, aiming to collect 24,000 species by 2010. Millions of dried seeds from over 120 countries are stored in sub-zero underground vaults—to enable them to survive for centuries. The bank acts like an insurance policy to protect the world's plant heritage for the future. These plants may offer great benefits for society— in medicine, agriculture or industry—that might otherwise be lost.

Rock started out by looking for plants and simply branched out— into collecting animal specimens for museums, into ethnography studies of the Naxi and the Tibetans, and into photography for National Geographic. Home for the next few decades was a Naxi-style courtyard villa on the outskirts of Lijiang at the village of Nguluko, now known as Yuhu.

The Tibetan world of the 1920s and 1930s was tribal—the authority of Lhasa extended only to central Tibet. Beyond that, lawlessness and brigandage prevailed, particularly in the north and east, where brutal warlords reigned. Private security was the order of the day—in the form of men armed to the teeth. On expeditions, Rock rode up front, wearing boots, riding breeches and a pith helmet—and with firearms at the ready. If he was sick or felt indisposed, he would instead travel by sedan chair, carried by four porters.

Rock's caravan could consist of up to 200 men—a large number of them heavily armed to keep bandits at bay. The caravan moved in a long line of riding and pack animals: bodyguards, muleteers, cargo handlers, porters, specimen collectors, photographic assistants and interpreters. The core of the group was a Naxi team trained by Rock; the armed escort was often provided by local rulers or officials, helping

Rock rides again—with his own posse of Tibetan cowboys

Rock through their territory. In exchange, Rock might offer an official a much-prized Colt .45 pistol. Despite the heavy protection, Rock's caravan was attacked several times. Of one encounter, Rock writes: 'Thanks to the bad aim of the brigands we lost only one soldier killed.' River crossings were treacherous—sometimes achieved by using rafts buoyed with inflated goatskins, and other times involving the use of perilous overhead ropeways. Pack and riding animals were dispatched across these in slings—using blindfolds so as not to cause the horses to panic.

Although the going could be rough, Rock liked to live in style on the trail. The pack animals bore some unusual cargo in their bags. Rock carried a battery-powered Victrola phonograph on which he played opera—*La Bohème* and *I Pagliacci*—in camp for himself, and on occasion to incredulous Tibetan nomads or monks at monasteries. Rock noted that sadder snippets of opera elicited howls of laughter from the nomads: in such remote realms, this was the ultimate ice-breaker.

During a march, Rock's personal retainers were divided into a vanguard and a rear guard. In the advance party would be a cook, an assistant cook and a butler who would select a sheltered campsite with a good view. Rock's sturdy tent would later be pitched here, with his folding bed—and his folding rubber bathtub, from the New York outfitters Abercrombie & Fitch (Rock liked to take frequent baths). Meanwhile, the advance guard would unfold a table and chairs on a leopard-skin rug, and lay out clean linen, china, silver and napkins. By the time Rock arrived, an Austrian-style-meal of several courses would be served, followed by tea and liqueurs. Rock had bottles of the finest European wines on hand: which he would savour as he listened to German opera played on a portable phonograph.

It was into an idyllic scene like this that two young German adventurers strayed in December 1931. Ernst Schafer and Hugo Weigold had just been detained and booted out of the Muli kingdom for breaking the taboo of hunting within its precincts, and were heading toward Lijiang when they came across the camp of Joseph Rock. The amazed Germans were bedraggled, unkempt and smelly—as Rock made a special point of telling them. Schafer, in return, greatly annoyed Rock by recounting how he'd bagged a spectacular specimen: a great white bear. In May of 1931, Schafer became the second white man to shoot a giant panda (the first white men to shoot the panda were Kermit and Theodore Roosevelt, in 1929—they shipped their trophy to a museum in Chicago).

Joseph Rock had a keen nose. And at camp, he would sniff around for a particular acrid odour—that of opium. He once fired his personal chef, Wang, because he suspected the man of smoking opium. But cooks experienced in preparing Austrian cuisine were hard to come by in these parts: two days later, Rock took Wang back upon his solemn oath he would never touch opium again. Rock was infuriated by the smoking of opium—in an area of Yunnan that was rife with the use of the drug. Opium-smoking was rampant throughout Yunnan, where the stuff was cheaper than cigarettes. Huge fields of opium poppy were common sights on Rock's travels. Rock could do little to control the recreational use of opium among the muleteers and soldiers he hired, except to forbid them from smoking the drug in his presence. For the Naxi who were his full-time servants, however, it was a different story—he was constantly watching them, and sniffing around for telltale odours.

In these remote parts, status and rank had to be established: it was important to keep up appearances and earn the respect of local leaders. So Rock arrived as a true leader would: by limousine. The limo of these remote areas was the sedan chair—a compartment borne on two long poles and carried either by four porters or four ponies. It was accompanied by an armed escort. On arrival, Rock would dramatically alight in a white shirt, tie and jacket. He acted like royalty—and carried a business card in Chinese.

Probably his grandest entrance like this was a meeting in 1924 with Chote Chaba, the king of Muli—who doubled as High Lama of Muli Monastery. Chote Chaba was the short name. Rock deciphered the king's longer name on his calling card:

> Hsiang tz'u Ch'eng cha Pa, by appointment self-existent Buddha, Min Chi Hutuktu, or Living Buddha, possessor of the first grade of the Order of the Striped Tiger, former leader of the Buddhist Church in the office of the occupation commissioner, actual investigation officer in matters relating to the affairs of the barbarous tribes; honorary general of the army, and hereditary civil governor of Muli. Honorific: Opening of Mercy...

The king of Muli—six-foot-two and corpulent—towered over Rock, who stood five-foot-eight. The 36-year-old king had a large head, and a powerful frame that was tucked into a red, toga-like garment, with one arm bare; below the tunic was a gold-and-silver brocaded vest. On his left wrist, he had a rosary. Ushered into the king's stone palace, Chote Chaba treated his unusual guest from America in a very dignified manner. But the king was not so kind to his own people. The monarch ruled over his tiny kingdom with absolute authority—which included frequent public executions. He employed spells and magical incantations to reinforce his power.

Rock played down the nasty aspects of Chote Chaba and harped instead on the theme of a long-lost kingdom. This was perfect prose for National Geographic—it appeared in the April 1925 issue under the title 'Land of the Yellow Lama.' Rock relates how the inquisitive monarch of Muli peppered him with inane questions like: Did Rock have binoculars that could see through mountains? Could a man ride a horse from Muli to Washington? Rock tried to keep a straight face when the king demanded to know where the kingdom of Puss in Boots was located. When Rock showed Chote Chaba a picture of an airplane in flight, the monarch inquired if the Americans could fly to the moon. Back in the 1920s, that made the monarch sound like a dum-dum, but today, his comment would be viewed in an entirely different light.

Joseph Rock rarely talked about food or what the local people ate in his writings, but there are some prize snippets in his National Geographic story:

> After the lecture, the king urged me to partake of Muli delicacies. There was gray-colored buttered tea in a porcelain cup set in exquisite silver filigree with a coral-studded silver cover. On a golden plate was what I thought to be, forgetting where I was, Turkish delight, but it proved to be ancient mottled yak cheese, interspersed with hair. There were cakes like pretzels, heavy as rocks. It was an embarrassing situation, but, in order not to offend His Majesty, I took a sip of tea, which was like liquid salted mud.

Rock, however, passed up on some other delicacies that the king dispatched to his campsite:

> As the king's porters left, a hungry mob of beggars gathered outside our gate. The dried legs of mutton and yak cheese were literally walking all over the terrace of our house, being propelled by squirming maggots the size of a man's thumb. I was informed these were the choicest delicacies from the king's larder. As none of my party wanted the lively food, we gave it to the beggars, who fought for it like tigers.

On a second visit in 1928, Rock curried favour with Chöte Chaba by bringing him copies of the 1925 issue of National Geographic, with photos of the king prominently displayed. Appealing to the king's great vanity, Rock used the National Geographic issues to gain leverage, for it was only through the diplomacy of the king of Muli that Rock was able to enter the sacred Konkaling mountain range in mid-1928. A number of explorers had tried to penetrate this region but failed, due to brutal weather conditions (alternate heavy rains or heavy snow), but mainly due to the threat of bandits—who were in the habit of robbing pilgrims coming to pay homage to the sacred peaks. These bandits included 400 monks from Konkaling Gompa (Snow Mountain Monastery) who used to rob pilgrims blind and then return to their quiet meditations—apparently not a contradiction in these parts. The resourceful Dr Rock got the king of Muli on the case: the king dispatched stern missives to the bandit chiefs telling them to back off—at least long enough for Rock to photograph the area and gather information for a National Geographic article.

The notorious Snow Mountain Monastery of Konkaling is still in business today—though not in the business of robbing pilgrims blind

Rock rode into the Konkaling region with an armed posse of Naxi and Tibetan bodyguards. The expedition visited twice during the monsoon season when torrential rain left the peaks obscured by cloud. When the clouds finally parted for Rock, the panorama knocked him out: 'In the cloudless sky before me rose the peerless pyramid of Jambeyang, the finest mountain my eyes ever beheld.' Rock was pumping it up for National Geographic: there are plenty of peaks that rival Jambeyang in the Himalayas. Rock was the first Westerner to lay eyes on this region, and the very first to photograph these peaks: he lugged heavy glass plates around and developed pictures on the spot in tents in primitive conditions.

Rock planned a third visit to the region in the dry season but never made it: the area's robber chief bluntly said next time round he would go after Rock and his escorts. Rock explains:

His reason was the obvious displeasure of the gods. Shortly after our last trip around the peaks the wrath of the deities was aroused and hailstones descended in such size and quantity as to destroy the entire crop of the Tonyi Besi outlaws.

Rock took the hint and stayed away: he knew when to quit. In fact, he never made another attempt to enter Konkaling. All bets were off

Horse riders heading for the sacred peak of Jambeyang, where Rock was the first Westerner to set foot.

when Rock lost his key protector: Chote Chaba, the king of Muli, was executed by the Chinese in 1934.

In his National Geographic articles, Rock often gloated over being First White Man on the scene. What he failed to mention was that he couldn't tolerate having another white man on his expeditions. In 1926, he took a young Pentecostal missionary, William Simpson, with him on his Amnye Machen expedition. Simpson, an American who spoke fluent Tibetan, was later described as 'taken by too much brotherly love and sweet words while these ruffians here look upon such conduct as becoming to a silly woman'. Rock told him to go take a hike back to his mission, and replaced him with a native interpreter. In 1929, he took on a young assistant, William Hagen, who held a post at the US Consulate in Yunnanfu, to join him on a trip to Minya Konka. Hagen lasted longer than Simpson, but fared no better. In 1931, Rock escorted American journalist Edgar Snow on a trek through bandit country to Dali. They got off to a bad start and ended up arguing over Rock's treatment of his caravan staff and numerous other matters. Upstart newcomer Edgar Snow was quite frank: he spoke his mind to Rock. In his

diary, Rock wrote: 'he is a greenhorn of the first order and an impertinent sponger.'

After this, Rock swore never to travel again with another white
man. But less than three months later, in April 1931, he invited two
Pentecostal missionaries, Mr and Mrs Andrews, to join him on a camping trip out of Lijiang. No sooner had they pitched their tents than Mr
Andrews went to work on Rock, telling him in graphic detail what he
could expect on Judgement Day if he didn't act quickly to redeem himself. Rock listened for half an hour before telling Andrews he would
not put up with any such nonsense. Mrs Andrews was even worse,
in Rock's view. He wrote that she was 'really silent and stupid, and on
nearly everything she possesses is written *Jesus Loves Me*, even on her
eyeglass case...'

Central Tibet had proved barren ground for the most resolute of
missionaries—over the course of several hundred years of attempts,
only a dozen or so Tibetans had been converted, and the missions
themselves had been vigorously expelled by Tibetan officials. The
missions ended up on the fringes of the Tibetan plateau, where Chinese officials were more protective of them, sharing a common disdain toward 'Lamaism'. Through this liaison, the missionaries came
to be considered Chinese agents by Tibetan tribes like the Khampas.
During sporadic anti-Chinese revolts, the Khampas not only targeted
the Chinese—they set about destroying mission stations and killing
European priests. This was a compelling reason for Rock to steer clear
of the missionaries—if he actually needed a reason. Rock sometimes
wondered whether all the crackpots in Christianity had not convened
along the Tibetan borderland to annoy him (Rock was an agnostic).
The remote areas that he travelled had more than their fair share of
hardcore evangelists, faith healers, and people who spoke in tongues.
Rock did see some worth in missionaries who had skills to offer the
local population, such as those who were doctors.

But living in Lijiang suited him fine, because there were very few
white men around at the time. Rock got so used to his wild lifestyle
that he found he could not adapt to life back in America. The problem
was most likely that there were just too many white men in America—
and Rock was no longer special. On his infrequent visits to the US—
shopping for expedition sponsors and equipment—he would gorge
himself on haute cuisine, opera and fine hotels; he would be the star
attraction at social gatherings. But then he would become homesick

for his simple villa in the backwaters of Yunnan—and would declare he was repelled by 'automobile-mad America' and 'the so-called civilized world'. He wrote, 'unless I can work in the wilderness and unexplored regions, I would have no incentive to living.'

As for White Women, well, that was entirely another story. In October 1932, Edgar Snow entertained Rock in Shanghai at the Rose Room, a nightclub-restaurant known for its exotic dancers. Rock recorded in his diary the outrage and disgust he felt at being confronted with gyrating female pelvises and breasts. Two days later, he was still berating Snow over the excesses of the nightclub. Rock's unusual sex life—or rather, lack of it—gave rise to numerous theories among those who knew him. Some suspected him of homosexuality—but as far as is known, he had no intimate relations of this kind, unless he was incredibly discreet. And as far as is known, he never had any intimate relations with women, regarding them with a mixture of fear and suspicion. He probably remained celibate his entire life. One very good reason for this would be that Rock worried that emotional attachments might restrict his movements—and he had an advanced case of wanderlust. The few women he befriended or admired were those who did not threaten him sexually: among them was fellow adventurer Alexandra David-Néel.

Moving on down the long list of the people that Rock held in contempt, you would arrive at his denigration of the Yellow Man. There was a strong anti-foreign sentiment among the Chinese of the 1930s and Rock was the object of frequent jeers and insults. Rock derided the nationalists and detested the communists. He wrote this diatribe about the Chinese in his diary:

> People, white people, are depraved enough and silly enough to want to save the souls of such a despicable people. They have souls no more than lousy, flea-ridden dogs have. Why not let them sleep in their filth and ignorance and leave them alone, let them rot in their bandit-ridden country? The best thing that could happen in the world would be a huge catastrophe which would annihilate that miserable, mean, selfish, filthy, degenerate race...

You have to wonder how Rock managed to survive in China at all. His diaries (held at the Royal Botanic Garden in Edinburgh, Scotland) and letters reveal a very different side of Rock than his reader-friendly

National Geo alter-ego. 'Eccentric' seems somehow inadequate to describe Rock's ranting and raving in the diaries. Some thought him quite mad. Rock himself worried about his sanity in his journal entries—with wild swings of mood and flawed logic.

At one time or another, Joseph Rock railed against just about every group he met in southwest China: he detested the Chinese, hated missionaries, and despised Muslim soldiers ('absolute robbers'). But he was fascinated by the minority groups of southwest China—especially the Naxi and the Tibetans. He praised the Naxi as 'noble savages' and 'pure children of nature'. It's ironic that Rock, who loathed women, should spend half his life studying the Naxi, a quasi-matriarchal group. Rock called them the 'Na-khi'—the name is pronounced 'Na-shi'. Under the pinyin spelling system, this pronunciation is rendered 'Naxi', which has the potential to be confused with 'Nazi'. The Naxi are a Tibetan-related ethnic group with similar customs and beliefs, but they wear different dress and have a completely different pictograph script. Rock became intrigued by their ways—which had not been documented by any outsider.

Rock's interest in the Naxi blossomed around 1930. The previous year he considered abandoning his Lijiang base and moving back to Hawaii. National Geographic was losing interest in his stories, but with new studies on the Naxi, he promised fresh stories. As his research into Naxi culture continued, he veered away from the National Geographic approach toward more scholarly writing. This paid very little, so he had to fund the research on his own. The Naxi were formerly matriarchal—the women ran the show—and traces of this remained, with women managing household and finances. There was a high rate of 'love-suicide' among the Naxi. Harking back to the ancient Bon faith of Tibet were Naxi shamans, or *dongba* wizards, who conducted fantastic rituals—dipping hands into burning oil, leaping into bonfires. The wizards chanted from strange pictograph texts that nobody else knew how to read. Rock decided to crack the pictographs, which was rather like taking on Egyptian hieroglyphs—using Naxi wizards as his Rosetta Stone.

The Naxi held Rock in high regard as he boosted respect for their culture and provided medicines (mostly free) for the needy. And his expeditions provided a lot of work for the Naxi, whom he often

Rock (in middle) with Naxi assistants on snowcap near Lijiang

trained for specific tasks. In the 1920s, he took two Naxi assistants back to Washington for training—one of them studied taxidermy, the other photography. Other Naxi assistants were trained in how to collect and store botanical specimens. Rock had a steady team of faithful Naxi assistants with him on expeditions.

Among the Naxi of Lijiang, Rock lived like a potentate. In fact, he was nicknamed 'the foreign prince'. It was a role he enjoyed—a role with power and prestige. As he moved around the remote borderlands of Tibet, he encountered Tibetan tribal 'royalty' like the prince of Choni. Between December 1924 and August 1929, Rock made three journeys to Choni, spending several months as guest of the prince.

The October 1935 issue of National Geographic carried an article by Rock on 'Demon-Possessed Tibetans and Their Incredible Feats.' In this piece, about a visit to Yongning Monastery in northwest Yunnan, Rock claims he witnessed an oracle in a trance twisting the blade of a sword into a knot. While in a trance, a Tibetan oracle is thought to possess superhuman strength: he convulses like an epileptic—hissing, groaning, gnashing his teeth, beating his breast, foaming at the mouth. A Tibetan oracle is a diviner: when questions about present or future events are posed, the oracle answers in high-pitched cryptic language that listeners interpret to their satisfaction. In the West, maniacs might end up in a lunatic asylum; in Tibet, they end up as schizoid oracles. This was Rock's last National Geographic piece, but his pioneering photography continued. In 1936, he chartered a plane

Rock photographed this shaman dance in Lijiang for National Geographic

to fly over the mountains around Lijiang to conduct aerial photography and surveys. This was the first plane to land in Lijiang.

When the Japanese invaded China in 1937, Rock refused to evacuate Yunnan: he stayed in Lijiang—growing vegetables, consulting his Naxi sorcerer, and listening to war bulletins on shortwave radio. Then he abruptly left—heading for Hanoi and Bangkok—and air-hopped across to Europe. Later in 1937, Rock showed up in Berlin, where he said he wanted to see the Nazis with his own eyes. Horrified by what was transpiring in Berlin, he bid a hasty retreat to Kunming, which came under attack from Japanese planes. Rock departed by air for Hanoi and later spent a year in Indochina, but in mid-1940 the Japanese invaded Vietnam. Rock repaired to Honolulu, engaged in a dispute over storage of his books—and headed back to Lijiang. He figured Lijiang was as safe a place as any to sit out the war and indulge in research on the Naxi.

In early 1944, the ever-restless Rock took a short trip to India. He turned up in Calcutta, where the US Army Map Service took a sudden interest in him. Military officers hustled Rock onto a top-priority flight to Washington, promising that his voluminous belongings would follow. Rock's invaluable knowledge was needed by the US Army to draw maps for pilots flying 'the Hump'—the mountainous region lying between China and India. These supply flights departed India and flew over Burma to southwest China, landing at Kunming. With large parts of China and Burma occupied by the Japanese, the flights were a lifeline for southwest China. The pilots kept reporting a sighting of 'the Thing'—the same Minya Konka peak that Rock had described back in 1930 as being higher than Everest. Some pilots even backed up Rock's assertions.

While Rock was flown to Washington, his precious Naxi research was packed into trunks in Calcutta and dispatched to the US by ship. The trunks included all the research for his Naxi encyclopedia and dictionary—a project he had laboured on for the last decade—plus translations of Naxi religious ceremonies and notes on Muli. The ship was torpedoed by a Japanese submarine: a decade of research sank to the bottom of the sea. Rock went ballistic when he heard the news. For a few days, he was perilously close to suicide.

Once he got over this, he decided he would just have to go back and start the Naxi research all over again. There were a few hitches: Rock calculated he'd invested $18,000 of his own money into Naxi research, and he didn't have the funds to kick-start the project. At sixty, he was too old to lead expeditions. But Rock was stubborn, and he had good connections. He talked Harvard University Press to agree to publishing a two-volume Naxi history, and secured guarantees that they would help finance his return to Yunnan to complete the rest of his Naxi research.

In September 1946 he was back in Lijiang again. He put in some productive years, reassembling his Naxi material—he found a good Naxi wizard, traced manuscripts, recorded religious ceremonies.

Meanwhile, Harvard published Rock's two-volume work *The Ancient Na-Khi Kingdom of Southwest China* in 1947. The text ran to over 800 pages, with 256 plates as illustration. British author Bruce Chatwin later called it 'the most eccentric book ever produced by Harvard University Press'. Coming from Chatwin, highly eccentric himself, that's a kind of weird compliment.

Time for Rock's research was running out. A new tribe of 'bandits' was on the horizon in 1949—the Red Chinese, as they were then called. Championing their cause was none other than journalist Edgar Snow, whom Rock had shown around Yunnan in 1931.

Rock escaped from the Red Army in August 1949 by flying out. But he had not given up on Lijiang. He went to Europe to talk about continuing his work in the Tibetan borderlands with Tibetologist Giuseppe Tucci. He kept a vigil of sorts in Kalimpong, Himalayan India, waiting for his chance to return. But with the entry of the PLA into Tibet in October 1950, Rock knew it was the end of an era. By mid-1951, with the Chinese bolstering the North Koreans against the US-backed south, Rock realised that his hopes of ever returning to Lijiang were gone.

Rock ended up in Hawaii, where he spent his last years hunting plants and writing. He had drafted a book about his adventures, and was putting together the final research for his epic Naxi encyclopedic dictionary—the lexicography he'd worked so hard to complete. He arranged for its publication by the Istituto per il Medio ed Estremo Oriente in Rome—the scholarly institute founded by Giuseppe Tucci. Rock subsidized the publication with his own funds. Publication of the first volume was timed to coincide with his 79th birthday on January 13, 1963. But on December 5th, 1962, Rock died from a heart attack. Volume I of the encyclopedic dictionary appeared the year after his death; Volume II was published in 1972. Combined, the two volumes run to over a thousand pages. The book Rock drafted about his adventures was never completed or published.

Numerous collections today house 'Rockiana'—his voluminous papers, notebooks, diaries, letters, photographs, 16mm films, plant and animal specimens—the Royal Botanic Gardens at Kew, the Royal Botanic Garden at Edinburgh, National Geographic, Harvard's Arnold Arboretum, Harvard's Museum of Comparative Zoology, the Harvard-Yenching Institute... Harvard University complains about stacks of Naxi pictograph manuscripts that nobody knows how to read. As it turns out, however, Rock's Naxi material has become important because during the 1966–76 Cultural Revolution, the Naxi culture was not only forbidden, it was targeted for annihilation: many Naxi manuscripts were burned. Rock himself predicted that the Han Chinese would seek to subjugate or destroy the culture of minority groups in China—and this is exactly what came to pass. In the 1990s, the Naxi culture was revived, and Rock's magnum opus on the history of the Naxi—translated into Chinese—was part of that revival.

In January 1997, Joseph Rock appeared in National Geographic again— this time as the subject, as in retracing the explorer's footsteps. The story, 'Our Man in China', juxtaposed Rock's archival pictures with modern ones. Meanwhile, back in southwest China, something very strange was happening. After being booted out by the communists in 1949, Joseph Rock was not only being revived, he was being rehabilitated. He was being turned into a hero by the Chinese—because of a tenuous link with the utopia of Shangri-La.

Rock made his name by stretching the truth whenever it was expedient. His vanity knew no bounds: in the Tibetan borderlands, he often

boasted about being first white man on the scene. So he would've revelled in the knowledge he has found new fame in the 21st century—
and at the same time, he would've been appalled to learn why. Joseph
Rock is a Communist Party poster boy. His story is being heavily promoted in a campaign to attract tourists to a brand-name paradise: the
realm of Shangri-La.

Shangri-La: a remote valley where the ageing process has slowed
down, where people do not succumb to disease. A place where knowledge is exalted, and where goldmines take care of any cash-flow problems. Shangri-La lies in the fertile Blue Moon Valley, a realm bordering
the frontiers of Tibet: a monastery with mixed Tibetan and Chinese
features is perched on the flanks of a towering pyramidal snowcap. A
monastery with central heating, stocking a superb collection of books,
music and Chinese art—and one that allows the luxury of ample time
for their contemplation. The High Lama is an expert on the passage of
time: this wizened Capuchin monk, originally from Luxemburg, stumbled into the valley more than 200 years ago, and is still alive to tell
the tale. The people of the valley are stocky Tibetans in sheepskins,
fur hats and yak-skin boots, but at the monastery, Chinese cuisine is
served—probably augmented by medicinal herbs from the valley—
and Chinese attendants are among the staff. And this, of course, is all
fiction. Shangri-La is an impossible composite that sprang from the
imagination of British writer James Hilton—whose novel Lost Horizon
appeared in 1933. Hilton never set foot in Asia: for Tibetan material, he
got no further than the British Library in London.

The movie version of Lost Horizon, released in 1937, spread the fame
of Shangri-La far and wide. The movie was dubbed in Chinese in 1938
and released in major Chinese cities under the title Romance in the
Peach Blossom Village—alluding to a classic tale of earthly paradise from
ancient Chinese literature. The theme song This Beautiful Shangri-La
was made widely popular by a Shanghai star. But it was not until some
60 years later that a resemblance was noticed to a real part of China.

American researcher Ted Vaill caught up with ageing actress Jane
Wyatt, who starred in the original Hollywood version of Lost Horizon.
She'd met Hilton, who was hired as special consultant for the making
of the movie. According to her, Hilton hinted that his sources were
based in part on Rock's feature stories for National Geographic—and
in part on British archival sources and other material. But Rock wrote
about a number of mountain regions in southwest China for National
Geographic. And the researcher overlooks the fact that Jane Wyatt's

character is not even in the book—she was added into the movie to provide romantic sizzle, enticing the lead character with a skinny-dipping session in a lotus pool, where she burbles: 'I'm sure there is a wish for Shangri-La in everyone's heart… Oh, I wish the whole world would come to this valley.'

This is exactly what tourism authorities in southwest China are hoping too. The Shangri-La paradise branding is a powerful marketing tool. Hilton claimed in his book that Shangri-La would not be found on any map, but that hasn't prevented mountain realms from Ladakh to Bhutan from staking claims. For over 70 years, debate has raged over the exact location, citing the author as being inspired by a real model. The Chinese have been rather slow off the mark, but they've joined the debate in truly spectacular style.

In March 2002, three counties in northwest Sichuan were renamed Shangri-La County by official decree from Beijing. The previous year,

Rehabilitated Rock: as a key link in Shangri-La marketing in Yunnan, Rock has popped up everywhere, from maps to magazine covers, like this one published in 2002.

the main county seat of Zhongdian opened Deqin Shangri-La Airport, with a runway that handles Boeing jets. Odd but true, Rock never wrote about Zhongdian in National Geographic stories, though he did write about Konkaling in upper Yunnan. In western Sichuan and upper Yunnan, dogfights have broken out between a dozen places vying for the Shangri-La crown. So bitter have the disputes become that another solution was proposed: the creation of 'China Shangri-La Ecological Tourist Zone', embracing all the greedy contenders from the highlands of Sichuan and Yunnan—and keeping them logo-happy. That zone is a chunk of territory approaching the size of Switzerland. But the concept seems to have since disappeared into thin air.

Joseph Rock is all over the brochures, the glossy photobooks, the maps. However, Rock is difficult to pronounce for Chinese, so typos like 'Doctor Lock' creep in, or even worse, 'Joseph Lark' and 'the Rocker'. The Naxi could not pronounce Rock's name either: they called him Luo Boshi. *Boshi* means 'doctor', and *Luo* is about as far as they got with pronouncing 'Rock'.

The communist reception for Dr Rock was rather different in 1949. In July 1949, when Rock flew into Lijiang by chartered plane, he stepped onto the airfield to Peter Goullart's wry greeting: 'Welcome to the Red paradise!' Rock nearly collapsed from the shock of hearing this, but gathered his composure and ordered his supplies unloaded. Within minutes, a band of 30 armed men descended and searched all Rock's belongings. They were soldiers from an advance guard of the Red Army. Rock made periodic visits to Lijiang after WWII, keen to get his Naxi research completed—but now with the communists around, he knew this would be impossible. Rock was jeered at the on streets of Lijiang as a despised Westerner; his Naxi assistants were called slaves of the foreign devil. The Naxi *dongba* wizards had gone underground; soldiers were smashing temples and sacking monasteries. Within a few weeks, Rock had reached the end of his tether—he packed up his substantial library, his stack of photographs and his treasured artifacts. On August 3rd 1949, Rock and Goullart managed to board another chartered plane out of Lijiang, bound for Kunming.

Peter Goullart, a Russian refugee who worked in Lijiang, gazed wistfully out the window of the plane—a droning Dakota turboprop—at the place he'd called home for the last eight years. And surely Rock must've felt the same (in Rock's case, it was home for considerably longer). Goullart wrote a nostalgic book about Lijiang titled *Forgotten Kingdom*, published in 1955, which he concluded with these words:

I had always dreamed of finding, and living in that beautiful place, shut off from the world by its great mountains, which years later James Hilton conceived in his novel Lost Horizon. His hero found his 'Shangri-La' by accident. I found mine, by design and perseverance, in Likiang.

Goullart saw the parallels between Lijiang and Shangri-La, but Joseph Rock never mentioned the Asian utopia in his work—and he was around for 30 years after the publication of *Lost Horizon*. Who knows—maybe he hated Shangri-La too, or was jealous of James Hilton's success.

❖　　❖　　❖

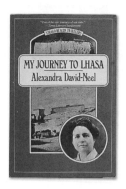

MY JOURNEY TO LHASA
Alexandra David-Néel

Camera or gun? Alexandra opted for the gun on her epic journey to Lhasa, but that left her scrambling for visual material for later book publication. The drawing at left is a recreation of an image taken in 1924 in Calcutta (photographer unknown). The picture replicates the pilgrim gear she wore en route to Lhasa, complete with furry backpack—and walking staff to fend off vicious dogs.

 # Alexandra David-Néel
1868–1969

anarchist, occultist, spiritual seeker,
opera singer, journalist & late bloomer

Hot Chocolate for the Mystical Soul

Alexandra indulges in Psychic Sports

❖   ❖

Into the Mystic: as a child, the rebellious young Alexandra escaped into other worlds by devouring the science-fiction fantasies of Jules Verne. She promised herself that she would one day outdo the heroes of these fantastic stories—and travel to faraway lands. She lived up to that promise—becoming the first Western woman to meet a Dalai Lama, and the first Western woman to set foot in the Sacred City of Lhasa. In old age, settled in France, she found fame and fortune by writing books that revealed the secret rites of Tibetan breath training and trance-runners. But she continued to be restless: at the age of 100, she renewed her French passport— ready for the next voyage…

❖

 THE READER WILL HAVE noticed by now that this book is somewhat skewed toward male explorers. The men seem to monopolise exploration in Tibet. This is not entirely the case—female adventurers did make it to Tibet, though they were few in number. And the women just didn't seem to hang around long enough to become really eccentric stars in the Tibetan firmament. But there were exceptions.

In the 1920s, French writer Alexandra David-Néel put to rest any suggestion that adventuring in Tibet was the sole domain of men. Though she did no mapping or measuring, Alexandra was readily accepted as one of the great explorers of Tibet by the other explorers themselves. She was part of the club.

Nowhere is that more readily revealed than in Alexandra's relationship with Joseph Rock. Rock hated women, but he got along just fine with Alexandra. In fact, he carried on a 40-year correspondence with her. They had lots in common—they both loved hot baths, they both loved opera (you have to wonder: did these two explorers sing opera together at the edge of Tibet?). And they loathed missionaries. Alexandra, however, readily took advantage of what the missionaries had to offer if she was in trouble and there was a missionary outpost in the vicinity. She would lodge with French Catholic nuns or American Pentecostals at the drop of a hat. Joseph Rock even offered Alexandra a job assisting him with plant hunting. She declined, but took him up on an escort through bandit-infested country of eastern Tibet.

Previous profiles in this book mention that Lhasa lost its lustre after the British invasion of 1904 and that the explorer's race for the Sacred City lost its appeal. But that lost appeal was for white men, not for white women. The trophy for being the first white woman to reach Lhasa was still up for grabs.

Alexandra started out on her long path as a journalist and scholar who simply had a keen interest in the East: somewhere along the line she got derailed—and ended up becoming a legend.

Tibet was new ground for female explorers. A number of female adventurers had gained access to 'Little Tibet'—the Ladakh area in northwest India—but very few had made it across the border into Tibet proper. If it was tough for male explorers to reach Lhasa, it was doubly difficult for female explorers, as the Tibetans had a strict policy of barring Western women. This was probably a remnant of China's trade with Europeans during the 17th and 18th centuries, when no foreign women were allowed on the Chinese mainland. In Nepal a similar policy held sway.

Initial forays by female adventurers into Tibet were very different from Alexandra's quest to learn about Tibetan Buddhism: the earliest attempts were made by female missionaries who pitied the poor Tibetans because they knew nothing about Jesus. Annie Royle Taylor, driven by missionary zeal, was the first Western woman known to enter Tibet. She embarked on the ambitious project of bringing the Presbyterian gospel to Lhasa's residents—and to the Dalai Lama himself. This feisty Englishwoman was small in stature: she possessed two great assets to mount the journey—she spoke good Tibetan and she dressed like a native. She learned colloquial Tibetan in Darjeeling, where she taught in a Presbyterian mission school.

In 1884 Annie transferred to the China Inland Mission. She honed her Tibetan language skills when she visited Kumbum monastery in 1887 to deliver Tibetan text cards to astonished lamas. These cards bore translations of Gospel messages, handed out in the belief that once received, the Word would triumph. Although missionary activity was forbidden in central Tibet, it was tolerated on the fringes of the plateau in Amdo and Kham, where missions attracted locals with schooling or medical assistance. Annie did manage to convert one Tibetan—a young man called Pontso, who had run away from his master in Tibet due to maltreatment. Annie gave him medical treatment in Sikkim, and in gratitude, Pontso became her servant—for the next 20 years.

In September 1892, Annie and Pontso set off to answer a Divine Call to reach Lhasa. In Tauchau, in Amdo, they met a Chinese ruffian called Noga, who was planning to ride to Lhasa along with his Tibetan wife. Noga agreed to accompany Annie as her guide. The small entourage comprised Annie, her faithful Tibetan servant Pontso, two Chinese servants, Noga and his Tibetan wife, and 16 horses. Annie's game-plan was roughly this: disguised as a Tibetan, she would make it through to Lhasa—where she would throw herself at the mercy of the Dalai Lama and, having won his confidence, would proceed to convert him.

Then 36 years of age, Annie endured a harrowing four-month journey from western China, braving ice and snow, windstorms and freezing passes. Those of lesser faith would have turned back: Annie developed stomach problems and suffered from the glare of the sun off the snow. Harassed by bandits, she lost most of her horses and her camp and bedding supplies; one of her servants turned back; another died. This left Annie and Pontso at the mercy of Noga, who at one point threatened to kill her. Then Noga absconded with several horses and other valuables, saying he wanted to ride ahead to Lhasa. On January 4th 1893, at Nagchu—only three days' march away from Lhasa—Annie and Pontso were arrested by Tibetan officials—who had been alerted by the treacherous Noga.

When questioned, the fearless Annie said her reason for going to Lhasa was that she wanted to cross Tibet to get to Darjeeling. She wisely made no mention of any conversion motives. A senior magistrate from Lhasa patiently listened to her story and her accusations of theft against Noga. He is said to have remarked: *Dear Me! The English people are odd creatures.* Instead of executing Annie and beheading Pontso, the magistrate compassionately supplied them with fresh horses, clothing, a tent and blankets—and an escort—and told them to go back the same way they came. Soundly rebuffed, the disconsolate Annie and Pontso made their way back to Sichuan, reaching Tachienlu in April, 1893. In seven months, they had covered some 1,300 miles, surviving the rigours of a howling Tibetan winter.

Not one to give up her divine quest so easily, Annie returned to England to found her own missionary group, called the Tibetan Pioneer Mission. Annie became an overnight celebrity in England: she was in great demand as a speaker—appearing at venues like the Royal Scottish Geographical Society. However, she was not astute at describing scenery or customs in Tibet—she was focussed on her mission to convert the Tibetans. The advance group of her mission—the Tibetan Pioneer Band—consisted of nine men, dressed in Tibetan robes and hats, dedicated 'to live and die for Tibet'. Within a few months of arriving in Sikkim, however, Annie had a falling-out with her workers, and told them to push off and join the China Inland Mission.

In 1895, Annie and Pontso showed up at the town of Yatung. Due to trade regulations negotiated in 1893, British traders were allowed to reside in this southern frontier town, lying within Tibet just near its border with Sikkim. Although she was clearly only interested in

trying to convert Tibetans, Annie wrangled a permit to open a general store and medical supplies shop in Yatung. Pontso and his new
Tibetan wife were in charge of the trading post. Two or three other
female missionaries joined Annie at various junctures but did not stay
long, finding her company rather difficult. She had no success in con-
verting Tibetans, but did succeed in arousing the wrath of China Customs Officers in Yatung, fighting with them over who had first rights
to open the weekly mail-bag.

The full story of Annie's adventures might never have surfaced if
not for a writer named William Carey, who passed through Yatung
in 1899. Planning to write a book about Tibetan customs, he sought
Annie out. Noticing that Annie referred to a slim diary to answer his
questions, Carey asked if he might transcribe it. The diary duly arrived:
Carey said it was 'very odiferous', redolent of the yak-butter, foxskins,
goatskins, dried mutton and yak tails that it had been packed with.
Carey painstakingly transcribed 160 pages of hieroglyphics by poring
over the diary with a magnifying glass. Annie's diary was published
in 1901 in a book compiled by Carey titled *Adventures in Tibet.* It is not
known how much Carey tampered with the original manuscript—he
mentions editing it for 'crude forms of expression'—which could mean
awkward phrasing, or could refer to nasty swearwords.

When Colonel Younghusband entered Tibet at the head of a British army in 1903, Annie was waiting for him outside Yatung. She questioned him closely about his religious beliefs before giving her seal
of approval to proceed with the invasion. Indeed, her nursing skills
proved useful to Younghusband's mission. She removed her red
Tibetan robes, fur boots and yellow peaked cap—and donned English
clothing again to become a nurse at a British field hospital. Annie, it
appears, may have even contributed to motives for the British invasion—a few years earlier she wrote a letter making the fantastic claim
that the Tibetans were about to attack India and that 20,000 Russians
were on their way to help the Tibetans.

Annie returned to England for most of 1905, but in December that
year she was back in Yatung, crossing the frontier at night without a
pass. She was greatly disturbed that the Younghusband campaign did
not open Tibet to missionary activity: she had her heart set on widespread evangelizing in Tibet. She took up residence at Yatung Customs house, refusing to pay rent on the grounds that the building
needed repairs. After firing off a volley of abusive letters to government

authorities in India (more than a few complaining about China Customs in Yatung) she was finally removed to a lunatic asylum in October 1906, most likely by fellow churchpeople, and her possessions were auctioned off in Yatung. Nothing more is known about her.

Pardon that long-winded aside on Annie Taylor, but it sets the scene for female explorer attempts to reach Lhasa—and reveals the extreme difficulty and pitfalls of the quest. And so back to Alexandra David-Néel. After 1904, the British blocked access to other Europeans—and that meant Alexandra, who was French. Even the British approached no further than Gyantse in the period 1904–1930. During this time, a handful of British Political Officers and Trade Agents gained access to Lhasa, but if there were wives around, the Tibetans never invited them along. When she set off in 1923, Alexandra was aiming to be the first Western woman to reach the Sacred City of Lhasa. And she would do this to spite the British, who had barred her from visiting Tibet—after she managed to sneak up to Shigatse in 1916.

Call her 'Alexandra the Late'. She was definitely a late bloomer. Born in the late 19th-century, when a career of a woman as an explorer of remote places simply wasn't on, she was a daring woman. 'Visionary' might be closer to describing what she accomplished. She was not an explorer in the conventional sense but she delved deeply into the world of Tibetan Buddhism. Hers was a spiritual quest—a journey as much internal as external. In this way, she was more in the mould of Thomas Manning, driven by curiosity and a thirst for knowledge.

Very little was known about the esoteric practices of Tibetan Buddhism in the early 20th century. Alexandra was among those who fostered the new field of Tibetology and who introduced Tibetan Buddhism to a wider audience in the West. She was among those questioning whether spirituality and human dignity had been sacrificed in the West—sacrificed to the relentless quest for scientific advances and for accelerated speed, and the preoccupation with time. Tibet embodied a world very different from Western values, a kind of counter-balance. Never conquered or occupied, Tibet had developed completely apart, with only a slight intrusion of technology.

Alexandra traces her infatuation with the Far East to the Musée

Guimet in Paris. The museum's library held the largest collection of oriental books in Paris, and was the focal meeting point of a small group of orientalists. Presiding over the library was a large seated Buddha statue (no longer there). Something about the library haunted Alexandra—she could not explain its pull. She imagined that she could commune with the large Buddha, who bore the faint flicker of a smile on his face. The Buddha was telling her to get to the source—to go to the East.

Born in Paris on October 24, 1868, Alexandra David grew up in Brussels, after her family moved there—or more accurately, was 'exiled' there, as her father was a radical journalist who had incurred the wrath of French authorities. An only child, Alexandra studied music at the Royal Conservatory of Brussels but did not complete her courses. She led a flamboyant early life—running away from home several times in her teens, becoming an anarchist at 19, and a freethinking and militant feminist. At 20, she left Brussels for London to improve her English, with her accommodation under the unlikely patronage of the Society of the Supreme Gnosis—a group that she had somehow strayed across. Through this group, she was introduced to the teachings of Madame Blavatsky of the Theosophical Society. Among Blavatsky's disciples was Annie Besant, a strong-willed feminist and advocate of free love— whom Alexandra greatly admired.

In 1892, funded by a small inheritance from her grandmother, the bohemian Alexandra departed for India. She joined the Theosophical Society in 1892 in Adyar and studied Sanskrit there before moving on to Benares to practice yoga. Then she ran out of money and had to return Brussels. Not having any financial success in her chosen field of writing, Alexandra decided to return to studying music at the Royal Conservatory of Brussels. She became an opera singer: for seven years she toured with various troupes, going to far-flung places like Vietnam and Greece.

In Paris, she engaged in an affair with a composer, living with him for three years—but she suddenly took off in the summer of 1900 on tour to Tunis, North Africa. Singing at the Casino de Tunis, she caught the eye of wealthy French railway engineer, Philippe-François Néel. In Tunis, Alexandra was in the full bloom of beauty, but at 36, a late bloom—one that might easily wilt—and Philippe was a wealthy catch. He owned a spacious Moorish-style home in Tunis overlooking the Mediterranean, and had a yacht and a string of mistresses. Playboy

Philippe was in the habit of photographing his conquests—usually loose women—aboard the yacht. Although Alexandra had risen to the position of 'artistic director' at the casino, she knew that her financial prospects were shaky. When Philippe invited the fashionable opera singer to his yacht for dinner, she stayed the night.

She married Philippe in August 1904—thus adding the 'Néel' part to her surname. Seven years her senior, Philippe was affectionately nicknamed 'Mouchy' after his handlebar moustache. Within a month of tying the knot, Alexandra and Mouchy went their separate ways— she to Paris, he to the south of France. It was a stormy relationship: periodically the two reconciled and spent time together. She did warn Mouchy: 'I am not pretty, I am not fun, I am not a woman... Why did you persist? Were you deranged?'

But he took no notice. There were some side-benefits for Mouchy from Alexandra's wayward travels. On her initial visit to India, she'd keenly studied tantric sex rites at Madurai's Meenakshi temple. Alexandra wanted to try out all the Kama Sutra positions, so she practiced on Philippe, although she never wrote about this. A French author mused that there are two Mme David-Néels: the one who writes and the one who knows.

In December 1904, Alexandra's father died. This had a profound effect on her—returning to the family home in Brussels reminded her of her ambitious childhood dreams, and her father's death reminded her of her own mortality. After a period of anxious self-examination, she decided to embark on a new career as a journalist—writing for both French and English magazines, mainly about feminism, Buddhism and the East. Mouchy did not enter into these plans, except as banker. In Paris, she studied Sanskrit at the Sorbonne and attended lectures by famed Orientalist, Professor Sylvain Levi. But theories were not for her—she longed to experience everything first-hand, see it with her own eyes. She boarded a ship, bound again for the Orient. When she arrived in the Far East in 1911, she planned a visit of 18 months, hoping to write articles for the press.

She ended up staying almost 14 years—during which she learned the Tibetan language and absorbed Tibetan Buddhist practices. She did not see Philippe once during this period. They kept in touch by mail—and occasionally Alexandra would hit Philippe up for a transfusion of money. She addressed him as 'my dear Mouchy' or 'my poor Mouchy'. In one letter to the long-suffering Philippe, Alexandra wrote:

> Sensuality is something each one of us experiences according to our own sensibility; in my own case it is related to solitude, silence, virgin lands revealing no sign of cultivation, wide open spaces and the rough life, under canvas, of the nomads of Central Asia.

And she indeed found all this in the Tibetan borderlands. It's ironic that this same sensuality excluded Philippe himself. Philippe became the absentee husband, bankrolling his wife's wild escapades. He was her lifeline—saving her letters, having her manuscripts typed, forwarding her articles to publishers, acting as her agent in France for any matter she needed.

In her earlier travels in Ceylon and Burma, Alexandra was initially drawn to Theravada Buddhism. But in India, she shifted her focus. She stayed at the Theosophical headquarters at Adyar, near Madras, luxuriating in a vast room by the sea. At night, lunatics abroad: the other guests wandered the vast grounds, lanterns in hand, keeping an eye out for venomous snakes. Among the guests was a European count, a beautiful circus performer turned missionary, and a Swedish woman who vowed to starve herself to death (she was persuaded otherwise by a cable from Theosophist head, Annie Besant). Alexandra eventually drifted north to Sikkim, where she fell under the spell of Tibetan Buddhism.

Few of the Dalai Lamas lived long enough to attain their majority to rule. In the 18th and 19th centuries, power in Tibet was in the hands of regents. The 9th Dalai Lama (the boy Manning had met) died at the age of ten, rumoured to be poisoned. The 10th, 11th and 12th incarnations all died before reaching the age of 21—some poisoned, one rumoured to have been crushed when a ceiling fell on him while sleeping. Fingers could be pointed at the regents, who were said to practice black magic to reduce the life expectancy of their charges in the interests of retaining their own power. Fingers could be pointed at the Chinese, who had a vested interest in curbing the influence of the Dalai Lamas. Or it could be sheer coincidence that these Dalai Lamas all died so young.

By dodging the odd assassination attempt, the 13th Dalai Lama turned out to be long-lived—and a shrewd ruler. The 13th travelled quite a bit, but not because he liked travelling. When the British invaded in 1903, he fled to find sanctuary in Mongolia. When there was trouble with Chinese troops in 1910, he fled in the opposite direction, to British India—actually to Sikkim. In early 1912, British representative Charles Bell hosted the Living Buddha in Kalimpong. Bell says that his wife was careful not to speak to the Dalai Lama,

> for that would have offended Tibetan custom. My wife never had an interview with him. In view of the gulf between him and the opposite sex, I did not think that would be right...

No such gulf for Alexandra. She was granted an extraordinary one-hour audience—the first meeting between a Dalai Lama and a Western woman. The 13th Dalai Lama was a man of striking appearance—piercing eyes, large pointed ears, long thin twirled moustache (horrible pun on names, but the moustache greatly resembled that of Salvador Dali).

The Dalai Lama was impressed by Alexandra's command of Tibetan and the breadth of her knowledge about Tibetan Buddhism. He urged her to study the Tibetan language so that she might better understand Buddhist doctrine. Alexandra seemed to have few reservations about offering him her wisdom as well. Thinking of writing an article for a French magazine, Alexandra persuaded the 13th Dalai Lama to pose for photographs—another unprecedented break with protocol. These would be among the first-ever photographs of any Dalai Lama. To Alexandra's astonishment, when the film was developed, there were only vague ghostly images of the Dalai Lama. She was convinced she was the victim of some occult phenomenon. But even so, she had scored a coup—she managed to arrange a second interview with the Dalai Lama.

Charles Bell managed to photograph the Dalai Lama in exile (and later in Tibet) thus overcoming a long-standing taboo against depiction of reincarnate monks. Once the taboo had been overturned, the Tibetans took it in stride: Bell's pictures made very special gifts, as the highly revered images were eagerly sought to be placed on altars around Tibet.

Word about Alexandra's feat in interviewing the Dalai Lama spread among the Tibetans themselves. The rumour was put forward that she could become a voice for Tibet in times of trouble—and that in fact she might be an emanation of venerated Dorje Phagmo, Tibet's only

The 13th Dalai Lama, photographed in temporary exile in Kalimpong, India, circa 1911. He was the first Dalai Lama ever to be photographed.

female incarnate to preside over a monastery—in turn thought to be a reincarnation of Tara.

Alexandra's lengthy stay in Sikkim could be written up under a separate thick chapter, titled 'Meetings with Remarkable Men.' Indeed, Alexandra wrote about these encounters at length in her book *Magic & Mystery in Tibet*. In Kalimpong, she met Sidkeong Namgyal, Crown Prince of Sikkim, and his special assistant Lama Kazi Dawa-Samdup. It was Sidkeong who facilitated her interviews with the Dalai Lama. The dashing young prince had been educated at Oxford, spoke English fluently, was handsome, rich—and a lama to boot. The 33-year-old prince evidently took a liking to Alexandra, a dozen years his senior. He invited her to his opulent English-style mansion in Gangtok. They whiled away the hours over afternoon tea, discussing the arcane practices of Tibetan Buddhism.

These discussions often included Lama Kazi Dawa-Samdup, who was a Sikkimese scholar of some renown. He was a schoolmaster in Gangtok: not the least bit interested in teaching, but consumed by books. Alexandra reported that he could become enraptured by a particular text—falling into a spellbinding 'trance' over it, and delaying all other pressing matters until the trance passed. His other main passion was drinking. He was an occultist and mystic who 'sought for secret intercourse with the Dakinis [ravishing female deities] and the

Ngakpa (shaman) from Amdo with outlandish hairdo

dreadful gods hoping to gain super-normal powers.' His reputation was such that an American Theosophist by the name of Walter Evans-Wentz later sought him out as his guru and arranged with him to translate an arcane Tibetan text, *The Tibetan Book of the Dead* (published in English in 1927) and a companion volume *Tibetan Yoga and Secret Doctrines* (published 1935). Both texts have become classics in the West.

Alexandra soon became involved in intrigue at the Sikkimese court. Sikkim was firmly under the thumb of British India as a protectorate, but the British permitted the charade of Sikkimese royalty. Not known for her subtlety, Alexandra wrote to Mouchy that all her life she longed for a grand passion—and that he definitely did not fit the bill. But evidently, the prince did. He plied her with expensive gifts—jewellery of solid gold, gold objects. She wrote to the alarmed Mouchy that the prince took her for hikes in the hills, where they dined in a bungalow by candlelight, talking well into the night about spiritual matters. Then, she wrote, the prince retired to his private quarters. Mouchy didn't believe a word of it: he demanded that she come home to her husband or else he would pursue other muses.

On the death of his father in February 1914, the prince ascended the throne as Maharaja of Sikkim with much pomp and ceremony, which Alexandra witnessed. Sidkeong's private life was somewhat complicated: he had fathered a son by a Sikkimese mistress, and was set up to marry a Burmese princess by the British. But in December 1914, Sidkeong died quite suddenly—rumoured to be poisoned because of his outspoken criticism of the British and because of reforms he wanted to introduce. Alexandra was heartbroken.

Meanwhile, WWI had broken out: Alexandra had no desire to return to the battlefields of Europe—nor to be sunk in a ship on the way to France. The outbreak of war suited her purposes—she was running out of excuses for telling Mouchy why she could not return. More distracting news for Mouchy: another young man had entered Alexandra's life. Earlier in 1914, when studying at various monasteries around

Sikkim, Alexandra's assigned translator, Lama Kazi Dawa-Samdup, told her that he had to go to India. Before he departed, Alexandra requested that he help find a boy to serve as her companion and valet when travelling. He recommended a 15-year-old novice monk called Yongden. It was an auspicious choice: she forged a strong karmic bond with Yongden—the two were to remain together for the next 40 years. Yongden later became her legally adopted son, over the objections of the jealous Philippe. Because he was born in Sikkim, a British protectorate, Yongden eventually obtained a British passport. The passport gave his name as Arthur-Albert David. Occupation: Buddhist priest and explorer.

Yongden and Alexandra journeyed north to the hills of Sikkim, where she glimpsed the landscape of Tibet for the first time—and was immediately smitten. She loved the brisk high-alpine air, the solitude, the silence. Alexandra had come north to find the lair of a hermit-sorcerer, the gomchen of Lachen, who lived in a cave. She'd encountered him a few years earlier when he'd conducted a tantric ceremony at the court of Sidkeong in Gangtok. The sorcerer was supremely ugly—a lama of around 50, with hair plaited in a long thick braid that touched his heels, turquoise-studded gold rings dangling from his ears—and eyes that blazed like hot coals. Rumour had it he could fly through the air, command demons, and kill people at a distance. Tracking him down, and determined to unlock the secrets of Tibetan Buddhism, Alexandra asked if she might become his disciple.

The hermit accepted her as an apprentice: she passed two winters with him. Yongden rested close by. In his cave, the yogi taught her Tibetan in Lhasa dialect, and shared his secret knowledge of such practices as *tumo reskiang*—raising body-temperature through meditation. Practitioners would take a decidedly odd 'final exam'. This consisted of sitting cross-legged, and naked, by the banks of an icy river in the dead of the night, preferably with a biting wind. A sheet would be dipped in the river and draped over the practitioner's torso: the adept was expected to dry the sheet using the force of inner heat. The exercise would be repeated until daybreak—by which time as many as 40 sheets might be dried out.

Alexandra had first crossed into Tibet in the fall of 1914, when she and Yongden had visited Chorten Nyima, a tiny nunnery near the frontier. Here Alexandra heard of a cranky hermit-sorcerer who sent *tormas* (ritual rice cakes) whirling through the air to wreak havoc on those

Monasteries were strictly a man's world, but Alexandra managed to talk her way into some of the major monasteries like Tashilhunpo and Kumbum

who disobeyed his orders. Alexandra exclaimed, 'Oh! To talk with this magician who shot avenging cakes through space!... I was dying with desire to meet him.' But the wizard turned out to be so mild-mannered that Alexandra concluded that he could not have harmed a fly.

In July 1916, Alexandra and Yondgen ventured much further up the line: they made their way on horseback north to Shigatse, the second-largest town in Tibet. She studied at famed Tashilhunpo Monastery, and so impressed the abbot with her ability to debate on Buddhist doctrine that he conferred on her the robes of a graduate lama. She and Yondgen eventually made their way back to Gangtok, where Alexandra received notice of deportation from the British Raj, on the grounds that she had crossed from Sikkim into Tibet without a permit. The deportation order was drummed up by none other than Charles Bell, her former host in Kalimpong. Incensed, she and Yondgen left Calcutta at the end of 1916. They took a leisurely route through Burma, Vietnam and Japan.

In Japan they tarried for six months, studying Zen, and meeting scholars and mystics. Among them was Ekai Kawaguchi, who'd travelled across Tibet in disguise for three years, from 1899 to 1902. This philosopher-monk was an old man with a flowing white beard. Alexandra took mental notes about the secrets of his success in reaching

Debate is an important part of monastic education. Tibetan-style debating involves slapping the right hand off the left palm when making a point.

Lhasa. He got there because he was low-key: just himself and a couple of sheep as companions. The sheep were porters, of sorts—he had them carry his minimal provisions. In adverse situations, he never lost heart. And he threw himself on local hospitality when desperate. After surviving an icy river crossing in the Kailash region of west Tibet, he chanced upon a nomad yak-herder encampment. Exhausted, starving, and looking wild and unkempt, he approached the first tent, where he got a flat rejection. The second tent was even colder, with the master accusing him of intention to rob them:

> I turned away, and a great sadness came over me as I stood in the snow. My sheep bleated pitifully, and I felt like crying myself. A third tent stood near, but I could not muster courage enough to repeat my request there. The sight of my sheep was melancholy in the extreme, and with an effort I made an appeal at the fourth and last tent. To my great joy, I met a ready welcome. I was utterly tired out, but a quiet rest near a comfortable fire made me imagine the joys of paradise, and this I was allowed to enjoy all that evening and through the next day.

Fired up by her meeting with Kawaguchi, Alexandra's attention turned once more to the Land of Snows. She and Yongden took a train from Korea to Peking in October 1917: their initial objective was Mongolia, where Alexandra wanted to study with Tibetan lamas, but chance sent her and Yongden in a different direction. Through the French Ambassador at Peking, Alexandra met a Tibetan lama from the Kokonor region of northeastern Tibet. Tall, strong and charming, the lama invited Alexandra and Yongden to join his caravan on its return trip to Kumbum, the great monastery of the Kokonor region, and stay at the monastery. He indicated he wanted Alexandra to help him write a book on astronomy.

To reach Kumbum, a well-armed caravan was essential. The lawless region of Amdo was rife with bandits and warlords—and saw sporadic skirmishes between Tibetans and Chinese. The lama's caravan proceeded by rail as far as possible, then switched to mules and wagons. The party rode from inn to inn. One morning, Alexandra woke up to find some freshly severed heads impaled on a wall in front of her door: she was informed they were bandits. One evening at another inn, Alexandra witnessed young women in green pants and pink jackets parading around the lama's room for his perusal. The lama evidently had a shadier side. Somehow the lama got into a fight with a Chinese officer, whose soldiers burst into the inn—to be confronted by the lama's men, guns in hand. Alexandra managed to defuse the situation.

No sooner did the caravan enter the walled town of Tungchow than the place was assaulted by bandits. Bullets whizzed through the air. The invaders, using ladders to try and scale the high walls, were repulsed by defenders who hurled stones down at them, being short on ammunition. The defenders held their ground. In due time, people inside the town emerged from their hiding spots. Alexandra, it turned out, had jumped into a hot tub. Convinced that the rebels would storm the city and take her prisoner, she had decided to get a good bath in first.

After harrowing adventures, Alexandra and Yongden reached Kumbum. At the time, Kumbum housed some 3,000 monks in a vast citadel. Although it was unusual to accept a female practitioner, the abbot allowed Alexandra and Yongden to set up at a comfortable quarters in Kumbum. They used Kumbum as a base for several years, undertaking several lengthy trips. Then Alexandra had a fateful encounter: she

Chortens at Kumbum Gompa in Amdo, where Alexandra and Yongden bided
their time before lurching toward Lhasa

met an English geographer who showed her his maps, and pointed out
an unexplored route up the Salween River from Yunnan, continuing
along the Tsangpo River to join a major caravan route—on to Lhasa.
Chance had thrown this route information her way, and she meant to
capitalise on it.

You might by now have conjured up a picture of Alexandra as an
Amazonian, a woman of remarkable powers. But she was tiny—barely
five feet tall—and when she made her final break for Lhasa in November 1923, she was not in great shape. Freeze-frame: the photo shows
Alexandra surrounded by 'gentlemen brigands'—Khampa warriors
holding their matchlock rifles, with antelope-horn prongs used to
steady them when taking aim at a target. Alexandra is dwarfed by the
tall brawny Khampas. But they respected her. Not only respected her:
in some parts she was treated like a lamessa and nomads flocked to get
her blessing.

When she set off on her clandestine trip to Lhasa, she wanted none
of this attention—she wanted to be totally anonymous. Early on in the
book *My Journey to Lhasa,* she describes trying to skirt past a village
without being seen—and she counsels:

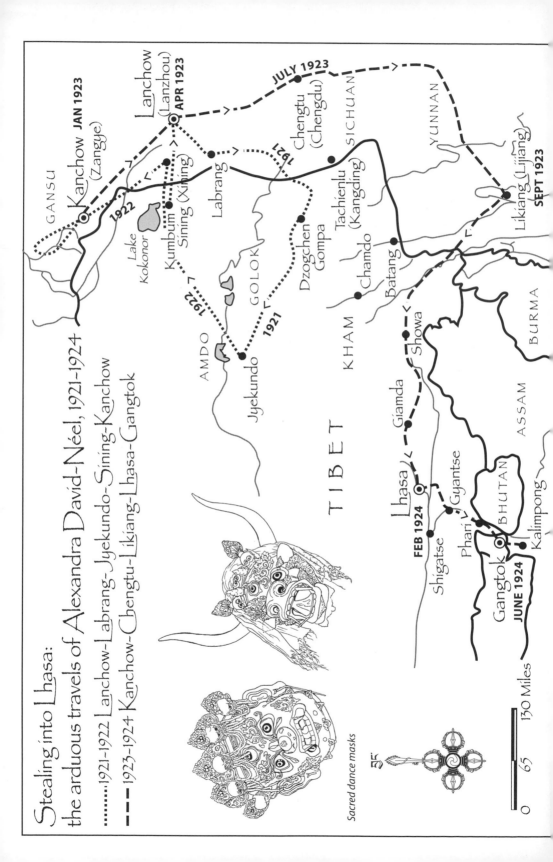

Stealing into Lhasa:
the arduous travels of Alexandra David-Néel, 1921-1924

.... 1921-1922 Lanchow–Labrang–Jyekundo–Sining–Kanchow
– – – 1923-1924 Kanchow–Chengtu–Likiang–Lhasa–Gangtok

Kanchow (Zangye) **JAN 1923**
Lanchow (Lanzhou) **APR 1923**
JULY 1923
Chengtu (Chengdu)
Likiang (Lijiang) **SEPT 1923**

GANSU

1922
1922

Lake Kokonor

Kumbum
Sining (Xining)
Labrang
1921

SICHUAN
YUNNAN

Tachienlu (Kangding)
Chamdo
Batang
Dzogchen Gompa

AMDO
GOLOK
1922
1921
Jyekundo

KHAM

BURMA

TIBET

Showa
Giamda
Gyantse
Lhasa **FEB 1924**
Shigatse
Phari
Gangtok **JUNE 1924**
Kalimpong
BHUTAN
ASSAM

Sacred dance masks

0   65   130 Miles

People whose hearts are not strong and who cannot sufficiently master their nerves are wiser to avoid journeys of this kind. Such things might easily bring on heart failure or madness.

Yet here was a 55-year-old woman undertaking such a journey—and she was heading right into a Tibetan winter. Travel in Tibet is rough enough: travel in winter verges on the suicidal. And travelling in disguise as a pilgrim made the trip even rougher—pilgrims were not given cushy beds at the sparse lodgings en route. More often, pilgrims would be sleeping in a crude shed shared with farm animals, or else out in the open. It was her iron will and powers of endurance that got her through. The reasons for the winter odyssey were two-fold: security on Tibetan borders was much laxer at this time, and Alexandra wanted to reach Lhasa for the Monlam (new year) festivities in February—which would also be the object of a number of other pilgrims.

FACE CREAMS

Face creams should be used with circumspection especially in Tibet. It will be found in many cases that the skin exposed to the sun and wind will crack and peel off, but on no account should face cream be applied to such chapped surfaces during the actual march. If this is done, the face will practically fry. Only when in the bungalows, after the march is over for the day, should lanoline, cold cream, or some such preparation be applied... Protection from the wind can be obtained by wearing a silk scarf across the lower part of the face, or by wearing a face mask, the latter being easily made in a few moments from an old handkerchief. In Tibet, one frequently meets the Tibetans themselves wearing these masks, on which they paint grotesque features.

This paragraph is from the booklet *Touring in Sikkim and Tibet*, by David MacDonald, for many years the British Trade Agent in Gyantse. The first edition of the booklet was published by Macdonald in Kalimpong in 1930. His clothing recommendations for female travellers include:

FOR A LADY
1 Riding Suit
2 Pairs Walking Shoes
1 Pair Slippers
1 Warm Skirt and Jumper
2 Sets warm undies

3 Sets Silk or Cotton undies
4 Pairs Warm Stockings
2 Washing Frocks
1 Topee
1 Soft Felt Hat
1 Dressing Gown
3 Nightdresses or Pyjamas
1 Pair Warm Gloves
1 Muffler
For the heights, for winter, and for travelling in Tibet, where the wind is drying, the following additions should be made:—
1 Warm Greatcoat
1 Extra Set Very Warm Underclothing
1 Warm Tweed Suit

Walking wealth: a Lhasan beauty parades with chunks of turquoise braided in her hair and a necklace of precious stones. Alexandra went to the opposite extreme—applying make-up to turn herself into an old crone.

This information was mainly directed at British women travelling in Sikkim. The Tibet slant had an audience that could be counted on the fingers of one hand. MacDonald had met Alexandra David-Néel in Tibet—she didn't wear a Tweed Suit or Silk Undies, and she didn't have any spare sets of Pyjamas for icy nights on the plateau. But she did carry a Soft Felt Hat to ward off the fierce high-altitude sun—and she praised her rubber-soled American boots. Those were among her precious few 'luxuries'—she dressed in Tibetan garb, or to put that bluntly, the rags of a pilgrim. She dressed like a harmless old crone so as not to be a target for bandits. She would masquerade as Yongden's mother—they would claim to be wandering pilgrims, begging their way to Lhasa.

As for face creams, Alexandra used cocoa powder and crushed charcoal. To disguise her brown hair, she blackened it with ink and lengthened her tresses by weaving in black yak-hair:

> ...and in order to match that colour I rubbed a wet stick of Chinese ink on my own brown hair. I hung huge earrings on my ears, and they altered my appearance. Finally I powdered my face with a mixture of cocoa and crushed charcoal, to obtain a dark com-

plexion. The "make-up" was rather strange, but suppliers to the theatrical trade, from whom I could have obtained better ingredients, have not yet opened branches in the Tibetan wilds!

Filth was essential to her disguise, keeping her skin dark. Tibetans are the Great Unwashed—but layers of dirt protect the skin from the harsh rays of the sun at this elevation, and Tibetan rivers can be freezing cold. Tibetans revel, however, in bathing in hotsprings. At one point, when a thermal hotspring came up on the trail—offering the rare chance of a bath—Alexandra faced the agonising dilemma: should she partake? At the risk of exposing her light skin? Yongden advised her not to bathe. That must've been very difficult for a woman who, until this trip, had made a ritual of indulging in two luxuries on the trail: drinking large quantities of hot tea, and taking a hot bath whenever possible.

Alexandra wrote later that she envied Swedish explorer Sven Hedin for his modern equipment, particularly his stove. But to employ such equipment would be to draw unwanted attention, which would defeat the purpose of the journey. Sven Hedin never made it to Lhasa, though he tried a number of times. Alexandra dispensed, too, with porters and guides, who had turned explorers in—like Annie Taylor, for instance. Alexandra was determined to avoid the mistakes of her predecessors. She and Yongden would travel without porters, horsemen or escort of any kind—or else use them only for short hauls.

'Into what mad adventure am I about to throw myself?' pondered Alexandra as she and Yongden slipped into Tibet over a high pass pelted with snow. She did not have to wait long for an answer.

Walking by night to escape detection and robbers, they tramped along a frozen river. By the light of the moon, the country was barren but starkly beautiful. They were on the march for 19 hours, writes Alexandra, hiking till two in the morning. Motion alone kept them warm, but they were exhausted and frozen. Stopping to try and light a fire, they found the flint and steel were wet. Telling Yongden to go in search of fuel, Alexandra sat down to meditate—she used her secret breath training to heat up her core temperature:

> ...my mind continued to be concentrated on the object of the *thumo* rite. Soon I saw flames arising around me; they grew higher and higher; they enveloped me, curling their tongues above my head. I felt deliciously comfortable.

Putting the wet flint and steel next to her body, she managed to dry them out, and started a fire that astonished Yongden. After all this, she needed a very hot drink. No hot chocolate, but they managed to brew some hearty yak-butter tea.

To Alexandra David-Néel goes the explorer's prize for attempting the most dangerous river crossing. Along the upper Salween, high above a deep gorge was a leather cable suspended between two cliffs. The cable 'sagged terrifyingly.' Alexandra and a Tibetan girl were bound together backwards with rough straps and tied to a wooden hook that would glide along the cable, pulled by a man using a towing rope. Alexandra recalls: 'a push sent us swinging into the void, like two pitiable puppets… Each jerk they gave at the long towing rope caused us to dance in the air a most unpleasant kind of jig.' Suddenly a towing rope snapped—this was not life-threatening, but it left the two of them dangling a few hundred feet above the swift current while hasty 'repairs' were made. 'My nerves are solid,' wrote Alexandra, '…But what of my companion. She was rather pale…'

When they finally made it to the other side, her Tibetan co-passenger became hysterical—weeping and shrieking. Yongden capitalised on the occasion to beg for food for his aged mother who had suffered so much on this cable crossing, and they continued on. They had to beg for hospitality at isolated farms or villages; they survived on a meagre diet of butter-tea and thin barley-flour soup that reminded Alexandra of dishwater. They fought off vicious guard dogs with their walking staffs. Once, a wolf trotted straight past them with the 'busy but calm gait of a serious gentleman going to attend some affair of importance.'

Alexandra carried a revolver—and was not afraid to use it. She was a straight-shooter, trained by her father, who used to take her out hunting with him in Belgium. Yongden carried a revolver too, but was clearly not as fast on the draw as Alexandra, nor as accurate. Closer to Lhasa, two ruffians showed up at the cave where Yongden and Alexandra had slept the night. They said they wanted to barter goods, but one man started to tussle with Yongden over their tent, and the other man picked up some spoons. When Alexandra demanded he give them back, he laughed and started to pick up more objects. Alexandra fired a shot from under her dress—the bullet grazed the man's head, sending him flying backwards. 'Flinging the spoons and the tent on the ground, the two ran like hunted hares across the thicket,' writes Alexandra. Only rich traders or chiefs carried revolvers, and passing

Alexandra and Yongden battle through biting snow on a high pass
in this drawing, recreating their epic four-month journey to Lhasa

pilgrims assumed that Yongden had fired the shot. When asked by
the curious about the weapon, he produced a small vintage revolver.
Which might explain why Alexandra was a better shot—she had an
automatic pistol.

Alexandra had a very good set of lungs: as an opera singer, she
was trained in breathing techniques that undoubtedly helped her deal
with altitude problems. And once or twice, she used that lung training
for quite different purposes. Confronted by a group of robbers, Alexandra decided that firing a pistol would be too risky—she might take
down one or two men, but not seven. Which was the number of robbers she and Yongden were faced with, blocking their path. A robber
took two rupee coins from Yongden and indicated he wanted to search
their bags for more booty. There was much more than robbery at stake
here: if their compass was discovered, Yongden and Alexandra could
be turned in as foreigners to collect a reward. What to do? Mustering all her theatrical expertise—and her fine set of lungs—Alexandra
let loose of torrent of filthy curses. She screamed and howled, calling
upon the most dreaded demons of the Tibetan pantheon to avenge

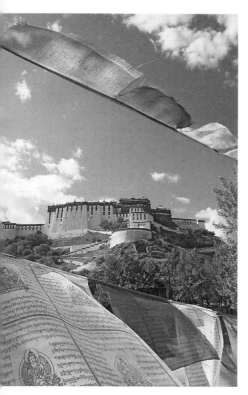

Lhasa by the back door: a view of
the Potala Palace from the rear,
from the pilgrim circuit

the loss of the two rupees—their only money for their pilgrimage to Lhasa. Awestruck by this blood-curdling outburst from such a small old woman, the robber chief stepped forward and returned the two rupees—begging her not to curse the men any further. He was evidently afraid that she was some kind of demoness herself. And then the robbers quickly turned tail and left, wishing them a safe journey to Lhasa.

Alexandra's strategy worked: in February 1924, after four months of strenuous tramping, and myriad trials and tribulations, she and Yongden sighted the Potala in the distance. Alexandra became the first Western woman to set foot in the Sacred City of Lhasa. Here, Alexandra's descriptions are anticlimactic, even bordering on the bland. But she's determined to enjoy her hard-won prize:

> Although I had endeavoured to reach the Thibetan capital rather because I had been challenged than out of any real desire to visit it, now that I stood on the forbidden ground at the cost of so much hardship and danger, I meant to enjoy myself in all possible ways… I would climb to the top of the Potala itself; I would visit the most famous shrines, the large historical monasteries in the vicinity of Lhasa, and I would witness the religious ceremonies, the races, the pageants of the New Year festival. All sights, all things which are Lhasa's own beauty and peculiarity, would have to be seen by the lone woman explorer who had had the nerve to come to them from afar, the first of her sex.

She joined excited throngs of pilgrims witnessing a great spectacle called Serpang—a pageant that filled the streets of Lhasa with hundreds of silk flags and banners, a procession by nobles and clerics, marching bands with longhorn trumpets, and fantastic costumed monsters performing all kinds of antics. Alexandra described this as an 'unforgettable spectacle which alone repaid me for my every fatigue and the myriad dangers that I had faced to behold it!'

Alexandra spent two months in Lhasa without being unmasked, though she had some close calls. She and Yongden found it imperative to leave because she was called as a witness for court case. Leaving not the same as arriving. They changed disguise, adopting lower middle-class dress. Alexandra had purchased a number of books and manuscripts in Lhasa and wanted to carry them out to India; they acquired a horse for onward transport. Alexandra knew that checks on those leaving Lhasa would not be as stringent as on those arriving.

Next stop: Gyantse, where Alexandra gave the British trade agent, David Mac-Donald, the surprise of his life. MacDonald was the son of Sikkimese Lepcha woman and a Scottish tea-planter. He married a Nepalese woman—they had nine children

A statue of the goddess Palden Lhamo, kept on the third floor of the Jokhang Temple, was paraded around the inner circuit of Lhasa once a year—with throngs of worshippers waiting with white scarves to offer. The statue was destroyed during the Cultural Revolution.

(one of his daughters described herself as a 'Himalayan cocktail'). When David MacDonald was informed of the arrival of a European woman and a lama, he assumed that his daughters were playing another practical joke on him, so he instructed the servant to show the woman into his bedroom, where he pretended to be asleep:

> After she had been in the room awhile I said, without turning, that I knew who she was, and told her to go away and not be silly. Imagine my confusion when a strange voice informed me that the speaker was Madame Néel. At once I conducted her to the sitting room, where tea had been served, and there questioned her as to how she had come, and the reason for her wearing Tibetan clothes.

Discussion over tea was limited: the cat was out of the bag—Alexandra had finally revealed her true identity, but would not talk much about her journey because she had book publication in mind. She got Mac-Donald to sign a slip of paper to say she'd come from the direction of Lhasa, and rested up a few weeks in Gyantse, developing a friendship of sorts with MacDonald. Leaving to the south, Alexandra and Yongden arrived in Gangtok, the capital of Sikkim, where she was guest of the British Political Officer, Eric Bailey. By the time Alexandra reached Kalimpong in India, MacDonald's wife had heard all about her—and took care of her much-travelled soul.

Alexandra's feat preceded her to France. By the time she reached French shores, she was already a celebrity. She embarked on a triumphant lecture tour with Yongden in 1925, promoting herself as 'the first white woman to reach Lhasa'. Her adventures were serialised in five monthly installments in the American magazine 'Asia', in 1926. The following year, her book *My Journey to Lhasa* was published in London, Paris and New York—to rave reviews.

Alexandra certainly got the scoop on her arch-rivals, the British. Thyra Weir, the next white woman to reach Lhasa, would get there in 1930 by official invitation. That didn't count as exploring—she was the wife of the British Political Officer in Sikkim, Colonel Leslie Weir. Luckily for Alexandra, several previous requests by British cadres to bring their wives along on visits—by Charles Bell and Eric Bailey—had been refused by the Tibetans. In the late 1920s, the Chinese had sent a female envoy to Lhasa and it was after this that the Colonel Weir and his wife were invited by the 13th Dalai Lama. The Weirs visited Lhasa in 1930 and again in 1932. The second time, they brought their 18-year-old daughter, Joan Mary: the entire family was granted an informal audience with the Dalai Lama on this visit. In the 1930s, as the policy loosened, more wives of British Trade Agents were allowed to stay in Gyantse and visit Lhasa.

In the mid-1920s, not long after Alexandra's triumphant lecture tour was launched, a woman even older—and tougher—than Alexandra made an unauthorised attempt to reach Lhasa. Gertrude Benham was obviously cut in the mould of Alexandra. Following in the footsteps of

Alexandra David-Néel is a sport now very popular among backpackers, particularly French and female. Gertrude was not French, however. She was English. Around 57 years old at the time, Gertrude got as far as Gyantse on her initial foray. Colonel Eric Bailey—who was then the 'gatekeeper' in Sikkim—reported that Gertrude 'made a thorough nuisance of herself', although he did not elaborate on why or how.

One thing's for sure: Gertrude was no amateur. Born in London in 1867, she spent most of her life travelling the world. As a young girl, she travelled to Switzerland with her father and became hooked on climbing. She climbed Mont Blanc and numerous other peaks in the Alps. Fearless on the slopes, she did not like to stop when she climbed, sometimes leaving guides in her wake. In 1904 she became the first woman to climb Mount Assiniboine, a Matterhorn-like-peak in the Canadian Rockies, towering at 11,870 feet.

And then she set off to climb the rest of the world's peaks—in New Zealand, Japan, Nepal and Africa. She climbed Kilimanjaro (19,335 feet) in 1909—the first European woman to achieve this feat. In fact, she climbed the last 4,000 feet of Kilimanjaro alone as her porters had deserted her upon discovering the bones of previous climbers embedded in an unknown white substance (snow).

Kilimanjaro sparked a lifelong interest in things African. Gertrude's idea of a good trip was to take three years off and start walking. In 1911, she walked from South Africa to Kenya, a distance of about 2,000 miles. In 1913, at the age of 46, Gertrude tramped 3,700 miles across Africa from west to east—a journey taking 11 months. She walked alone, with African bearers carrying her boxes and guiding her. She exclusively ate local food, but drank no alcohol. Along the way, she traded her handmade embroidery for food and local artefacts with tribal chiefs. In the course of her world travels, she amassed over a thousand artefacts and curios, including jewellery, clothes, weapons and toys—her collection was left to the Plymouth City Museum in England. She sketched and painted en route—sketching the mountains she explored—and was fond of collecting wildflowers, particularly alpine varieties. In the Himalayas, she collected thousands of them.

On her journeys, she always carried her knitting, Bible, pocket Shakespeare, a copy of Kipling's *Kim*, and an umbrella. It's not clear which of these items she relied upon for protection and defence purposes—a jab with a knitting needle or a bang over the head with the Bible. Gertrude shunned publicity and fame, but according to family legend, she walked the world to study nature and native cultures, 'armed only with an umbrella'. In a rare interview with the Daily News (UK, January 1928), she said:

> I am a lone wanderer. I have no home that is generally under-stood and so there is nothing to prevent me enjoying to the utter-most the spirit of wanderlust that has entered my soul. I am never lonely. How can I be when there is so much to see and admire in the world?

Here was a kindred spirit to Alexandra David-Néel. Gertrude found great pleasure in walking, and sallied forth alone, not worrying about security measures:

> I walk everywhere I can, using steamers, railways and motors only when necessity demands it. I have been quite close to lions and leopards in the bush, but they never harmed me or any of my carriers. I always go unarmed, and I think wild animals in the forest know by instinct that I have no desire to kill. I just wear an ordinary khaki skirt, puttees, strong shoes and a pith helmet.

Gertrude must've had a guardian angel watching over her: she was only robbed once—in South America in 1908—and miraculously never suffered any illness or fever during her travels.

Though she loved walking, climbing was Gertrude's passion—and in recognition of her mountaineering firsts, she received awards from the Royal Geographical Society in 1916 and the Ladies' Alpine Club of England in 1935. Travelling in Asia, India and Tibet, Gertrude most likely had her eyes on pristine peaks. Perhaps it was her well-thumbed copy of Kipling's *Kim* that inspired her in this direction. She wanted to reach sacred Mount Kailash, lying to the far west of Tibet. In 1929, at over 60 years of age, she was still trying to get into Tibet. It is not known what Colonel Bailey thought of this tough, determined Eng-lishwoman, dressed in khaki skirt and pith helmet, with umbrella at the ready, but it's clear that Bailey was equally determined to keep her—and other interlopers—out of Tibet.

Foiled in her Tibetan quest, in 1931 Gertrude turned her attention to the supreme challenge of climbing Mt Kamet. This 25,447-foot Hima-layan peak, lying in northern India right near the Tibetan border, was first conquered in August 1931 by veteran mountaineer Eric Shipton—at the time, the highest peak ever climbed.

After an adventure-filled life, the indomitable Gertrude died at sea in February 1938 at the age of 71 while returning home from one of her 'African tours'. She was buried at sea off the west coast of Africa.

Uncharitably, others would later dispute the details of Alexandra's trip—some saying she never reached Lhasa; others saying that the entire trip never took place. The latter claim was voiced in a book titled *Alexandra David-Néel au Tibet*, by Jeanne Denys, one of her former physicians—who appears to have been intent on some kind of personal vendetta to prove Alexandra was a charlatan. However, Denys' book was published in 1972, which was three years after Alexandra's death—somewhat cowardly timing, as Alexandra was no longer alive to contest it.

At the centre of the faking controversy are eight photos taken in and around Lhasa. Credited to Alexandra David-Néel, they appeared in the English edition of *My Journey to Lhasa*. However, the contents of Alexandra's travel kit did not include a camera. Pistol or camera? Alexandra went for the seven-shot automatic pistol—it was easier to hide and it was defence against bandit attacks. The travel kit consisted of pistol, glacier goggles, compass, watch, jewellery pouch and money. Cooking utensils were shared with Yongden. Alexandra later admitted she did not carry a camera because it would have been too bulky and liable to be discovered—although a beggar with a pistol was also rather suspicious.

So where did the photos come from? There were certainly no Tibetan photographers around in the 1920s except for innovators like Tsarong, the commander of the Tibetan army. And Alexandra would not have dared ask a British official to take such pictures. There was at least one resident Ladakhi photographer who was up to the task, but he would have used an old wooden-body camera with a black cloth draped over his head and the camera—which was bound to have attracted big crowds in 1924. The question then arises how that film would have been processed: film from Lhasa was mostly sent to India for processing. This photo of Alexandra (face blackened), Yongden and a little Lhasa girl against a backdrop of the Potala is claimed to be fake by Jeanne Denys. Others have suggested it might be a composite. Others say it is the real thing, but made with primitive equipment.

On the dust-jacket of the first editions of *My Journey to Lhasa* is a photograph of Alexandra in Tibetan dress with a pack on her back and a walking staff in one hand. If she looks immaculately clean and composed, it's because that photograph was taken after the trip—in a Calcutta studio.

The 1920s was an era where decent photography required lugging around of heavy supplies and developing on the spot. Joseph Rock managed this feat—but he had a large caravan to back him up with horses and porters. Alexandra didn't. In the Tibetan hinterlands she took mostly black-and-white photos, with the possibility of having these hand-coloured later. She returned from her 13-year sojourn in Asia with some 3,000 photographs—ample enough to illustrate her writings.

At almost 60, Alexandra decided it was time to settle down—somewhat. She bought a rambling house in 1927 at Digne-les-Bains, a quiet town surrounded by the Alps, in the south of France. The mountains reminded her of 'Lilliputian Himalayas'. Though the house was French, the interior décor was Oriental—created from treasures she had acquired in India, China, Tibet and Japan. She christened the place Samten Dzong or 'Fortress of Meditation'.

Indeed, one room was reserved for meditation and study. The décor for the meditation room was pure Tibetan temple-style: low Tibetan couches and cushions, a figure of Buddha, a Tibetan altar, *tankas* on the walls, and Tibetan woodblock-printed books. With its wide view of the mountains and its large pleasant garden, the house was a tranquil spot—ideal for writing books. Alexandra had, over her many years in the east, amassed a large collection of superb Tibetan artifacts: *tankas*, statues, ritual objects, rugs—and an especially fine array of masks. Samten Dzong was where they could all be arrayed and displayed. It made for the wildest interior décor—particularly in France.

At Samten Dzong, Alexandra settled into a routine of steady writing. Although she went on to author dozens of books, none achieved the impact of her first, *My Journey to Lhasa*, with its idiosyncratic mix of travel and occultism. In 1931, her version of *The Superhuman Life of Gesar of Ling* was published in France, and several years later in England. The ancient Tibetan epic of Gesar of Ling is thought to be the longest verse saga ever written—even longer than Homer's *Odyssey*. If you can imagine a Tibetan *Lord of the Rings*, this might come close.

Alexandra and Yongden experimented in writing in several genres—three novels are attributed to Yongden's authorship, and Alexandra wrote learned books about Buddhism. But Alexandra seems to have found her stride with the publication of a book called *Magic & Mystery in Tibet*, published in 1931. Through her lectures and first publications, Alexandra had picked up on public thirst for spiritual and bizarre practices. Catering to this niche-market, *Magic & Mystery in Tibet* delves into paranormal and occult: reincarnation, telepathy, clairvoyance, necromancy and other psychic phenomena.

Tibetan Buddhism is intimately linked with meditation practices—far more so than any other religious tradition. Yet in the 1920s, little was known in the West of Buddhist meditation practices—about the practices of Vipassana (initial focus on the breath) or walking meditation (initial focus on foot-falls). And even less known about the arcane Tibetan practices like Dzogchen—cultivating a clear but even-keeled awareness. They're so arcane that it's only recently that science has caught up with meditation, with new devices allowing neuroscientists to test and verify through science what Tibetans have known for centuries.

Alexandra recorded these phenomena, sometimes providing an explanation. She speculated that Tibet was a good host for the paranormal because of its high altitude and its great silences—permitting one to hear another's thoughts. But above all, she said it was due to the absence of cities, crowds and electric devices—she maintained these caused whirlpools of distracting energy. In Tibet, the spirit world came out of the animist Bon tradition that predated the arrival of Buddhism—spirits were present in the mountains, lakes and streams. Tibet embodied the fantasy of Shangri-La—a remote place with enlightened masters who could impart secret knowledge. And Alexandra found her personal paradise right where Madame Blavatsky had said it would be—in the Himalayas. Alexandra had studied with the great masters—the yogis of Sikkim—and returned to the West to impart this knowledge.

One of the arcane arts she described was *tumo reskiang*. Practiced by Tibetan monks in eight-hour sessions, this technique enabled them to raise their core body temperature high enough to overcome earthly defilements, or—more practical—to dry wet sheets on their backs while withstanding freezing Himalayan temperatures. On her way to Lhasa, Alexandra had used the technique herself to start a real fire. *Tumo* is an

Sacred masked dance being performed in a monastery courtyard—only monks danced in old Tibet, not nuns

ancient practice: the great Tibetan poet and singer Milarepa was said to travel in the Himalayan snows in a cotton loincloth by generating heat. Other times, not wanting to leave his meditations to search for food, he subsisted by eating nettles that grew near his cave: he is often portrayed in paintings with a green skin—the result of consuming too much nettle soup.

While raising body temperature through meditation is within the realm of the possible, a number of Western critics pooh-poohed another practice that Alexandra described. This was *lung-gom* or trance-running. Alexandra christened *tumo* and *lung-gom* 'Psychic Sports' in *Magic & Mystery in Tibet*.

According to Alexandra, *lung-gom* is the ability of monks to bound along in a trance, covering huge distances over rugged terrain, without the need to stop for food or water. She saw a *lung-gom* runner through field glasses, bounding through the desert, but was warned by others in her caravan not to stop the runner nor talk to him as this would break his meditative trance and result in certain death:

Large monasteries have a locked room where ritual items are stored—like these skeleton-dance masks

By that time he had nearly reached us; I could see clearly his perfectly calm impassive face and wide-open eyes with their gaze fixed on some invisible far-distant object situated somewhere high up in space. The man did not run. He seemed to lift himself off the ground, proceeding by leaps. It looked as if he had been endowed with the elasticity of a ball and rebounded each time his feet touched the ground. His steps had the regularity of a pendulum. He wore the usual monastic robe and toga, both rather ragged. His left hand gripped a fold of the toga and was half hidden under the cloth. The right hand held a phurba (magic dagger)...

There are some plausible explanations for what she saw. It's eminently possible Alexandra was hallucinating. Mirages like this can be induced at high altitude, and Alexandra was known to regularly take small pinches of cyanide—which would certainly have enhanced hallucinations. Or she might have seen a yeti. The King of the Yetis is said to move around by bounding rather than running.

Or she may have misconstrued, through field glasses, the figure of the postal runner. In the absence of any motorised vehicles, postal runners were used in relays to deliver messages in Tibet. Though horse-relays were sometimes used, the messages were largely delivered by foot-runners, who ran at different speeds, depending on urgency of the message. Monasteries had their own runners—perhaps Alexandra saw an express postal runner from a monastery. She might well have seen an express courier drugged to the eyeballs on stimulants. The pundit Sarat Chandra Das wrote a description of conditions for express couriers on the Lhasa-to-China route. The runners were required to subsist on a special diet (no onions, garlic or red pepper, for instance) and apparently took some sort of drug to keep them bounding along—possibly opium:

> At midnight they are allowed to sleep in sitting posture for three hours, after which they are awakened by the keeper of the stagehouse. It is said that these couriers are in the habit of taking certain medicines to give them the power of endurance against fatigue...

There is always the intriguing possibility that Alexandra was telling the truth: she saw a real live *lung-gom* runner. As if to drive this point home, she recounted three separate sightings of *lung-gom* runners. Odd that other travellers to Tibet have not witnessed this, however.

According to some sources, trance runners were trained at Shalu Gompa, lying close to Shigatse. The *lung-gom* runners were reputed to build their leg muscles by running on a pile of grain—while meditation masters provided mental training. During important religious festivals, the monk with the greatest physical and mental abilities would be selected to run to Lhasa without food, drink or rest. That's a distance of more than 140 miles. If these supernatural feats were true, imagine what the psychic sport of *lung-gom* could do to marathon races at the Olympics (assuming the contestant could pass drug-screening tests). If a contestant could bound along effortlessly for several days at a stretch, the record books would need to be rewritten.

In fact, certain sports have benefited from Tibetan meditation methods. Meditation and mindfulness have been used as techniques to sharpen focus by NBA teams, for instance. And in the spring of 1985, the amazing phenomenon of Sidd Finch surfaced in a story in *Sports Illustrated*. According to the story, Finch showed up at the New York Mets spring training camp firing baseballs at the ballistic speed of 168 mph—a talent learned from a Tibetan yogic master. So many readers were convinced of the truth of this story that two weeks later the magazine felt obliged to formally announce that the piece was an April Fool's Day joke, perpetrated by wacky author George Plimpton.

The Tibetans take psychic phenomena for granted: trance-runners who cover 300 kilometres at a stretch without stopping, adepts who can raise their body temperature through meditation, monks who can levitate—seeming to fly. But think about this: how would a Tibetan villager react to the news that a man has walked on the moon, that people can speak across the globe with a little gadget they carry in their pockets, or that people accumulate Airmiles when they go shopping? All that would sound mighty strange to Tibetan ears.

Alexandra's most extraordinary achievement lies in her ability to come to grips with arcane Tibetan Buddhist rituals—and being able to convey in print. By 1931, three of Alexandra's most influential books were in print: *My Journey to Lhusa, Magic & Mystery in Tibet,* and *Initiates & Initiations in Tibet.* With their strange mix of adventure, travelogue, scholarship and autobiography, these works occupied a middle ground between popular occultists and sober oriental scholars. The scholars berated her for not keeping to popular aspects of Tibetan Buddhism, while the occultists complained that she was too rational and skeptical.

For her more contentious claims about the incredible meditation practices of Tibetan Buddhism, Alexandra may yet be proved correct. Neuroscientists are beginning to discover, through use of sophisticated brain imaging technology, that meditation is an observable phenomenon. Richard Davidson, a University of Wisconsin neuroscientist with a special interest in the brain circuitry of emotions, has taken to wiring electrodes to the skulls of meditators to see what is transpiring. One of his subjects is Matthieu Ricard, a French practitioner of Tibetan Buddhism and an ordained monk—and formerly a molecular biologist. Davidson claims that scans of Matthieu Ricard's brain showed high activity in the area of the brain associated with positive emotion. 'They [Tibetan Buddhists] are the Olympic athletes of mental and emotional achievement.' says Richard Davidson. 'It's very, very exciting to think what we can learn from them and help other people.' It would appear that Tibetan Buddhists can not only regulate their emotions through

A *tanka* depicting esoteric Kalachakra Wheel of Time deities. There were subtle layers of meaning attached to *tankas*—often used to focus mediation practice.

meditation, they can also focus on compassion at will. In a world hell-bent on destroying itself through war and hatred, such skills and techniques might truly come in handy. To save the planet.

In 2003, the 14th Dalai Lama took part in a session on mental imaging at MIT. This was part of an ongoing series of dialogues between the Dalai Lama, his entourage, and MIT neuroscientists and psychologists. The session dwelled on the ability to hold a visual image in the brain. Harvard University psychologist Stephen Kosslyn lobbed questions at the Dalai Lama, like 'what shape are a cat's ears?'

The Dalai Lama claims that experienced monks can visualise many of the 722 deities of the Kalachakra (Wheel of Time) initiation. These deities are considered manifestations of aspects of consciousness and reality. Sometimes practitioners would visualise the deity up close, sometimes far away. He added that experienced meditators could keep a mental image like this for minutes—or even for half an hour. Or hours at a time (senior meditators only). This claim seems preposterous to researchers like Kosslyn. The longest they've ever had a Western subject hold a mental image is for seconds—and never an image

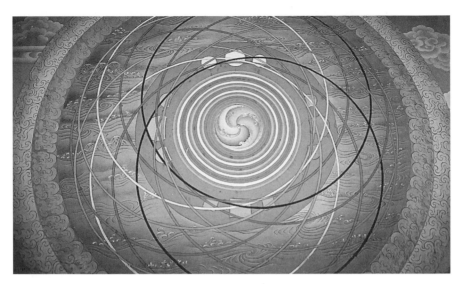

The eccentric Tibetan cosmos, depicted in a Bhutanese temple fresco, places credence in a huge snowcapped peak at the centre of the universe.

as complex as a Tibetan deity, which can be many-headed and multi-armed. Testing continues—can the Dalai Lama's claim be true?

The dialogue between Western scientists and Tibetan Buddhist monks is an intriguing one. As the Dalai Lama explains: while the West concentrated on Outer Space, the Tibetans focussed on Inner Space—the workings of the mind. The Western scientific ability to measure, describe and explain the physical world is infinitely more advanced than anything in Tibetan Buddhism. But after 2,500 years of training the mind through meditation and other practices, Buddhist have a lot to offer modern science, too. As the Dalai Lama phrases it: 'Western psychology, compared to Buddhism, is still very young. Like a baby.' Of all the unsolved mysteries of the human body, it is the brain that most rigidly resists our efforts at understanding. Witness the total lack of strategy for dealing with clinical depression and mental illness— fast becoming the major health issues of the 21st century.

Tibetans may be light years ahead of scientists in techniques for calming the brain, but they are aeons behind in the world of physical science. The Tibetan cosmos is—like most things in Tibet—based on a spiritual source of inspiration, harking back to an ancient Indian model. The Tibetan universe is not heliocentric or terracentric—it is Merucentric. At the centre of the universe lies Mount Meru, the abode of the gods, who live in a celestial city at its summit. Above Meru float twenty-five more heavens of the gods, while under the mountain lie the hell-realms, including the forest of razors. Meru is surrounded by seven rings of golden mountains and seven oceans. Across the oceans lie a few spin-off worlds, like the one we're on (rendered in mandalic diagrams as flat and trapezoidal in shape). Tibetan Buddhists have had to seriously reconsider their traditional cosmology in the light of modern discoveries.

In the 1940s, the young 14th Dalai Lama was fond of using a telescope to spy on the comings and goings of people in the city below the Potala. But at night, he turned the telescope to the skies to study the stars. He was astonished when he saw that the craters and peaks on the moon cast shadows—meaning that the source of light came from outside the moon, not from inside the moon as the Tibetan scriptures taught him. A 1,200-year-old Buddhist teaching claimed the moon was light-emitting; the Dalai Lama worked out that the moon was illuminated by the sun. He deduced that the sun and moon are not the same size, nor the same distance from Earth—again contradicting what he'd been taught under Buddhist cosmology. And then one day, he was tinkering with a clock (a gift to his predecessor, the 13th Dalai Lama) which rested atop a round object that gradually moved throughout the day—when it dawned on him that the round object was a globe showing countries, and that the turning of the globe was designed to indicate time zones. From this, the Dalai Lama deduced that the world was round—but his monastic tutors had taught him it was flat.

Exploring outer space versus exploring inner space—which is more important? In an age when satellite-guided missiles rain down and destroy a city like Baghdad, the concept of promoting inner peace and harmony—and non-violence as a means of conflict resolution—could prove more important in the end.

Truthfully, I am homesick for a land that is not mine. I am haunted by the steppes, the solitude, the everlasting snow and the great blue sky "up there"!... The campsites in the snow, sleeping in the frozen mud, none of that counted, those miseries were soon gone and we remained perpetually submerged in a silence, with only the song of the wind in the solitude... A land that seemed to belong to another world, a land of Titans or gods? I remained under its spell.

Alexandra wrote those lines in a letter to Mouchy in 1917, but they came back to haunt her forty years on. Her 'homesickness'—combined with restlessness and a thirst for more Tibetan source material for her writing—propelled her back to China. In January 1937, she and Yongden boarded an express train bound from Paris to Moscow, connecting on to Peking. China was chaotic, with Japanese incursions and widespread unrest. The pair made their to Tachienlu (Kangding), the gateway to Kham and eastern Tibet. By this time, the Germans had marched into Paris, so Yongden and Alexandra hung on in Tachienlu. In February 1941, she received a devastating telegram informing her that Philippe Néel had died.

She was caught in limbo—not able to enter British-dominated Tibet, not able to return to Paris. They stayed in Tachienlu till mid-1944 before making a break for Chengdu and Kunming, and flying over 'the Hump' to Calcutta in 1945. Post-war India was a chaotic and dangerous place, but they managed to make a nostalgic trip north to Darjeeling—where Alexandra had first glimpsed the Himalayas and the hidden realm of Tibet so many years before. In June, 1946, they boarded a plane from Calcutta bound for Paris—and returned to Samten Dzong in Digne.

After the war, Alexandra slipped into obscurity—but not into retirement. Approaching 80 years of age, she continued with her output of books, but they did not sell well. With her legs growing worse, she purchased a Citroen 4CV—a tin can of a car that Yongden drove when shopping in the town of Digne. The tranquillity of Samten Dzong was disturbed, from time to time, by some peculiar visitors. Like the one who fell to the ground and kissed Madeleine's feet when she opened the door (Madeleine being Alexandra's housekeeper). Or the woman who was anxious to find out whether her dead husband had been reincarnated. Another time, Alexandra was excited to hear that some explorers in their sixties would be visiting. But she said later they were boring old bats.

Alexandra David-Néel's far-reaching influence on other writers is apparent from the 1933 publication of James Hilton's *Lost Horizon* to the 1956 publication of Lobsang Rampa's *The Third Eye*. And the 1958 publication of *Tintin in Tibet* by Belgian cartoonist Hergé. None of these authors had set foot in Tibet, but they borrowed freely from Alexandra. She was particularly jealous of the great success of *Lost Horizon*, which bore echoes of her own writing—including, for instance, a description of the practice of *tumo reskiang*.

Much later, in the late 1950s, the comic book *Tintin in Tibet* was created by Belgian cartoonist George Remi under the alias Hergé (rather like the pundits, this name derived from his initials reversed, as pronounced in French). In the comic, Tintin goes into Tibet in search of his Chinese friend Chang, missing after a plane-crash on the plateau (it turns out he has been abducted by a yeti). Using Hergé's original files, a researcher traced the visual sources of *Tintin in Tibet*: newspaper clippings, climbing pictures, some issues of National Geographic. For the customs woven in, however, Hergé relied heavily on French editions of Alexandra's books—drawing on both text and photography. From her, Hergé took material on Tibet's monasteries, monks, people and way of life—as well as magical acts like levitation.

Herge's work went a lot further than Alexandra's—*Tintin in Tibet* has been translated into dozens of languages, including the elegant Tibetan script itself. Tintin is considered innocuous enough that copies have even been spotted for sale in the lobby of Lhasa Hotel—one of the very rare Western books allowed into Tibet by Chinese overseers. Pirated T-shirt bearing 'Tintin in Tibet' images are also on sale.

There is even a bar within the hotel featuring large murals copied from the comic book.

In the 1960s, Alexandra 'had a profound influence on the Beat generation and the emergence of American Buddhism', according to biographers Barbara and Michael Foster. The first English translation of her book *The Secret Oral Teachings in Tibetan Buddhist Sects* was a slim tome published in 1967 by City Lights Books in San Francisco, known as a publisher of beat poets. In the foreword Alan Watts cited Alexandra as 'wonderfully lucid,' although the book is replete with dense, esoteric prose. Alexandra influenced writers Jack Kerouac, Allen Ginsberg and Peter Matthiessen—fostering a new brand of American mysticism.

In her twilight years, Alexandra was a canny woman who cut a hard deal. She made a pact with the town of Digne whereby she lived rent-free at Samten Dzong, but would donate all royalties from her books to Digne upon her death. The town of Digne was gambling on the fact that she would not live to an advanced age. But she outlived the man who made the deal. In fact, she outlived all her contemporaries. She outlived her frustrated husband, Philippe. She even outlived her adopted son, Yongden—30 years her junior—who was supposed to take over when she died and look after all the paperwork and her writing. Yongden died in 1955 of a bad liver—too much alcohol—at the age of 56. Alexandra described his premature departure as impudent—and highly inconsiderate.

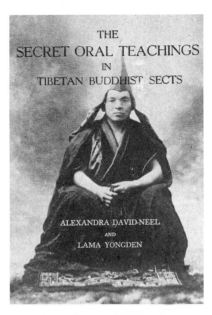

Some claimed that Alexandra extended her lifespan through diligent adherence to yoga and arcane practices, but actually she did no such thing. Inexplicably, in her writings she remained completely silent on the subject of traditional Tibetan medicine, based on herbal remedies. Alexandra's remedy was to ignore pain: she suffered terribly from arthritis and other debilities and hobbled around her fortress with a walking-stick. When the pain became unbearable, she occasionally resorted to taking some narcotic, or consulted a number of physicians— but took none of their advice.

Lama Yongden appears on the cover of this thin edition, published by City Lights Books, San Francisco, in 1967. City Lights published radical beatnik writers and poets—some drew inspiration from the esoteric works of Alexandra David-Neel.

Her favourite physician was Dr Maille, whose services she engaged in 1953 because she heard he had a strong interest in Buddhist philosophy, having lived with monks in Indochina and Burma. He described her condition thus: 'She was enormously fat with swollen, painful knees and legs.' She loved to talk with handsome sprightly Dr Maille about tantric sex and other esoterica. Later interviewed, Maille said that Alexandra claimed to have actively participated in sexual rites of left-handed tantrism, a secret teaching completely unknown in the West. Scholars like Giuseppe Tucci and David Snellgrove wrote about it only from hearsay. However, Alexandra never put these experiences down on paper. With Dr Maille, she would talk about anything except improving her health. Maille turned on her one day and said: 'What doctor? you refuse to take drugs. You don't give a damn about medicine.' Alexandra retorted: 'At least we could talk more often about things Tibetan'. She got little sleep now, due to arthritic pain, and lived in a chaos of books, papers and manuscripts.

Enter a new housekeeper: Madeleine Peyronnet—a young woman raised in French Algeria. She shuddered when shown the shrine room, with its table covered with human skulls and phallic symbols, a *tanka* with multi-armed deities engaging in *yab-yum* (sexual fusion of opposites), a devilish collection of Tibetan masks and a case that contained the ashes of Yongden. After getting over this initial speed-bump, Madeleine went on to become Alexandra's trusted secretary, nurse, confidant and driver. Though suffering from multiple health problems, Alexandra kept up appearances. When writer Lawrence Durrell interviewed her for *Elle* magazine, he came armed with a gift to soften up his notoriously grumpy subject. Durrell had blown up a picture of Alexandra at a much younger age. Alexandra accepted the picture in great delight and flirted with him. Durrell called her 'the most astonishing woman of our times.' Another interviewer was not so lucky: for a short TV program about her exploits, she variously replied to questions in French, English or Tibetan—as the mood caught her.

In her late nineties, Alexandra had a visit from a London agent intent on negotiating book royalties. If he was expecting to deal with an old woman with half her marbles missing, Alexandra gave him a rude shock—she fought tooth-and-nail over percentage points, demanding all royalties up front. She knew she wouldn't live long enough to see the money in delayed royalty payments.

In 1968, the town of Digne decided to celebrate her 100th birthday. Alexandra dressed in a robe of Chinese silk, her hair in a chignon. Dignitaries arrived. Champagne flowed. Television crews and reporters invaded. Local schoolgirls presented her with roses. Scholars paid her homage. Alexandra had been showered in honours and awards in her long lifetime: in her 100th year, she was promoted to the highest order of the French Legion of Honour.

And at the age of 100, Alexandra David-Néel renewed her passport. Never one to give up on travel, she announced to Madeleine that she wanted to go for a drive in the Citroen. First to Berlin, where she knew of a doctor who claimed to be able to cure arthritis. And then on to Moscow—to see how Red Square was coming along. And after Moscow on to Vladivostok, from where they could embark for New York. She always dreamed of going to America. Madeleine demurred, claiming her long legs would get cramps in the tiny Citroen over such a long trip. In reality, she feared for the frail health of Alexandra on such a trip.

Alexandra never got to New York. Nor back to Tibet. She died on September 8, 1969, just short of her 101st birthday. As she had requested, there was a minimum of ceremony at her funeral in Marseilles: Madeleine was there, along with some old explorer friends. Her remains were cremated and her ashes placed in an urn, to be kept with Yongden's at Samten Dzong.

Madeleine became the custodian of her home and her papers and photos, and editor of her posthumous works. Samten Dzong remained under the care of Madeleine, but she could not prevent others removing vital parts. Alexandra had talked of preserving Samten Dzong as a combination of museum, library and research facility for visiting scholars, but this was not to be. Her precious collection of Oriental artefacts and masks was packed off into 12 containers and sent to Paris intended for museum collections—but it largely vanished. Her Tibetan books— some 450 tomes—were bequeathed to the Musée Guimet, to the same library that had inspired her so many years before.

In February 1973, Alexandra's spirit embarked on a final journey to Asia. As she had requested, Madeleine took her ashes to India, along with the ashes of Yongden, and scattered them in the River Ganges. In 1992, another homecoming, of sorts: Madeleine was involved in the return of an exquisite statue of the Buddha to the state of Sikkim. The statue had been given to Alexandra 80 years earlier by Sidkeong Namgyal—the dashing young prince who'd captured her heart. The Buddha statue, unfortunately, was later stolen from its last resting place in Sikkim, most likely by art thieves.

Tucci, with a mind of boundless curiosity,
was drawn to Tibet's ultimate riddles. He used his
intimate knowledge of Tibetan script as a way to break in.

 # Giuseppe Tucci
1894–1984

iconographer, art historian, archaeologist,
master linguist, cryptographer, scholar & Tibetologist

Cracking The
Tibetan Code

❖   Stumbling into   ❖
the lost kingdom of Guge

Sometimes, great explorers are not the first ones on the scene—
they are just very good at finding what others have ignored
or overlooked. Italian professor Giuseppe Tucci found facets
that the British had overlooked—or dismissed as superstitious
nonsense. The professor loved puzzles, and Tibet provided the
ultimate ones: from 1933 to 1948, Dottore Tucci mounted a
number of expeditions in Tibet hunting for sacred texts and
sacred art. He was pilgrim and pioneer in both quests—and
a pilferer too. Whether altruist or temple raider, his books
inspired a lust among art collectors around the world
for Tibetan sacred art, and sparked a market
in stolen artifacts from Tibet.

❖

 AMONG THE RASH of books published in 1905 in the wake of Younghusband's invasion of Tibet are these titles: *Lhasa and its Mysteries, The Unveiling of Lhasa, The Opening of Tibet, To Lhassa at Last*. The titles suggest that Tibet's mysteries had been revealed for the world to see. But the British authors could not come to grips with Tibetan culture because they could not read Tibetan. The books were glorified travelogues, full of misconceptions and British colonial bias. The author of *The Unveiling of Lhasa*, Edmund Candler, was driven by more than bias: before the British campaign, he'd married Miss Tooth in Calcutta and had a wife and child to support—and was hoping sales of his book would assist in this endeavour. Offering a very different perspective was *The Truth About Tibet* by Alexander Macallum Scott—an attack on the motives of the Younghusband Mission.

At this time, very few Tibetans had ever left the country's borders—and they mostly did not get beyond neighbouring Asian countries. Tibet had no diplomats abroad; it had no roads. But it had an extensive literature about which precious little was known. Tibet was the keeper of texts which had long since disappeared in India itself—the birthplace of Buddhism—due to Moslem invasion and ruthless persecution from the 11th to 13th centuries. To come to grips with Tibetan culture, religion and history, its literature had to be translated and analysed—and its complex iconography decoded.

Shortly after the Younghusband Mission to Tibet concluded in 1904, Tibetan curios were being sold to the British Museum and were being offered at major London auction houses: Tibetan painted scrolls were auctioned at Christie's, for instance. Some curios had been purchased from markets in Lhasa, but most had been looted from sacred sites. Dr Waddell alone was responsible for the removal of 400 mule-loads of artifacts and books. Waddell served a dual role in the Younghusband expedition—as chief of the medical team, but also its archeologist, bent on collecting objects of interest to scholars in the West. He was the mission's self-appointed cultural expert. In particular, he was after Tibetan manuscripts.

The 400 mule-loads ended up in Calcutta: according to Waddell, the cargo comprised 'rare and valuable manuscripts of Lamaist sacred works, images, religious paraphernalia of all descriptions, armour, weapons, paintings and porcelain'. This booty was displayed at the Indian Museum in Calcutta, and later divided up between that institution, the British Museum, the Bodleian Library and the India Office Library. A Berlin museum later bought part of Waddell's collection. In 1909 a complete set of the *Kanjur* that came into Waddell's possession was auctioned at Sotheby's: the *Kanjur* comprises translations of the Buddha's discourses in 108 thick volumes. In 1906, Waddell was appointed Professor of Tibetan at London University, before retiring two years later to Scotland.

In his book *The Buddhism of Tibet or Lamaism* (1897) Waddell advanced the theory that Tibetan Buddhism was a perverted offshoot of the teachings of the Buddha, and corrupt devil-worshippers held sway over the country. Tibetan priests were lazy, corrupt and parasitic. Waddell dismissed Lamaism as an animistic creed that was full of black magic and dark gods. That was before he even got to Tibet. When he reached Lhasa in 1904, Dr Waddell—a follower of the Theosophists—was very disappointed to learn in Lhasa that there were no teachings of ancient wisdom preserved by the 'Mahatmas' after the sinking of Atlantis. Waddell found the central shrine of Buddhism, the Jokhang, to be a dark and dismal. A staunch Scottish Presbyterian, Waddell railed against the evils of the lamas and their superstitious practices in his book *Lhasa and its Mysteries* (1905). The colonial British were blinded by their motives: they justified invasion of Tibet by claiming that they were bringing light to the darkness of heathens, bringing the benefits of science and technology to the Tibetans. As Candler phrased it in his 1905 book, *The Unveiling of Lhasa:*

> I question if ever in the history of the world there has been another occasion when bigotry and darkness have been exposed with such abruptness to the inroad of science, when a barrier of ignorance created by jealousy and fear as a screen between two peoples living side by side has been demolished so suddenly to admit the light of an advanced civilisation.

The only problem was that the Tibetans never asked for any of these benefits, nor wanted them. They got along just fine on their own— they were quite content with their own enlightened civilisation. This was something the British failed to recognise—writing off the Tibetan culture as superstitious, backward and medieval. But there was a kind of 'Shangri-La Effect' that came into play. In James Hilton's novel *Lost Horizon*, the High Lama of Shangri-La is a wizened Capuchin priest from Luxembourg who set out to refute Tibetan Buddhism by the force of logical argument. Over time, however, he found himself more attracted to Buddhist philosophy, and had no desire to spread his own faith—nor leave the valley of Shangri-La. He quietly put aside his grand project of refuting Tibetan Buddhism.

Tibetan Buddhism could be a serious threat to the faith of the person who sets out to critique it. It has all the trappings of a religion—chanting priests, temples, devout pilgrims—but it is not a religion, if you define religion as a belief in a superior being. The faith is more akin to refined agnosticism: the Buddha taught that all the answers to problems are here on this earth. Even Waddell found some good things to say about Tibetan Buddhism after a while. And Francis Younghusband had some sort of revelatory experience on the eve of his departure from Lhasa when he gazed at the Potala Palace, bathed in the radiant light of sunset. The man who had lifted the veil on Lhasa, pulled the curtain on Tibet, and finally opened the door to Inner Asia, evolved into a mystical nutcase. In later years, after writing about his military exploits wore off, Younghusband found new celebrity as initiator of a group known as the World Congress of Faiths, turning his back on his Christian upbringing and staking the case for inter-faith dialogue. Younghusband went on to write *Life in the Stars: An Exposition of the View that on Some Planets of Some Stars Exist Beings Higher than Ourselves, and on One a World Leader, the Supreme Embodiment of the Eternal Spirit which Animates the Whole*. That book was published in 1927. In 1933 he followed up with another corker called *The Living Universe*, in which highly evolved asexual aliens inhabit the far-off planet of Altair—a work apparently not intended as fiction.

Giuseppe Tucci had none of the motives of British explorers—which varied from trade incentives (18th century) to Great Game political manoeuvring (20th century). Tucci was a seeker of humanist knowledge, on a quest for personal spiritual fulfilment. In this, he was much like Alexandra David-Néel: in fact, the two competed in translations of Tibetan books. Tucci recognised the texts of Tibetan Buddhism as a treasure-trove of spiritual wisdom. The British thought Tibetan art and literature was a whole lot of hogwash and dark superstition, but Tucci saw it as extraordinary.

Tucci took an elliptical approach to most things: he could be quite barmy. He had an incredible thirst for knowledge: his genius lay in being able to break into a field of his choosing, take it by the horns—and master it. Tucci was not articulate about himself or his personal feelings in his books—but his colleague and fellow-expeditioner Fosco Maraini managed to capture the man in action in his book *Secret Tibet*. Here is Maraini's description of Tucci in 1948 at the monastery of Kyangphu, central Tibet:

> The master is in good form today...He's a hound off the leash. He runs hither and yon, he wants to see, to unlock secrets, grab millennia by the throat. There is something of the shaman in him... His hair stands up like antennae ready to capture the unknowable. Which then does become knowable for the simple reason that it is processed and digested by a brain in which entire libraries lie in ambush, in a babel of different tongues. Poor old problem, it doesn't stand a chance! That extraordinary mind collars it, grinds it up, mashes it to bits, pulverizes it and extracts from it a synthesis, a bloom.

The key to Tucci's code-cracking was his remarkable facility with language. He soaked languages up like a sponge. In his student days in Rome, he mastered the ancient tongues of Sanskrit, Latin, Greek and Persian. He spoke English well. He learnt Chinese. In India, he tackled Bengali, Hindi and Tibetan. For Tibetan, he mastered not only the spoken language but the complex written one—and was able to hold his own when debating with learned Tibetan monks. Tucci was an extraordinary autodidact—self-taught in many subjects.

Professor Giuseppe Tucci is a slippery person. Dates are hard to track, photos are hard to come by. He was born on June 5th, 1894 in Macerata, central Italy. As a student, he was interested in history, archaeology, sociology, philosophy and language. Gradually he became drawn to Indian philosophy and Buddhism. And that caused him to seek out more direct experiences in India itself.

In 1925, Tucci arrived in India to teach Italian, Chinese and Tibetan at Shantiniketan University in Bengal—an institution founded by Nobel laureate, poet and philosopher Rabindranath Tagore. In the late 1920s, Tucci oscillated from Italy to India, lecturing at various universities, before launching a series of archeological expeditions to northwest India. He was allowed to travel in the Indian border areas of Ladakh and Lahaul in 1928, which whetted his appetite to go further—into Tibet. In 1931, he applied for a permit to cross into western Tibet: he approached the Government of India in Calcutta through the Italian Consulate-General, on the basis of being a genuine scholar, praising the British for their sympathy and intelligent assistance. He was granted a permit, but too late in the season, so he bided his time—and took up a teaching post in Naples. In 1933 he applied for a permit to Tibet again, this time specifying that he would dedicate his forthcoming book to 'the British authorities of India, who have always been so kind to me.' Flattery like that will get you everywhere. Tucci was on his way to the unexplored region of west Tibet.

In the summer of 1933, Tucci made a glorious crossing of Shipki pass into west Tibet. At his side was his faithful Tibetan mastiff Chanku—who'd taken part in his previous expeditions to this region. And in the entourage: medical captain Dr Ghersi and a Tibetan lama—whom Tucci used as a translator and guide. Lama, doctor, dog: Tucci was sniffing things out with a novel approach. On all his expeditions to Tibet, he took along a learned monk to assist in 'code-cracking'. And Dr Ghersi proved to be an excellent ice-breaker, offering his medical expertise to villagers en route.

After arduous overland travel, Tucci's yak caravan eventually reached the 'gateway' to the Guge Kingdom. The access route proceeded along the bed of a deep gorge, which Tucci describes as an elaborate labyrinth of gullies, like:

> ...corridors in fantastic castles; from time to time, wide spaces on which stand vertical towers and peaks—contorted, ponderous—or there rise solitary monolithic columns with enormous capitals.

On the other side of that gorge, Tucci stepped back a few centuries:

> To enter Tibet was not only to find oneself in another world. After crossing the gap in space, one had the impression of having trailed many centuries backward in time.

How far back? There was some debate among the Italians about this. Fosco Maraini hazarded this guess:

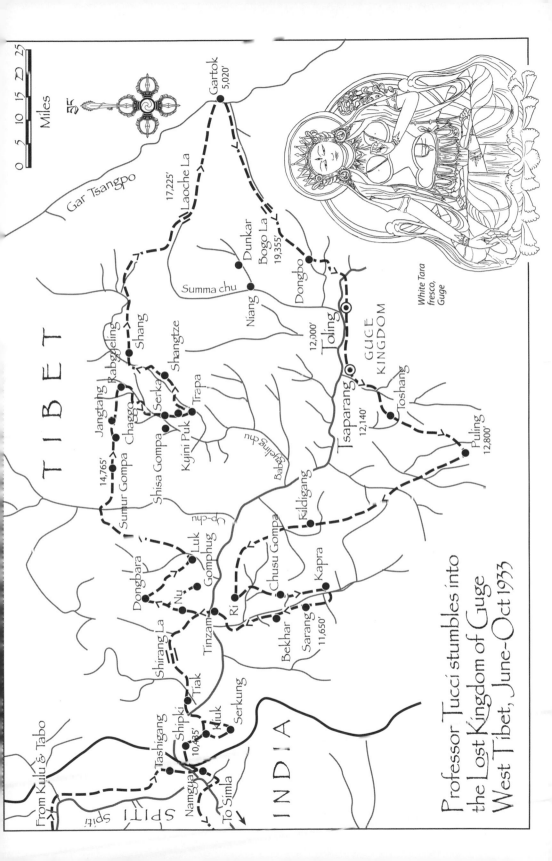

Miles
0 5 10 15 20 25

Gar Tsangpo

Laoche La
17,225'

Gartok
5,020'

TIBET

Rabgyeling
Jangtang
14,765'
Shang
Sumur Gompa
Chaggo
Serka
Shangtze
Shisa Gompa
Kyini Puk
Trapa

Dunkar
Summa chu
Niang
Bogo La
19,355'
Dongbo

Toling
12,000'

GUGE
KINGDOM

Tsaparang
12,140'

Toshang

Puling
12,800'

Babi Byeling chu

Up-chu

Dongbara
Luk
Gomphug
Nu
Ri
Tinzam
Kildigang
Chusu Gompa
Kapra

Shirang La
Tiak
Shipki
10,485'
Kiuk
Serkung
Bekhar
Sarang
11,650'

Tashigang
Namgya

SPITI

To Simla

INDIA

From Kulu & Tabo

White Tara
fresco,
Guge

Professor Tucci stumbles into
the Lost Kingdom of Guge
West Tibet, June–Oct 1933

> Visiting Tibet...means travelling in time as well as space. It means
> for a brief while living as a contemporary of Dante or Boccaccio...
> breathing the air of another age, and learning by direct experi-
> ence how our ancestors of twenty or twenty-five generations ago
> lived, loved and thought.

By that clock, Tibet was much further back in time than Dante—it was
back into ancient Egypt. Another Italian writer, Luigi Barzini, estimated twenty or thirty centuries back in time, citing parallels with
ancient Egypt. He was looking at photos of stone buildings in Lhasa
taken by the invading British of 1904. Like British writers, Maraini puts
a 'medieval' spin on Tibet—medieval hierarchy, medieval feasts and
festivals, medieval tourneys, princesses, pilgrims, brigands, hermits,
lepers, medieval minstrels and story-tellers and prophets.

For Guge, you could settle on the Renaissance—some 500 years
ago. And this would be fitting as Guge kingdom artists were very special. Guge is associated with a revival of Tibetan Buddhism after it
was snuffed out in central Tibet: the rulers of Guge promoted cultural
exchanges with Indian Buddhists from Ladakh. Eventually, the Guge
rulers became wealthy enough to import artisans from regions like
Kashmir. This is what Tucci determined from inscriptions at the site.
He stumbled into a world of impeccable artistic pedigree—and one
overlooked by others who'd ventured to this remote corner of Tibet.
British officers who'd visited some 20 years before Tucci simply wrote
that the place merited further investigation.

Tsaparang, the main ruins remaining of the Guge kingdom, is
sculpted entirely from a mountain of clay—a sort of whimsical surre-
alistic creation that architect Antonio Gaudi would've been proud of.
At the lower levels are 'cave-condos' fashioned from clay, and small
fort-like structures with watchtowers poking up. Then reddish cha-
pels appear—temples with interior walls adorned with frescos. Temple
walls at Tsaparang were made of rammed mud and mortar: artisans
prepared wall surfaces for painting by applying layers of plaster, using
much the same method employed by Italian Renaissance masters—
and comparable in quality and technique to those masters. Tibetan
master artisans at Guge were skilled in woodcarving and the casting of large statues as well. While the artistic style at Guge has strong
Kashmiri elements, it is also distinctly Tibetan. Tucci recognised 'an art

Kashmiri-style frescos at Tsaparang—a rare artform in Tibet

peculiar to Guge, distinctive in itself and independent of the art movements in other parts of Tibet.'

The power of the murals resonates—mute testimony to the bril-
liance of the Guge Kingdom—huge, beautiful Tara frescos; paintings
of mythical creatures—half-beast, half-human. Some details turned
out to be stunning miniatures—entire works of art in themselves.
There were paintings of Tibetan tantric deities, tangled in embraces
with their consorts. But not all portrayed here was mythical—some
frescos showed high lamas giving teachings, or depicted the arrival of
an important envoy.

This unknown art-style was superb in technique and style. Oddly
enough, 15th-century Tibet, in parallel with 15th-century Europe,
was experiencing a Renaissance in high art. And both cultures, with
no known connection, were constructing wall paintings using similar technologies. The Tibetans applied successive layers of plaster,
starting with a coarse mix of mud, straw, clay and dung—and adding
progressively finer clay layers. A similar technique was vital to Michelangelo—who used a 'wet plaster' method for the Sistine Chapel—and
Leonardo Da Vinci, who used a 'secco' (dry plaster) approach when he
painted The Last Supper.

Some 70 years after Tucci's expedition to Guge, two Italian art
experts made a trip to Mustang, a Tibetan enclave in the west of the

plateau, to assess conservation of temple murals. Rodolfo Lujan, an Asian art conservator from Rome and one of Europe's premier experts in art restoration, set about removing eons of yakbutter-lamp soot from the frescos, revealing brilliantly coloured scenes depicting the life of the Buddha. Lujan trained in the restoration of the Sistine Chapel, removing layers of soot, dust and smoke, and so is in a unique position to make comparisons. He places the Mustang murals in a class with Italian Renaissance masters: 'Maybe the quality is even better than…a Leonardo, Michelangelo, Raphael.' He marvels at the perfect technique, the quality of the pigments, the refined execution of the paintings. His compatriot, Luigi Fieni, uses an infrared camera to find out what is beneath the surface of the paintings. He discovers guidelines and blueprints for the final images, with grids revealing strict iconometry—where deities were painted to precisely determined proportions. Special markings conveyed instructions, mainly for colour: the master artists created the blueprints, and assistants filled in the colour, grinding their own pigments. Pigments made from precious materials, like gold leaf, were the final stage of painting.

Unlike the Italian Renaissance masters, none of the Tibetan artisans is known by name. A rare exception is 17th-century Mongolian sculptor Zanabazar, also a highly revered lama—and known to posterity because of that reason. Artwork in Tibet is largely sacred—artists use set formulas for drawing deities and other icons: every pose or hand position of the Buddha, for instance, has a specific meaning. Since this is done for religious reasons, the creation is considered exponentially more important than the creator—who expects no credit. Another great departure from Western religious art is in theme. Tucci divined that the murals and tankas of Tibet are used for bringing focus into meditation, and for teaching key aspects of history, culture or religion. In these artworks, Tibetans are not shy of depicting sex or death—considered integral to existence. Sex is viewed as a powerful force that must be dealt with: indeed, it is incorporated into some meditation practices. At Guge, the Yamantaka Chapel is dedicated to tantric deity Dorje Jigje: the walls bear murals of deities locked in sexual union with their consorts—which Tucci interpreted as signifying the fusion of opposites.

Tucci and company scouted some other engrossing areas in west Tibet—they went up Kyunglung Valley, the possible site of the ancient Bon kingdom of Shang-shung.

Wrathful multi-armed female deity appears in fresco at Tsaparang

Somewhere in this region lies the legendary Khyunglung Ngulkhar, or The Silver Palace. The name was unknown to the West until Paul Pelliot unearthed the Dunhuang documents in 1908 in a Silk Road cave. Written records speak of a vast palace with foundations of gold, doors of silver, and walls encrusted with agate. And a treacherous queen, who betrayed her husband—which caused all of the preceding to be reduced to rubble in battle. Or was it? At the dawn of the 21st century, the hunt for the long-lost Shang-shung kingdom continues. Archeologists have unearthed a series of walled foundations behind Gurugem that look promising.

The year 1933 proved to be a very busy one for Tucci. In Rome, he founded his own institute to promote cultural relations between Italy and Asian countries, called Istituto Italiano per il Medio ed Estremo Oriente (ISMEO). He built a large collection of Tibetan books for this. And set to work, writing furiously. Tucci's *Secrets of Tibet* (published in Italian in 1934 and in English in 1935) provided the first detailed account of long-abandoned temples of the Kingdom of Guge. This was a find of great importance on several levels: filling in major gaps in the history of Tibetan Buddhism, and reconstructing the course of Tibetan style, architecture and artistic sensibility. The mysteries of Guge have

The mantra *Om Mani Padme Hum*, recited by pious Tibetan pilgrims, is chiselled in stone at many sacred sites. A rough transliteration is 'Hail to the Jewel in the Lotus'.

yet to be unravelled: caves adorned with intricate murals continue to be discovered in the arid valleys of this region.

The 'puzzle palace' of Guge and the vanished Bon kingdom of Shang-shung were fresh ground for exploration—Tucci managed to make some sense out of the artwork and inscriptions of this region. He soon moved on to other puzzles: the arcane Tibetan language with its elegant script, the secret teachings of the sects.

Tucci was hooked on Tibet—he started planning more forays. In common with Joseph Rock, Giuseppe Tucci had a disdain of modern life in the west—he yearned for the simplicity of Tibet, without modern machines. Writing in 1950, Fosco Maraini captured Tucci's nostalgia for west Tibet, quoting him verbatim:

> ...now those were voyages, expeditions, enterprises! Passes of five and six thousand metres high, snow, ice, yaks rolling down into the precipices, whole buried cities to unearth, hermits, brigands, sorcerers, deserts, hunger and thirst often enough, but glimpses of paradise. Lake Manasarovar, Mount Kailasa!

Tucci was not the first foreigner to see the splendours of the Guge Kingdom. Not by a long shot. Some 300 years earlier, in March 1624, two Portuguese Jesuits, Father Marques and Father Andrade, followed up on rumours of a lost Christian-like sect. They set out from Ladakh disguised as Hindu pilgrims, on a route similar to Tucci's. They were on foot with pack animals, crossing passes that were 18,000 feet or more. At times, they sank into snow up to their chests. They complained of frozen feet, or blindness, and of suffocating 'poisonous vapours'—probably the first Western accounts of altitude sickness by the first European known to enter Tibet. Their round trip from India took eight months.

Arriving in Tsaparang, centre of the Guge Kingdom, the Jesuits were warmly received by the king: they were invited to celebrate a special occasion, with over 2,000 monks in attendance. The Jesuits found the temple rituals bore superficial similarities to Christian ones—monks in robes spent hours chanting—but drinking from human skull-cap vessels was definitely a little different. Andrade was the first to publish to the world the sacred chanting mantra *Om Mani Padme Hum*, but could not determine its meaning (which experts still debate today). In any case, a bestseller penned by Andrade got Europeans excited by describing this part of the planet they'd overlooked.

Andrade returned to Tsaparang in 1625 with fellow missionaries, and the Jesuits eventually built a small church there. Andrade died in India in 1634, poisoned by a colleague who evidently did not share his enthusiasm for the Inquisition. Around 1650 (some sources say 1630), Tsaparang was suddenly abandoned. It is said that the king angered his lamas by favouring Father Andrade, and that factional fighting ensued, tearing the kingdom apart. Other sources claim that a two-year siege by Ladakhis led to the fall of Guge. The reason: the king rejected a bride who happened to be the sister of the king of Ladakh, who was supremely insulted. At the fall of Guge, the king of Guge and the royal family were either killed on the spot or sent into exile. Their followers were reduced to slavery. Guge fell into obscurity—and ruins. Not only that: successive waves of invaders went to great lengths to wipe out all traces of the kings of Guge, making it near-impossible to recount the history of the place.

The father of adventure travel, Marco Polo, never made it to Tibet, though he wrote second-hand reports about the dangers of brigands in these realms, and the charms of loose Tibetan women. But other Italians figure prominently in early exploration of Tibet—notably missionaries.

In 1661, the first Europeans known to reach Lhasa were two Jesuits—Johann Grueber (Austrian) and Albert d'Orville (Belgian). They found their way overland from China to Tibet, heading for India. They stayed a month in Lhasa, but were not permitted to see the Dalai Lama because they had announced their unwillingness to make prostrations in his presence. Grueber's account of the journey, published in Latin in 1677, excited a great deal of interest as it made the first references to the Dalai Lamas and presented Grueber's sketches of the strange customs of the Tibetans. Grueber's drawing of the Potala is the first known image of this amazing building—then still a work-in-progress (it was called the 'Bietala' by Grueber).

Grueber and d'Orville arrived in Lhasa at a seminal point in Tibet's long history. By the 17th century, Tibet's line of ruling kings had been supplanted by one of the most unusual forms of government the world has even seen—a line of reincarnate Dalai Lamas. The 5th Dalai Lama consolidated this theocracy or 'Buddhocracy'. The title 'Dalai Lama' (meaning 'Great Ocean' or 'Ocean of Wisdom' in Mongolian) was bestowed by Mongol leader Altan Khan in 1578 on Sonam Gyatso—who was recognised as the 3rd Dalai Lama (his two predecessors were given the title retrospectively). The 4th Dalai Lama was most likely murdered. It was the 5th Dalai Lama (aka 'the Great Fifth') who got it all off the ground.

The Great Fifth was instrumental in seeing through the construction of the monumental Potala Palace. A project of great daring and imagination, this thousand-room 13-storey castle was constructed using very basic equipment. Stones were lugged on the back of animals and porters; no nails were used in the woodwork. The Great Fifth oversaw the completion of phase one (the White Palace) but did not live to see the completion of phase two (the Red Palace). The death of the Great Fifth was concealed by the Regent for a dozen years to maintain political stability and to ensure completion of the colossal Potala project. The deceased Dalai Lama was replaced by a double and was announced to be engaged in long meditation retreats.

Meanwhile, behind the scenes, a young boy, Tsangyang Gyatso, was being groomed as the 6th Dalai Lama. But his monkish minders lost control of him. The Sixth took over as an adolescent, not an infant like his predecessors. He refused to take any celibacy vows and was never fully ordained as a lama, emerging as the strangest and most whimsical of all the Dalai Lamas. He showed little interest in either his political or religious duties. His passions lay elsewhere. With long braided hair, blue silk dress, and rings on his fingers, the handsome Sixth serenaded lovers in the taverns of Lhasa. Despite his outlandish behaviour, the Sixth was revered by the people, who came to the conclusion that the living Buddha had two bodies—one which stayed in the Potala and meditated, and the other that got rotten drunk and chased Lhasa women. The Sixth echoed this in verse:

I dwell apart in the Potala
A god on earth am I
But in the town the chief of rogues
And boisterous revelry

He was a prolific rake—no woman in Lhasa was said to be safe from his indulgences. It was considered a great honour to have a daughter sleep with him—after which event, the house exterior was permitted to be painted a regal yellow. The Sixth was renowned for his erotic songs, along these lines:

Sweetheart awaiting me in my bed
Yielding tenderly her sweet soft body
Has she come to cheat me
And disrobe me of my virtues?

The 6th Dalai Lama was eventually discredited as not being a proper reincarnate. He was deposed and sent into exile: he disappeared under suspicious circumstances in 1706 at the age of 23—variously rumoured to be poisoned, stabbed, or otherwise disposed of. His body never found. His untimely death led to political turmoil: fighting erupted between Mongols, Chinese and Tibetans for control of central Tibet.

An eye-witness to the last years of the 6th Dalai Lama was Tuscan Jesuit priest Ippolito Desideri, who portrayed him as a 'dissolute youth, addicted to every vice, thoroughly depraved, and quite incorrigible, because of the blind veneration and stupid faith of the Thibettans.' Desideri reached Lhasa in the early 18th century—at the same time that Italian Capuchin missionaries were staking out the region. Both groups were bent on establishing a permanent mission—setting the stage for a showdown over who had the right to claim the souls of the Tibetans for Rome. Jesuit father Ippolito Desideri faced off with Capuchin friar Orazio Della Penna. The rival Italians eventually waived their differences to tackle the pressing problem of Tibetan grammar. Desideri became proficient enough in Tibetan language that he was able to debate with the monks of Sera Monastery on religious matters. He wrote a book in Tibetan refuting the 'errors' of Tibetan Buddhism, which caused a big stir in Lhasa.

Desideri left Tibet in 1721 on orders from Rome. After leaving Tibet, he wrote a report of his travels—which was suppressed by the church because it did not want to create tensions between Capuchins and

Jesuits. It was not published till 1904. In 1902, another long-lost narrative saw the light of day—the diaries of Cassiano Beligatti. Beligatti hailed from Macerata—the same town where Tucci was born. His narrative was unearthed at Macerata's library—a manuscript of 200 pages written in Italian, with pen and watercolour sketches of Tibetan rituals and plans of edifices in Lhasa. Scholars think this is only the first part of his narrative and that the other part was destroyed in a fire. The narrative probably lay unpublished because proselytizing had been a dismal failure in Tibet—the total number of converts for the entire Capuchin campaign could be counted on the fingers of two hands. Not good numbers to broadcast for all the money spent on these missions.

Despite strong opposition from the Jesuits, the Capuchins finally prevailed in the quest for souls in Tibet—the Vatican, persuaded by Della Penna, backed another Capuchin mission to Tibet. Della Penna had remained in Tibet for some 16 years—after he left in 1733, the Lhasa mission lapsed. But in 1740, Cassiano Beligatti approached Lhasa bearing gifts from the Vatican for the 7th Dalai Lama, including a fine drawing-room clock. The welcome mat was no longer out—the mission's status went from bad to worse, and the Capuchins were forcibly ejected from Tibet in 1745. Although missionaries were barred from central Tibet after this, there were still openings for spreading the gospel at the fringes of the plateau—in the Kham and Amdo regions. French, Belgian, British and American missionaries of all stripes and creeds—Capuchins, Jesuits, Lazarists, Presbyterians, evangelists—all had a stab, but gained precious few converts. Tibetan Buddhism stood firm.

From 1933 to 1939, Professor Giuseppe Tucci mounted expeditions to Tibet roughly every two years—during which he continued to study the sacred art and architecture of Tibet, particularly at Gyantse. While Tucci was passionate about Tibetan art, it was another hunt that was to consume his later interest: Tibetan texts. The secret to decoding the world of Tibetan Buddhism lay in its texts, written in Tibetan and Sanskrit. Some were ancient texts that came up from India, where Buddhism originated but had been wiped out by Mughal invasion. Between the 11th and 13th centuries, many texts were brought from India to Tibet to safeguard them from invading Islamic armies—these

Gyantse Kumbum—a rare form of circular architecture

texts were translated into Tibetan and held in Tibetan monasteries. For centuries, Tibetan monasteries amassed the knowledge of the ancient Indian world, with books 'delivered' in mule caravans over the Himalayas—or on horseback. In 1959, the outflow of refugees from Tibet reversed the process: India returned the favour, becoming a safe haven for Tibetan sacred texts that were being destroyed under Chinese rule.

Tucci dedicated his first book (*Secret Tibet*) to one of the first sacred text hunters, Alexander Csoma de Koros. His is a romantic story, the stuff of legends. Born in Transylvania in 1784, at a very young age he became obsessed with the origins of the Hungarian people. In 1819, in pursuit of these childhood dreams, he left Transylvania with little money and few possessions and headed east—on foot. His amazing quest took him to the Himalayas.

Approaching the Ladakhi capital of Leh in 1822, Csoma had a fateful encounter with William Moorcroft, a freewheeling British agent intent on opening new markets for British goods (and through this, to bring them into the British orbit). Moorcroft was on a mission to reach Central Asia and find the legendary fair where the horses of Attila the

Hun were traded. As a veterinarian specialising in horses, he hoped to find the perfect horse—sponsored by the East India Company's Stud, which supplied the British Indian army. Moorfcroft was outfitted with a small army himself—an entourage of 50 men, and assorted animals, including horses, mules and dogs—even the odd camel or elephant on occasion.

Moorcroft travelled in style—he slept in a large tent equipped with carpets, folding furniture, and a collapsible brass bedstead that folded into a leather case. Plus a portable writing desk and more than 100 reference books.

He carried supplies of sugar, chocolate and brandy—along with weapons, ammunition, surveying equipment, medical supplies, and a large stash of trade items for bribes and gifts.

Recognising Csoma's unusual scholastic talents, Moorcroft invited him to accompany his deluxe caravan on several long forays in the region. He proposed that since Csoma had already mastered 13 languages, learning another one (Tibetan) should be a breeze. Moorcroft gave Csoma a volume from his reference library—the only known work in Latin about the culture and language of Tibet, the *Alphabetum Tibetanum*, published in Rome in 1762 by Catholic priest Antonio Giorgi. This was an incoherent rambling volume of 900 pages, replete with third-hand rumours derived from missionaries—most of it misinformed. Moorcroft figured that a dictionary and grammar of Tibetan would be invaluable in intelligence gathering about this unknown nation—and so gave Csoma initial support to carry this object out, sparking his first voyage into Ladakh.

In November 1824, having run out of funds and energy, an emaciated Csoma showed up in Sabathu, the East India Company's frontier station closest to Ladakh. Though an outpost, the British commanding officer had a taste for style and luxury—which extended to fine horses, champagne and gourmet dinners. Into this refined world walked Csoma, in ragged clothing like an Indian beggar. The British had no idea who this extraordinary visitor was, since Moorcroft was still gallivanting around Central Asia and had neglected to mention anything about him. Since Csoma spoke English with a heavy accent, the British at first suspected he was a Russian spy. When told to change into smarter clothing, he reappeared in the only European outfit he possessed: the Hungarian national costume, with baggy trousers, longtailed coat and waistcoat.

Csoma showed enthusiastic letters of introduction penned by William Moorcroft as his patron. As it turned out, Moorcroft was considered a meddlesome crackpot by his superiors—and certainly had no authority to delegate deals on behalf of the British Raj. Csoma was placed under house arrest: missives were dispatched to Calcutta about what to do with him. But his story checked out, and his mission was one of great interest to the British. After a lengthy delay, Csoma was granted official patronage with a stipend of 50 rupees a month, and dispatched back to Ladakh to complete his work. Csoma ended up spending a total of nine years in the cold cells of monasteries in Ladakh and Zanskar trying to crack the Tibetan language, mustering material for his Tibetan grammar and Tibetan-English dictionary.

Csoma de Koros did not find the origins of his people, but he did tap into a vast mine of literary riches, entirely unknown to Europeans. He is widely regarded as the founder of Tibetology. In April 1831, Csoma de Koros arrived in Calcutta to oversee the publication of his lexicons. He stayed in Calcutta for the next decade, working as librarian for the Asiatic Society.

Csoma de Koros put in a lot of time cataloguing Tibetan texts presented by young scholar Brian Houghton Hodgson. Hodgson was just 20 years old when he first set foot in Nepal in 1820: he became the British representative in Nepal from 1824 to 1843. Hodgson's interests were wide-ranging, covering everything from geography to ethnography. He had an immense curiosity—and a passion for collecting. As a naturalist, he collected numerous bird and animal skins for museums, and as a scholar, he collected stacks of manuscripts and ancient texts. He was in a virgin field—only himself and Csoma de Koros had attempted to collect Tibetan and Sanskrit texts. Though the Tibetan language was a mystery to him, Hodgson wrote in a letter to the Asiatic Society that the first task was to collect the texts—and that translation and interpretation would surely follow.

Hodgson's collecting enriched not only the Asiatic Societies in India and England, but also the India Office Library, the British Museum, the Bodleian Library of Oxford, the Institute of France, and the Société Asiatique de Paris. He eked out manuscripts from obscure monasteries in Nepal, as well as sourcing what he could from Tibet. Among the rare manuscripts Hodgson presented to British libraries are some dating back to the 11th century. He procured two complete sets of the *Kanjur* (108 volumes) and *Tenjur* (over 220 volumes) which together constitute an encyclopaedic analysis of the philosophy of the Buddha.

Hodgson's lucid essays on the religion and literature of Nepal and Tibet, dating from 1828, were a revelation to European scholars—giving the first account of northern or Mahayana Buddhism. In publishing these essays, Hodgson narrowly beat Csoma de Koros into print—unaware of each other, the two had been researching the same field at different ends of the Himalayas. Csoma de Koros highly praised Hodgson's essays, and used the texts that Hodgson sent to Calcutta as a basis for his own writing. The two corresponded over the next decade as Hodgson carried on collecting texts from his base in Kathmandu.

In 1842, at the age of 58, Csoma de Koros set forth from Calcutta once more on his quest to find the origins of his people. His destination was Lhasa, where he hoped to dip into the treasure-troves of monastic libraries. But barely a month later, he succumbed to fever and died in the foothills of the Himalayas. Hodgson resigned his official post in Nepal in 1843, but moved along to conduct research on his own bat in India until 1858. Then he set sail to start a new life as a married country squire in England. Despite his prodigious output and generous contributions to museums and libraries, Hodgson's work was largely overlooked. It was not until he reached his ninetieth year that Oxford University deigned to confer an honorary degree on him. Hodgson seemed indifferent to praise or criticism—ultimately, he was in search of truth. This remarkable scholar, who pioneered so much in unravelling the riddles of Tibet, died in 1894—the exact year that Tucci was born.

It was due to the efforts of Csoma de Koros and Houghton Hodgson that little-known Buddhism made its debut in Europe. By the 1850s, translations began to appear—such as the Lotus Sutra, translated into German in 1852. The arrival of Buddhism was greeted with some alarm by Christians—it seemed nihilistic yet rational, and a formidable rival. To others, the wisdom of Buddhism was spellbinding: they simply had to find out more. British, French, German and Russian scholars set to work collecting Tibetan and Asian texts—and translating, annotating and analysing them.

In the early 1880s, British undercover agent Sarat Chandra Das pulled off a literary coup of sorts. Sengchen Tulku, chief minister at Shigatse, was fascinated by Western science: in exchange for presenting a printing press and smallpox vaccine, Das was allowed to examine

At Ramoche Temple in Lhasa, monks strike up deep throat-singing chants. Over-
doing the chanting like this can render the singer mute, due to intense vocal-
chord strain.

sacred texts at the library of Tashilhunpo Monastery. On these forays,
Das spirited over 200 volumes from Tibet back into Sikkim. The Japanese explorer and scholar Ekai Kawaguchi sought out manuscripts in
Tibet, and Charles Bell, British liaison officer in Tibet in the early 20th
century, collected a fair number of Tibetan texts. In the mid-1920s,
Alexandra David-Néel arrived in France with 400 Tibetan books and
manuscripts from many years of wandering in Tibet and India. Outdo-
ing all these sacred text hunters was Professor Tucci, who carted many
loads of books back to Rome during his expeditions of the 1930s. In
1939, Tucci explored the temples of Sakya, but above all its libraries,
with a number of works written in Sanskrit on palm leaves and carried
into Tibet from India.

Miraculously, the sacred texts at Sakya Gompa mostly survived
the ransacking and theft of the 1966–76 Cultural Revolution. This was
due to the efforts of caretaker monks who hid the material behind a
huge Buddha statue in the Great Sutra Chanting Hall. Inside this hidden vault is a dark enclosure, where a flashlight will trace an astonishing contour: the library shelving here is about 180 feet long, 30 feet
high and three feet deep. Seven huge shelves are filled with thousands
of Buddhist scriptures, many hand-copied by Tibetan calligraphers.
Near one corner is a huge manuscript illuminated in gold called the

Written in stone: a man chiselling sacred mantras into stone by copying text from a looseleaf Tibetan book

Prajnaparamita Sutra. The book is so large it requires its own special rack: the pages are five feet wide.

The musty atmosphere is evocative of a powerful, ancient world, like the fabled lost library of Alexandria in Egypt. The papyrus scrolls of Alexandria were painstakingly made by hand, copied by scribes. Credit for the oldest printed book goes not to Egypt, nor to Europe, but to Central Asia around the eighth century. The oldest known dated book is a woodblock copy of the *Diamond Sutra*, printed in Chinese in 868 AD, with elaborate illustrations of Buddha and his disciples. This rare tome now rests in the British Library, and is related, content-wise, to the *Prajnaparamita Sutra* sitting on the shelf at Sakya.

The Tibetans were actually ahead of Europe with their version of woodblock printing—done with blocks that were beautifully engraved specimens of very graceful penmanship. The woodblock printing might be supplemented by illustration by hand—sometimes using inks derived from gold, silk or turquoise. The trouble is that the Tibetans got firmly stuck in the woodblock stage of printing, never advancing beyond that. Their technology became fossilised. Everything was done with woodblock printing: Tibetan postage stamps were printed from woodblocks, all the prayer flags were printed with woodblocks.

It was—and is—an enormously complex process to print a Tibetan

Monk reading Tibetan looseleaf book, printed by using a mediaeval system of woodblocks

Mythology on the money: panel from a 100-*sang* paper bill from the 1940s shows a pair of snow lions. The bills were printed by woodblock.

sacred text from a set of woodblocks. A *pecha* (Tibetan book) is loose-leaf, with pages printed both sides with long narrow woodblocks. The *Tenjur*, or commentary on Buddha's discourses, requires some 25,000 separate leaves to be run off—using woodblocks originally carved by monks. To produce a Tibetan book, rows of monks work in a machine-like rhythm, bobbing up and down with alarming rapidity—one inking a woodblock, the other rolling a strip of paper. Then the printed pages are left to dry—and have to be sorted, collated and bound in cloth. The text is not glued—all the oblong loose leaves are stacked in order between two boards, and the entire assembly is wrapped in cloth. Books of prayers are sacred—never allowed to touch the ground and must be stored in high places.

There were once four great monastic printing presses in Tibet— two were razed to the ground under Chinese rule after 1959. The press at Kumbum survives in a scaled-down version. The main surviving woodblock operation is at Derge Gompa, in northeast Tibet, which ships sacred texts to other monasteries of the plateau. This monastery also uses copper blocks for printing. At Derge, everything connected with printing of text is considered holy—even the ink. Pilgrims have been known to smear gooey run-off ink in their hair. Some pilgrims— bless them—even attempt to drink it.

Tucci was a leading scholar but in a rather obscure field—he relied heavily on grants and sponsorship for funding. For support, he pandered to both the Tibetans and the British imperial government of India. To the Tibetans, he revealed himself as a true follower of Tibetan Buddhism— but on earlier expeditions he presented himself to the British as non-Buddhist, to ingratiate himself with those who controlled the access routes to Tibet. Professor Tucci was a follower of the Kagyu order of Tibetan Buddhism. His kept a shrine in his apartment in Rome—which was full of Tibetan ritualistic objects and books.

Tucci's reputation rested on his scholarly publishing output, sponsored by various Italian institutions. Tucci says that most of the money for expeditions came from 'private sources'—which included the pockets of Benito Mussolini himself. Tucci had ties with fascist intellectuals at the University of Rome and appears to have been in the good graces of Mussolini—indeed, a friend of Il Duce.

In an academic paper titled *The Tibetan Travels of Professor Giuseppe Tucci*, British scholar Alex McKay poses some thorny questions:

> But do we not also learn that Tucci was a master of telling officials what they wanted to hear—that he was an assiduous cultivator of powerful and influential officials, a skilled manipulator of his contacts, and an arch-flatterer of men more familiar with criticism?.... when we judge Tucci by the company he kept, fascists, neo-Samurai and the like, we should ask whether he would not have been equally assiduous in cultivating and flattering communists, monarchists, or any other ideological leaders who could

give him what he really wanted—access to fields of scholarship. Nor should we assume he enjoyed supping with the devil.

Tucci's 1935 book *Secrets of Tibet* lists among its sponsors the Royal Italian Academy—but also the National Fascist Federation of Public Works, the National Fascist Confederation of Agriculturalists, and the General Fascist Confederation of Italian Industry. In the same breath, Tucci goes on to rhapsodise about the extent of the co-operation of English authorities in India. That support continued even after rival Tibetologist Marco Pallis wrote to authorities in Delhi roundly condemning Tucci's use of Royal Italian Academy funds to buy up manuscripts and antiquities in Tibet. British-Greek scholar Pallis accused Tucci of ransacking entire villages, stripping them of valuable tankas and sacred texts. Tucci's response, in 1939, was a letter advising the Tibetan Government to set up a Department of Antiquities which would preserve its heritage and, among other duties, prevent the removal of artifacts from Tibet! Tucci's letter had no apparent effect in Lhasa, but it seems to have been condoned in imperial government circles. The colonial attitude of authorities in Delhi was that it was better that Tucci took valuable items than that they perished by Tibetan neglect. Alex McKay picks up the story:

> Tucci's suggestion that the Tibetans control their own antiquities was in many ways ironical, but to the British—let us not forget the vast hordes of relics in the British Museum—it was a mature and appropriately material response; Asian treasures were best kept by Europeans until the Asians could look after them themselves.

The European colonial argument of removal artifacts for 'safe-keeping' opens a whole can of worms—the Egyptians are after the French for Napoleon's looting of stone statuary (now in the Louvre), and the Ethiopians are hounding Italy to return stone artifacts plundered by Mussolini as booty during his 1935 invasion.

By the end of WWII, Tucci had lost his chair at the University of Rome for supporting Mussolini, and his chief publisher, the Royal Italian Academy, had been closed down. And yet, *despite* the fact that Tucci openly supported the fascists, and *despite* the fallout from the war, and *despite* accusations of grand theft of artifacts, when Tucci applied in 1946 for travel permits for Tibet, the British smoothed the way with Tibetan authorities. How did he get away with this? It boiled down to the fact that he was a highly respected scholar who spoke and read Tibetan, and he cultivated good relations with important British cadre in Tibet like Basil Gould and Hugh Richardson. He sent them his reports, his books—and his maps. Tucci's painstaking cartography was invaluable to the map-crazed British intelligence because Tucci often roved through parts unknown. Among the books that Tucci diligently dispatched to Hugh Richardson were volumes from his seven-part series *Indo-Tibetica*. These books—devoted to art, literature, iconography and architecture of Tibet and the Himalayas—were published over the period 1932 to 1941 by the Royal Italian Academy.

By contrast, Swedish explorer Sven Hedin had been hauled over the coals by the British for supporting the Germans in the first world war. Hedin, who explored in west Tibet, was stripped of his Royal Geographical Society gold medals—and his membership—and stripped of his British knighthood. Unbowed, Hedin remained a strong supporter of Germany: at the 1936 Olympic Games in Berlin, he was Hitler's special guest. When Harrer and Aufschnaiter took up residence in Lhasa in the mid-1940s, Hedin struck up a correspondence with both of them.

A lot has been written in this book about encounters of Westerners with Tibetans—but what about exploring the other way? How many Tibetans made it to the West? And what resulted from these encounters?

Well, Tucci was responsible for a prominent transplant himself: he brought the young Namkhai Norbu to Italy where he developed a world-renowned Dzogchen Buddhist practice. Writing in 1950, Fosco Maraini gives a glimpse of Europe through Tibetan eyes:

> To the Tibetans a white man represents a world of fascinating mysteries. To them we represent the exotic in reverse—the exotic of aeroplanes, cameras, clocks, penicillin, the world of controllable, repeatable miracles... Our exotic characteristic in Tibetan eyes is our magical mastery of the elements.

Maraini goes on to cite how a lama can learn to suspend himself in mid-air by levitation—but only after years of preparation and ascetic ordeals, and even then he may not succeed. But anybody can fly in an aeroplane.

By exploring the lands of airplanes and motorcars, Tibetans could familiarise themselves with modern machines and perhaps even introduce Western technology to Tibet on their return. That was the idea behind a grand experiment that got under way in 1913 when four Tibetan boys, sons of nobles, were sent by Charles Bell to Rugby School in England. The four Tibetan boys were Ghonkar, Kyipup, Mondo and Ringang. And strange tales their lives became. They were dispatched to the UK with two 'handlers'—Laden La (a Sikkimese official who later worked with Eric Bailey) and Lungshar (whose meteoric fall from grace and sticky end is chronicled in the Aufschnaiter chapter).

The arrival of the 'Rugby Boys' in 1913 was very inauspicious timing, as WWI shortly broke out. While Tibet itself escaped WWI, the Tibetans got to see the fabulous machines of the West used for purposes of mass destruction. This was a useful demonstration for one of the Rugby Boys, Ghonkar. After Rugby, Ghonkar was sent to Woolwich Military Academy with the idea of training him to modernise the Tibetan Army. By a strange turn of events, Ghonkar fell in love with an English girl and declared his desire to marry her. When the Dalai Lama disallowed the marriage, the disconsolate Ghonkar returned to Tibet. For political reasons, he was posted to a frontier station in Kham, where he died shortly afterward—some say from a broken heart.

Kyipup turned out to be a lazy fellow. He took surveying courses, and on his return to Tibet was assigned the task of developing the telegraph line. Although the British-built Sikkim-Gyantse telegraph line had been open since 1904, it was not until 1923 that permission was given for the line to be extended to Lhasa, with several foreign experts lending assistance. A major problem was that Tibetans kept stealing wire along the route for their own construction projects. One foreign inspecting telegraph master had a unique solution to the rampant problem of pilfering. He had a glass eye, and would cause considerable consternation among the Tibetans by removing this and showing it to them: he would often leave this eye to watch his property—none of his belongings was ever pilfered. After a shaky career as superintendent of telegraphs, Kyipup was appointed City Magistrate and Chief of Police. But he lost his position when a great pole erected for the celebration of Tibetan New Year collapsed—a highly inauspicious incident. Then he went into the Foreign Office, acting as guide and interpreter for foreign visitors—one of whom was Tucci.

Mondo (aka Mondro) was trained in geology and became a mining engineer. He returned to Tibet keen on fossicking for precious metals—in particular, gold. However, he ran up against conservative

abbots who claimed he would disturb the spirits of the earth by digging—and this would cause the crops to fail. After moving through
several towns in Tibet to start mining—and getting booted out of each
one—Mondo gave up. He headed the police force in the early 1920s,
but was exiled to the Ladakh border after being implicated in a plot
to depose the Dalai Lama in 1924. He became the *dzongpon* of Gartok, and was considered rather avaricious. Mondo was pardoned for
his transgressions in the mid-1930s and made a comeback in Lhasa,
where he proceeded to terrify the Tibetans by hurtling around town
on a motorcycle purchased in India—a Tibetan rebel without a cause.
That is, until the day a minister was thrown from his skittish horse—an
incident that brought Mondo's motorcycling days to an abrupt halt.

Ringang was the most effective of the Rugby Boys. After graduating from a course in electrical engineering in England, he dreamed of
setting up hydroelectric stations in Tibet. With Herculean resolve, Ringang arranged for equipment to be carried over the Himalayas from
India—and constructed a small hydroelectric station in Lhasa at the
foot of a mountain stream. He laid a power line to the city and to the
Norbulingka. Except for the winter months when the stream was frozen, this provided the city with some electric lighting. But as time wore
on, and parts wore down—and replacement parts did not arrive—the
plant fell into disarray, and eventually yielded only enough power to
drive the machines at the Mint.

Sadly, any gains that the Rugby Boys were able to make were wiped
out by conservative backlashes of the clergy. One of the few successful
results of the Rugby experiment was that these Tibetans could speak
excellent English, which spooked the bejasus out of foreign visitors to
Lhasa in the 1930s. In fact, Mondo and Ringang both served as interpreters for the 13th Dalai Lama. In 1948, Briton Robert Ford met the
last surviving Rugby Boy, Kyipup—but by the following year, Kyipup
too was dead. And so was the Rugby experiment.

In Tibet itself, another British educational experiment floundered.
This was the setting-up of a British-run school for the sons of Tibetan
nobles. In the early 1920s, a school in Gyantse operated for about three
years before being closed down under strong pressure from jealous
Tibetan lamas. The British schoolmaster, Frank Ludlow, was deeply
disappointed: he wrote that the Tibetans 'will regret this decision one
day when they are Chinese slaves once more, as they assuredly will
be.' There was an alternative way to access British-style education:

progressive Tibetan nobles like Tsarong sent their sons and daughters to fashionable boarding schools in Darjeeling and Kalimpong, where they acquired mastery of English and were exposed to modern ideas.

In the early 1940s in Lhasa, another attempt was made to open a British school. That too suffered an early demise: it was closed down by the ultra-conservative Regent Taktra. Regent Taktra had taken over from Reting Rinpoche, who at least was receptive to Western ideas—he rode a motorcycle and played football. In 1947, Reting Rinpoche was charged with sending a parcel bomb to Regent Taktra. In a battle that followed at Sera monastery, some 300 monks-supporters of Reting Rinpoche died. Reting Rinpoche was condemned to having his eyes put out, but fearful of his incarnation powers, his jailors instead resorted to crushing his testicles. He died from poisoning in May 1947.

Thrown into a dank dungeon in Lhasa by the same Regent Taktra in the same year was a man named Gendun Choepel. He was a very rare Tibetan—a rebel intellectual. While Tucci came north to decode Tibetan culture, this former monk went south to India to study English and to pursue studies of the Western world—unprecedented for the time. Gendun Choepel, who was born in 1905 in Amdo, was fond of provoking monastic scholars in debate—a skill at which he excelled. Choepel was an iconoclast—he took such unusual positions in debate that his opponents were often frozen in silence. Choepel was also an accomplished artist. In the mid-1930s, he set off to visit important pilgrimage sites in India and Sri Lanka. He went on a binge, developing an intense interest in liquor, sex, meditation and art—and opium. The chain-smoking Choepel had formidable powers of concentration—he could debate with the best of them, even when totally inebriated. He laughed at Tibetan superstition; he translated parts of the Kama Sutra into Tibetan. And he stepped on imperial British toes in Kalimpong through his research showing Tibet as an independent nation—whose borders extended into British India. He stepped on the toes of the Tibetan government with his religious iconoclasm and his suggestions about modernisation. Then he jumped up and down on more Tibetan toes by participating in the drafting of a constitution (by disgruntled Tibetans in India) calling for parliamentary rule in Tibet—thus challenging rule by the powerful aristocrats. Choepel stepped on far too many toes belonging to powerful people.

After 13 years in India and Sri Lanka, Gendun Choepel decided to return to Tibet in the mid-1940s to write the definitive history of independent Tibet. For this purpose, he assembled a large black metal box packed with notes, drawings, books and papers. He also imported a life-size rubber woman that he had painted with the face of a nomad. He claimed this was to take care of his sexual needs without the time-drain of a wife to distract him from his history book. Choepel was arrested in Lhasa: he never saw the black box or the rubber woman again. He was thrown in jail on trumped-up charges of having communist leanings and was flogged to induce confessions. Ironically, in 1949, when communist invasion of Tibet seemed imminent, a general amnesty for prisoners was declared in Lhasa. Gendun Choepel emerged from jail in an emaciated condition, filthy and dressed in rags. Tibet's foremost intellectual died in 1951 at the age of 46—a shadow of his former self.

The year 1947 was notable for one other significant Tibetan interaction with the Western world. Realising that its extreme isolationism, lack of technology and lack of diplomatic links left it wide open to Chinese invasion, the Tibetan government embarked on a last-ditch stand to drum up support for Tibet's independence in the West. Four delegates were issued with Tibetan passports and, wearing traditional robes, were packed off on an official world trade tour. They even made it to America. But by then it was too late: the Communist Chinese were already declaring their intention to invade Tibet.

Meanwhile, back in Rome, in 1948, Professor Tucci—having survived WWII somewhat intact—was preparing to embark on another expedition to Tibet. His sidekick, Fosco Maraini, had not weathered the war so smoothly. After his 1937 expedition with Tucci, Maraini won a scholarship to go to Japan: he arrived in 1938 with his wife and daughters. Maraini fell under the spell of 19th-century Japanese master painter Hokusai. He had lots of time to contemplate: the whole family was interned in Japan in 1943 because of Maraini's anti-fascist views. Maraini went on to carve out a career as photographer, filmmaker, ethnographer, climber, adventurer—and writer. In his book *Secret Tibet*, Maraini brought Tucci's expeditions to life—something Tucci himself failed to do because he was stuck in scholarly mode. Maraini told it like it was—not sentimental or gushy or awestruck—a radical style of travel writing for the time.

Spring 1948: Maraini returns for another Tucci expedition to Tibet—

on board a ship bound from Naples to Bombay. The trip is sponsored by the Italian Geographical Society. Maraini describes the departure dock:

> There is a great bustle on the quay, opposite the little ship. A lorry arrives from Rome with packing cases, sacks and boxes, all labelled "Professor Tucci's Expedition to Tibet". A crane hoists it all on board, while one of the professor's assistants, armed with spectacles, pencil and notebook, carefully checks it...

Tucci's son Ananda waves goodbye at the dock—another trip is under way. Maraini provides a verbal sketch of Tucci:

> He is a small man, half-way through his fifties, with a strange philosopher's bead of hair, and side-whiskers...he doesn't take much interest in his appearance. Under his arm he has the inevitable book. I am prepared to swear that within five minutes he will be curled up in some corner, reading it. Reading it? That's not the right word.... Tucci ploughs through books. He sprinkles them with pencil notes, underlines passages, reads the paragraph headings aloud, grows furious if the author says anything stupid...Then when the book has yielded all it can, like a field of wheat after a huge harvest, it falls worn and exhausted to the deck.

Through Maraini, we get a glimpse of Tucci's cabin: it is chaotic and more resembles a library, a sanctum. Maraini talks to him on deck one evening: Tucci tells him he is only interested in things that contain a mystery—in the inexplicable, the tangled, the obscure. He adores paradoxes. He hates certainty and clarity. He hates science, he says, for that reason. Science postulates that matter is governed by fixed, immutable laws, while Buddhism teaches that all everything changes, evolves, mutates.

Tucci's entourage includes two photographers—Pietro Mele and his assistant Fosco Maraini, plus surgeon Regolo Moise of the Navy Medical Corps. In Darjeeling, Tucci added a sirdar—Tenzing Norgay—and he hired Geshe Sangpo, a middle-age lama who'd been educated in Tibet, to help with specialised research. With a caravan of 20 horses, the expedition moved up the 'wool route' to Gyantse. Loaded on some of those horses was canned food from Italy—meat, vegetables, noodles and preserved fruit—as Tucci admitted his stomach did not

These Liebig cards (written in Italian) were printed in the 1930s—the time of Tucci's trips to Tibet. Liebig Meat Extract—a molasses-like black spread that was packaged in a glass bottle—was used by European adventurers in places like Africa as a dietary supplement. It is not known if Tucci packed along any Liebig Meat Extract, but he certainly packed a lot of canned food from Italy, and his own olive-oil supply—because he found Tibetan food hard to stomach. The top card shows hats and haute coiffure in Lhasa; the lower picture shows a sacred mask dance performance near the Jokhang Temple.

readily adapt to the Tibetan staples of *tsampa* and yak meat. Perhaps his Roman taste buds might have played some part in this: Tibetan food must be the blandest and most tasteless in Asia, with spices rarely used except for salt (and dollops of yak-butter). Tucci also noted in his book *To Lhasa and Beyond* that they had on board a 'liberal supply of olive oil to guarantee our daily intake of vitamins'—kindly donated by the Olive Growers' Association of Italy.

Although Tucci had been on half a dozen expeditions to Tibet, he'd never made it to Lhasa—which was the major objective of this trip, along with important monasteries of central Tibet. One of these was Samding—highly unusual because it was commanded by female incarnates in the Dorje Phagmo lineage. Tucci was presented to the current abbess, 'a pretty girl of 13' who laid her hands on his head to bestow blessings. They exchanged scarves and gifts. Samding commands a hilltop near Lake Yamdrok Tso: pilgrims were gathering for a festival at the gompa.

Tucci does not go into details about the lineage here, but it was embroiled in controversy. In Tibet, incarnate figures occupied positions of great wealth and power: this resulted in considerable pulling of strings—and legs—to have a favourite 'recognised'. The Dorje Phagmo lineage at Samding dates back to 1717: trouble with the lineage started up almost immediately. In 1740, Capuchin friar Cassiano

Beligatti was part of an ill-fated mission to Lhasa bearing gifts from the Vatican to the Dalai Lama. The mission passed by Samding en route to Lhasa and Beligatti recorded:

> The Tibetans have for this Lhamessa the same veneration as for the Grand Lama... She lives celibate, having made a vow of chastity; notwithstanding which, about 5 years previous to our arrival, she had brought forth a Lhamessina, which fact—in spite of the great diligence exercised—they had been unable to prevent from being made public. This for a little while had cooled the veneration for her...

More serious veneration problems surfaced in 1937, when the acting regent of Tibet announced that the 6th Dorje Phagmo had been recognised in a baby girl, even though the 5th was still at large. The regent argued that the transference of souls actually took place in this case *before* death. The 5th Dorje Phagmo died the following year, but the Tibetans would not accept the 6th as the true incarnation and three other candidates were put forward. The matter was hotly disputed by the nominated 6th's father—and a costly legal battle ensued.

Fosco Maraini and Pietro Mele, as non-Buddhists, were not allowed to proceed to Lhasa on this trip. On entering Lhasa, Tucci—like Manning long before him—was puzzled by the architecture of the Potala Palace, which he records as 'irregular and whimsical' and yet 'built with such inner consistency that each corner and each line falls in with a necessary plan, as it were, and gives you the impression of order where waywardness prevails.' Tucci's caravan, filing past the Potala, suddenly broke ranks when the horses became skittish at the sight of the Dalai Lama's elephant, out for a stroll. The elephant—the only one in Tibet— was a gift from the Maharaja of Nepal.

Dottore Tucci and Tenzing Norgay were introduced to Peter Aufschnaiter and Heinrich Harrer, with whom they got along very well. Tucci and Aufschnaiter held a common interest in archeology, and Norgay and Harrer talked about climbing. Once, before a large gathering, Harrer was trying to convince the Tibetans that the earth is spherical, not a flat disk, so he appealed to Tucci for support—which backfired, as Harrer reports: 'To my great surprise he took up a sceptical attitude, saying that in his opinion all scientists ought continually to be revising their theories, and that one day the Tibetan doctrine might just as well prove to be true!'

Tucci surprised his hosts, too. He arranged an audience with the 14th Dalai Lama at the Norbulingka, but when requested to wear Tibetan dress, suddenly declared himself 'the enemy of any masquerade' and decided to visit in European dress—which he knew would only upset the monk attendants. The Dalai Lama, then a boy of 13, did not normally grant formal interviews as he had not reached his majority, so Tucci apparently got the next best thing: a silent audience. The young Dalai Lama was very good at these, with a commanding presence. When he was enthroned in Lhasa at the age of four in 1940, Basil Gould (the British representative in Lhasa) wrote: 'I have never seen anybody assume more complete and natural control of great assemblies.' Tucci followed a ritual presentation of a gift scarf, and the Dalai Lama blessed him by laying his hands on his head and binding a red scarf around his neck. Tucci could not help noticing the Dalai Lama's 'glistening, inquisitive stare' directed at 'the foreigner whose unwonted garb was set off against the red of the lamas.' Seated on a lower throne near the Dalai Lama was the stern man responsible for banning the wearing of European clothes—the 78-year-old Regent Taktra. Tucci does not record what the Regent's eyes looked like, but he must've been livid.

Tucci stayed for a week in Lhasa. At the end of his stay, he was personally given a copy of a rare religious text by the Dalai Lama. Tucci was delighted—as the news spread, Tibetans shed their reluctance to give away sacred texts, and Tucci bought up all he could through using agents. This precious hoard of books was loaded onto yak-hide boats, as Tucci was leaving Lhasa the traditional way—floating downstream along the Kyichu River. This method saved considerable time over the horseback version. And Tucci and crew stayed aboard as the Kyichu turned a bend into the Tsangpo River—and they continued on eastward to their destination. Which was Samye monastery, reckoned to be the oldest in Tibet—with architecture based on Buddhist cosmology and geomancy principles.

In 1949, Tucci's three-volume magnum opus, *Tibetan Painted Scrolls* was published—at the time, the largest and most important study of Tibetan painting and iconography ever produced. This lavish scholarly work was printed as a limited collector's edition, with maroon cloth binding. Volumes I and II are text, running to 800 pages; Volume III is a portfolio containing 26 colour plates and 231 monochrome plates. In his preface, Tucci states the case for a new appreciation of Tibetan art:

> Tibetan painting has not met so far with the same appreciation as that received by its Indian and Persian counterparts...it has been difficult to overcome the impression that Tibetan painters have little originality and are so subservient to the rules of iconography that they are hardly able to give individual forms to their own fancy.

Fresco of the female deity White Tara, from Tsaparang. The hand-gestures used by Tibetan deities convey special meanings. In this fresco, an eye is embedded in each palm of the hand, and a further vertical eye in the forehead. Tucci was among the first to decode the subtle layers of meaning in these frescoes.

After the 1950 Chinese invasion of Tibet, Tucci switched his focus to neighbouring Nepal, which was becoming more accessible to outsiders. He conducted two major expeditions to western Nepal. In 1952, he journeyed to Mustang, a remote Tibetan enclave on the Nepal-Tibet border. Publishing a brief book about this trip, Tucci introduces Signorina Francesca Bonardi as expedition photographer and logistics person: by the end of the trip, she became Signora Bonardi Tucci, his third wife. In 1954, Tucci made another expedition to western Nepal, in search of a forgotten ethnic group—the Mollahs.

That was his last hardy trekking foray. Leaving behind the Tibetan world, Tucci shifted his attention to Swat (Pakistan), Afghanistan and Eastern Iran, conducting archeological digs with teams from ISMEO. Important finds are displayed at the National Museum of Oriental Art in Rome—which came into existence on Tucci's initiative.

Professor Tucci, the president of ISMEO for decades and director of publications, became something of an institution himself. A number of scholars were associated in research under his leadership—among them was Joseph Rock; papers on obscure Tibetan subjects by Peter

Aufschnaiter were also published by ISMEO. Although Tucci remains the great pioneer of studies in Tibetan art history and archeology, his influence has waned because of considerable advances in these fields and because of new approaches.

Tucci kept a house in Rome but on weekends repaired to the villa of Francesca, his wife, at San Polo dei Cavalieri, a small hill station about 40 miles from the capital. In 1969, after teaching religion and philosophy in Rome for three decades, Tucci retired. He donated his entire library to ISMEO and pulled up stakes: keeping only a few thousand books, he shifted to San Polo dei Cavalieri. Fosco Maraini said Tucci loved this place because it reminded him of Tibet—it was peaceful and was ringed by mountains. Tucci passed away on April 5, 1984 at the age of 89. His most dedicated follower and biographer-of-sorts, Fosco Maraini, died in Florence in June 2004.

Tucci was one of the last foreigners to see Tibet under the rule of the Dalai Lama. And Tucci left a strange legacy. The year 1959 proved to be a decisive turning point for Tibetan art and literature. Tibetan sacred texts were in grave danger of destruction after the Tibetan uprising of 1959 was crushed by the Chinese, who went on a rampage—looting, sacking and burning. Tibetan sacred texts were used as toilet paper by Chinese troops.

With the refugee exodus from Tibet in 1959, a large amount of Tibetan art became suddenly available to dealers and collectors in the West. Some were works that Tibetans carried out and sold to support themselves. In the early 1960s, Tibetan art was systematically looted by the Chinese, with valuable works launched on the international market through dealers in Hong Kong. The madness of the 1964–74 Cultural Revolution involved large-scale destruction of temples in Tibet and ransacking of its precious artworks.

Giuseppe Tucci was caught in a conundrum. Nobody had done more to have Tibetan art recognised as one of rare skill—and broadcasting that message to the world. Yet in doing so, Tucci had raised its value—and unwittingly sparked a worldwide market in art theft from Tibet to feed the appetite of greedy foreign collectors. Interpol estimates that the black market in stolen art and antiquities worldwide results in upward of $10-billion changing hands annually, making it the world's largest illegal trade after arms and drugs. The motivation is vast profits with a short turnover time. Original Tibetan art is highly sought after, and there is little doubt that Chinese smugglers have been involved in the traffic, dismantling Tibet's heritage piece by piece.

Cases of Tibetan art theft are hard to track, but some are well-documented. In April 1993, two Chinese men arrived with a mini-van at Drolma Lakhang, a small temple outside Lhasa with exquisite statuary that somehow escaped destruction during the Cultural Revolution. The two men took a 1,200-year-old statue of the Buddha, which was immediately sold to smugglers in Chengdu for an estimated $300,000. It then disappeared without trace, until Lhasa customs discovered it had been shipped to the US, where a buyer was prepared to pay eight million dollars for it. The FBI seized the Buddha statue, but demanded photographic evidence that it had come from Drolma Lakhang before they would return it. The Tibetans did not have such evidence. Finally, after two years of wrangling, Lhasa customs found a picture taken by a foreign tourist, and the FBI returned the statue to Drolma Lakhang in late 1997.

Statues of this scale are no longer made in Tibet—and very few tanka painters remain in Lhasa. The Tibetan skill of casting large Buddha images is still practiced in Dharamsala, India—the centre of the Tibetans-in-exile. The world's best tanka painters perfect their skills in Dharamsala today. Kalsang, a painter who trained for six years in Dharamsala, says tankas in Lhasa are of poor quality, more like Nepalese factory-type efforts. The entire tanka-trade around Barkor Bazaar in Lhasa is controlled by Chinese shop owners. Old tankas are rarely seen in Lhasa these days—most have been smuggled out to Nepal for collectors. Looking at 'older' tankas in one of the Chinese shops on the Barkor, Kalsang noticed something strange: Chinese brush strokes. 'There's a difference in technique. And not just the Chinese brush strokes—it's the colours and the shadings. These tankas were very different from any others I've seen.' It would appear that somewhere in China is a peculiar cottage industry: Chinese artists hard at work painting 'aged' tankas for sale to tourists who think they're getting ancient Tibetan ones.

Peter Aufschnaiter was at home in high places,
and had great rapport with Tibetan nomads. In the background
is Aufschnaiter's photograph of Mount Shishapangma,
the first ever taken of this peak.

 # Peter Aufschnaiter
1899–1973

engineer, cartographer, mountaineer,
tireless trekker, selfless aid worker & unsung hero

Land of Snows & Silence

❖   Eight Years in Tibet   ❖

There are those who instantly find the rhythm, the heartbeat, of a different tribe—and want to join them. Austrian mountaineer Peter Aufschnaiter found his kin in Tibet—he loved the simplicity and humour of the nomads. The first foreigner ever to be employed by the Tibetan government, he would happily have lived the rest of his life there were it not for Chinese invasion of Tibet in 1950. Having escaped a British POW camp in India in 1944, Aufschnaiter went running the other way to escape advancing Chinese soldiers. And while fellow escapee Heinrich Harrer became a very wealthy man from telling their incredible tale, Aufschnaiter said nothing. He just kept on walking.

DURING THE MAKING of the movie *Seven Years in Tibet* in 1996, an Austrian researcher revealed that the original writer, Heinrich Harrer, had glossed over a few important facts. The researcher unearthed a photograph of Harrer shaking hands with Hitler. Indeed, Harrer was discovered to be a member of both the SS and the SA in the 1930s. At the last minute, after negotiations with Harrer's lawyer, director Jean-Jacques Annaud inserted some references to this: mainly a brief scene at Graz railway station, showing an official thrusting a Nazi flag into Harrer's hands—a flag to be planted on top of Mount Nanga Parbat. In the same scene, Harrer coldly said goodbye to his pregnant wife—something else he forgot to mention in his memoirs.

Harrer, then in his nineties, sheepishly admitted this was all true, but maintained that he had joined the SS only because he needed the sponsorship for mountain climbing. In the same breath, he said that joining the SS was the biggest mistake in his whole life. Probably his second biggest mistake was not coming clean about it: *Seven Years in Tibet* was written post-war, when a confession like this would have made his journey to Tibet seem so much more poignant.

Harrer, played by Brad Pitt, comes off as an arrogant egotist in the movie, while Aufschnaiter—played by David Thewlis—fares considerably better, with a kind of contemplative poise and a manner that wins him the heart of a Tibetan woman, acted by exotic beauty Lhakpa Tsamchoe. With no acting experience, she steals the show from the veteran Western actors—as do two brothers from Bhutan, Jamyang and Sonam Wangchuk, who play the younger Dalai Lama. Also stealing the show, as far as director Jean-Jacques Annaud was concerned, were the real-live monks he imported for the making of the movie: they made splendid actors. Annaud said that years of Buddhist meditation training had taught them to focus their energies totally in the moment. Annaud said they required no acting lessons. But were they acting? The monks were playing monks, after all.

The movie left a few matters up in the air. At the end, the viewer knows that Harrer left Tibet, but what about his companion Peter Aufschnaiter? Aufschnaiter is left in limbo, left behind in Lhasa with his

Tibetan wife. So do they try to escape the Communist Chinese? Or are they arrested by the Chinese, condemned as spies and tossed in some dark dungeon? Though Aufschnaiter and Harrer were thrown together in one of the most remarkable POW escapes of all time, their destinies diverged in Lhasa—and they followed very different paths. This short biography follows up on Peter Aufschnaiter's path.

If the British were obsessed with summiting Everest as a national endeavour, the German equivalent was Nanga Parbat. In any case, the British stymied attempts of other European nations to access Everest: they maintained a monopoly on the mountain. The resident spirits of Mount Nanga Parbat (located in what is now Pakistan) were even nastier than those of Everest: on the 1934 and 1937 German expeditions, a staggering total of 29 Germans and Sherpas perished in summit attempts.

Aufschnaiter and Harrer were part of a joint Austrian-German reconnaissance of 1939 on Nanga Parbat and Rakaposhi. The expedition was organised by the German Alpine Club, sponsored by the Reichssportsfuhrer—a Nazi organisation aiming to show how the Teutonic race excelled at sports. The same year, Harrer had conquered the north face of the Eiger—a feat that so impressed Hitler, he personally congratulated the summit team. Naturally, the Nazis used this for propaganda value—boasting of the great strength of the Austrian climber.

Aufschnaiter, the leader of the expedition, was about 20 years senior to Harrer. The movie did not show this age difference, but it got their heights right: at six-foot-four, actor David Thewlis stands almost a head taller than Brad Pitt—and that's approximately the real-life ratio. Aufschnaiter was tall, thin and wiry. Of the two, Aufschnaiter had much more experience climbing the peaks of the Himalayas. In the 1920s, he had nearly twice reached the summit of Kangchenjunga—long before anyone had summited one of the 26,000-foot-plus giants of the Himalayas. From that time, he had dreamed of one day climbing in Tibet.

For the 1939 reconnaissance on Nanga Parbat, there were just four climbers plus three Sherpas from Darjeeling (the real expedition was slated for 1940, with a big group of climbers). The four climbers were to scout the northwest face of the peak as a possible summit route.

They reached a ridge on Nanga Parbat at 22,000 feet and decided to abandon the climb at this point. They returned to Karachi to take a ship back to Germany.

The ship never showed up: war had broken out. The group was intercepted by the British and trundled off to Dehra Dun, where 1,500 Germans were eventually interned, along with those from other axis nations. At Dehra Dun, they had food, they had books, they were well treated. But they were bored out of their skulls after four years in the camp—and several failed escapes. Aufschnaiter passed his time studying Tibetan language and customs, poring over maps, plotting escape routes.

On April 29th, 1944, seven prisoners made their desperate bid for freedom. They were disguised as a work-unit for fixing barbed wire. Rolf Magener, Heins von Have and Sattler were dressed as British officers. Four more were disguised as Indian porters with hair dyed black and faces darkened. Hans Kopp and Heinrich Harrer carried a heavy roll of barbed wire; Bruno Treipel and Peter Aufschnaiter carried a ladder.

After bluffing their way out of the camp, Rolf Magener and Heins von Have quickly split off from the group. Their destination was Calcutta, where they hoped to find a route overland into Burma and then to Japan. The other five escapees headed north, into the hills. Because they travelled mostly by night to escape detection, there were some odd nocturnal encounters, as Aufschnaiter describes in his diary:

> I started to go round a large rock in the middle of the path. Suddenly the 'rock' jumped up howling, and then hurled itself down the slope. It was a leopard. All happened so quickly that I had no time to be afraid.

As the group proceeded into the Himalayan foothills, Sattler discovered he could not stand the altitude and decided to turn back. Treipel teamed up with Aufschnaiter, while Harrer and Kopp hiked together. On May 17, 1944, they saw prayer flags marking a pass—the heights of Tibet. Shortly after, they reached their first Tibetan village, described by Aufschnaiter as:

> ...six flat-roofed houses on a hill, tiny fields and a few people, mostly women, dressed in black. We were in a different world, barren and almost uninhabitable, but wonderfully beautiful.

The people too were quite different—strange, self-willed, but intensely human. A strange environment, and yet somehow we do not feel we are strangers.

A day later they were in Toling, the seat of the ancient Guge Kingdom. Treipel saw his goal of Japan slipping further away and suddenly decided to turn back. Aufschnaiter, accompanied by a Tibetan, forged on: he met up with Harrer and Kopp in Gartok.

The governor of the tiny summer camp of Gartok knew something of the outside world, and decided it was not fair to send the escapees back into captivity in India. He was willing to give them a travel pass allowing them to carry on east to Tradun if they swore to return from that point via Mustang to Nepal. Aufschnaiter and Harrer later used this travel document to trick every official they subsequently met into believing they had the right to travel eastward across Tibet, toward Lhasa. Aufschnaiter even dispatched a letter to the King of Mustang to back up this ruse.

After staying in Tradun for several months, Hans Kopp decided to head south into Mustang, believing Nepal to be a neutral place where he could remain during the war. And then there were two: Aufschnaiter and Harrer were directed to proceed to Kyirong, close to the Tibet-Nepal border, where they expected to be deported to Nepal:

> When we reached Kyirong in January 1945, we felt as if we were in paradise. After months spent in a highland landscape devoid of trees and shrubs, we were suddenly transported into a region that could compare with the most beautiful parts of the Alps. The slopes, covered directly with dark green forests, rose almost directly out of the valley to mighty shining snow peaks.

The pair of fugitives rested up in this idyllic alpine village for ten months, staying at a simple inn. There was time to regain their strength, lick their wounds—and polish Tibetan language skills. And even time to try out some winter sports—like skiing. Harrer recounted how he carved some skis from birchwood. But before he or Aufschnaiter had a chance to use them, he was summoned before the governor, who implored him not to ride on wooden planks in the snow. Local farmers complained that 'flying' was the sole privilege of the demonesses, who would surely destroy the next harvest if Aufschnaiter and Harrer took to skiing the slopes.

Caravaneers take a tea-break. On the boil is yak-butter tea; horse and mule saddles are used to form a temporary windbreak. On their long march across Tibet, Aufschnaiter and Harrer encountered rough-and-ready caravaneers—who were not always friendly.

The POWs took a long break in Kyirong—with plenty of time to reflect on the past. Aufschnaiter kept his past to himself—he was highly secretive, and modest about his achievements. He was born in Kitzbuhel, Austria on November 2nd, 1899, son of a master carpenter. From an early age, he developed a passion for skiing and mountain climbing, joining various expeditions in the region close to his home. In 1917 he was called up to serve in WWI—he was subsequently captured and interned. After the war, he went to Munich to study, graduating as an agricultural engineer in 1927. In the meantime, he had pursued a quite different career in mountaineering, starting from the time he joined the Munich Alpine Club in 1921. In 1929, Aufschnaiter was the leader of the first German Himalaya expedition to climb Mt Kangchenjunga in Sikkim. He led another expedition two years later, remarkably reaching the altitude of 24,500 feet without oxygen—the attempt was foiled by constant threat of avalanche. During this attempt, his team breached a region bordering on Tibet: Aufschnaiter was bewitched. He wanted to see the Himalayas from the Tibetan side. And now his wishes were granted—though not under the best of circumstances.

In November 1945, Aufschnaiter and Harrer decided they could no longer remain in a state of limbo in Kyirong. They sneaked out one night and made a break northward, on a circuitous route to try and

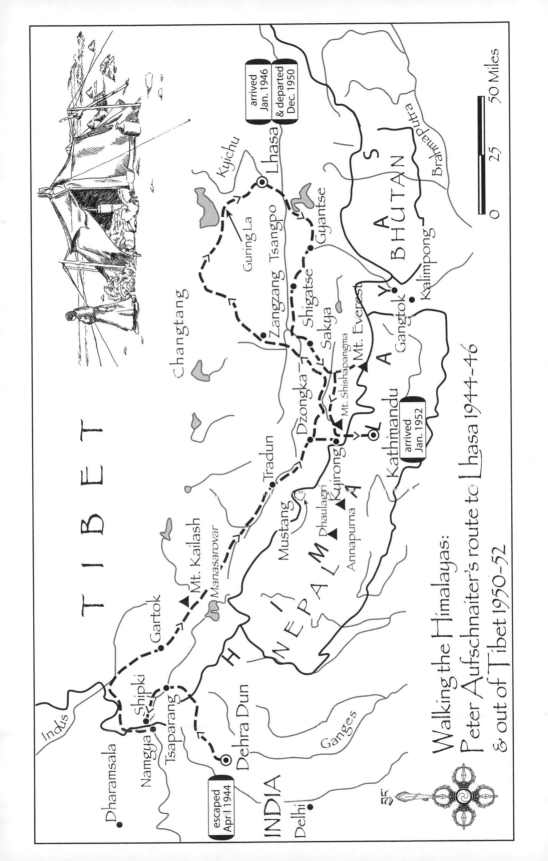

TIBET

Indus

Dharamsala

Shipki
Namgya
Tsaparang

Gartok

Mt. Kailash
Manasarovar

Changtang

Kyichu

Guring La

Zangzang Tsangpo

Lhasa

arrived
Jan. 1946

departed
Dec. 1950

Shigatse
Gyantse

Sakya

BHUTAN

Brahmaputra

Gangtok

Kalimpong

Mt. Everest
Dzongka
Mt. Shishapangma
Kyirong

Tradun

Mustang

Dhaulagiri
Annapurna

HIMALAYAS

NEPAL

Kathmandu

arrived
Jan. 1952

Dehra Dun

INDIA

Delhi

Ganges

escaped
April 1944

Walking the Himalayas:
Peter Aufschnaiter's route to Lhasa 1944–46
& out of Tibet 1950–52

0   25   50 Miles

A pack-yak with wooden saddle and rug, ready to transport goods. Yaks are good pack animals, but they hate to be ridden.

reach Lhasa. When questioned, they variously claimed to be on pilgrimage, or else said they were making their way to salt stores in the north. They dodged hunger, severe cold, bandits and a raft of other hazards. The walk across Tibet was arduous, but on a brighter note, they managed to skip the entire war. They had their freedom, and they were in a dreamland of stunning landscapes and strange people.

Aufschnaiter loved snow, loved high places, loved solitude. Tibet had all these in abundance—and one special quality that mesmerized Aufschnaiter: its profound silence. A number of explorers in Tibet have remarked on the hypnotic quality of silence in Tibet, partly due to the absence of modern machinery of any kind—no trains, no cars, no radio. Combined with pristine Himalayan vistas, this quality most likely enhanced the development of meditation arts in Tibet. Giuseppe Tucci wrote about 'its vast silence that at once humbles man and uplifts him.' Tucci's expedition photographer, Fosco Maraini, waxed poetical on silence. He claimed that the defining elements of Tibet were butter, bones and silence. Yak-butter gets into everything—into tea, in lamps, as a cosmetic, used for every conceivable purpose. As for bones, Maraini writes:

> ...nowhere else in the world, so far as I know, do you see so
> many carcasses, skulls, thigh-bones, vertebrae and ribs scat-

tered along the roads, outside the houses, along the mountain passes... The bones of animals are not buried, or hidden from sight, or destroyed; they are just left, like stones on the road outside the doorstep.

And then Maraini weaves the butter, the bones and the silence together:

Modern science talks of a four-dimensional space-time continuum. Tibet consists of a four-dimensional space-silence continuum. There is the yellow, ochre silence of the rocks; the blue-green silence of the ice-peaks; the silence of the valleys over which hawks wheel high in the sun; and there is the silence that purifies everything, dries the butter, pulverizes the bones and leaves in the mind an inexpressible, dreamy sweetness, as if one had attained some ancient fatherland lost since the very beginning of time.

On January 15, 1946, Aufschnaiter and Harrer slipped past dozing sentries at the West Gate of Lhasa. The Austrians were exhausted, penniless, and dressed in rags—and their knees were much the worse for wear after an amazing trek of 1,500 miles over rough mountainous terrain. It was one of the greatest escapes of all time. Their training as extreme mountaineers gave them the grit and muscle to accomplish this incredible feat: few could have survived such an ordeal. Hiking over the Himalayas had taken 21 months, including a pit-stop of four months in Tradun, and ten months in Kyirong. This persistence in overcoming hardship so astounded Tibetans in Lhasa that they took a shine to the Austrians. The Tibetans never tired of hearing how the POWs had deceived those along the route to reach Lhasa—their story brought tears to the eyes of delighted listeners.

But in other quarters, reception in Lhasa was frosty, especially at the British Mission. Although the war was over, the POW camp in Dehra Dun was still operational—and Aufschnaiter and Harrer had escaped from that camp. The head of the British Mission, Hugh Richardson, had experienced a great deal of trouble with a German expedition under Dr Ernst Schafer in 1939. Schafer and his five-man crew of 'scientists' and filmmakers bumbled their way into Tibet, stayed a few months, and left just a month before the outbreak of war between

Britain and Germany in 1939. The expedition was patronised by Herr Himmler and the Ahnenerbe, or 'Ancestral Heritage' office of the SS. This bizarre institution carried out archeological digs at various sites around the world, trying to give scholarly credence to German racial superiority.

Expedition motives were complex. There was definitely an element of spying: Schafer made a detailed map of Tibet, which would come in handy if Tibet turned out to be a good location to launch attacks on British India. A bit of light ethnic research: measuring up Tibetan heads to check for the origins of the Aryan race. Some delving into occult Tibet, which probably would have delighted Hitler. Another objective was to establish relations with Tibetan nobles, to tell them that Germany was the most powerful nation on earth, and to swap swastikas with them. The Tibetans use both clockwise and counter-clockwise versions of the ancient *sva-as-tika* as sacred and auspicious symbols. The Nazis stole the symbol around 1920 and set it on an angle—and tarnished it forever. Although rounds of swastika-swapping with nobles in Lhasa proceeded well for the Schafer expedition, the Germans were stoned for taking pictures during a religious festival involving the state oracle. They were lucky to escape with their lives.

Aufschnaiter and Harrer were not German—they were Austrian. But then so was Hitler. At first the British attempted to evict the Austrians from Lhasa, but Harrer pleaded he was unable to leave due to a medical condition—severe sciatica. Hugh Richardson decided the Austrians were harmless and helped them make a case. Besides which, the athletic Harrer made a fine tennis opponent for Richardson. Harrer constructed a tennis court at the British Mission—not out of grass or clay, but from compressed yak-dung. And he played bridge at the British Mission. Richardson found the Austrian pair useful for carrying gifts to the Dalai Lama: for reasons of protocol, he could not manage this himself.

When they first arrived in the Sacred City, Aufschnaiter and Harrer lodged with the Master of Electricity—a noble called Thangme, who was Lhasa's chief electrical engineer. Not long after, they received an invitation to live in a side building on the Tsarong estate. They had gone from being penniless beggars in rags right to living at the wealthiest estate. Tsarong House was among the most opulent mansions in Lhasa—a modern concrete structure on the southern outskirts of Lhasa with glass windows, a modern library, and even a working bathroom. It was filled with modern gadgets imported from Calcutta. But the gadget the Austrians were most interested in was on the roof: a radio aerial. Tsarong's radio gave the Austrians access to stations around the world—they were able to listen to news for the first time in two years. And Tsarong had newspapers and magazines 'delivered' from Calcutta—including copies of National Geographic.

Aufschnaiter and Harrer had metamorphosed from POWs into gentlemen of status. It was a fairytale transition. There was one detail, however, that did not fit. They shuffled off their rags and got new clothing, but it was harder to change their accents. Lhasa was the most sophisticated town of the Tibetan world—a place peopled with aristo-crats who spoke their own toffee-nosed dialect. There was also a regal form of Tibet, spoken at the palace. Aufschnaiter and Harrer spoke like country bumpkins—they'd picked up their Tibetan from peasants and nomads. This was rather like showing up at Buckingham Palace with a strong Cockney accent: it elicited guffaws of laughter from officials in Lhasa. By contrast, Hugh Richardson, the head of the British Mission in Lhasa, spoke impeccable Lhasa dialect with a British twang.

But Tsarong got a real kick out of the earthy speech of the Austrians because he himself had once been a country bumpkin. Dasang Dadul Tsarong was around 60 years old—a short stocky man with broad shoulders and hair done up in two topknots. The double topknot indi-cated noble rank—though to Western eyes, it gave the wearer a comic Mickey Mouse touch. Tsarong was not born a noble. He was born a commoner—the son of an arrow maker from central Tibet. Engaged as a retainer at the Summer Palace, he worked his way up the ranks to become the 13th Dalai Lama's personal assistant. In 1910, he fought a brave rearguard action against Chinese soldiers that saved the Dalai Lama's life.

An extraordinary change of fortune was in store for Dasang Dadul. In the political turmoil of 1912, Tsarong Shapé, head of the powerful Tsarong family, was accused of being pro-Chinese and was beheaded at the Potala: his son and several ministers were similarly dispatched on the same day. This left Tsarong Shapé's lineage without a male heir. In order to preserve the family lineage, a solution was proposed: that Dasang Dadul step in and fill the void. He married the widow of Tsarong Shapé's son as his first wife, and the eldest daughter of Tsar-ong Shapé as his second wife (later he married two more daughters of Tsarong Shapé). After he was firmly established at Tsarong House,

Dasang Dadul was promoted to Supreme Commander-in-Chief of the Tibetan Army. He also became Master of the Mint, responsible for producing Tibetan money. Between the marriages and the mint, Tsarong was a very busy man.

It was no accident that Aufschnaiter and Harrer were invited to stay with the progressive Tsarong family. The jovial Tsarong was into all things foreign. His moves to modernise—and his involvement in a 1924 showdown in Lhasa with conservative forces—had cost him his position as head of the Tibetan Army. Although he'd lost much of his political power, he was reckoned to be one of the richest men in Tibet due to his trading enterprises. The wealth and the trading allowed him to indulge in importing the latest gadgetry from India. Tsarong was the voice of reform: he wanted a stronger Tibetan army with modern weapons. He wanted Tibetan embassies abroad. He wanted to drag Tibet headlong into the 20th century—removing centuries of dust—but his reformist words fell on deaf ears, rejected by suspicious lamas.

Tsarong's domestic arrangements were complicated even by Tibetan standards: he eventually had ten children by three wives, running three separate households. He was a firm believer in Western-style education and sent his children to British-run schools in Darjeeling. He gave them English names—Daisy, Nancy, Kate, Tess and George. Aufschnaiter and Harrer struck up a friendship with George Tsarong, who spoke excellent English. George was a keen photographer and filmmaker—very rare for the time. Trained by Reggie Fox, he built his own radio receiver. He brought up many things from Calcutta—gramophone recordings, diesel generators, and a motorcycle (never ridden because of a conservative ban).

Lhasa was home to a privileged aristocracy with a rigid system of ranking. Aufschnaiter and Harrer were able to dodge the whole ranking system simply because Tibetans didn't know where to slot them in—foreigners weren't meant to be in Lhasa in the first place. As a great novelty, the two Austrians were in demand at parties, which might go on for three or four days. Fairytale land, fairytale princesses: Princess Kuku-la, daughter of the Maharaja of Sikkim, was a beauty married to the heir of the powerful Punkhang family. She was a woman of considerable beauty, charm and intelligence. Her slim figure was not hidden under layers of thick clothing in traditional Tibetan style, but draped in closer-fitting silk garments. She had long eyelashes, a clear musical voice, and slowly exhaled cigarette smoke—into the faces of besotted diplomats and aristocrats. Kuku-la had received a Western education: she spoke English and French fluently, and some German. Heinrich Harrer later wrote he was most attracted to her, but under the circumstances (her marriage) could do little about it. Aufschnaiter was drawn to her charisma as well.

Aristocrats like Kuku-la and Tsarong tried to introduce Western ideas, but with little success. Even the progressive 13th Dalai Lama could make no headway. In the 1920s, the 13th Dalai Lama had some telephones installed—one of them in the Potala. Gifts from British political officers included two 1920s Baby Austin cars and a 1931 orange Dodge, carried in pieces over the Himalayas by yaks and porters—and reassembled in Lhasa by an Indian chauffeur. The 13th Dalai Lama mused about the idea of making roads and introducing motor vehicles into Tibet, but his monk advisers counselled against this.

Upon the death of the 13th Dalai Lama in late 1933, a power struggle broke out. Somehow, by default, Reting Rinpoche, an anemic-looking youth with jug ears, was chosen as regent. Another power broker, Lungshar, thought he could control the new Regent, but underestimated the man with the strange ears. During a fracas at an official function, Lungshar's arm was broken, and his Tibetan boots were ripped off him and turned upside-down. According to one version of this story, two pieces of paper fluttered out of the boots. Lungshar managed to seize and swallow one, but the other piece was intercepted. It bore the name of Trimon Shapé, a leading minister—in Tibetan lore, trampling a person's name underfoot is a magical way of doing harm, tantamount to a voodoo curse. Lungshar was thrown into the Potala dungeon, where one of his eyeballs was forced out of its socket by means of a yak's knucklebone; the other eyeball was hacked out with a knife. He died a broken man.

Meanwhile, Reting Rinpoche was instrumental in leading the search party that found the reincarnate Dalai Lama—a young child brought to Lhasa and enthroned as the 14th Dalai Lama in 1940. Reting Rinpoche was fond of motorcycles and played football regularly—and he had some disturbing sexual peccadillos. The randy bi-sexual regent worked his way through both the clergy and the wives of aristocrats. After 'retiring' from his post, Reting Rinpoche was replaced in 1943 by ultra-conservative 73-year-old Regent Taktra, who set about banning everything European and modern. He banned the use of motorcycles, bicycles, felt hats, modern leather boots or shoes, and foreign-made leather saddles. All of which would serve to explain why Aufschnaiter and Harrer stood out like sore thumbs in the streets of Lhasa in 1945. The foreign clothing restrictions did not apply to the handful of foreigners resident in the capital. Aufschnaiter wore a tweed jacket, woollen trousers and battered Panama hat; Harrer wore a suit. In colder weather, they wore trench coats.

During their five years in Lhasa, Aufschnaiter and Harrer were privileged to experience a fantastic world seen by very few outsiders. There were only four other Europeans resident in Lhasa of the late 1940s: three of them were connected with the British Mission in Lhasa. Scotsman Hugh Richardson came to Lhasa in 1936 as first official representative of the British government in Lhasa. He stayed until 1940, then returned for a second period from 1946 to 1950. In August 1947, the British Mission in Lhasa was replaced by the Indian Mission—but since Richardson spoke excellent Tibetan and knew everybody, he was asked to represent the new Indian government.

Reginald (Reggie) Fox came to Lhasa in 1937 as radio operator for the British Mission and stayed on, marrying a Tibetan woman and starting a family in Tibet. One of Fox's duties was spying on the Chinese Mission in Lhasa—intercepting their radio transmissions. A young RAF officer, Robert Ford, was brought to Lhasa from May to October 1945 to replace Reggie Fox on leave, and so did not cross paths with Aufschnaiter and Harrer then. But when 'Phodo' returned to take up a contract with the Tibetan government in the summer of 1948, he stayed a year to set up Radio Lhasa—and interacted with the two Austrians. Ford was trying to set up a radio network in Tibet: in 1949, he left Lhasa to establish a radio relay in the town of Chamdo, near the Chinese border.

A latecomer to Lhasa in the 1940s was Nedbailoff, a White Russian refugee fleeing from Stalin's dictatorship. He had been interned in the same camp at Dehra Dun as Aufschnaiter and Harrer. Nedbailoff had been wandering around Asia for a considerable time—he had walked right down through China to Calcutta. In 1947, when the British threatened to deport him back to the USSR—to certain death—Nedbailoff fled toward Tibet. The British caught him near the Tibetan border, but he was allowed to remain in Sikkim because of his skills as a mechanic. In the summer of 1949, Nedbailoff was hired as assistant to Aufschnaiter and Fox to install the generators for the new Lhasa hydropower project.

A handful of Western visitors passed through Lhasa during the five years Aufschnaiter and Harrer were resident there. French journalist Amaury de Reincourt visited in 1947. Italian Tibetologist Giuseppe Tucci managed to gain entry in 1948. In 1949, American radio journalist Lowell Thomas and his son visited. And in early 1950, CIA agent Frank Bessac and White Russian Vasili Zvansov sought refuge in Lhasa after being ambushed by border guards in the north.

Modern technology was never a high priority in the monastic-dominated world of the Tibetans. Indeed, technology even took a few steps backwards: the Tibetans lost the art of bridge-building, for instance. In the 15th century, master bridge-builder Tanton Gyepo built many structures—his masterpiece was a suspension bridge made of iron chains at Chaksam, near Lhasa. The invading British found this bridge derelict in 1904. In 1938, Tsarong arranged for fabricated steel sections to be portered in from India—to complete the only steel bridge in Tibet, near Lhasa. The ancient Tibetan art of bridge-building remained strong in Bhutan, however, where elaborate wooden structures are found.

There were more oracles than engineers in old Tibet. Aufschnaiter found himself in a very unusual position: he was the sole trained engineer in a land of zero engineering. Aufschnaiter had plans to modernise Tibet's sad lack of engineering—and to improve its agricultural practices by importing seed and so on. He can lay claim to being the first foreigner ever employed in the service of the Tibetan government, starting in December 1946. After the British Mission folded in 1947, Robert Ford and Reggie Fox followed in his footsteps, taking contracts with the Tibetan government. They talked about ranking: Ford joked he would become Minister of Radio Communications. If that were so, Aufschnaiter would be Chief Digger and Minister of Agriculture. Harrer dabbled in lots of things—teacher, tennis coach—but did not gain official status until 1948. He had plans to modernise education—to open schools and the first Tibetan university. Aufschnaiter wrote in a letter to Sven Hedin, dated 25 March 1948:

> The Dalai Lama is now fourteen, a healthy and fresh looking boy. Up to now we have seen him twice, the last time at the New Year, when we joined the line of monks and Drogpas [nomads]

who daily file past him and the Regent to receive his blessing...
The Tibetans treasure their independence above all things, and
every decision is taken almost exclusively from this single point
of view...Harrer and I feel very grateful to this nation, and sometimes think of taking Tibetan nationality.

Meanwhile, Aufschnaiter was digging Lhasa. This was virgin ground:
Tibetans are afraid of digging because they believe it disturbs the spirits of the earth. It certainly disturbed the worms—in the course of the
work, women diggers would run away screaming when a worm surfaced. Worms had to be carefully relocated to a safe home. This gave
rise to a memorable line in the movie *Seven Years in Tibet* where a
Tibetan worker holds up a worm and says: 'In a past life, this innocent
creature could have been your mother.'

Aufschnaiter was asked to dig several drainage canals around
Lhasa in 1947. Following the success of these, he was asked to construct a dike to stop the annual monsoon flooding of the Dalai Lama's
Summer Palace grounds. A whole new raft of problems arose: workers would disappear after being paid because they couldn't see the
point of continuing to labour when they had enough money for the
next few weeks. Aufschnaiter and Harrer finally recruited beggars, but
after several days of pay, they drifted back to their old trade. Finally
500 bodyguards of the Dalai Lama had to be bought in to finish the
job. An unexpected result of digging by Aufschnaiter was archeological finds—the first in Tibet. These digs—unearthing artifacts hundreds
of years old—were of particular interest to visiting Italian scholar, Professor Tucci.

After bouts of digging and dike-making, in 1947 Aufschnaiter
turned his attention to surveying. He'd been asked to survey the town
because distribution of electric mains and installation of a sewer system in Lhasa would required a good map. In its long history, Lhasa
had never been properly surveyed. Aufschnaiter conducted the survey
with measuring tape and an antique theodolite belonging to Tsarong.
Harrer assisted: in the centre of town and at the Summer Palace, they
were not allowed to use measuring tape because it offended religious
sensibilities, so they had to pace out distances just like the pundits. A
National Geographic photographer on assignment in India learned of
the plan to survey the Holy City from Tibetan traders, and dispatched
a gleaming new theodolite to Aufschnaiter to use.

At the time, Aufschnaiter produced the most accurate map of Lhasa ever drafted—surveying 600-odd buildings. This sparked a new sport, whereby nobles crowded round the map-in-progress—a huge draft on paper—to try and pinpoint their place of residence. Aufschnaiter's map of Lhasa was so accurate that it was used as the basis for Western cartography of Lhasa from the 1990s onward. By then, there were radical demographic changes: the city's population expanded ten-fold, with a skyline filled with Chinese-built apartment blocks and highrises. Most of the original 600 Tibetan stone buildings surveyed by Aufschnaiter had been knocked down to make way for Chinese concrete structures.

The map was mostly Aufschnaiter's work, but Harrer claimed joint credit in his later articles and books—odd for someone not trained as a surveyor. Credit for making the map must have led to friction between the two. Copies of the final work were made for the Tibetan government and the Dalai Lama. Harrer handed over a copy to Frank Bessac to give to the American government. This copy was a scroll that measured five feet by nine feet.

Harrer and Aufschnaiter stayed at Tsarong House for almost two years. Having established good incomes, they moved on to their own mansions. By early 1948, Aufschnaiter was living in a simple rural cottage at Perong, five miles east of Lhasa to be closer to the new hydroelectric project he was working on. Harrer took over a house from the Serkang family: it had lots of modern glass windows, and was sited right opposite the residences of the Dalai Lama's family, near the Potala. He lived a gregarious lifestyle, mixing it up with Lhasa nobles, while Aufschnaiter lived like a recluse on the fringes of town. After leaving Tsarong's house, the two Austrians saw much less of each other. Aufschnaiter explained that he was very busy—too involved in his work for such socialising.

In the movie *Seven Years in Tibet,* it is ironic that Aufschnaiter comes off as a more likeable character than Harrer. British actor David Thewlis plays Aufschnaiter with such convincing compassion that he seems to be the truly enlightened one in the film. Thewlis virtually embodies the Buddhist ideals to which Harrer aspires but does not attain (the Dalai Lama apparently attempted to convert Harrer to Buddhism, but was unsuccessful due to Harrer's lack of interest). And Aufschnaiter wins the hand of lovely Pema, in competition with Harrer.

Fiction or fact? Somewhere between the two, it seems. When interviewed much later, Harrer said he considered dallying with Tibetan

Fact or fiction? In the movie *Seven Years in Tibet*, Aufschnaiter's character (played by David Thewlis) marries a pretty Tibetan tailor called Pema (played by Lhakpa Tsamchoe).

women, but could not find any condoms—and so thought better of it because of the risk of syphilis. But on a more practical note, there was less chance of this occurring if staying with one woman. Aufschnaiter wrote in letters that he planned to spend the rest of his years in Tibet and he was thus thinking of marriage to a Tibetan woman. There were precedents. British radio operator Reggie Fox married a Tibetan woman and had four children—with fair hair and almond eyes. And a British signalsman in Gyantse had twice been married to Tibetan women.

Aufschnaiter appears to have set up with his housekeeper, who may have been a local woman—or could have been from a noble family from the east. An aristocratic residence in Lhasa of the 1940s contained a servants' quarters, with a cook, cleaner, horse-handler and so on. When the master went out on horseback, a servant would usually accompany him to assist with tasks. Aufschnaiter's country house in Perong employed several Tibetans—and it seems the housekeeper was not living in the servants' quarters. This was a very casual arrangement, and Aufschnaiter did not broadcast the fact. Robert Ford, who visited Aufschnaiter house outside Lhasa several times, met the Tibetan woman in question, but said she was never presented as anybody special. The liaison was low-key.

This 'arrangement' would've been quite possible in Lhasa of the day. There was a surfeit of women in a land where up to a quarter of the male population dedicated themselves to being monks. When CIA agent Frank Bessac passed through Lhasa in 1950, a pretty young woman was 'offered' to him. She stayed with him for the duration of his visit. Harrer elaborated, 'sometimes it happened that a pretty young servant girl was offered to one, but the girls don't give themselves without being courted.' In Bessac's case, courtship lasted two nights. Then the woman was his nightly companion for as long as he was in Lhasa, which was about a month. Harrer and Aufschnaiter met Bessac and learned of his bizarre tale: he and his American cohort Mackiernan, along with three White Russians, had been gunned down when attempting to enter Tibet from the north on an important diplomatic mission. Frank Bessac and Vasili Zvansov survived: the others did not. Both Bessac and Zvansov were paired up with Tibetan women in Lhasa.

British radio operator Robert Ford was offered a 'temporary wife' after he arrived in Chamdo in 1950. He declined the offer, citing several obstacles. One was the high incidence of venereal disease and absence of condoms; the second was personal hygiene, which the Khampas were not big on—rarely bathing. At a dinner get-together, however, Ford found himself flirting with Pema, a pretty young Khampa woman. When she asked what he thought of Khampa women, he said he thought they were very beautiful. '...I looked at her rosy-cheeked oval face, full lips and clear black almond eyes. Her lips smiled invitingly, her eyes flashed, and she stroked her cheek.' This gesture had a precise meaning in Khampa courtship rituals: it meant she had the hots for him. Usually, if an interested man caught a girl's eye, he would pull the lobe of his ear, or, if a Khampa, would rub the crown of his head. Responding to this, the woman would stroke her cheek (If not interested, she would look away and raise her chin). Dragged onto the dance floor, Ford joined in a boisterous circle, indulging in loud singing and foot-stamping. But within several days, the Khampa maiden was claimed by another man.

In the 1920s, a Tibetan called Ringang pulled off a remarkable feat. Ringang was sent to England in 1913 as part of an educational experiment. He studied engineering at London University and Birmingham University, and returned to Tibet fired up with a dream: to harness the plateau's mighty hydro power. Against all odds, he arranged for hydro-electric components from Birmingham to be shipped to India and then carried over the Himalayans to Tibet. Because porters were not enamoured of their heavy burdens, some loads disappeared over cliffs 'by accident'—leaving the project with parts missing. But eventually,

Ringang got the hydroelectric plant functioning in 1928. It was used to power a coin press. A few years later, the mint was moved closer to Lhasa at Drapchi, with power still supplied from the same hydro plant brought in by transmission line. The mint workshop extended to producing banknotes, rifles and cartridges.

However, as the machinery wore down, and little maintenance work was done, Ringang's pet project languished. By 1947 (by which time Ringang had passed away), the old power-house was practically out of commission. Lhasa's élite powered everything with generators using batteries brought in from India. Making banknotes at Drapchi Mint was under the direction of Tsarong. Work was hampered by frequent power failures. When an urgent need to bring out a new commemorative issue of 25-sang banknotes arose, George Tsarong suggested using a 10hp diesel engine he'd imported from India for home lighting. He was unsure how to use it, but Reggie Fox used the same-size engine to power up the Indian Mission. Under the guidance of Fox, George got the diesel engine working and the mint was able to print the new banknotes.

This exposed the shortcomings of Drapchi: constant use of a small diesel engine would not be adequate for future needs. So Tsarong proposed a new hydroelectric power station be imported from India. Fox advised that bringing heavy equipment overland from India was impractical: it was decided to purchase several lighter-weight pieces—three 125-kilowatt hydroelectric generating plants from England. Aufschnaiter wrote in 1947:

> Since an expansion of the old works (on the Doti River) was not a possible option, I was requested by a commission headed by Thangme, Tsarong and Fox to see whether a new electric station, powered by the water of the Kyi Chu, could be built. The Kyi Chu, which even in the winter was a big river, swelled in summer to a mighty torrent.

The new power project—meant to provide all of Lhasa with electric lighting—got under way in late 1947, but was interrupted while Aufschnaiter completed his survey of Lhasa. The power project resumed again in 1948. Although Tsarong was Master of the Mint, his son George was in charge of Shangdap hydroelectric project. George invited Nedbailoff up from Gangtok to work on the project. According to Ford:

Peter Aufschnaiter with the team involved in a new hydropower scheme for Lhasa. From left to right: Tsedon Thubetn Tsenlek (monk official), Mr Reid (contract manager of General Electric, India), Tsarong (finance minister), Peter Aufschnaiter (chief engineer), and Reggie Fox (British radio operator in Lhasa).

Aufschnaiter had done all the spadework—literally—for the hydroelectric scheme, and Fox had designed the plant. Nedbailoff came to help him install it.

Freeze frame: a photo taken by George shows the power-station crew, minus the elusive Nedbailoff. Who is in charge? It could be George, it could be Aufschnaiter—but in the photo credits, George says it was Tsedon Thubten Tsenlek, a monk official who stands at the left in robes—perhaps appropriate if Lhasa were to be illuminated. Next to him stands Mr Reid, contract manager of General Electric in India, who was invited to plan and estimate the cost of transmission line and city lighting. Next in line is Tsarong senior. Then a smiling Aufschnaiter, the surveyor—standing tall—and finally Reggie Fox. The project was doomed—it was never completed, due to circumstances way beyond Aufschnaiter's control...

Tibet remained neutral through both world wars. Tibetans passed the days of WWII and up to 1950 in blissful ignorance of what was happening in the world. The monks offered prayers for their friends the

British in their great war—and that was about the extent of Tibetan participation.

In 1942, two American intelligence officers, Brooke Dolan and Ilya Tolstoy arrived in Lhasa to negotiate overflying 'The Hump'—a mountainous piece of Tibet lying between southwest China and northern India. This was an essential air-link to by-pass Japanese lines in Burma. In December 1943, an American B-24 bomber flying The Hump got blown off-course and circled Lhasa at night, believing it to be an Indian town. With no radio response from the town and rapidly running out of fuel, the crew decided to parachute out of the plane. The first plane to arrive in Tibet crashed into a mountainside at Tsetang— just like Shangri-La. Startled villagers in Tsetang fed the airmen and clothed them in fur-lined garb. Escorted to Lhasa, the airmen faced mobs angered because they'd flown over the Potala Palace, thus committing great sacrilege. The airmen were quickly hustled out of the country.

Picnics were the big thing in Lhasa in the summers. Nobles were out in force, cruising the Kyi Chu river in yak-hide coracles, shaded under parasols. Embroidered tents were set up on islands in the Kyi Chu, with willow-shaded resting spots that served ten-course luncheons. Digestion was eased by the pleasant refrains of the Tibetan lute, the *damnyen*. Peasants—men, women, children—bathed nude on the banks of the river.

Lhasa's social calendar was chock-full of religious and secular festivals: New Year festivities, horse-racing and stone-lifting competitions, masked Tibetan opera performances. Betty Sherriff at the British Mission introduced the Tibetans to table tennis and croquet, noting that the lamas used their long robes to manoeuvre the croquet balls into better positions. Harrer and Aufschnaiter introduced the sports of tennis and skating. The Austrians realised Manning's fantasy—what the Tibetans called 'walking on knives'—by repairing skates left behind by British diplomats.

British diplomats gained a foothold in Lhasa in 1936, when the British Mission was established to counter the influence of the Chinese Mission, across town. The Chinese had set up this up in the early 1930s under the pretext of a special mission to convey condolences following the death of the 13th Dalai Lama. The same mission had a radio transmitter installed in Lhasa, which got British hackles up— they were determined to match this with a British radio transmitter.

In the early 1930s, the Tibetans lent Colonel Leslie Weir and his family a house called Dekyi Lingka (Garden of Happiness), which eventually became the home of the British Mission. One of the reasons British officials liked to visit Lhasa was to collect plants from this botanically rich area. At the outbreak of WWII, the Mission was headed by plant-hunter Frank Ludlow, and later by botanist George Sherriff. A side-effect of this was the development of a dazzling garden at the British Mission. The exact nature of the British Mission was vague—it never had any official status, although it flew the Union Jack to irritate the Chinese Mission. Lhasa hosted only one other foreign envoy—at the Nepalese Mission.

Men carrying car: importing a car into Tibet in the late 1940s was a bit of a problem. For one thing, there were no motor roads, just caravan tracks. The shell of this car, a Humber, is being carried over the Himalayas by a team of porters—it was a gift for the Dalai Lama. The engine arrived by the same method, as did the wheels—and the fuel.

Easily the most subversive idea introduced by the British Mission was the game of football. The Brits set up the Mission Marmots, which took on an opposition team from the Nepalese Mission, and later a Tibetan team formed from the robust men who served as the Dalai Lama's bodyguards. A constant problem was theft of the goalposts for firewood. Footie became all the rage in Lhasa, with 14 teams in competition: football boots were even on sale in the market. The clergy regarded the sport as thoroughly evil—a great threat to social and cultural stability. In 1944, a hailstorm erupted during a football match—an event regarded as highly inauspicious because of the damage hail caused to crops. Seizing upon this, conservative Regent Taktra banned the game.

The lamas of Tibet were determined not to become slaves to the gadgets and whirring wheels of the industrial age. But certain innovations did appeal. Technological marvels of the 1930s and 1940s were introduced by the British Mission. The Dalai Lama, then a young boy, delighted in receiving gifts brought from Calcutta by the British

The 14th Dalai Lama, painted in a temple fresco. In the late 1940s, the 14th Dalai Lama—then a teenager—met both Aufschnaiter and Harrer in Lhasa.

Mission—a pedal-car, a bicycle, a toy train set and picture books. Also arriving in saddlebags from Calcutta were 16mm movie reels. During WWII, Allied troops were shown the Hollywood Shangri-La epic *Lost Horizon* to bolster hope in world peace by showing the legend of Tibet—a sanctuary of peace and serenity, a repository of wisdom. But in Tibet itself, head lamas and high officials were clamouring for Charlie Chaplin movies.

The addiction of cinema proved so great that the 14th Dalai Lama, then a boy, asked Heinrich Harrer to construct a projection-room at his Summer Palace in the winter of 1949. Harrer powered it from the engine of an abandoned car. By the spring of 1950, when the Dalai Lama returned from the Potala, the projection-room was ready. The Summer Palace, known as the Norbulingka ('jewelled garden'), was in full bloom with peach and pear blossoms. Roaming the extensive garden grounds were peacocks and deer; bar-headed geese swam in the lakes. This place delighted the young Dalai Lama, who far preferred it to the gloomy Potala. And now he had more reason to like it, with his own movie theatre. His preference in film was for animal adventure and non-violent stories.

The Red Army was on the way, but the Tibetans reckoned their protector gods and high mountain barriers would stall them. The sheer scale of the invasion took Tibetans by surprise: there were about 40,000 Chinese troops amassed in the east. The Tibetans fielded no more than 5,000 troops.

A short stroll to the east of the Norbulingka, the British Mission ran its own mini-theatre, with a projector operated by Reggie Fox. Movie night at the British Mission could easily last four hours at a stretch, with an audience of nobles and dignitaries and their families packed into a tiny room—some 60 or 70 souls. Spencer Chapman described the odour in the projection-room as 'the clinging musty smell of old silk robes, smothered by the rancid pungence of monk and servants' butter-sodden garments.' To attune those who'd never seen an 'electric picture', Fox would start out by showing a 16mm reel shot in Lhasa. Next up might be Rin-Tin-Tin—a tremendous hit with so many requests to view it that the British became heartily sick of the wretched film.

An unreal air pervaded Lhasa: the nobles were picnicking and watching Chaplin and Rin-Tin-Tin movies while war raged across Europe, Asia and Africa. Lowell Thomas Jr, who visited Tibet in 1949

One dramatic reason why Aufschnaiter's engineering skills were in great demand: river crossings were dangerous affairs in Tibet. This bridge is somewhat advanced for old Tibet: it was supported by wires, and people walked on wooden boards placed on animal skins, which were held together by leather straps.

just before Chinese invasion, suggested appropriate gifts to bring to Lhasa:

Incidentally, Reggie Fox, who runs the Dalai Lama's 16-mm projector, said that 16-mm Tarzan films or Marx Brothers films would make a big hit with the Dalai Lama and those around him.

Closer to home, in China, the Marx Brothers were on the way—in a more sinister guise of Mao Zedong, Zhou Enlai, Lin Biao and Zhu De. On August 15, 1947, the Union Jack was pulled down at the British Mission and the Indian national flag was hoisted—the newly independent Indians simply inherited Britain's entire infrastructure in Tibet, including the post offices and trade agencies. In Lhasa, the same staff were kept on under Hugh Richardson because nobody else spoke such good Tibetan.

There were only a handful of radio transmitters in Tibet in 1950—at the foreign missions (Indian, Chinese, Nepalese), one owned by the Tibetan Government, one owned by Tsarong. After setting up Radio Lhasa, Robert Ford rode east to set up another relay point in Chamdo. He left Lhasa in charge of a caravan of 20 riding animals, 80 mules and yaks, ten muleteers, 40 porters, and an armed escort of 12 soldiers: besides all the radio equipment, he took 400 gallons of petrol for the engines to run everything. In October 1950, when a desperate official from Chamdo radioed that the Red Army was invading, he was told that the Lhasa cabinet could not be disturbed because they were at a picnic on the banks of the Kyi Chu River. The radio transmitter in Chamdo suddenly went dead.

The Chinese claimed the object of their invasion of Tibet was to root out all foreign imperialist oppressors. There were exactly six foreigners living in Tibet at the time: three of them were former prisoners-of-war from Dehra Dun; the other three were British. The Chinese captured their first foreign 'spy'—Robert Ford. Harrer and Aufschnaiter knew their days were numbered.

In Lhasa of 1950, Aufschnaiter had pretty much everything he dreamed of having: a high-ranking position with the Tibetan government, a house in the country, a Tibetan woman. And more than this—he

Visiting Lhasa in better days: the Marahani of Sikkim (at left), Yangchen Tsarong (middle) and Princess Kula Namgyal (at right) at a festival in Tibet in the 1940s

had limitless opportunities to innovate and assist the Tibetan people, whom he had grown very fond of. Tibet was virtually untouched: Aufschnaiter didn't even know where to start when it came to projects for agricultural engineering. The scope was enormous. Aufschnaiter had few relatives left in Europe: he planned to live in Tibet for the rest of his life as a small-estate owner and special consultant to the Tibetan government.

Another great attraction for Aufschnaiter was the mountains: apart from Everest, few Himalayan peaks had been attempted in Tibet—here was a vast playground for an avid mountaineer. Up until this point, British climbers had monopolised access to the peaks in Tibet. But with Aufschnaiter's inside position with the Tibetan government, it would have been easy for him to wrangle permits.

Aufschnaiter never got the chance to tackle the virgin peaks. Dark clouds were gathering in the east. Aufschnaiter was a soldier in WWI: in the Dolomites, he was captured and held in a POW camp for nine months. He spent more than four years in Dehra Dun POW camp in WWII. Now a different kind of war was on the horizon—and threatened to make him captive once again. Neither he nor Harrer could envisage life under the Chinese—they knew they would most likely be arrested as spies.

On December 20, 1950, the Dalai Lama and his entourage departed Lhasa, to decamp in the Chumbi Valley and negotiate at a safe distance with the invading Chinese. Aufschnaiter and Fox departed the same afternoon. Harrer accompanied the Dalai Lama's caravan to the

Yak-hide express boat: departing Lhasa for parts south was often done by floating downstream on the Kyichu River to Chushul—an overnight trip of one day on smooth waters (with boatmen singing), as opposed to two bumpy days of riding horses. Aufschnaiter left this way in December 1950 as Chinese troops advanced toward Lhasa.

Chumbi Valley. In Gyantse, February 1951, Harrer crossed paths again briefly with Aufschnaiter— who asked Harrer to take his baggage on to Kalimpong in India.

Harrer left Tibet in March 1951, crossing the border to Sikkim, but Aufschnaiter was intent on staying in Tibet as long as he could. He travelled light and dropped out of sight: nobody heard from him for a period of almost a year, leading to rumours that he had died or had been captured by the Chinese. Princess Kuku-la from the royal family of Sikkim even sent out a search party to look for him in southern Tibet. But Aufschnaiter was not lost—he simply kept on walking. As the communists advanced from eastern Tibet, Aufschnaiter was on the move in central Tibet with his friend Draba Angdi—sleeping rough in scores of basic tents and simple houses of the Tibetans along the way. While this must've been arduous at times, exploring was what Aufschnaiter loved to do—it gave him a great sense of inner peace. He loved the simple nomad lifestyle. He was a Tibetan nomad at heart: he said they were just like Tyrolean shepherds. He explored the high mountain ranges—visiting Rongbuk and climbing to Camp I on Everest. He scaled lower Himalayan peaks to gain viewpoints to sketch maps of unknown parts of the Himalayas. Although aerial pictures were taken of Mount Shishapangma in 1950, Aufschnaiter was the first Westerner to sight and photograph the peak on land from the vicinity of the basecamp. He fixed the position of Shishapangma, the only 8,000-metre peak lying wholly within Tibet—and the last of the world's 14 highest peaks to be explored and climbed.

Finally, he drifted down to the village of Kyirong—the place where he and Harrer had spent ten blissful months previously. Aufschnaiter

Nomad tents made from yak-hair, with the tent-ropes also woven from yak-hair

held out in Tibet as long as he could, crossing the border into Nepal on January 22, 1952. He arrived in Kathmandu six days later.

In August 1950, Hugh Richardson, head of the Indian Mission in Lhasa (and the ex-British Mission), had departed Tibet—ostensibly into retirement, but in fact to plead Tibet's case at the United Nations. After the Chinese invaded, Richardson accompanied a delegation to New York to lobby for the Dalai Lama's appeal for help at the UN. But only El Salvador had the courage to condemn the unprovoked invasion of Tibet. The British delegate at the UN, pleading ignorance of the events, asked that the matter be deferred.

In 1959, when a Tibetan uprising was put down with ferocious brutality, Chinese military occupation was complete. Again at the UN, when a joint resolution was put forward on the dire situation in Tibet, the British delegate abstained from voting. Hugh Richardson bitterly concluded: '...the British Government...sold the Tibetans down the river...I was profoundly ashamed...' India turned its back on Tibet—as did America and a number of European nations. The best that could be mustered at the UN were some stern resolutions warning the Chinese not to break the UN Human Rights Declaration (which China blithely ignored). And that was it. A thousand years of Tibetan civilisation down the tubes, abandoned to the clutches of the Chinese, keen to exploit Tibet's untapped wealth.

Newly created after WWII, the UN was specifically set up to prevent another Holocaust. An important part of the UN charter is that if a situation like wholesale ethnic slaughter were to occur (as in Germany) then the UN members would have to act to stop it. Tibet was the first test case, and the UN did absolutely nothing. What fits the definition of 'genocide' is still debated at the UN today. It's all a matter of semantics: at what point can 'genocide' be declared? When 30,000 people have disappeared? When 100,000 have been killed? When half a million have been systematically exterminated? The sad case of Tibet represents the first failure of the newly formed United Nations to act on its mandate—to stop deliberate genocide. And a number of other cases would follow: from Cambodia to Rwanda. Subverted in its chief mandate, the UN simply has no moral authority left.

In 1952, Heinrich Harrer's book *Seven Years in Tibet* was published in German. It came out the following year in English, becoming an instant bestseller. In the book, Harrer speculated about Aufschnaiter:

> He is still a willing exile in the Far East, endeavouring to satisfy his insatiable thirst for exploration. There are few men alive with such a thorough knowledge of the Himalayas and the 'Forbidden Land' as he possesses. What will he not have to tell when he returns to Europe after all these years?

But Aufschnaiter was very different in character to Harrer: he remained silent about his experiences, living like a hermit in Nepal—working as an agricultural expert for the Nepalese. Aufschnaiter was the more pure adventurer of the two. Martin Brauen, his friend and biographer, claims that Aufschnaiter was in deep shock over the fall of Tibet, but also mentions that he did not wish to exploit his Tibetan experiences for personal gain. Unlike Harrer—who went on to become a very wealthy man from his various projects, receiving generous commissions from National Geographic, Life Magazine and other prestigious publications.

This must've been hard for Aufschnaiter to take: knowing that he was barely making ends meet, yet his former climbing partner was making money hand over fist by selling their story—rapidly becoming a millionaire. Harrer's *Seven Years in Tibet* is one of the biggest-selling books on Tibet ever written. But in the book, Harrer gives Aufschnaiter scant credit for his leading role in both the climbing expedition and the escape. Aufschnaiter was the expedition leader at Nangpa Parbat—something that Harrer glosses over. The flight to Tibet was only made possible by Aufschnaiter's extensive knowledge of Tibetan language, acquired during months of imprisonment at Dehra Dun. He studied Tibetan customs, religion and history, and was plotting out escape routes. Aufschnaiter had the knowledge that got them through. Harrer deftly edited Aufschnaiter out of most of his Lhasa story, or resorted to using a nebulous 'we' at key places—for an audience with the Dalai Lama in Lhasa, 'we' means the two Austrians. Other times, he referred to Aufschnaiter as his 'associate' or 'companion', but not by name.

Upon arrival in Kathmandu, Aufschnaiter was hosted by Major Kaisher Bahadur, the former head of the Nepalese Mission in Lhasa. Kathmandu in 1952 was very different place from the buzzing tourist Mecca it is today. The town was quiet, with high mud walls—and no concrete. There was only one paved brick road. There were no buses, no taxis, no trishaws, and fewer than a hundred vintage cars. No crowds, no radios blaring, few newspapers. The mountains were always in view except during the monsoon. Nepal had been closed to foreigners for a lengthy period under the aristocratic Rana family. In 1951, when the Rana Prime Minister resigned, King Tribhuvana regained power and set in place a new dynasty. His elaborate coronation in 1951 entailed invitations to delighted foreign guests, which sparked thoughts of tourism. And so the doors to Nepal opened a crack—though these were early days.

Aufschnaiter stayed Kathmandu from January to November 1952 and was transferred to Delhi (against his will) to work on Tibetan frontier maps for military purposes. He was based there from January 1953 to September 1956. Aufschnaiter had leave periods during this time—he took the opportunity to return to Europe for the first time in over a decade. There he met Heinrich Harrer, and caught up with news on fellow adventurers in Tibet. After departing Tibet, Nedbailoff found safe haven in Australia, working as an electrical engineer. Reggie Fox, the radio operator in Lhasa and Aufschnaiter's associate on the hydro project, started up a radio operator school in Kalimpong—but succumbed to various illnesses and died in 1953. Robert Ford, the radio operator in Chamdo, was held in dark dank dungeons for five years—subjected to constant interrogation by the Chinese. He was released in May 1955 and returned to England, where, by bizarre coincidence, he married a woman by the name of Monica Tebbett. He wrote a book about his experiences in Tibet, entitled *Wind Between the Worlds* (published 1957). Then he embarked on journeys to more trouble-spots— landing up in the fiery cauldron of Vietnam.

Aufschnaiter learned that he and Harrer had been very lucky with their wartime escape: the other escapees from Dehra Dun POW camp had passed some miserable years. The strangest story belonged to Rolf Magener and Heins von Have, who were trying to reach the Japanese lines in Burma. They both spoke fluent English: the pair kept up their disguise as British officers, bluffing their way to Calcutta, over a thousand miles away from Dehra Dun. They used forged documents, and shared railway compartments and station restaurant tables with unsuspecting British passengers. Switching disguise to Swiss businessmen, they took a river boat upstream and started to walk toward Burma. After some hair-raising adventures, they surrendered to the Japanese—and came close to being executed as spies. After exhaustive questioning by Japanese intelligence agents, they were declared genuine—and were thrust into a room full of journalists in Rangoon. They were front-page news in Japan, where they ended up working as Honorary Consuls in the German Embassy in Tokyo for the duration of the war. Magener even settled into married life—he wed Doris von Behling, who was working for the German Air Attaché in Tokyo.

When the Japanese surrendered in 1945, the American army arrested Magener and von Have, not believing their story about escape from Dehra Dun. They were not released by the Americans until August 1947—a year after all other prisoners in Dehra Dun had been set free. In Germany, the Americans held them prisoner briefly once again. Finally gaining his freedom, Magener went on to become a prominent businessman, working for corporations like BASF and Mercedes. He wrote a book about his war experiences—in German entitled *Our Chances were Zero* (published in English as *Prisoners' Bluff* in 1954).

Back in India, Aufschnaiter had a surprise reunion with Hans Kopp, who was working on a dam project on the Sutlej river. Kopp was the third POW in Tibet from the 1944 escape bid from Dehra Dun. And he was the third POW of the group to write a book in German about his experiences. In English, his account was published in the mid-1950s under the whimsical title *Himalaya Shuttlecock*—which refers to Kopp's desperate crossing of the Himalayan range six times during several escapes (twice reaching Tibet). After leaving Aufschnaiter and Harrer, Hans Kopp had headed south into Nepal, which he believed to be neutral—but was actually pro-British. He was recaptured by the British and sent back to the camp at Dehra Dun, where he joined Sattler and Treipel—two other escapees from the original group of seven.

On leaves in India, Aufschnaiter climbed in the Garwal Himal. He got lots of ideas from a climbing circle of Sherpas—among them, Tenzing Norgay, whom Aufschnaiter had met in Lhasa in better days, when Tenzing was sirdar on a 1948 expedition with Giuseppe Tucci. Aufschnaiter met Tucci again, too, in Nepal. Tucci was intrigued by Aufschnaiter's discovery of unusual frescoes in caves in the Nepalese region of Mustang. Tucci wrote:

> What surprised me most, and what I admired in him, was his remarkable simplicity, a gentleness of spirit, and the fact that he preferred to be alone rather than with people. The mountains were his real home, and simple people his companions... He was a living example of a man who had gained in silence and peace, in contemplation and meditation, that sense of spiritual freedom which was praised by the Buddha as the ideal for suffering humanity.

Returning to Nepal, Aufschnaiter went to work as an agricultural engineer for the Swiss Association for Technical Assistance (NGO group in third-world countries). In 1957, he took up a post in Nepal with the UN Food and Agricultural Organisation. To strangers, Aufschnaiter appeared to live in a state of chaos. He preferred to live in a single room. At the best of times, his entire possessions were packed up in 17 suitcases—and he spread the entire contents all over the room on arrival. George Tsarong bumped into him on the streets of Calcutta. 'Peter was a recluse,' he said. Michel Peissel, who met Aufschnaiter in Kathmandu, described him as a withdrawn—shellshocked by the fall of Tibet. Aufschnaiter was suffering from an ailment rare for a foreigner: the loss of a homeland that was not his to begin with, but which became his. He had post-invasion-shock-syndrome. Many Tibetan refugees suffered from it—and a number went crazy—or died from it. They simply could not handle the loss of their great culture and their homeland.

The first road connecting Kathmandu with India was not completed until 1956. For the rest of Nepal, supplies moved as they had for centuries—on the backs of mules and porters: it was a case of hoofing it. And that's what Aufschnaiter loved to do. His real home was the mountains. He was at his happiest in the mountains with few possessions, camping out under the stars. This was a time when trekking was unheard of in Nepal, although mountaineering had opened up since 1950. And Aufschnaiter was a true pioneer in the sport of trekking in Nepal: a hardy hiker who was also a mountaineer. Aufschnaiter had been granted Nepalese citizenship, which enabled him to get to areas like Dolpo and Mustang—long before any other foreigner. Visiting Mustang allowed him to actually roam part of the Tibetan plateau and relive the lifestyle of Tibet.

Meanwhile, in 1959 in Tibet, the situation had taken a serious turn for the worse. While co-operation between the Dalai Lama and the Chinese appeared to work for a period, revolt against the Chinese was simmering. In March 1959, fighting erupted in Lhasa, with monks taking up arms against the Chinese. Tsarong, the generous Lhasa host of Aufschnaiter and Harrer, was arrested in the uprising and perished in prison. According to Heinrich Harrer, Tsarong always carried a small bag of diamond splinters with him—if he ever got into problems and was taken prisoner, he said he would swallow the splinters.

The Dalai Lama fled into exile, riding out of Tibet with a guard of Khampa warriors. After reaching Sikkim, he made a long haul back westward across India, by train to Mussoorie. Mussoorie is near Dehra Dun, the same place Harrer and Aufschnaiter had escaped from. The Dalai Lama had escaped from Lhasa to Mussoorie in a mirror route from that of the two Austrians. And the Dalai Lama arrived, like Harrer and Aufschnaiter, as a refugee—no passport, no status—having lost everything.

Tibetan refugees crossed into Nepal, Bhutan and Sikkim in droves. Aufschnaiter, who was in semi-retirement, rallied to the cause. He acted as translator and mentor—a compassionate move on his part. He carried on with his selfless NGO-related work in Nepal until poor health got the better of him. As well as hiking into remote Tibetan enclaves in Nepal, like Mustang, Aufschnaiter managed to pull off one brief visit back to Tibet—though just across the border, not to Lhasa. Aufschnaiter had a lot of trekking mileage on him by the time he reluctantly left Nepal, and headed back to Austria for medical treatment. In fact, he had more mileage on him than any Western adventurer to Tibet—in the course of walking across Tibet to escape the British to reach Lhasa, walking back across Tibet to escape the incoming com-

munist Chinese, and then trekking extensively across Nepal in ensu-
ing years.

On his deathbed, he whispered that his most beautiful memories
were of the times when he was in Tibet—walking, walking under open
skies in the mountains, with just the sound of bar-headed geese honking. He died in Kitzbuhel, the town of his birth, on October 12, 1973—
just shy of his 74th birthday.

In the mid-1990s, the long-departed Aufschnaiter found fresh fame
among Tibetans through the translation of *Seven Years in Tibet* into
the Tibetan language. The book has been translated into over 50 languages—but translation into Tibetan is a rarity. This version, appearing
in 1995 (or 43 years after the German original edition), was published
by the Amnye Machen Institute in Dharamsala—run by a group of
Tibetan scholars trying to drag Tibetans headlong into the modern
world by providing translations of authors like George Orwell and
Vaclav Havel. Very few texts from the Western world have appeared
in the Tibetan language—most of what has been translated consists of
religious texts from India and elsewhere.

More fame for Aufschnaiter came with the release of Annaud's
movie in 1997. The movie found an emotion-charged audience among
Tibetans-in-exile in Dharamsala, India (the movie is banned in Tibet
itself). In the town's video theatres, Tibetans could see Tibetan actors
and actresses up on the screen for the first time in a big-budget
Hollywood-style movie. And experience the optical illusion of Lhasa
of the 1940s, recreated as huge sets in the wilderness of Argentina.
Among the 'actresses' was Jetsun Pema, sister of the Dalai Lama, who
played her own mother in the movie. Jetsun Pema, who'd never acted
before, said it was an amazing experience to step back in time onto the
set of a recreated Lhasa. No doubt boosted by the popularity of the
movie, the book *Seven Years in Tibet* had racked up sales of over 10 million copies worldwide by 2004.

Seeing the movie potential, Harrer himself had been involved in
a celluloid version of the book in 1957. Directed by Hans Nieter, the
black-and-white movie *Seven Years in Tibet* was more like a documentary than a drama. It featured voice-overs from Harrer, with himself in
the lead role—playing himself, naturally. This hokey melodrama was
eminently forgettable—it was badly put-together, badly acted, and had

an atrocious soundtrack. Harrer revealed himself as a goofball when it came to commentary on Tibetan Buddhism. The only saving grace of this low-budget movie was that it contained real footage of the 14th Dalai Lama shot by Harrer himself.

For four decades, directors had tried to bring the book to the silver screen, but none succeeded. The trouble lay with the story. It was a tremendous journey but Harrer told it like a trip to the corner grocery store—as one critic put it. The book had no focus—it told many stories, thrown together without a cohesive narrative. It lacked a beating heart, a theme. There were blisters on the feet, but no blisters of the heart. French director Jean-Jacques Annaud finally got the story up on the big screen in 1997, by embroidering Harrer's story and taking considerable liberties with it. Scriptwriter Becky Johnston focussed on the coming-of-age of the Dalai Lama and his friendship with Harrer, and added in the unknown story of Harrer's pregnant wife and his longing to see his son, plus hints about his Nazi background. A tale of redemption: crass egoist Harrer discovers his better qualities in Tibet. Facts were altered to make the story more dramatic: the scriptwriter had the Austrians arrive in Lhasa while WWII was still going on; the movie claimed the Austrians were the only foreigners in Tibet at the time; and the story left Harrer still in Lhasa when Chinese troops invaded in 1951.

Aufschnaiter had one last trump card to play—as author of a posthumous book entitled *Eight Years in Tibet*. The title was a deliberate swipe at the over-inflated ego of Heinrich Harrer. But Harrer's book *Seven Years in Tibet* was hardly unique in its title anyway: two books published long before his were *Three Years in Tibet* (Ekai Kawaguchi) and *Twenty Years in Tibet* (David MacDonald). Heinrich Harrer, the longest-lived of the original group of seven escapees from Dehra Dun, went on to author a number of books about Tibet and the Tibetan realm—though none as popular as his first. In 2003, his hefty autobiography *Mein Leben* (My Life) was published in German (it later appeared in English translation under the title *Beyond Seven Years in Tibet*). The books are all sold at Harrer's own museum in the town of his birth—the Harrer Museum in Huttenberg, Austria. Harrer died in Huttenberg at the age of 93 in January 2006—a man who lived a very full life of high adventure.

Like Thomas Manning, Aufschnaiter's eccentric streak lies in his silence—and his secrecy. Aufschnaiter stuck to his guns, stuck to his principles. He had fabulous stories to tell, but he committed little to paper. And like Manning, others later collated what he wrote for eventual publication. Aufschnaiter's earliest visit to the Himalayas was as part of an expedition to Kangchenjunga, led by Paul Bauer of the Munich Academic Alpine Club. Starting in 1939, Aufschnaiter had studiously kept maps and surveys of the remote Tibetan regions of his travels, and also letters and shorthand notes. In the 1950s, Paul Bauer urged him to assemble this material into a book, and even arranged for typing out his notes by two Swiss women in Kathmandu. But the book idea went nowhere, and Aufschnaiter appears to have shelved it.

The Brauen family had not forgotten, however. Some years after Aufschnaiter's death, scholar and friend Martin Brauen put together a biography, with letters, notes, reports, observations, cartography, sketches and photographs from Aufschnaiter. It was published in German in 1983, but it was not until 20 years later—and nearly 30 years after Aufschnaiter's death—that this reached a wider audience, when it was published in English as *Eight Years in Tibet* (2002). The book is a rough diamond, more a series of impressions than a carefully crafted account. In the back jacket is a reproduction of Aufschnaiter's painstaking map of Lhasa, though not at its original size of five feet by nine feet.

Lobsang Rampa at home in Montreal, with crystal ball, circa 1972. This picture was taken by publisher Alain Stanké, who discovered upon developing it that a weird light and ghostly patterns had crept into the film somehow. And this would not be the first time this happened when attempting to photograph Rampa.

Lobsang Rampa
1910–1981

Reincarnate Lama? Bigamist?
Omniscient Guru? Imposter?

Tales from the Three-Eyed Lama

Concerning a New Age guru, cats with occult powers & some stellar voyages

❖　　　　　　　　　　　　❖

What is reality? What is truth? Tibetan monks have been debating the nature of reality and illusion for centuries. In 1956, along comes an Englishman who sparks debates of a similar sort. Is he real? Is he telling the truth? Well, according to his cult following, if Rampa did not visit Tibet in person, he certainly did in spirit— the ultimate astral voyager. At the cutting edge of paranormal and occult phenomena emerges a highly unlikely guru—and New Age trailblazer. Rampa created so much of a stir that he had to bid a retreat from the news hounds—to find refuge in Canada.

❖

BACK IN THE 16TH CENTURY, Confucian scholar Wan Hu strapped himself into a wooden chair with 47 rockets attached. When he ignited the rockets, he perished in a massive explosion. Despite this failure to get off the ground, today he is regarded as China's first rocket scientist—and honoured with monuments. Some 400 years after Wan Hu vaporised himself, the Chinese space program achieved his lofty dream. In October 2003, astronaut Yang Liwei blasted into orbit to become 'China's first space-probing warrior', as the official news media rapturously phrased it. The nation that invented gunpowder and rockets had finally recaptured its glorious past—and could look to a bright future competing in the frontier of military weaponry in space.

Overshadowing the achievement was a disappointing statement by newfound hero Yang Liwei. When asked if he had seen the Great Wall from outer space, he replied that he had not. He thus exploded a widely held belief that the Great Wall is the only man-made object that can be seen by the naked eye of an orbiting astronaut. For decades, Chinese elementary-school textbooks proclaimed that their most famous creation was visible from space. These have to be rewritten: the Great Wall cannot even be made out from a low orbit of the earth.

Far more successful at getting off the ground are the Tibetans. The concept of astral travel is built into Tibetan legend and common belief. Tibetan deities, demi-gods and high lamas seem to have no trouble flying through space—and transcending time while they're at it. Many high lamas are credited with magical powers like levitating, hovering and outright teleporting. And the power of being in two places at the same time—and being able to direct their rebirth into a specific body. The legendary King Gesar of Ling got around on a flying horse. Tibetan Buddhist masters were said to shoot up sunbeams to mountain tops (the dwelling places of the gods) and to cross the Himalayas on flying tigers.

But the Tibetan lama who showed up in London in 1956 was a bit hard to take at face value. For one thing, he didn't look Tibetan. For another, he had apparently developed a mental block to speaking the Tibetan language. But he swore black and blue that he was Tibetan, and he could explain everything clearly. With a Devonshire accent.

The third eye is a feature shared by numerous deities in the Tibetan pantheon, like this one appearing in a temple fresco in Tibet

In November 1956, British publisher Secker & Warburg came out with a book titled *The Third Eye*. It proved to be the publishing event of the year, a runaway bestseller. Purporting to be the autobiography of a Tibetan lama and doctor called T. Lobsang Rampa, the book detailed the painful opening of the Third Eye, the wisdom eye, the power to see things clearly.

In the Tibetan pantheon, there are numerous three-eyed deities—particularly wrathful ones. The third eye is sited vertically on the forehead, between the two regular eyes. One meditation technique used by a Tibetan practitioner is to close the eyes and imagine connecting with the mystical third eye of a particular deity. For instance, he or she might imagine the light of divine wisdom emanating from the third eye of Manjusri and entering into his or her own 'third eye', filling the consciousness with clarity.

Rampa's use of the third eye was rather different—he claimed to use it to read auras. He said he was initiated at Chakpori Medical College in Lhasa at the tender age of eight: to put it bluntly, a hole was drilled in his forehead to enable him to see auras, which in turn enabled him to divine the intentions of those around him. However, in traditional Tibetan medicine, surgery is never used, so this seemed a bit

In *The Third Eye*, Rampa claims to have used his special third eye to read the auras of high-level visitors to the Potala (while in the service of the 13th Dalai Lama, seated at left)

far-fetched. Trepanation—drilling holes in the head—was an ancient Egyptian and Sumerian specialty. Rampa also described 'temple cats', who attacked those trying to steal jewels from shrines—a concept also of Egyptian origin. In *The Third Eye*, Rampa wrote about monks flying around on giant kites and sightings of yetis. Most remarkably, Rampa claimed that he was hired by the 13th Dalai Lama to hide behind a screen and read the auras of members of a visiting Chinese delegation to determine if their intentions were honest or treacherous. Rampa determined that the auras were full of hate.

Just as Rampa's book was about to be published, Heinrich Harrer came into London to see his British publisher Hart-Davis, which was moving great quantities of *Seven Years in Tibet*—a book that had no competition. Until Rampa loomed on the publishing horizon, that is. The publisher was very concerned about Rampa muscling in on their turf. Harrer looked over the galleys for *The Third Eye* and declared it to be a literary swindle, and a complete fraud as a documentary report (he later pinpointed more than a hundred slip-ups in the book). He requested a meeting with Rampa to enable him to chat to him in Tibetan about Lhasa. The publisher received back word that the lama was in a mediation retreat and could not be disturbed under any circumstances. Several other Tibet experts, such as Marco Pallis and Hugh Richardson, were also keen to find out the identity of this mysterious author. Richardson challenged Rampa to meet him face-to-face to debate the authenticity of the story—in the Tibetan language if he so desired (which Rampa evidently did not). With no responses forthcoming from the Rampa publishing camp, the Tibetologists regrouped and hired a private detective, Clifford Burgess, who went undercover and slipped into one of the lama's séances as a student. Burgess reported that Rampa wore a mighty beard, and delivered his talks while lying in bed stroking two Siamese cats. Among the students were several members of the English aristocracy. House cats are rare in Tibet—and Tibetans do not sport beards. Burgess conducted more investigation to unmask the true identity of Rampa—this enlightening data was duly passed along to the press.

In January 1958, when *The Third Eye* was at the height of its success, the *Daily Mail* revealed that Doctor Rampa was in fact not a Tibetan monk—but the unemployed son of a plumber from Devonshire by the name of Cyril Henry Hoskins. The *Daily Mail* claimed he was married to a registered nurse by the name of Sarah Anna Pattison. Further investigation revealed the extent of Hoskins' medical background was that he'd once been employed in a company making surgical fittings—actually, making corsets. In fact, he had originally submitted two manuscripts to publishers: one on Tibet, the other on corsets. And his experience of other-worldly phenomena seems to have been limited to a stint when he was employed as an accident photographer.

After the *Daily Mail* story broke, Rampa was hounded mercilessly by reporters from rival newspapers. He got a visit from some dim-witted detectives who demanded to see his Tibetan passport. Finally, having reached the end of his tether, Rampa decamped with wife and cats in tow. He took up residence at a cliffside mansion in the seaside resort of Howth, near Dublin. Rampa claimed the move was necessary because of seriously failing health—the same reason that he refused to give interviews to reporters. He also developed a mysterious mental block in speaking Tibetan: he refused all contact with Tibetans. The publisher, Fred Warburg, recounts an incident in his London office

MAP OF THE MIND OF RAMPA

Actually, this is Rampa's coat of arms, used on his letterhead. Instead of heraldic lion supporters, Rampa's crest features two Siamese cats, holding a candle aloft over the letters TLR (Tuesday Lobsang Rampa). On the heraldic shield, symbols shown clockwise from top-left are: the Potala Palace, a Tibetan prayer wheel, a crystal ball, and the author's books. At bottom is the motto 'I Lit a Candle'. Enclosing the entire design is a Tibetan rosary of 108 prayer beads.

where he spoke a few words in Tibetan that he'd practiced with a Tibetologist: *Did you have a nice journey, Mr Rampa?* When Rampa realised what language he was using, he fell to the floor writhing like an epileptic. Recovering his composure, he told Warburg never to use the Tibetan language ever again. Rampa said that because he had been tortured by the Japanese during WWII, he had developed a complete aversion to his own language and was in complete agony when he heard it.

In the interests of a better PR image, Fred Warburg dispatched his own writer to track down Rampa at his Irish lair. The man he sent was young Eric Newby, later to make his mark as one of England's greatest travel writers. Rampa's residence in Howth was a fort-like structure backed onto a cliff overlooking the sea. The Rampa entourage was under virtual siege from members of the press, keen to bag a story. It was an early case of persecution by paparazzi: the press hounds were going through Rampa's garbage, and trying to spy over high walls with periscopes. None had made it through the front door.

Newby gingerly approached, explaining his official mission from the publisher, but he was repulsed. The best he could manage was a brief exchange through the letter-slot of the front door with Mrs Rampa. Madame Rampa said she would relay his questions to Rampa, whom, she mentioned, was on his death-bed. Newby refused to give up so easily. He was insistent on seeing the lama, and eventually the plump matronly Madame Rampa allowed him a brief face-to-face. And what a face it was: Rampa was one weird-looking dude. Newby describes the lama as having a long nose, luminous, powerful eyes, a beard, a completely bald head and a high-domed forehead with a slight dent in it (not a third eye).

By promising to show the lama in a more favourable light than the hatchet job of the *Daily Mail*, a photographer from the *Daily Express* actually managed to take some pictures. When these were later being developed, the photographer was shocked to discover a ghostly effect. 'He had a ruddy great halo round his head!' was how he put it. Maybe there was something to this aura business after all.

Citing a heart condition, Rampa refused to meet any Tibetologists face-to-face—or any reporters for that matter. He responded to accusations through reprints and new translations of *The Third Eye*. For one reprint, he adamantly insisted he was telling the truth—the whole truth—and had his wife contribute a piece as a sworn witness. And then a slightly different tack emerged. Cyril Henry Hoskins had offi-cially changed his name to Carl Ku'an So, with Lobsang Rampa being his nom-de-plume for books. In 1958, in response to reporters' ques-tions, his wife asserted that her husband had written *The Third Eye* for the real Dr Ku'an, a Tibetan whose family was in hiding from the Chi-nese Communists. For security reasons, she said Dr Ku'an's identity could not be revealed. If true, Rampa was the ultimate ghostwriter.

And a very rich ghostwriter at that. *The Third Eye* had become a bestseller in the US and Europe—where it was translated into a dozen languages. It was running neck-and-neck in bestseller sales with Hein-rich Harrer's *Seven Years in Tibet* (first published in English in 1953). So Rampa followed up his phenomenal success with a sequel, *Doc-tor from Lhasa* (published 1959). He acquired a cult following. He received an enormous amount of fan mail from readers. He milked his fans, shamelessly indulging in spin-off marketing—selling meditation robes, incense, instructional audiotapes, you name it. From being an unemployed layabout, Hoskins had metamorphosed into a very rich guru, held in high esteem by scores of readers.

But not held in high esteem by the press. The British press hounds were having a field day. An attractive young woman, Sheelagh Rouse, had moved into the Rampa household. She was either an adopted daughter or Rampa's secretary—or perhaps both—but the press started rumours flying about bigamy. Sheelagh Rouse was somehow con-nected with a publishing associate of Rampa's—the press made out that the evil Rampa had 'poached' his colleague's love-interest.

Fed up with the unwanted attention, in 1960 Rampa and entourage fled Ireland for the Land of the Red Indians (as Rampa phrased it). That translated to the quiet seaside town of St John, New Brunswick, on the east coast of Canada; the 'entourage' consisted of Mrs Rampa, Sheelagh Rouse and several cats. Here, Rampa could quietly work on new books. Sheelagh Rouse typed the new work up, and Mrs Rampa proofed it for errors. And what the cats did, we may never know.

Despite his huge success, the three-eyed lama was evidently ran-kled by his detractors. His behaviour as a writer would have been per-fectly acceptable if he labelled his works 'fiction', but Rampa stuck like Velcro to his identity as a real lama, most likely because this is what gave the books their credibility and their authority. If written by an ordinary Englishman, the sales figures certainly would not have been the same.

To confound the skeptics, Rampa penned a third book, *The Rampa Story*, making an autobiographical trilogy. *The Rampa Story* was completed in Windsor, Canada, and published in the UK in 1960. In the book, he tried to weasel his way out of monstrous contradictions. He made the startling claim that he was a Tibetan lama who had transmigrated—shifted souls—into the body of an Englishman after his own body had been rendered useless through illness and debilitation and unemployment. In other words, he was the spirit of a Tibetan lama who had possessed Hoskins' body, and Hoskins had been snuffed out. This was later identified in New Age lore as the 'walk-in' phenomenon—someone had walked in on Hoskins and taken over his soul—or hijacked it, whatever.

In *The Rampa Story*, Lobsang claimed he left Tibet in 1927. After lengthy voyages as a Tibetan monk and doctor through civil-wartime China, he was captured by the Japanese, tortured, and sent to Hiroshima. When the atom bomb was dropped on Hiroshima in 1945, Rampa seized the opportunity to escape (*are you still with us?*). He made it by fishing boat to the Russian coast, and then to Moscow, and set off across Europe to deliver a stolen Mercedes. When encountering various Mafia types with knives or broken bottles, he simply dispatched them with his knowledge of martial arts, learned from the great masters of the east.

Then he went to America, and finally back to Tibet, which he found occupied by the Communists and not to his liking—

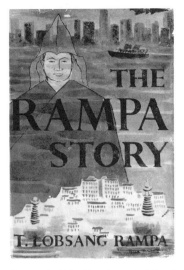

Rampa's third book, published in 1960, is not a sequel but a prequel—explaining his early life.

While Rampa's books were selling like hotcakes in Europe, back in Tibet, this man was moving millions of copies. By the 1960s, the little red book of quotations by Mao was compulsory reading in Tibet at enforced commune meetings

The family name Rampa is as rare in Tibet as men with beards, but older Tibetans occasionally sport wispy beards, like this Rainman, pictured here sounding his human thigh-bone trumpet at the heavens. He is using the trumpet as a magic dagger either to summon rain for crops or to deflect crop-damaging storms (weather oracles handily performed both functions). There was no shortage of paranormal feats performed in Tibet for Rampa to draw on for his books. The place abounded in oracles of many kinds, both male and female.

This grainy picture shows the State Oracle, dressed in a special brocade costume with a circular mirror on his chest. As the oracle goes into a trance, a huge helmet piece (weighing in at 40 pounds or more) is strapped onto his head. Once in a trance, the oracle's strength increases considerably: he is said to dance around as if the headdress were made of feathers. Members of the cabinet pose important questions to the

oracle in a trance: the answers are delivered in high-pitched Tibetan cryptic fragments. These riddle-answers are analysed for significance in making important decisions. The State Oracle is considered a medium who conveys messages to the Dalai Lama from Dorje Drakten, a protector-deity. The 14th Dalai Lama fled Tibet in 1959 based on a consultation with the State Oracle (who also fled). Due to the rigorous demands of their position, oracles like this were not long-lived. Since 1959, State Oracles in exile in India have a dismal track record for prophecies that are on target. They have predicted a number of times that Tibet would soon be free—later modifying this to forecast a major international change that would benefit Tibet.

monks and nuns were being killed and tortured. So while in a deep meditative trance in Lhasa, Rampa succeeded in travelling by astral projection to London, England. Rampa revealed that he could transport himself in space—through astral travel or teleporting—had the power to travel backwards and forwards in time (within the same century, at least). The summer of 1949 was when he claims to have taken over the body of Hoskins, the unemployed Englishman. Hoskins fell from a tree in his garden, banged his head, and temporarily knocked himself unconscious. When he revived, his body had been usurped. The Englishman claimed to be sick of being unemployed and was only too willing to give up his body, but forewarned the good lama about the extreme mental unease of being unemployed. But no problem for the lama. Racking his brains about how to make a living, the Rampa-inherited-Hoskins-body hit on the brilliant idea of writing a book, which was, of course, *The Third Eye*.

More howlers were to follow. It was revealed that the initial 'T' in his full name (T. Lobsang Rampa) stood for 'Tuesday'. And how exactly had Rampa acquired this English first name? Was that the day that the Tibetan lama had taken over Hoskins' body? The day he fell out of the tree? Was it the day he had drilled a hole in his forehead? Wisely, Lama Rampa's publishers chose to ignore the full name in the interests of higher sales figures.

His last name is just as curious. Rampa is a Tibetan family name, but a very unusual one. Otherwise, the closest thing to Rampa is 'Lharampa', which is a high-level Geshe degree or doctorate of Buddhist philosophy. Since Tibetans place their credentials after the name, Rampa could be interpreted as a title. In that case, it would come out as 'Lobsang, Doctor of Metaphysics'.

Rampa was not the first to claim astral voyaging to Tibet, or time travel on the plateau. Not by a long shot. The crackpot founder of Theosophy, Madame Helena Petrovna Blavatsky, claimed to have visited Tibet for an extended period—if not in person, then in spirit. She said she'd spent a total of seven years in Little Tibet (Ladakh) and Great Tibet (Tashilhunpo Monastery, Shigatse). She referred to her Masters as 'the Brotherhood of the Snowy Range.' She claimed that the Mahatmas, keepers of the ancient wisdom of the lost continent of Atlantis, lived in Tibet—where they congregated to escape increasing levels of magnetism produced by civilisation. The secrets of this lineage were archived in Tibetan monasteries, according to Madame Blavatsky, who claimed to be in touch with these keepers of ancient wisdom through telepathy. Thus the secret wisdom of Tibet became the fountainhead of her newly founded Theosophical Society.

About the closest Madame Blavatsky was a Russian who travelled around the world, supporting herself by working variously as a bareback rider, pianist and medium. She married an American and emigrated to the US, where she turned herself into a powerful medium and female guru. In 1875, she was instrumental in founding the Theosophical Society in New York—a secret society with secret signs, along the lines of others like the Freemasons or the Illuminati. And for a society handbook, she wrote a monumental work of gibberish entitled *Isis Unveiled* (1877), running to two volumes and 1,500 pages of text, which she said had been dictated to her daily by a tall Hindu—what she called 'automatic writing'. While good for the spirit, the dictation was evidently bad for the body, as she barely moved from her chair during the long period of transcription. Blavatsky became somewhat monumental herself—a 'hippopotamus of an old woman' (her own description) weighing in at 245 pounds. Though publicly maligned as an imposter and a fraud, her brand of mysticism continued to flourish.

About the closest Madame Blavatsky got to Tibet was Darjeeling, in the early 1880s, where it seems that she encountered the pundit-explorer Sarat Chandra Das and purloined his knowledge about Tibet. The rest she stole from Hindu scriptures like the *Rig Veda*. Madame Blavatsky ran into a spot of bother in India after fraudulent charges were levelled against her. In December 1884, Richard Hodgson, a member of the London-based Society of Psychical Research, arrived in India to investigate. A year later, his scathing report branded Madame Blavatsky 'one of the most accomplished, ingenious and interesting imposters in history'. For good measure, he accused her of also being a Russian spy. Blavatsky left India in a huff, never to return.

Out of her Indian sojourn, Blavatsky produced her magnum opus, *The Secret Doctrine* (1888)—a monumental account of human origin and destiny, running again to two volumes and 1,500 pages of gibberish. There are some morsels that Rampa might have picked up here: Blavatsky describes the third Root Race, the Lemurians—egg-laying hermaphrodites with a third eye in the back of their heads. After they interbred with beasts and turned into apes, the Lemurians learned the arts of fire-making, metallurgy and agriculture from space-travellers from the planet Venus, which had a highly developed civilisation.

Blavatsky's books bore swastika-decorated covers—Blavatsky adopted the Vedic *sva-as-tika* symbol (known in Tibetan as *yungtrung*) as the logo for the Theosophists. The *sva-as-tika* is an ancient Vedic symbol for peace, longevity and good luck. Rudyard Kipling, who described Blavatsky as an 'unscrupulous imposter', also used the *sva-as-tika* to embellish his book covers. Blavatsky died in 1891—long before the Nazis stole the swastika from the Theosophists and imbued it with such terrible associations that the Theosophists had to abandon the logo. Then again, the Theosophists were the ones who advanced the theory of an Aryan master race or Great White Brotherhood— which the Nazis followed through on. It's hard to believe that Blavatsky's brand of gibberish could be taken seriously, yet at the time of her death, her followers were estimated to number 100,000.

Rampa himself cited the phenomenon of 'possession' of a body by another as deriving from the Theosophists. And there was another key Theosophist whose work Rampa most likely helped himself to: Alexandra David-Néel. She became a member of the Theosophical Society in 1892. The essence of Rampa's writing involves Tibetan paranormal phenomena: reincarnation, telepathy, clairvoyance, and so on—which Alexandra David-Néel investigated and introduced to the world.

In the mid-1960s, Rampa ran into a spot of publishing trouble. He met his match when he came up against some UFOlogists. The trouble came in the form of a very slim volume titled *My Visit to Venus*. This was published by Saucerian Press, run by Gray Barker, a UFO-specialist living in West Virginia. Barker was a theatrical film booker who moonlighted by making money off promoting hoaxes, particularly UFO hoaxes. In 1952, there were reports of a spaceship-riding creature in West Virginia: Gray Barker interviewed witnesses and wrote it up for a magazine. Realising that this UFO material was eliciting great interest, Barker investigated further.

In 1956, the same year that Rampa's *Third Eye* was published in London, Gray Barker's book *They Knew Too Much About Flying Saucers* was published in New York. The book gave birth to an urban legend: that after strange aircraft are observed, black-clad men descend in shiny new black shoes from shiny new automobiles and hush up the witnesses. Suggesting complicity of Western governments in a vast UFO cover-up conspiracy, Gray Barker carved a career out of writing about the sinister Men in Black, who later inspired comic books and the *MIB* movies of the 1990s. There may have even been a glimmer of truth in the MIB conspiracy, but not linked to UFOs—more likely CIA agents trying to hush up sightings of super-secret US spy planes spotted on test flights.

Gray Barker's success with his first UFO title spawned his own profitable enterprise, Saucerian Publications—which printed books under the Saucerian Press imprint and a magazine, *The Saucerian*. And here's where Rampa stepped up to the plate. In 1959, Saucerian Press was the US publisher for Rampa's second book, *Doctor from Lhasa*. A little later, Gray Barker also acquired US rights for a short story that Rampa wrote for a UFO magazine in England, about a visit to Venus. Gray Barker obviously decided there was money to be made from selling the Rampa name, so he issued Rampa's Tibetan UFO story as a separate 'book'. He padded the story out with his own introduction, plus a write-up by UFO collaborator John Keel, and Saucerian Press published it around 1966. Keel is author of *The Mothman Prophecies*, a story about a seven-foot-tall winged mothy apparition that haunted a town in West Virginia in the mid-1960s—the story was later turned into a thriller starring Richard Gere.

My Visit to Venus amounts to only 12 pages of text: padded out with illustrations and an extended preface, it came to about 30 pages. That could hardly be called a book; furthermore, the pages were photocopied and bound with homemade equipment. But it continued to sell because of Rampa's cult following. Rampa junkies would snap up any morsels from the master.

Rampa, the man who dressed in black, was pitted against Gray Barker, creator of the Men-in-Black mythos. Rampa knew that *My Visit to Venus* could damage his reputation for telling the truth, the absolute truth and nothing but the truth. Astral voyages in Tibet were one thing; astral voyages in UFO vessels from Tibet to a paradise on Venus were quite another. If Rampa wanted to stop Saucerian Press from publishing the work, he would have to go to court—and he was definitely not willing to attract public attention because of embarrassing and probing questions that might have resulted. A sensational court case would most likely cost him a fortune in legal fees, and would only have resulted in increased sales of *My Visit to Venus*.

Gray Barker was a joker who was in the business of squeezing as much cash as he could from hoaxes—his own and those created by others of similar bent. He later offered cassette tapes purporting to be the voice of Rampa, entitled 'My True Story' and 'Miracle Healing through the Power of Prayer'. Incensed, Rampa sent Barker a letter telling him that he had never recorded such a tape—and threatening him with dire consequences in the next world:

> I think you should be put in prison and the key thrown away. I can assure you most definitely that when you leave this world, you are going to bitterly regret the way you have treated me in plagiarizing my material.

Was Rampa ahead of his time? In December 1970, Russian spacecraft Venera 7 touched down on the surface of Venus, transmitting data for a short time before being consumed by the fiery Venusian atmosphere. No signs of life, but a visit to Venus had been made—and the gap between reality and science fiction had just narrowed.

Rampa continued to crank out new titles—which were snapped up by his cult followers. Among these was *Living with the Lama,* which Rampa claimed had been dictated to him telepathically by his cat, Mrs Fifi Greywhiskers. Since the creature spoke Siamese cat language, Rampa added a note at the front to the effect that he had diligently translated this Siamese into English for the reader's benefit.

Rampa seems to have gotten two very ancient cultures mixed up: the worship of cats and employing of cats as temple guardians is of Egyptian origin, not Tibetan. The Egyptians have a cat goddess, but Tibetans are not fond of cats at all. They prefer dogs. A simple reason is that cats take lives (they catch mice) while dogs are less likely to. So guardian cats never caught in Tibet on the same way guardian dogs did. And dogs are supposed to be reincarnates of monks who didn't make the grade. But nothing about cats in the same league. So from a Tibetan point-of-view, Rampa's use of cats in his books is very strange. If it was ancient Egypt, it would have been more acceptable—the Egyptians mummified their cats for the Pharaoh to take along into the next world.

Rampa and his wife doted over their cats, far preferring them to human company. And cats found their way onto the covers of later books. If you want eccentricity, go no further than Rampa's coat of arms. This sometimes appeared at the top of his letterhead, with a list of his books in the left column. In place of the normal set of rearing lions on an English coat of arms, Rampa's crest shows two Siamese cats standing on their hind legs holding up a large candle in their raised front paws, with the letters 'LTR' below. The coat of arms is divided into four quadrants: one shows the Potala Palace, while the others show a prayer-wheel, a crystal ball and some books (presumably Rampa's own books). The motto is: 'I Lit a Candle'. This feline coat of arms is enclosed by an oval string of 108 prayer beads.

Mrs Rampa shared Lobsang's passion for Siamese cats as highly evolved creatures. In a blatant attempt to cash in on the Rampa legend, Mrs Rampa wrote several books that promised to reveal the inside story with the truth about Rampa. She was well-placed for this task, after all—she was the closest to the truth. But she wrote gibberish about their Siamese cats (in books titled *Pussywillow* and *Tigerlily*). She took up writing when her husband's use of the pen was growing weaker due to worsening health. She cranked out three titles under the name Mama San Ra-Ab Rampa. 'Ra-Ab', she explained, was an Egyptian thing. Her three books, however, fail to come to the point and tell us how a lama acquired a wife like her in the first place. The simple explanation would be that she was baggage: she came with the body that the lama possessed. Hoskins was already married to her when the body was taken over. Ergo, the Tibetan lama that possessed the body inherited the wife—and she must have proved difficult to get rid of. So he made the best of the situation and employed her as his proof-reader and his nurse.

On January 7, 1971, a Rampa manuscript titled *The Hermit* landed on the desk of Alain Stanké in Montreal. This was the first he'd heard of Rampa. He went on to become Rampa's editor and agent, and more remarkable still, his confidant. Stanké, then the publishing director of Les Editions La Presse in Montreal, was living in a luxury building called Habitat 67—an avant-garde structure thrown up in the Cité du Havre for the Centenary of Canada during Expo 67. Habitat 67 was a design well in advance of its times—even today, this hodge-podge building looks futuristic, like some sort of child's bizarre toy. By coincidence, the Rampa Family was living incognito in the same jumble of buildings. So through Stanké, we catch a brief glimpse of the weird world of Rampa.

Stanké rings Rampa's doorbell. There is a long pause. Stanké is wondering how on earth to address Rampa—as doctor, master, father, brother, eminence, sir—how is an reincarnated lama addressed so as to avoid offence? The door opens: a large woman with grey hair. It's Sarah Rampa, the great guru's wife. There's a haughty air about her. She seems awkward and suspicious. Her role? Probably Rampa's nurse as much as his wife. Rampa is not in the greatest health, though he seems to have recovered somewhat from his supposed death-bed state in Ireland.

Stanké follows Mrs Rampa down a long hallway. In the air is a strong whiff of incense, perhaps sandalwood. Rampa, international man of mystery, is dressed in a black robe. Definitely a powerful presence. His head is bald with some white hair clinging to the sides; his fuzzy white beard is that of a patriarch, peppered with grey. A wart under his right nostril. Cat hairs cover his robe at pot-belly and chest level. This is his bedroom, and he appears to compose his works in bed. The room is sparsely furnished: in one corner is a motorized wheelchair; on the wall, a large map of the world and a collection of clocks—pendulum and alarm clocks. Rampa's health is declining—which explains why he spends so much time in bed. According to his nurse (wife Sarah), his body is racked with a raft of ailments—ranging from arthritis to diabetes—and he has suffered from coronory thrombosis. On the occasions when he goes outdoors, he gets around in a motorised wheelchair of the latest design.

Rampa studies Stanké with intense eyes. He tells him that he can see the colour of his aura, revealing his mental, moral and physical state. He also reads Stanké's hand and examines his handwriting. Satisfied that his guest is trustworthy, Rampa launches into a spiel on how it's all true—his books are true, everything he says is true. He reminds Stanké that he will be acting in the role of an editor, not a journalist. Rampa harbours great disdain for journalists who relentlessly harass him for interviews. He lives like a hermit, refusing to meet fans or journalists. Everything he has to say is in his books—he has nothing more to say. Rampa presents a tricky challenge for a publisher like Stanké. The guru over the years has managed to upset Catholics, teenagers, feminists—and simultaneously, both the Chinese communists and the Tibetan government-in-exile. But his greatest venom is reserved for

Rampa was a gadget man, and he had oodles of money to indulge his whims. In Montreal, in the early 1970s, he was one of the very first to own a paper shredder—which he used to destroy manuscript drafts.

journalists and literary critics who try to savage his books—or worse, his reputation.

To let off steam, Stanké says that Rampa liked to amuse himself with constructing miniature model trains, cars and boats. But his grand passion was photography. Stanké said he had all types of equipment—from Polaroid to 3-D cameras, and many lenses. Rampa confided that this passion was linked with his other-worldly research: he hoped soon to be able to photograph what he claimed to see with his own naked eye: the human aura.

As Rampa's confidence in Stanké grew, he even permitted rare photographs to be taken of himself. Stanké reports that when developed these pictures mysteriously contained ghosted images—he has no idea where these came from. Stanké captured Rampa using what was then a high-tech piece of equipment: a paper shredder. Rampa is photographed shredding manuscript drafts and hundreds of letters from fans. This, he said, was to foil admirers who had been caught in the garbage room of Habitat 67, sifting through the guru's garbage for unpublished nuggets of wisdom.

Stanké and his wife managed to see Rampa a few more times and to find out more about his ménage. Or is that menagerie? Next up: two Siamese cats, Cleopatra Rampa and Tadalinka Rampa. Cleo and Taddy are treated just like humans: they communicate telepathically with the Rampas. In the background hovers Sheelagh Rouse, a tall pretty young woman, according to Stanké, and an efficient secretary. She types out his manuscripts and sometimes illustrates them. She is said to be Rampa's adopted daughter, but rumours persist that Sheelagh Rouse is part of a ménage à trois, making Rampa a bigamist. Asked about this by Stanké, Rampa laughs it off, saying in fact he lives with four women—two female cats as well. Stanké finds out that the Rampa Family all go by nicknames—the Guv (Rampa), Ma (Sarah Rampa), Buttercup (Sheelagh), and Cleo and Taddy (the cats).

To mark the launch of Rampa's first book published in Canada,

Stanké asked if he might write a short profile for a magazine, which duly appeared, along with his photo. Rampa liked it, and on the strength of this, Stanké talked him into a much bigger scoop—an appearance on television. A profile on Rampa was filmed for TV in Montreal—the only formal interview with Rampa known to be recorded, given his extreme aversion to journalists and to public appearances. Cut to: the high lama's bedroom at Habitat 67. He is filmed in bed—with crystal ball, Tibetan prayer-wheel, his books and his two cats. Uncannily like the Rampa coat of arms (only missing the Potala). On Stanké's first attempt to film, the camera is somehow knocked out of commission. So he has to come back again the next day. The final version—edited to 20 minutes of film—was aired on CFTM-TV in Montreal.

Stanké's close contact with the lama lasted about a year and a half—till mid-1972. Stanké went on to edit a dozen of Rampa's books in French, and even three penned by Rampa's wife. Rampa read Stanké's tarot cards: Stanké says these readings turned out to be remarkably accurate. Was the man a great master of clairvoyance? Rampa showered him with expensive gifts—sophisticated cameras, the latest typewriter, a tapedeck. When Rampa sent him a present of great value for his birthday, with a card signed by his two cats, Stanké tried to return the gift. Rampa was highly insulted, saying that if he refused the gift, he was refusing their friendship—and that since he could not take it back, he would break it on the spot. He made to throw the gift on the ground to shatter it—Stanké caught it just in time, thus saving both the gift and the friendship.

The relationship was smooth until the day that a journalist wrote a mocking article on Rampa, laying doubt on his incarnation. This enraged Rampa. He asked Stanké to come to his defence by writing a letter to the newspaper in question, stating that he believed in the reincarnation. Stanké refused. Stanké was heading off for travels in Africa. Rampa abruptly left Montreal, heading west with his entourage.

Among Canada's bestselling authors, a Tibetan lama does not spring readily to mind, and yet there was one—living in quiet obscurity in Calgary. Until some Tibetan refugees found out about him. In 1971, Canada opened the door to some 500 Tibetan refugees from India. This was a one-time deal only—the doors were promptly slammed shut again on this humanitarian gesture, and no more Tibetans were taken in after that. Some Tibetans ended up in the Rockies—and eventually in Calgary. Hearing about a renowned Tibetan lama called Rampa, some Tibetan refugees tried to meet him. And like the press hounds, Rampa did his level best to ignore them.

Otherwise, Rampa had found his perfect refuge in Calgary. He even wrote at the front of the book *As it Was!* a special note for turning a blind eye to his eccentricities: '*Dedicated to the City of Calgary, where I have had peace and quiet and freedom from interference in my personal affairs. Thank you, City of Calgary.*'

When not busy churning out books, Rampa found time to follow his passion of paranormal photography. This interest started years back in Ireland when he sey about photographing nude young women to determine the colour of the body aura—a process he christened 'auric photography.' Rampa maintained the female aura is brighter than the male one, and it was necessary to have women pose nude to capture the aura. Why they had to be attractive young women is anybody's guess, but from Dublin to Calgary, he found subjects willing to pose. Drawings along these lines appeared in his instructional book *You Forever*, which cobbles together material on how to read auras. Rampa was still working on his fantastic idea to create a machine that would enable the viewer to see the human aura. Or better yet, a set of goggles that could be donned for the same purpose. Rather similar in concept to the Man with X-Ray Vision, granting the viewer the ability to peer through walls—or through women's clothing—just like Superman. And that technology already exists. Developed for combatting terrorism in the UK is a remote body scanning device that uses tetrahertz radio waves to see through clothing—ostensibly for hidden weapons, but it can also profile everything else on your person, including your most private anatomical features.

In the back of his bestselling books, the canny Dr Rampa placed ads urging the reader to buy everything from monastic robes to sacred stones. At the back of *Wisdom of the Ancients*, for instance, he advertised Dr Rampa's Tranquiliser Touch-Stones. These were magical stones with the word 'Om' inscribed on them in English and Tibetan: they could be conveniently purchased in 17 different currencies via an agent in the UK.

But to Rampa's great horror, others tried to muscle in on this lucra-

Who was Rampa? How many personas did he have? Did he really exist? These photos were taken circa 1970, shortly before he passed on to another realm.

tive spin-off marketing. In the late 1970s, Rampa was still carrying on a running battle with Gray Barker of the Saucerian Press over unauthorised use of the Rampa name, particularly in selling instructional audiotapes supposedly recorded by Rampa. In California, meanwhile, a man did more than copy Rampa's voice: this impersonator claimed to represent the great sage himself. In 1979, Rampa complained in letters about a man in England who was offering a kind of other-worldly Rampa correspondence course.

This man claimed that Rampa was dead but that he could be contacted by Ouija Board in a séance. The man advertised his services as a medium: applicants could enrol for a special course to be taught by the great sage Lobsang Rampa, dictating his answers via the Ouija Board. The Ouija Board was one of the devices that Rampa wrote about, and Rampa endorsed just the idea of telepathic contact with departed loved ones—he claimed himself to communicate with some of his dead Siamese cats.

The English medium's odd business may have picked up in January 1981, when Rampa departed this physical plane. Or to put that bluntly: he died in Calgary. He was 70 years old, and had been laughing all the way to the bank for 25 years. His long journey—imaginary or not—

from the British Library to Lhasa, to Egypt, to Venus and back again—was over. Alain Stanké, who visited Rampa six months before he died, was later told a strange story by Mrs Rampa. She said he'd suffered a heart attack: she called an ambulance to take him to emergency at a Calgary hospital. And she said that while he was lying in an emergency operating theatre, the lighting system blew out—at the exact moment that Rampa passed on.

But in books, Rampa's flame burns on. At the time of his death, he had 20 titles on the go (23 if you count his wife's): his books had racked up sales of over four million copies. The sales figures are probably far higher today—by one estimate, over twelve million copies sold worldwide. The biggest seller is his first title, *The Third Eye* (reprinted more than 30 times), but once someone read this and liked it, this reader would seek out other titles by Rampa. The books have been translated into over 40 languages, and have acquired a huge cult following. In the late 1990s, Tibetan scholar Jamyang Norbu noticed a large influx of Israeli tourists in Dharamsala, the seat of the Tibetan government-in-exile. Why? Rampa's *The Third Eye* had recently been translated into Hebrew.

To this day, librarians do not know where to file Lobsang Rampa's books: under religion, mysticism, occult, paranormal, thriller, fantasy, sci-fi or autobiography. The best solution yet seen: New Age. And perhaps librarians should print at the front of each book the Rampa Mantra: *Abracadabra Pooh-Pooh Hocus Pocus*—inscribed under his Siamese cat coat of arms—with a rejoinder: *In Veritas Caveat Lector*.

In 1983 Mrs Rampa wrote a bubbling eulogy about Rampa—in which she revealed that the Rampa Family had been reduced to just herself and Cleopatra, the Siamese cat. Sheelagh Rouse, who typed all Rampa's manuscripts and illustrated his Siamese cat work (*Living with the Lama*) eloped with a man—disappearing in western Canada. Upon the death of Mrs Rampa, Rampa's will dictated that lucrative book royalties would largely go to the cats of Canada. The income was donated to a feline care organisation. Rampa had donated the royalties from an earlier book to Save the Cat League in New York.

Death usually puts a crimp in the productivity of most authors—but not Lobsang Rampa. His books just keep on selling. He even came out with a new book, posthumously. In 2003—over 20 years after Rampa's death—a book called *My Visit to Agharta* was published by Inner Light-Global Communications, clearly seeking to cash in on the Rampa legend.

THE LONG LOST BOOKS OF RAMPA FEATURING...

MY VISIT TO AGHARTA

T. LOBSANG RAMPA

The same press, Inner Light-Global, reprinted *My Visit to Venus*, taking over from the long-defunct Saucerian Press (Gray Barker died in 1984) and continued to sell Rampa Meditation Tapes (the same ones purporting to be the actual voice of Rampa). There's a definite link between the two small presses, with Inner Light-Global also specializing in UFOs and kooky paranormal phenomena. The head honcho of New Jersey-based Inner Light-Global, Timothy Green Beckley, used to write for Saucerian Press. He is a UFOlogist who penned such classics as *The UFO*

Spaceships and dubious authorship: this title came out more than 20 years after Rampa died, published in 2003 by Inner-Light Global Communications

Silencers: Mystery of the Men in Black (1991). His specialty, however, is not so much outer space as inner space. Beckley is a proponent of hollow-earth alien visitations: he wrote *Subterranean Worlds Inside Earth* (1992), a revamped version of a book he originally wrote for Saucerian Press. The book investigates a vast network of tunnels in subterranean realms, inhabited by troglodyte aliens.

In 1990, Inner Light-Global reprinted an old Rampa book *The Hermit*, which involves UFOs and subterranean caves. And then in 2003, the publisher put out the slim volume, *My Visit to Agharta*. This is purportedly a long-lost manuscript written by the great guru Lobsang Rampa himself, and concerns the high-Asian subterranean kingdom of Agharta. The realm of Agharta has long been known in Tibetan legend and long been sought by adventurers in Central Asia: it has even been linked with the legend of Atlantis. So *My Visit to Agharta* is a posthumous Rampa book—ghostwritten by a fellow hollow-earth fruitcake. The book is a 50-page 'original' manuscript about Agharta, padded out with an additional 75-odd pages of excerpts from previously-published Rampa books which have nothing to do with Agartha. Put a picture of Rampa on the front with some flying saucers and caves—and presto! A long-lost classic from the master is born.

This is a hoax within a hoax—Beckley regurgitating the work of Doctor Rampa. There's even in a reference to Men-in-Black in this bogus manuscript. At the back of the book, ads offer 'products inspired by Rampa', which include a Color Therapy Wand Healing Kit for the New Millennium, made up of seven semi-precious stones, 'to rejuvenate the body's chakra centres'. Also on offer are a Meditation Stone, and audiotapes featuring the real voice of Rampa—guiding the listener on a journey to inner realms.

Timewarp: we advance to the year 2005, when, after a silence of some 20 years, Rampa's secretary Sheelagh Rouse suddenly comes out of the woodwork, self-publishing a book titled *Twenty-five Years with T. Lobsang Rampa*. She burbles on for a few hundred pages—but the reader gets no closer to the character of Rampa, even from this insider who lived in close proximity with him for two decades. She doesn't explain how it came to pass that a beautiful young socialite with a house and kids in London would suddenly desert her family to join the Rampa household. She says that she experienced a kind of electric shock when she met Rampa for the first time—an awesome tingling all over her body. She was instantly drawn to Rampa's psychic powers. Her move into the Rampa household was meant to be temporary—something that she could not explain. But she is more forthcoming on why she suddenly left that household more than two decades later. In the late 1970s, the ageing Rampa was falling apart—and he wanted Sheelagh to take care of his wife after his departure to the Heavenly Fields. He threw in a bargaining chip: he suggested that his wife would not live long, and that Sheelagh would inherit his considerable fortune when Mrs Rampa passed on. Sheelagh felt a special connection to Rampa, but not to his wife. She felt insulted—she would have none of this bribery and blackmail. So she walked out, walking away from Rampa's millions. Rampa promptly disowned his 'adopted daughter' of two decades.

Sheelagh got married, got divorced, got married again. The only ones in the Rampa family who have not been forthcoming with books about him are his Siamese cats. And since they have the power to dictate entire books through telepathy, their versions might surface yet. Of course, the cats would have to come back from the dead first—but that could possibly be done through séances, and the services of a good Siamese cat-language interpreter.

In his own special way, Rampa was a pioneer. He pulled off a major publishing coup—it was not any writer who could do this kind of thing. There was definitely something behind his twisted talent. Rampa's genius lay in creating a sort of bogus cult, setting himself up as guru. He could easily have become a live guru with students—he had many requests for teaching from admiring followers. But he said he preferred to instruct through his books rather than talking directly to his followers.

When Rampa's book *The Third Eye* appeared in 1956, he was ahead of his time: no Tibetan lama had written a book like this in English. But reality was soon to catch up with Rampa's fantasies—in ways that he could not have envisaged. In 1959, following the dramatic escape of the Dalai Lama from Tibet, many high lamas followed him into exile in India. A number travelled further, to the West. Prior to 1950, Tibetan high lamas had no reason to ever leave Tibet: this was a highly esoteric faith and it guarded its secrets jealously. But suddenly, in the 1960s, Tibetan high lamas were popping up everywhere.

In early 1970, one of them even landed in Montreal, right where Rampa was at the time. His name was Chögyam Trungpa Rinpoche: to be more precise, he was a defrocked lama. Thirty years old at the time, he had renounced his monastic vows to elope with 16-year-old English schoolgirl, Diana Pybus, from an aristocratic family. Diana's mother fainted when she heard the news. This was a scandal of the first order: defrocked Tibetan lama marries teenage follower.

After escaping from Tibet to India in 1959, Chogyam Trungpa had landed a fellowship to study at Oxford in 1963. Following this, he became one of the first Tibetan lamas to teach in English. At his Scottish base of Samye Ling, Chogyam Trungpa's teaching promoted 'Crazy Wisdom'—a euphemism for wild parties, free sex and taking drugs. One night his car crashed into a practical joke shop: he suffered from partial paralysis at a result. After the accident, the Rinpoche walked with a limp, and was christened 'Rimp the Gimp'. Didn't seem to slow him down much. While normal people put on fancy dress once a year for Halloween, the Rinpoche did it on a regular basis—he revelled in dressing up in everything from a long Tibetan gown to a British naval uniform. Or full Scottish Highland regalia with sporran and kilt. Fellow Tibetan escapee Akong Rinpoche told him this was going too far—smashing up a car and tangling with a sixteen-year-old female follower would never have happened in Tibet. The two of them got into a serious tussle over methodology. The upshot was that Chogyam Trungpa decided to leave Scotland with teenage bride in tow. The couple arrived in Toronto, spent some time in Montreal, and crossed into the US, establishing a teaching centre at Boulder, Colorado.

Deciding that America was too materialistic, Trungpa eventually moved back to Canada, settling in Halifax, Nova Scotia. He said it was because the weather was extreme in Halifax and he wanted his followers to be constantly tested. Chogyam Trungpa became increasingly erratic—he started dressing as king of the mythical Tibetan kingdom of Shambhala, surrounded by bodyguards in a quasi-military regalia. He wrote a number of books, established a string of dharma centres in North America and Europe, and developed a considerable following—attracting minds like poet Allen Ginsberg.

Though a brilliant teacher, Chogyam Trungpa was derided as the 'cocktail lama' due to his compulsive drinking habit. He died of liver failure in Nova Scotia in 1987. There was considerable fall-out after his death because his second-in-command, the Vajra Regent, was diagnosed with AIDS—along with a male companion and a female companion. The Vajra Regent, Thomas Rich (known by the Tibetan name Osel Tendzin) was the first Westerner to be recognised in this lineage. He died of AIDS in 1990. The spiritual directorship of Shambhala International was handed over to Sokyang Mipham Rinpoche, who is Chogyam Trungpa's son by his Tibetan first wife. And Diana Pybus, Chogyam Trungpa's English wife, remarried and went on to manage a dressage school in Rhode Island called Windhorse Academy—incorporating mindfulness training into the riding discipline.

Where to search for answers for profound questions about the present and future? Turn to religion or to science-fiction? Well, why not mix the two and come up with a new cult—that appears to be the case with one of the greatest movie franchises of all times, *Star Wars*. The Jedi warrior code in *Star Wars* is based on Buddhist principles, particularly the wisdom of Yoda. In fact, on census forms in places like Australia, Star Wars fans have entered 'Jedi' as their religion.

New Age gurus, yuppie gurus, bogus gurus: in the Rampa-ish vein are weird sects and cults that milk susceptible followers. And North America is prime ground for the milking. It's eminently possible that American sci-fi writer L. Ron Hubbard borrowed ideas from the Theosophists and then took them in a whole new direction—nurturing the cult of Scientology, which claims movie stars Tom Cruise and John Travolta among its more high-profile followers. L. Ron Hubbard was born around the same time as Rampa, and died five years after him. At some point in his career, Hubbard decided that there was more money in creating a cult than in writing science fiction. Accessing the inner teachings of Scientology can cost an aspiring devotee up to $150,000, working through an endless course of sessions to reach the level of 'Operating Thetan'. Here, the grand truth is revealed: that the cruel Xenu, alien ruler of the Galactic Confederacy, brought billions of people to planet Earth in spacecraft and then nuked them with hydrogen bombs— the root of all problems today. L. Ron Hubbard did very well from his pseudo-religious mishmash. His Church of Scientology today claims over eight million followers worldwide—no doubt being bilked regularly by Hubbard's heirs and prophets. 'Writing for a penny a word is ridiculous,' Hubbard said on several occasions. 'If a man really wants to make a million dollars, the best way would be to start his own religion.'

And that's exactly what another self-made guru called Frederick Lenz attempted. His book *Surfing the Himalayas* is an account of how his snowboarding technique was perfected in the Nepal Himalayas through the tutelage of a Tibetan Buddhist monk with mysterious powers, Master Fwap Sam-Dup. According to Lenz, Master Fwap's lineage (the Rae Chorze-Fwaz Order of Tantric Buddhist Enlightenment) stems from the legendary Atlantis that sent great teachers to ancient Egypt and other places before it sank without trace due to its karmic depravity. Fwap tells us that the ancient wisdom behind true enlightenment is now contained in his mysterious Buddhist enclave outside of Kathmandu, Nepal. That should ring a few bells of the Theosophist kind—deafening bells of Blavatsky, chimes of Alexandra David-Néel, echoes of Lobsang Rampa. Fwap initiates Lenz into the 'metaphysics of snowboarding'—how to become 'one with the board', how to levitate and perform other neat tricks. Lenz says the first-person book is loosely fictional—but firmly grounded in the author's real experiences.

The book was self-published by Lenz in 1994 in a small edition, mostly for his students. It attracted the attention of Warner Books, which bought the rights for a hefty sum but then dropped it when they learned that Lenz was a controversial cult leader who sexually manipulated female followers. The deal was picked up by another New York publisher and went on to become a national bestseller—so successful that Lenz followed up with a sequel, *Snowboarding to Nirvana* (1997), which is dedicated to his dog, Vayu (Lenz was crazy about his dogs). This second book is very similar to the first, but with some new initiations—this time an explosive initiation into tantric sex by Nadia, a stunning young Danish woman with a visible aura—who claimed to be rekindling a love affair extending over many lifetimes with the author. Although it appears that Fred Lenz could not snowboard worth a damn, he again insisted that the book was based on 'real-life occurrences'. In the introduction, he says he has only altered time periods, shortened trekking experiences, and made other chronological and content changes—leaving the reader to conclude that everything is true except for some minor timing adjustments.

Flashback to Malibu, California, early 1983: Dr Frederick Lenz anoints himself 'Zen Master Rama'—an incarnation of the Hindu god of the same name. Lenz has been a follower of a Hindu guru called Sri Chinmoy in New York, but falls out with him and breaks away, taking with him a number of followers. Lenz then puts a unique spin on Buddhism—he calls his brand of philosophy 'Tantric Mysticism', which includes meditation, out-of-body experiences, and altered consciousness (read: LSD), but still allows for an affluent lifestyle and enjoying worldly pleasures. One ad shows a sexy blonde draped over a Porsche. Lenz is a lover of imported cars: he soon has a collection of Porsches, Rolls Royces and Mercedes Benzes—some 'gifts' from his students. He jets between luxury mansions he has acquired in different states. Lenz demands that his followers (known as Lenzies) contribute large sums of money on a regular basis to maintain the guru's lifestyle. Since many of his followers are computer programmers, he later demands shares in companies he has encouraged them to start up—this later generates a huge investment income.

Another demand in the guru's lifestyle: a supply of nubile young women. After recruiting followers through silver-tongued seminars, Lenz takes an awed female recruit aside and convinces her that they have been lovers in past lives—and that having 'tantric sex' with him again now will accelerate her spiritual development, speeding her along the path to attaining enlightenment. Female followers are taken in by this, convinced that Lenz has occult powers. But they later regret that the sexual encounter has happened under duress, and is thus not greatly different from rape. Questions are raised, eyebrows are raised, court cases happen.

On April 12, 1998, Frederick Lenz was found lying at the bottom of a bay in Long Island, overdosed on drugs in an apparent suicide pact with a female devotee—who survived. His three dogs, also drugged, survived. His estate, valued at $18 million, became the subject of a bizarre court battle. Two women, both claiming to be married to Lenz, showed up to stake their claims. The will specified his entire estate should go to a foundation to promote his ideas. However, it also said that if significant steps were not taken to establish such a foundation, all of his money would go to the National Audubon Society. The will's executor, Norman Marcus, promptly formed the Frederick Lenz Foundation for American Buddhism (of which he was president) and argued the money should go to this. Locking horns with the executor was the National Audubon Society, which took the unusual tack of arguing that Mr Lenz did not, before his death, properly set up a foundation to promote his screwball ideas, and that furthermore he was a fraud, a charlatan and a cult leader—and that the world would be much better off if the money went to the National Audubon Society (presumably, it would then go to the birds—as the society's strength is its conservation work with wild birds). In the end, the judge awarded funds to both claimants, with intellectual property rights going to the Fred Lenz Foundation.

Back in the 1950s, Lobsang Rampa could not stand being ridiculed in England—where there appeared to be too many Tibetologists lurking—so he fled to Canada. Canada later became safe-haven for another guru who was a laughing stock in France. This was because of his all-white baggy clothing and his strange topknot of hair—which he claimed was an antenna for receiving extraterrestrial messages. After a faltering career as a pop singer and racing car journalist, Claude

Vorilhon found his true calling as a prophet of free love, cloning and communing with extraterrestrials.

In France in 1973, Claude says he was abducted by a four-foot-tall alien with a large forehead and long hair, who took him back to his UFO and told him how aliens created the human race 25,000 years ago. In between classes, Claude says he received the attention of six voluptuous and bewitching female robots. The alien renamed him Rael and instructed him to build an embassy for the return of the aliens. Rael, who started up a cult called the Raelians in Quebec, called on his female supporters to offer themselves as hostesses for the aliens and for him, their prophet on Earth. He specified only good-looking women for his Order of Angels, whose tasks would range from sexual gratification to offering their wombs and eggs for cloning experiments. Rael published a book, *The Message Given By Extra-Terrestrials*, with a cover design that would have done Lobsang Rampa proud.

In October 2002, a national poll of 1,007 Canadians conducted by Ipsos-Reid revealed that fully 51 percent believe that angels exist, while 20 percent said they believed that extraterrestrials visit Earth on a regular basis (only three percent said they believe Elvis is still alive). Canada is obviously fertile ground for a cult like the Raelians: too much viewing of *ET*, *The X-Files* and *Star Trek*. In December 2002, Raelian bishop Brigitte Boisselier made a spectacular announcement: that Raelian 'scientists' had cloned a human, a baby girl named Eve—a genetic replica of her mother. This is either a nasty breakthrough in genetics—or the biggest hoax in history. Evidence later emerged that Clonaid, the Raelian cloning arm, had a staff of only two, and had never cloned even a sheep or a rabbit prior to this miracle. Baby Eve may well have been the result of too much group sex in candlelight, accompanied by the sounds of chanting, rather than cloning. But Raelians insisted the procedure was true—and not only that, it is the first step in a future in which scientists could reproduce an adult's body in a few hours and download his or her mind into the empty vessel. 'Then,' says Rael, 'you can live forever.'

While scientists remain highly skeptical of the cloning claim, the announcement sparked outrage from rabbis, priests and Muslim clerics—and sparked all kinds of questions from individuals. A man paralysed from the waist down wanted to know: could he be cloned so that he could end his paralysis? (and use the existing body for spare parts). A man who had tragically lost a nephew in a car accident wanted to know: could his nephew be resurrected through cloning? And a woman asked: if she had a lock of Elvis' hair, would she be able to clone the king?

Just pray that nobody gets round to cloning Rael himself: he makes Lobsang Rampa look positively angelic.

Michel Peissel on the balcony of his Paris apartment,
holding his book *Tibet: the Secret Continent*.

 # Michel Peissel
1937–

*anthropologist, inventor, filmmaker, dealer in mysteries,
adventurer & simply a very curious person*

Cavalier Of Curiosity

Encounters with
the fierce Khampa warriors

Michel Peissel is an unconventional explorer who longs for the grand 19th-century era of exploration—and finds his calling by stepping back in time on the Tibetan Plateau. The French explorer gets a lot more than he bargained for as he stumbles across an intrigue involving the CIA and the fierce Khampa warriors of Tibet. Much later, it is through his familiarity with the Khampas that he reaches the place where dreams and reality meet—locating the source of the Mekong.

 PARIS, AUGUST 2002: Michel Peissel ushers me into the small apartment and offers me a seat—but does not sit down himself. He is on the move, even in his own living room. He chats excitedly about his new projects. The phone rings. A courier has come to pick up a video Peissel has just finished editing. The phone rings again. He answers in French. 'That's my girl-friend,' says Peissel casually. 'Soon to be my wife.' I look at him quizzically. 'My third wife.'

At 65, Peissel shows no sign of slowing down—or indeed, of even sitting down. He dashes off into the adjacent study. 'Oh and here's my new baby,' he says, grinning from ear to ear. It's a hardcover book, *Tibet: the Secret Continent*, hot off the press. It is the fruit of Peissel's expeditions to the Tibetan Plateau—some 30 of them in the last 20 years—handsomely illustrated by his own photographs. He flips to a page showing stone towers in southeastern Tibet. 'These towers are a mystery. In the middle of nowhere. Some are over 50 metres high,' he says. 'Nobody knows what they are doing there, or who made them.' He goes into his study and returns with a drawing. 'And here's another mystery. This is a sketch I made from an amulet in Lhasa. The design is very similar to those of the ancient Scythians, from the Black Sea area, who worshipped griffins. But who were the Tibetan artisans who kept alive an artistic tradition that disappeared everywhere else 2,000 years ago? I have yet to find the answer.'

Michel Peissel is a dealer in mysteries. He is renowned as an explorer—though he will tell you otherwise, because he hates pigeon-holing. In the 21st century, you'd think that the planet has been thoroughly explored and picked over, and that explorers are redundant. But in the grand old 19th-century tradition of exploration, Peissel's quest goes on. 'I prefer to be called an adventurer,' says Peissel. 'Essentially, I am just a very curious person.'

That would be putting it mildly: Peissel embraces a broad range of interests. He loves solving riddles, especially geographical and historical ones. His intense curiosity has driven his entire life. 'Very few people receive grants for curiosity,' notes Peissel, wryly—but he seems to have managed the feat. So how do you become an explorer? By accident, he claims, though he always fantasized about it.

The son of a French diplomat, Michel Peissel was raised in England and France. Due to his father's posting to London, Peissel learned English at the same time as French—he is fluent in both languages. His childhood heroes were great explorers and adventurers. He initially studied to become an economist: his life went off at a tangent when he took time out from Harvard Business School to visit Mexico in 1958.

His 'spring break' was a little different: one night, he and a fellow European decided to set off along the uncharted coast of eastern Yucatán. His companion turned back when the going got tough, but Peissel forged on, chartering a native craft, and then—finding himself stranded—walking in sandals for 42 days along a coast normally only visited by smugglers. The young adventurer stumbled across 14 unrecorded Mayan archeological sites—quite a feat for someone with no experience in exploration. Peissel was just 21 at the time: the trip changed his life. It told him that the planet was still exciting and mysterious—and there were many secrets to uncover. Peissel's Yucatán journey resulted in his first book, *The Lost World of Quintana-Roo* (1963), and sparked a lifelong interest in Mayan coastal culture: he has returned several times on expeditions.

In May 1959, Michel Peissel turned up in Kalimpong, northeast India, wedged between the remote kingdoms of Bhutan and Sikkim. Here he was catapulted into another incredible adventure. Peissel knew nothing about Tibet or the Khampas when he bumbled into Kalimpong. But he was quick to find out—the place was buzzing with chaotic activity. 'It was a fucking mess,' says Peissel nonchalantly. Tibetan refugees were pouring in, close on the heels of the Dalai Lama who had fled from Tibet a few months earlier, escorted to the Indian border by the warrior tribesmen of eastern Tibet, the fierce Khampas. Revolt had broken out in Lhasa in March 1959, and refugees were streaming southward, out of Tibet. Kalimpong was a nest of spies—Taiwanese, Chinese, Indian, and CIA.

The sleepy outpost of Kalimpong at the time hosted some high-class refugees. Fleeing from Tibet, Princess Kuku-la was there, along with her sister Kula from the royal family of Sikkim. Elderly Afghan princesses might be spotted in the weekly market—or relatives of the deposed king of Burma. Kalimpong was where the 13th Dalai Lama had lodged in temporary exile in 1912—when Alexandra David-Néel

Partying with the princesses of Sikkim: Peissel (at left) with Princess Kuku-la, and her sister Princess Kula (at right), and Kula's husband Rigzin Yuthog (who is wearing Western jacket and tie, while Peissel is decked out in Sikkimese robes). The photo was snapped in Kalimpong around 1959.

was granted an interview with him. Poets, writers and painters graced the social circle in Kalimpong. And diplomats.

In centuries past, Kalimpong was the meeting place of emissaries from Sikkim, Bhutan and Tibet. The town used to belong to Sikkim, but in 1706 it was seized by the Bhutanese, who ruled until 1865—when it fell into the hands of the British. After 1904, the town shot to prominence as a key staging post on the new trade route from British India to Tibet. In its heyday, Kalimpong employed more than 10,000 men sorting mounds of dirty wool from Tibet into neat, compact bales for the onward journey to America or England. Mule caravans from Tibet brought yak tails, borax, musk and Tibetan curios; in the opposite direction they loaded up with manufactured goods from India. This trade dwindled after Chinese invasion of Tibet. Eventually the door was slammed shut—and Kalimpong lapsed into obscurity again. In 1959, after the fall of Tibet and the flight of the Dalai Lama, Kalimpong was a surreal place. It was a town of the mighty who had fallen. The Tibetans had fallen a long way: from living at altitudes of over 13,000 feet on the Tibetan plateau—and plunging to a mere 4,000 feet in elevation at Kalimpong.

Peissel had come to Kalimpong with one purpose: he had his heart set on getting into Bhutan. The Bhutanese aristocracy maintained summer villas in Kalimpong. Trying to curry favour with Bhutanese officials, Peissel came armed with a letter to the prime minister of Bhutan, Jigme Dorji. The letter was from Thupten Norbu, eldest brother of the 14th Dalai Lama.

Thupten Norbu and Gyalo Thondup (second-eldest brother of the Dalai Lama) were both based in Kalimpong at the time, and both known to be connected to the CIA, which was backing Khampa guerrilla activity in Tibet. Gyalo Thondup was married to the daughter of a high-ranking KMT (Taiwanese Nationalist) official. In 1950, when the Dalai Lama retreated to the Sikkim border, the Tibetan cabinet had discretely ferried hundreds of mule-loads of gold and silver across the border—worth at least $5 million, according to Peissel. And again in 1956, when the Dalai Lama was allowed to visit India for the 2,500th anniversary of the birth of the Buddha, pack-mules bearing gold and other treasures were unloaded in Sikkim at the Chogyal's palace. Would that money be used to back the Khampa guerrillas? The problem was that the swashbuckling Khampas were a law unto themselves—they never recognised central Lhasa authority, and were just as likely against Lhasa officials as they were against the Chinese. The Dalai Lama was a staunch advocate of non-violence, but his brother Gyalo Thondup backed the Khampas, setting up intelligence-gathering operations in Darjeeling in 1951. Both the Khampas and the CIA were heavily involved in the escape of the Dalai Lama in 1959.

Although the Dalai Lama's brothers were involved with the CIA and the Khampas, the Dalai Lama himself stayed aloof. Under pressure from the Chinese, he had stripped his brothers of their nationality and declared the Khampas 'reactionaries' and asked them to lay down their arms—even as monasteries in Kham were being bombed and strafed by Chinese aircraft. The Dalai Lama called for the path of non-violence. Given the timing, Peissel pronounced that a major mistake:

A word from the Dalai Lama, one single proclamation, and all Tibet would undoubtedly have stood up and faced the Chinese. The Dalai Lama's failure to understand this, his failure to act, to speak and to lead his people to war, is perhaps the greatest tragedy in Tibet's long history.

Khampa man with red yarn tasselled throughout his hair

Kalimpong was where Peissel first encountered Khampa guerrillas. While the Lhasan refugees and aristocrats milled around in tears and confusion, he noticed a group of tall men with daggers on their belts, proudly swaggering around. This warrior race from eastern Tibet had resisted the armies of Genghis Khan. Peissel describes Tsering, a Khampa commander he met:

> He was then a flamboyant and arrogant commander in the Khamba guerrilla forces. Wearing spotless black boots and a vast, flowing, dark blue gown slung over a white raw-silk shirt, his six-foot-three figure towered impressively head and shoulders over the emaciated Indians, squat Lepchas and short Nepalese who crowded Kalimpong's bazaar…when we first met he still wore his hair in long braids wound around his head. This typical Tibetan hairstyle gave him a wild, masculine appearance, in no way lessened by the gold-and-turquoise earring he work as a sign of his rank. Tsering's height and lean, aristocratic profile, combined with the leopardskin lining of his vast, flowing gown, gave him the rare elegance of a true warrior.

No luck with the Bhutan project, but Peissel acquired a very pretty Tibetan teacher by the name of Betty-la. She was from the aristocratic Tsarong and Taring families of Lhasa. Her sister, Tess-la, was married to the prime minister of Bhutan, making a good connection for Peissel. The sisters were from a group that had wielded great power and privilege in Lhasa. They were educated in Darjeeling, and mixed with royalty from Sikkim and Bhutan. Peissel tells us:

> The products of Elizabeth Arden held no secrets for the women who, like Betty-la, graced the perfumed houses of rich men like Lahu, Ngabo or Tsarong… It took hours for Betty-la's servants to do up her long brown hair on the silver and gold frames, studded

with turquoise and amber, which rose high above her head, an obligatory sign of her noble birth.

Peissel confides with a laugh that he fell in love with Betty-la—even if she was nine years older than him, and was married with four children. Thinking about those children was agony for her: she'd left them behind to travel down to Kalimpong on a shopping holiday with her husband—and then could not return when hell broke loose in Lhasa and Tsarong, her father, had died in a Chinese prison. And listening to these stories, Peissel was increasingly drawn into the plight of the Tibetans.

Stymied in his attempt to get into Bhutan, Peissel moved on to Kathmandu in neighbouring Nepal. He ended up writing a yeti-debunking story that appeared in Argosy magazine in 1960, titled 'The Abominable Snow Job.' Intense interest in yetis had come close on the heels of Everest expeditions of the 1950s: with the 1958 publication of *Tintin in Tibet* (which revolved around a yeti), interest was at fever-pitch. In the course of Himalayan expeditions, European mountaineers discovered quasi-human footprints with stubby toes in the snow of remote high-altitude valleys, which bolstered the case—although some may have been fabricated as practical jokes.

A simple explanation for the hairy yeti points to the Tibetan brown bear. In 1879, the pundit-explorer Kishen Singh described a brown bear to the northeast of the plateau whose feet are similar to human feet. This bear would often stand upright—most likely to survey the landscape. And it was aggressive—it mauled yaks and livestock, and would not hesitate to attack a human. The number of bears has dwindled due to hunting: it is rarely sighted today. To the eastern side of the plateau, renowned climber Reinhold Messner swears he sighted a yeti high on a peak. In fact, Messner spent the better part of the 1990s chasing this hairy apparition throughout the Himalayas: he concluded that sightings were most likely of a Himalayan brown bear. Legends of the yeti pop up in Nepal, Tibet and Bhutan under different guises. Unfortunately for the legend, a supposed yeti skull at a monastery in Nepal proved—under rigorous examination—to be that of a large monkey.

Having disposed of the yeti myth, Peissel took on the legend of Boris Lissanevitch. Boris was a Russian aristocrat and a famous dancer

On the trail into Mustang, with the ethereal Annapurna range floating above

with Diaghilev's Ballet Russe. He fled Russia after the Bolshevik Revolution and eventually made his way to Calcutta, where he opened a club for playboy maharajahs, sultans, heads-of-state, actors and diplomats. Boris was variously described as a Russian agent and an American agent: he led a glamorous life, mixing with his celebrity clientele. Then he married the belle of Calcutta—Inga Scott, a Danish beauty 25 years younger than himself.

When Boris travelled, he always wore a heavy overcoat lined with pockets that were filled with smoked salmon, black caviar, red caviar and herring. His overcoat was somewhat heavier than normal when he flew to Nepal in 1951. Asked to organise King Tribhuvan's coronation party, he chartered DC3s and filled them with live chickens, ducks, turkeys, geese—and several tons of ice. When the guests had departed, he convinced the king to allow him to open a first-class hotel in Kathmandu—the Hotel Royal. Boris fostered the opening of Nepal to wealthy tourists—who proceeded to snuff out Nepal's abundant wildlife. He accompanied members of the royal family and visiting maharajahs on hunting sorties, chalking up a record number of tiger kills himself. To support his travels, Peissel wrote a biography about Boris titled *Tiger for Breakfast*.

Meanwhile, Peissel took more Tibetan lessons in Kathmandu and bided his time, waiting for his chance to prove himself as a real

The Khampas hid out in caves high in the hills of Mustang: they were impossible
to dislodge from these 'cave-condos'.

explorer. In the summer of 1964, that chance came up. Peissel's studies
had switched to the Sorbonne in Paris, in the field of ethnology: for his
PhD thesis, he came up with a startling study area. He targeted the tiny
Kingdom of Mustang in the Nepal Himalayas, bordering Tibet. Peissel
has an uncanny ability to charm his way past officials and obtain permits for sensitive regions: his upbringing in a diplomat's family stood
him in good stead for this. His talent for languages has helped considerably—he speaks fluent English and French, and has mastered Spanish and Tibetan. Through his connections in the Nepalese royal family,
Peissel managed to wrangle a permit to visit Mustang.

Getting to Mustang was not easy. Peissel had arrived at a time
when Khampa guerrillas, backed by the CIA, were using Mustang as
a base to launch punishing raids on Chinese troops in western Tibet.
They had shifted their base to Mustang in 1962 and by 1964, numbered
about 6,000 Khampas, firmly entrenched in mountain caves. Peissel had trouble finding caravan companions for the journey to Mustang because the Nepalese feared the tall brawny Khampas, who had
a reputation for being ruthless brigands. Peissel ran into a number of
Khampas on his expedition. His knowledge of Tibetan helped smooth
things over, but more than once he found himself looking into the

The modest four-storey palace of the King of Mustang

muzzle of a sub-machine gun. He eventually made friends among the Khampas and developed great respect for them.

Dressed in a Tibetan long cloak and speaking Tibetan, Peissel was able to trek into the Kingdom of Mustang, staying for several months in the summer of 1964. Very few Westerners had penetrated the remote region: none had stayed long enough to research its culture and history. Apart from early Japanese visitor Ekai Kawaguchi, the only person who had done any real reconnaissance here was Peter Aufschnaiter, who roamed these hills and investigated cave dwellings back in the 1950s. Aufschnaiter revelled in being back in a pure Tibetan culture and landscape, and he spent some time trekking in the area. But since Aufschnaiter rarely seemed to put pen to paper, this left the way open for Peissel.

At Lo Monthang, Peissel found a walled citadel, locked in a medieval timewarp, ruled by a king from a lineage stretching back to the 14th century. The people of Mustang were flat-earthers with bizarre customs, rituals and beliefs. Speaking Tibetan, Peissel managed to ingratiate himself for a month's stay so he could study the culture. He was lucky to witness a demon-chasing ceremony. And the further he delved into the customs of Mustang, the odder he found the place. The Lobas of Mustang practice polyandry when expedient—a woman can have two or three husbands, and they all pile into bed together at night by the fire, naked, as is the custom of Tibetan nomads.

Even more startling to Peissel was one of the Loba burial customs. Corpses are normally cremated or given a sky burial, but in the case of a younger male dying without heirs, the body is placed in salt, wrapped in a blanket and buried inside the wall of a house. Peissel discovered, to his horror, that he'd been sleeping near such a corpse, entombed in the wall. Pemba, his host, cheerfully explained this was the embalmed body of his elder brother, who had died at the age of 17 without heirs. Then Pemba pointed out another section of wall where his younger brother, who died at the age of nine, was entombed. But not to worry, Pemba added. When one of his daughters grew up and married, the son-in-law would break open the wall, remove the bodies and take them far away. They must follow this tradition to appease the ghosts.

With the wealth of material he collected, Peissel not only completed his doctoral thesis, he landed a cover story for National Geographic in 1965. This was followed in 1969 by the publication of *Mustang: A Lost Tibetan Kingdom*, which went on to sell several million copies in France and won several prestigious awards. All this launched his dream of devoting his energy to exploration by giving him credibility—and a financial base.

Spurred by his early success, Peissel mounted more expeditions to hidden enclaves and kingdoms on the Tibetan Plateau on horseback. He says he felt a special kinship with Tibetan peoples and their customs— to the extent he even started to dream in Tibetan:

> Somewhere deep in my heart I feel truly Tibetan, connected in spite of myself to a certain basic humour and broad-minded approach to existence. Tibetans are a friendly, no-nonsense sort of people...

Peissel felt right at home here: for someone who longed to have been born during the great Victorian age of exploration, the Tibetan Plateau was a fantastic step back in time. Getting around was mostly accomplished on foot or on horseback: Peissel was in his element honing his riding skills on rugged expeditions to Ladakh and Zanskar. In 1968, after a decade of trying, he finally got permission to enter Bhutan. At the time, there were few roads in this reclusive kingdom: with a caravan of pack-animals carrying supplies, Peissel was the first foreigner to explore the eastern reaches of Bhutan.

A plain cover design for a book that caused a storm when it was published

But Tibet itself eluded Peissel because of a book he wrote. It was a spin-off from his Mustang trip—a book called *Cavaliers of Kham*, published in 1972. This tome, about Tibetan Khampa guerrillas operating in Mustang with CIA support, became a bestseller—and it got Peissel into lots of trouble. In the book, he detailed China's genocidal policies in Tibet and systematic destruction of monasteries, and although he was tight-lipped on CIA backing for the Khampas, it was enough to provoke considerable reaction. Peissel was blacklisted in China, which meant he was barred from reaching Tibet:

> The Chinese were furious with me—they banned me from visiting China. I upset the Americans—they were angry about this story leaking out. And I upset the Nepalese. But to the Tibetans I was a hero because I spoke up about the plight of the Tibetans—and at that time, nobody was doing that.

With US rapprochement with China in early 1972, the timing of Peissel's book proved embarrassing. Tibet was actually the first operation of the newly inaugurated CIA, which had come out of WWII, taking over as the American intelligence arm after the disbanding of the OSS. The CIA started operations in 1948—after Tibet, the CIA would be involved in covert operations in Cuba, Laos, Nicaragua, Angola and Afghanistan.

Peissel says he wrote the book to honour the memory of brave Tibetans, like his friend Osher. He flashes back to Mustang in 1964: the Khampas were desperate for any medical assistance and pestered Peissel for help, despite his limited medical knowledge. In the village of Tangya, he was dragged off to see a Khampa who'd been wounded in battle. He was stunned to recognise his friend Osher, his eyes bright with fever—his expression one of panic and fear. This was the bright young man he'd known from Kathmandu. The young man convulsed and died right before his eyes:

This strange and tragic coincidence affected me more than words can say. It was when I was outside again in the blazing sun that I resolved to write this book. More than anything, his death seemed to me symbolic of the Tibetan tragedy. Outside everything was so bright, while there, in that hovel, a young man of my own age had died, a friend, a victim of a war that nobody cared about…a war which lead Osher, the wild, arrogant, reckless man I had admired in Bodnath, to his premature, anonymous death, a lonely death in a strange land a thousand miles from the pastures he had called home, a thousand miles from where he had been born. I shall never forget that look of fear in Osher's eyes or the morning sun that was his last.

It was not till 30 years later that material about CIA involvement with the Khampas was declassified and a clearer picture emerged, with a flurry of publishing. Some titles were authored by former CIA operatives. The books essentially back up what Peissel wrote 30 years before—but reveal that the extent of CIA involvement was much greater than Peissel or anyone else had previously thought.

One of these books, *Into Tibet* by Thomas Laird, revealed that the first CIA agent killed in the line of duty was shot in Tibet. Not only was he shot: his head was lopped off and taken in a saddlebag to Lhasa. It was all a horrendous mistake. The agent in question, Douglas Mackiernan, was on the run from Communist-usurped Xinjiang in far-west China. Mackiernan was the former US vice-consul in Urumqi: his mission was to reach Lhasa and see the 14th Dalai Lama, who had requested American support against the new Communist front in China. Mackiernan may have been instructed to arrange shipment of modern American weapons to Tibet. Mackiernan and his sidekick, fellow-agent Frank Bessac—together with three White Russians—entered Tibet's northern border on camels on April 29th, 1950.

Six Tibetan border guards, told to shoot at any intruders on sight, levelled their guns at the small caravan. Douglas Mackiernan and two of the Russians were cut down in a hail of bullets. Frank Bessac and Vasili Zvansov miraculously survived: Bessac was unhurt, but Zvansov was wounded in the knee. Speaking no Tibetan, they desperately chanted the mantra *Dalai Lama Lhasa*. The Tibetan guards took them

prisoner and divided up gold bars and other booty from the small caravan. Meanwhile, not wanting to carry the bodies of those killed to
Lhasa, several guards lopped off the heads—much easier to transport
as proof of intruders shot.

Shortly afterward, an Arrow Letter arrived at the frontier post from
the office of the Dalai Lama. An Arrow Letter was an express deliv-
ery by horseback relay with a message wrapped around an arrow. Un-
furled, the message instructed the stupefied border guards to look out
for a small group of foreigners approaching at this border—and to give
them a regal escort into Lhasa. Though in rough shape, Bessac and
Zvansov made it to Lhasa, where they met Heinrich Harrer and Peter
Aufschnaiter. The border guards were severely punished for their
transgressions. On his return to the US, Bessac was ordered by the
CIA to remain absolutely silent about what had transpired: his story
did not see the light of day until more than 50 years later, with the
2002 publication of Thomas Laird's book *Into Tibet*.

In 1974, an Honor Wall was commissioned at CIA headquarters in
Virginia—rows of nameless stars in honour of those CIA agents who
gave their lives in the service of their country. The anonymous First
Star was whispered to be 'Mac', the nickname of Douglas Mackiernan.
If, in 1950, the Tibetans were looking to the Americans for support to
stave off the imminent threat of Chinese invasion, the arrival of Mackiernan's head in Lhasa was not an auspicious start.

In his book *Orphans of the Cold War* (published in 2000) former CIA
operative John Kenneth Knaus reveals that the backdrop to the secret
war in Tibet was the aftermath of the Korean War, pitting the US
and allies against the China-led communist bloc in Asia. This would
come to a head with American involvement in the Vietnam War of the
1960s. CIA operations in Tibet were codenamed 'ST Circus'. Between
1957 and 1961, more than 250 tons of equipment was air-dropped into
Tibet, including arms, radios, medical supplies, printing presses. Flying by night, the planes also dropped Khampa commandos, trained in
Colorado. After the 1959 escape of the Dalai Lama, clandestine operations were stepped up: from 1964 to 1967, Khampa operations from
their Mustang base were at their height. The CIA was pouring several
million dollars annually into the operation. And spurring the Khampas on was the soothing voice of Betty-la, whom Peissel had fallen for
in Kalimpong—she read news on Tibetan-language broadcasts on All
India Radio, in her refined Lhasa accent.

Knaus says that one of the greatest intelligence hauls in CIA history was a blue sack retrieved when 40 armed Khampa horsemen wiped out a Chinese military convoy in western Tibet in 1961. The documents in the blue sack were a goldmine of information—about worsening Sino-Soviet relations, about the extent of famine in Tibet and China created by the disastrous Great Leap Forward.

Other than gathering intelligence like this, according to Knaus the purpose of the Tibetan operation was to annoy and distract the Chinese, to throw them off-balance. The CIA had no intention of supporting a military force suffi-

A Tibetan armed brigade with foxfur hats— but one that is fictitious. This picture was staged for a Chinese propaganda spiel in the 1960s. The only armed Tibetans running around in the 1960s were Khampa guerrillas, who were a lot more disorderly.

cient to achieve Tibetan independence. In this, the Tibetans were not only misled, they were clearly betrayed. The CIA had scaled back their operations in Mustang by 1969, and pulled out support completely in 1971. The reason for this was a secret visit to Beijing that year by national security adviser Henry Kissinger. Kissinger gave the Tibetans the Kiss of Death. He dumped them as a Chinese precondition for establishing diplomatic relations. American rapprochement with China took place in early 1972, with President Richard Nixon cosying up to Mao Zedong.

Peissel's book was published before the final chapter could be written—the betrayal of the Khampa guerrillas, who were snuffed out in Mustang by Nepalese forces in 1974 under Chinese pressure: all the Khampas were either killed or captured. Peissel tells me he is no fan of the Dalai Lama, due to his handling of the Khampa issue. The Khampas have always viewed the Lhasa government as weak-willed flackeys of the Chinese—and that included the Dalai Lama, who asked the Khampas to lay down their arms. He sent taped messages to Mustang urging the guerrillas again to lay down their arms. Although Peissel never updated his book in later editions, he did fictionalise some elements in his novel *La Khamba* (1996), a thriller set in the 1980s Nepal, with a cast of Chinese secret service, shadowy CIA operatives, Tibetan rebels and a Khampa princess.

Michel Peissel has still not taken a seat. He relates all this as he paces up and down the living room of his Parisian apartment—or wanders off to adjacent rooms to bring back a magazine or a book he wants to talk about. This is more of a rambling discourse than an interview— the subject shifts easily from the Himalayan blue poppy to rafting the Brahmaputra—to how he fell in love with the daughter of a Tibetan aristocrat. The apartment is small, and cluttered with books, papers and recording equipment. On one wall hangs a classical painting; on another, a Tibetan scroll painting. If the place looks somewhat chaotic, it's because Peissel is in transit: he's just arrived back from Tibet, and tomorrow he's off to his villa in Cadaqués, on the Spanish coast. He leads a complicated domestic life, with four children from two marriages. He may see them intermittently, but how many kids can claim their father is an explorer? Sometimes he takes one of them along on an expedition—for the educational ride.

Peissel's approach to exploration is unconventional. Often he does not set out with specific goals—he simply bumbles his way through, and makes chance discoveries that often prove significant. He does not take a strictly scientific or academic approach to exploring: he prefers to play it by ear, staying open to possibilities. His explorations are usually low-key, working with a small team: to fill gaps in expertise, he may take along specialists in particular fields. 'I don't think you can specialise when you are exploring. Exploration comes from crossing different fields,' he says. Peissel often tackles those fields himself—he's qualified as an anthropologist, and skilled as an archeologist, geographer and zoologist. Not to mention documentary filmmaker, producer, director and television presenter. Some expeditions have involved film crews from England and France. Peissel was producer of his own seven-part television program in France, 'Frontiers of the Unknown.'

Juggling these multiple roles has provided essential income, but expeditions to remote parts require hefty budgets. Peissel admits to having had major problems making ends meet because he avoids working with sponsors, finding their demands limiting. However, he has found backing from foundations like Loel Guinness, Smithsonian, and the Kalpa Group. More recently, Rolex and National Geographic have contributed direct funding to support him.

Another unusual mantle Peissel claims is that of inventor. 'Throughout history, new technology has made new travel possible,' says Peissel. 'Look at rockets going to the moon, or the invention of the aqualung.' Peissel's fascination with maritime and river exploration led him to design and build a hovercraft that could travel upstream over white-water rapids. Rafters commonly shoot down rapids: Peissel pioneered the sport of shooting *up* rapids, intent on going where none had gone before.

In the course of five expeditions to the Himalayas from 1959 to 1969, Peissel travelled thousands of miles on foot and on horseback across remote parts of India, Nepal and Bhutan. During these marches he reflected how men could travel to the moon but still had no practical way of penetrating these mountain regions. Then he got to thinking about the Kali Gandaki gorge, a cleft in the Himalayas, a river road from Nepal into Tibet. 'What if I could follow its foaming course, and ride its waters from India to Tibet? Such a thought seemed sheer madness, an impossible feat. Or was it?'

If such a thing were possible, he could journey over swathes of remote territory in record time. And somehow Peissel launched himself on a fantastic Jules Verne quest. He turned into a hovernaut. The hovercraft was invented in 1958 by a British engineer who coupled his wife's hairdryer with two coffee tins to create his first model. The technology was still in its infancy: it was unknown if the hovercraft could traverse rapids, or handle waves, or how it would perform at altitude. In October 1970, Peissel started to delve into the world of hovering. Teaming up with British adventurer Michael Alexander, he tracked down a prototype model being tested by British company Hover-Air. This was an inflated rubber dinghy, similar to a Zodiac, powered by two small engines: a thrust engine and a lift engine. It seated one pilot in the cockpit. The whole thing could be loaded onto the roof of a Land Rover. And that meant it could be deflated, disassembled, and the parts fitted onto an aircraft.

The idea of hovering the Himalayas started to gain momentum. Peissel and Alexander set about customising the Hover-Air design to increase its power and lift. This was followed by months of trials all over England, France and Spain—to the delight of curious crowds, and to the consternation of local officials, who had no regulations governing this strange vessel thundering along rivers. The press had a field-day: Alexander was photographed putting money in a parking meter beside the hovercraft. On a test-run in France, Peissel talks of his rapture at gliding along a river like a dragonfly, although a noisy one due to the roar of the engine. Coming around a bend in a river, he surprised a fisherman: as there was little room for both fisherman and hovercraft on this stretch of the river, Peissel veered to an embankment, hovered up over it and around the fisherman and then continued along the river. The gape-mouthed fisherman dropped his rod: such are the origins of UFO sightings. Hovercraft are notoriously difficult to steer and handle in calm waters: turbulent waters promised great danger. Launching on the river in Spain, Peissel encountered a stretch of white water: to his amazement, the hovercraft simply raced over it. This trial was a success.

Peissel had to work feverishly to get financial backing for the Himalayan hovercraft expedition because nobody took the idea seriously. Then Peissel and Alexander had a stroke of luck: Hover-Air was holding a liquidation sale. They snapped up two more prototypes at bargain prices. In an effort to attract funding, Peissel and Alexander summoned the French press and television to the banks of the Seine in Paris. Alexander pulled up with a hovercraft on the roof of his car, and dramatically stepped out in black fur coat and hat. Out of the other door leapt a beautiful young woman in a leopardskin coat. Peissel duly climbed into the cockpit of the machine and hovered up and down the Seine—past the Louvre, back toward the Eiffel Tower, under the famous bridges. This demonstration netted some free Air France tickets, plus an advance from a publishing company—and that was enough to get the project off the ground.

In mid-1972 Peissel and fellow explorers Michael Alexander and Bob Cardukes packed their three customised hovercraft into crates, loaded them onto a Jumbo jet, and headed for Nepal. After numerous mishaps—one where Peissel almost drowned when his hovercraft overturned—the hovernauts ironed out the kinks, and carried on, testing different rivers. The hovercraft—and the hovernauts—took a terrible pounding after flipping a few times. And there was an unexpected hazard: something that they first mistook as floating logs, but which turned out to be gharial crocodiles.

For their last attempt, attempting to cross the Himalayan breach, they obtained a permit to proceed up the Kali Gandaki gorge to 9,000 feet—an altitude never before reached by hovercraft. They had negotiated a ride in the king's helicopter to a launch-point on the lower Kali Gandaki river. But only one hovercraft could be transported, and Michael Alexander and Michel Peissel decided to alternate hovering with hiking. Peissel took over the first leg, roaring up to the Thakali village of Tukutcha, where he hovered up a flat grassy field at the river's edge. The entire population of Tukutcha, some 600 souls, crowded around Peissel and his futuristic machine, talking excitedly—children, beggars, monks, traders, old women, herdsmen. Peissel, over six feet tall, was clad in rubber boots, baggy orange waterproof pants and blue anorak. The orange and grey hovercraft lay at his feet. His teeth were chattering from the cold.

> I surprised everyone by asking point-blank in Tibetan whether there was any house where I might get arak, as what I now needed most was a drink. It must have seemed as if a Martian had landed in Wales and, on stepping out of his module, had begun speaking Welsh! In a few seconds everyone was smiling and laughing and asking amazed questions. How was it that I spoke Tibetan, and from where had I come?

Peissel was about to tell them that he started that morning in Kathmandu, but then thought better of it: the trek from Kathmandu to Tukutcha normally takes 24 days.

A few days later, Alexander and Peissel took turns crossed the breach between Mt Annapurna and Mt Dhaulagiri, reaching 8,750 feet at the village of Marpha. At this point their energy was spent, and it was the altitude limit of their permit. Peissel must have gazed longingly up the Kali Gandaki, as the gorge lead directly into Mustang, the lost kingdom he had explored eight years before. He must've been thinking about what a grand entrance a hovercraft would make into such a remote land. But the hovercraft was in sorry condition. Michael Alexander piloted the battered hovercraft back as far as Larjung where he met ferocious headwinds and decided to abandon the machine. As they joined up again and hiked back down to civilization, Peissel and

Alexander had lots of time to reflect on what they had accomplished, as he wrote in his book *The Great Himalayan Passage:*

> Our three craft had totalled 1200 miles on nine different rivers, through gorges never travelled before, and up rapids too numerous to count. We had, it is true, been prevented from travelling the full course up the Kali Gandaki... But I had accomplished at long last my dream of reaching the fringes of Tibet, not as in the past on foot up a trail, but as a navigator on nature's own highways. Against all odds, we had triumphed... And in the process we had discovered an entirely new Himalayan world, one whose history was written on water.

In 1980, Peissel returned to hover up part of the Ganges, and later hovered in central America. He took out a patent on the now-customised hovercraft, to be marketed by a French company.

Peissel's hovercraft ventures produced few results except for a book: the hovercraft was a novelty of transport, an experimental fad. In 1968, an English expedition hovered some 2,000 miles through South America; the following year, another English expedition topped that by hovering some 5,000 miles through Africa. But nothing memorable was written about these expeditions: there were no earth-shattering discoveries.

On his long road to adventure, Peissel has gotten into lots of trouble—and controversy. His writing has caused him to be banished in a handful of countries, and has propelled him to cross swords with rival explorers and testy academics. He can be abrasive and short-tempered. An example of his unorthodox approach was a journey in disguise from India into Pakistan in 1982. Dressed as a local, with his skin darkened with walnut dye, Peissel sneaked over a ceasefire line on a horse. He wanted to study the obscure Minaro tribespeople of the upper Indus, but he was also bent on solving the legend of the 'giant gold-digging ants' described by ancient Greek historian Herodotus, who in the 4th century BC wrote in his *Histories:*

> ...in this desert, there live amid the sand great ants, in size somewhat less than dogs, but bigger than foxes... Those ants make their dwelling under ground, and like the Greek ants, which they very much resemble in shape, throw up sand-heaps as they

burrow. Now the sand which they throw up is full of gold. The Indians…go into the desert to collect this sand…they fill their bags with the sand, and ride away at their best speed: the ants, however, scenting them, as the Persians say, rush forth hotly in pursuit.

Then again, Herodotus also wrote about snakes that fly; dog-headed men; tribes who squeak like bats, build houses of salt and never dream; and tribes that paint themselves red and eat monkeys. Back to the gold-digging ants: Peissel discovered that there was indeed a creature that dug 'for gold'. Himalayan marmots dug large quantities of gold-bearing sands out of their burrows—and the locals would sift through this sand. The Iranians who told the story to Herodotus apparently called marmots 'mountain ants': Peissel claims these discoveries lay the 2,500-year-old mystery to rest. The description of Herodotus, dismissed as fiction, was based on reality says Peissel—it simply got warped in translation.

After *Time* published a story revealing how the trip was accomplished, Peissel was banned from traveling in India. Peissel shrugs it off. The doors close in one country, but open in another. The same year, the doors to China suddenly swung open. Peissel had been barred from entering China and Tibet since the publication of his book about Khampa guerrillas. But after a decade of persistence, Chinese authorities finally granted him a visa—oddly enough, allowing him to visit the very place the Khampas originate from, a vast area known as Kham. He received permission to trek around Mount Minya Konka in 1982—an area first explored by Joseph Rock. Peissel had one huge advantage over other explorers to the region: he speaks Tibetan Khampa dialect.

It was during this expedition that Peissel stumbled across a series of tall, star-shaped towers dotting the valleys of the Kongpo region. Joseph Rock had spotted the towers and photographed them, but had not investigated further. Peissel was intrigued. Who built these colossal towers and why? Peissel says he was blown away by the discovery, but wasn't able to follow up. 'I broke both legs on that trip. *Merde!*' he offers by way of explanation.

Peissel had a run of bad luck with his early expeditions to Tibet. His second wife, Missy Allen, was along for an expedition to the Tsangpo gorges—she had to be rushed back to Lhasa because of a miscarriage. Peissel met Missy Allen at Harvard, married her in 1981, and took her on several expeditions. They collaborated on a series of educational books for young adults—with titles like *Dangerous Mammals, Dangerous Insects*, and *Dangerous Water Creatures*. And then they parted ways: Peissel laments that his obsession with exploring and solving riddles has cost him two marriages.

The origins of polo can be traced to ancient Tibet—where the game was devised as a way of training warriors in cavalry arts during times of peace. Even so, players could be killed during the rough-and-tumble Tibetan version of polo. Instead of a ball, the Tibetans used a sheep carcass, and no mallets—they just dangled off the saddle to pick up the carcass.

And some of Peissel's greatest discoveries owe their origins to the game of polo. Playing polo in Spain, he came in contact with Sebastian Guinness (the Guinness heir) and they got to talking about horse breeds. Peissel broached the idea of tracing the bloodline of the hardy Tibetan ponies, and Guinness offered to back an expedition. Although the object of Peissel's expeditions to Kham and Amdo was to study Tibetan horse breeds, the equine research opened up permits to highly restricted areas. And then Peissel realised that there was something else quite spectacular within his grasp—something that had been overlooked for a century.

The source of the Mekong River has proved one of Asia's most elusive riddles—and one of the world's last great geographical mysteries. In 1866, a French expedition of six explorers set off from Saigon to trace the Mekong to its source, but failed to get far in China, let alone into the Tibetan highlands. In 1894, another French expedition edged closer to the source, but ended in tragedy after its leader Jules Dutreuil de Rhins was killed by Khampas in a dispute over stolen horses. For close on a hundred years, the Mekong riddle was somehow overlooked—perhaps related to the fact that the fierce Khampas and Goloks of this area of northeastern Tibet kept outsiders away. The Goloks not only had an eye on expedition animals and goods—they were after heads. They attacked all foreigners who ventured into their grasslands, whether they be Muslim trading caravans, Tibetan pilgrims, Chinese immigrants or Western missionaries. Joseph Rock had been forced to turn back by the Goloks. Russian explorers Przhevalasky and Roborovsky had been robbed by them.

The drainage basin of the Mekong has been known for many decades. It is really a question of narrowing down which feeder stream might be the source—and that is a tricky question, because it may vary with volume of water, depending on the time of year being visited, rainfall distribution, whether streams vanish underground for a short distance, and so on.

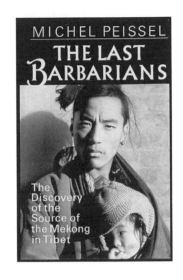

Peissel following up on clues left by Francis Grenard, the explorer-companion of Dutreuil de Rhins. Grenard theorised that the source lay along a river branch called the Lungmo. Armed with detailed maps, in September 1994, Peissel and two fellow adventurers—Sebastian Guinness and Dr Jacques Falck—set off in search of the elusive prize. Peissel's affinity with the Khampas and his command of Khampa dialect paved the way. Setting off on horseback on the final leg of their journey, the group located the Mekong's source in a spring field at the head of 16,322-foot Rupsa Pass in Kham. It was a mere trickle of water, a rivulet that you could stand astride (which Peissel did, for photos taken on-site).

The Franco-British expedition's discovery made headline news in *Paris-Match*, *Le Figaro* and the *New York Times*, followed by a flood of articles from Australia to Africa. Peissel stakes his Mekong claim in *The Last Barbarians*, published in 1997 (the title is a reference to the Khampas and Goloks, considered the 'last barbarians' of the Central Asian plateau by the Chinese). In the book, Peissel writes of taking altitude and GPS readings at the source:

> On the surface, these numbers were the entire purpose of our venture, the figures necessary to be able to pinpoint the source on any map of the world. This was what geography and exploration were all about. Just a few numbers, yet what a struggle to record them—how much bloodshed, tears, and sweat...

Peissel's documentary film on the discovery of the source of the Mekong was broadcast in 1998 in 28 countries—on the Arts & Entertainment Channel, National Geographic Channel, and as a Smithsonian Exploration Special.

Peissel was thrilled by the worldwide attention over the Mekong source discovery: he was over the moon about 'having reached the place where dreams and reality meet.' But the history of exploration is full of claims and counter-claims, and the source of the Mekong is a slippery prize. In 1999, two Chinese expeditions upstaged Peissel by discovering, in the same area, a northern branch of the Mekong that is further inland from the sea than Peissel's source.

Their data was based on the work of a joint Sino-Japanese expedition that searched the area exactly the same month that Peissel did—in September 1994. Seems ironic that two separate expeditions would find the source of the Mekong in the same month, after a search in progress for some 130 years. Peissel's co-ordinates for the Mekong's source were: Lat. 33.16.534 N, Long. 93.52.929 E, altitude 16,322 feet, at the head of Rupsa Pass. According to Tamotsu Nakamura, writing in the Japanese Alpine Club journal, the September 1994 joint Sino-Japanese expedition set the source at: Lat. 33.44.13 N, Long. 94.41.35 E, altitude 16,952 feet. And further expeditions of 1999 identified the source as being close to that, at the foot of a glacier on the north side of Mt. Guosongmucha: Lat. 33.42.31 N, Long. 94.41.44 E, altitude 17,135 feet.

There's an obvious tone of annoyance in Peissel's voice as he relates the Sino-Japanese claims. He concedes the Chinese claim on locating the true geographical source, but defends his claim on discovering the principal historical source or traditional headwater of the Mekong. Peissel says that in 1994, it was unknown if there was a single source or multiple sources for the Mekong. After the Chinese expeditions of 1999, he simply puts it down to two sources for the river: the valley of the Black Mekong (historical source or main headwater) and the valley of the White Mekong (geographical source, defined as being furthest from the sea). In this battle of the rivulets, the White Mekong source (Dza Kar) turned out to be a few miles longer than the Black Mekong source (Dza Nak). The controversy over the sources of the Mekong has yet to be fully resolved. And there's the question of giving the Tibetans some credit—they have known for hundreds, if not thousands of years, the source of the Mekong, which they identify as a sacred set of prayer flags.

In *The Last Barbarians*, Peissel details yet another significant discovery. On a 1995 expedition, in the remote valley of Riwoche in Kham, his party chanced across a herd of miniature wild horses. Peissel had initiated several expeditions to research horse breeds in Tibet: he has identified six distinct breeds and maintains that the Nangchen horse from Kham is a bloodline on a par with the Arabian horse. But on this trip Peissel got much more than he bargained for:

> We were now utterly convinced that the Riwoche horse was not only a breed apart, but that it was no doubt very, very ancient. In my mind's eye, I saw the horses of the Stone Age cave paintings.

Peissel was referring to French cave-paintings of horses in Chauvet—reckoned to be at least 17,000 years old—which, as it turned out, bear an uncanny resemblance to the Riwoche horse. Was this the missing archaic horse from prehistoric times? Domesticated horses dating back some 6,000 years ago (from skeletons found in tombs in Crimea) were small-bodied like the Riwoche horse. Blood samples taken from the Riwoche horse—tested by an equine geneticist—did not show any chromosomal abnormalities or variations, and Peissel's claims were shot down by some experts, but Peissel is convinced that this particular horse represents a missing link in equine evolution. Where were the world's first horses tamed? Who were the people who first dared to ride horses? The mystery remains unresolved.

By now I am convinced that Michel Peissel suffers from the same malady as Thomas Manning: restless-leg syndrome. He cannot stay in one place for more than a few minutes. Nor do we appear to stay on the same subject for long: Peissel has switched to describing Tibet's wildlife. The plateau is a wonderland for rare flora and fauna, evolved in startling ways to deal with the extreme climate. And very little is known about its natural secrets.

Tibet's abundant birdlife is intriguing, says Peissel: bar-headed geese fly over Himalayan peaks on their annual migration from Tibet to India, enduring temperatures down to minus 60 degrees Fahrenheit. The geese have been spotted flying at an altitude of 29,000 feet, which is just below the troposphere—making them astronauts on the wing. Also taking a high-altitude winter holiday over the Himalayas is the black-necked crane. The last of the crane species to be described, this rare creature was sighted in 1876 by Russian explorer Colonel Nikolai Prejevalsky at Lake Kokonor, on the northeast fringe of the plateau. In Tibet, even large mammals have eluded zoologists: Przewalski's horse is a wild miniature pony of the Mongolian steppes named after its Russian discoverer. The *kyang*—or Tibetan wild ass—is oddly more like a zebra without stripes than anything else. The *kyang*, admired for its fleetness and hardiness, has resisted all attempts at taming it. The British army attempted to domesticate them in 1904 for use as pack animals, but failed dismally. The yak, it seems, is one of very few wild animals on the plateau that has been domesticated.

Pursuing twin passions for zoology and ethnology, Peissel mounted several expeditions in the 1990s to the bleak Changtang desert region of northern Tibet, where he initiated studies on the Sengo nomads. The bleak, arid Changtang region is home to Tibet's last wild yaks and a number of other rare species, including the Tibetan grizzly—which Peissel managed to photograph. And he got a glimpse of an animal that had eluded him in more than 30 years of travel to the Tibetan plateau.

The animal is the Tibetan antelope or *chiru*. This mammal is so elusive it was not discovered until 1826 by British naturalist Brian Houghton Hodgson, who identified it from skins brought to him in Nepal. Hence the Latin name for the Tibetan antelope: *Pantholops hodgsoni*. Because of its obvious resemblance to African antelopes, Hodgson put it in that category, but recent DNA analysis classifies it as a caprid or goat family. However, it still acts and looks like an antelope—another weird wildlife twist in Tibet. And solving another riddle: the Tibetan antelope's long upright horns could make it the source of unicorn myths in Tibet that date back several centuries. If one horn is broken off during rutting season, the single remaining horn would make it appear unicorn-like.

Little is known about the *chiru*, about its migration cycles or its calving grounds. But in 1991, a great secret was unravelled. It concerns a riddle that goes back to 1774, to the early pages of this book, to the diplomatic expedition of George Bogle—and the search for the animal that bore the fine shawl-wool known as *shahtoosh*. Bogle never found out which animal this was, and for over 200 years those that did contrived to keep the knowledge secret. The secret of the wool's source was as closely guarded by Kashmiri weavers and Tibetan nomads as the origin of silk was by the Chinese. Kashmiris variously claimed that the wondrous wool was picked off bushes in Tibet after the ibex (Tibetan wild goat) passed through or that the ibex rubbed on rocks, leaving hair behind; others said shahtoosh came from the down of the 'toosh bird' or the Siberian goose.

Shahtoosh shawls were a sign of status—exclusive to royalty of India and central Asia, mostly worn by men. In fact, translated from Persian, shah-toosh means wool (*toosh*) of kings (*shah*). The wool is gossamer in weight and texture, soft as baby's skin, yet incredibly warm. Shahtoosh is so fine that even a large shawl can be pulled with ease through a finger ring, giving it another name—the 'ring shawl.' In the early 18th century, fine cashmere shawls were a fashion rage among elite society in England and France—most of these imported by the British East India Company. For reasons that are unclear, in the 1980s there was a sudden surge of interest in shahtoosh shawls and scarves in fashion boutiques in the West, sold to socialites and movie stars for up to $5,000 apiece. Larger shawls could sell for up to $20,000 each.

The elusive Tibetan antelope (*Pantholops hodgsoni*): the male sports long horns

In 1991, American wildlife expert Dr George Schaller received a letter from Michael Sautman, a Californian who was running cashmere processing plants in Mongolia and Tibet. Sautman had received a request from a firm in Italy for 500 kilograms of shahtoosh. Intrigued, Sautman and Schaller delved deeper. They knew the wool came from the Changtang region.

Traders said it was the underwool of the ibex, but Schaller knew there were few ibex in the Changtang. However, Schaller had seen a lot of antelope carcasses at a nomad camp in the Changtang, and Sautman had seen shahtoosh arriving in Lhasa for shipment to Kashmir. Comparing notes, the two men came to the conclusion that shahtoosh is the underwool of the Tibetan antelope. Drop-dead gorgeous: the antelope was being shot in large numbers in Tibet to feed a fashion craze in Hong Kong, Milan, Paris, London and New York.

Recent research has revealed that shahtoosh is the finest animal fibre in the world—finer than the hair of the vicuna (South America) or the Arctic muskox. The Tibetan antelope's wool is a special adaptation that traps layers of warm air close to its body so it can tolerate freezing temperatures—the key to its survival in the extreme environment of Tibet. To get this wool, Tibetan and Chinese hunters have to shoot the antelope. The chiru cannot be tamed or reared in captivity—and in any case, it would probably die from the cold if its underwool were shorn (and conversely, it might not grow the wool at all if conditions are not cold or windy enough).

Then Sautman and Schaller realised there was another identification problem: after the antelopes were shot and the underwool shorn off, this would be mixed in with fine cashmere wool for contraband transport. It was only with the advent of a specific DNA test that the raw wool could be identified as shahtoosh—or that a shawl could be determined to be made from shahtoosh rather than cashmere or pashmina. Of course, experts can determine this by hand, but DNA testing provided proof. George Schaller launched a campaign to have the trade in shahtoosh shawls completely banned.

In 1992, Schaller contacted Ashok Kumar, the director of TRAFFIC India—part of a cooperative effort to contain the international trade in endangered species. When Schaller explained the shahtoosh-antelope link, Ashok was incredulous. He went to shops in Delhi, where the owners told him the routine stories about the wool being collected off rocks and bushes from an animal that lives high in the mountains. Kashmiris are very nice people who would never kill any animals, he was told. Delving further, Ashok discovered that the Tibetan antelope was accorded the highest level of protection under India's own Wildlife Protection Act. So that this trade in shahtoosh shawls was in violation of India's own laws—if the link to the Tibetan antelope could be proven. Ashok said that the secretary of the handicraft association that represented the shahtoosh weavers and agents of Kashmir claimed the whole thing was an American conspiracy to close down the trade, that the Chinese wanted the market for themselves, and that Schaller was most likely a CIA agent.

Meanwhile, Peissel was in trouble again: he was making a study of the Sengo nomads—who are heavily involved with hunting the Tibetan antelope in the Changtang, and thus not keen on the idea of appearing on film. Sengo nomads still use old muskets that are steadied by two antelope horns, as a kind of tripod base. On paper, the Tibetan antelope is a protected species, with stringent penalties for poachers. But corruption is rampant, and poachers using 4WD vehicles and high-powered rifles have decimated numbers of the *chiru*. In 1900, the *chiru* population may have numbered a million in Tibet; today, it is on the verge of extinction.

This is a home where the wild yaks no longer roam, where the musk-deer and the antelope no longer play. Without the wildlife, warns George Schaller, Tibet's vast high steppe will have a great emptiness—depleted of some of the globe's most beautiful species.

Something that Peissel fails to mention: the Khampas are part of the antelope extinction problem. There is a two-way trade between Tibet and India in illegal species: sadly, one endangered species is being traded for another. The Kashmiris of India want to get their hands on the shahtoosh from dead antelopes, but coming north are the skins of tigers, leopards and otters. The tiger is highly prized in Chinese medicinal hokum, but the leopard and otter furs have another destination: Kham. In October 2003, three smugglers from Markham and Gonjo counties, which lie in Kham, were arrested when their truck was searched near the Tibet-Nepal border. The haul included 32 tiger furs, 579 leopard furs and 665 otter furs. The leopard and otter furs are highly prized for lining and for trimming of the elaborate sheep-skin cloaks worn by Kham nomads. Hats bear leopard-skin bands, and wooden trunks are covered with these skins for aesthetic reasons. Some use faux-leopard-skin trim or faux-otter, but the real thing is far preferred as a fashion statement, and as proof of the real thing, a claw may be retained, visible on a cloak.

It is a vicious fashion cycle. Rare animals from India feed the fashion demands of Khampas, who trade species, killing Tibetan antelopes to feed the fashion demands of socialites in the West. And yet there is a very simple solution to feeding demand for fine shawl wool: replace shahtoosh with high-quality pashmina—a high-grade cashmere wool from domestic goats and thus a renewable resource. The goats can shed this underwool in the summer and grow it back for winter. Shahtoosh is 9–12 microns thick, while pashmina is 12–16 microns thick.

Meanwhile, among the Khampas, demand for otter and tiger skins suddenly plummeted due to a speech given by the 14th Dalai Lama at a large religious initiation in India in January 2006. The Dalai Lama spoke out about the poaching of the Tibetan antelope and the devastating trade in shahtoosh shawls. He said that in previous times, Tibetans lived in great harmony with wildlife and nature, and that this admirable consonance should be revived. Then he said that he was

ashamed when he saw those pictures of nomads decorating themselves in skins and furs. As many as 10,000 pilgrims made their way to
this event from Tibet—and around 3,000 of them signed a pledge that
they would not buy, wear or sell rare animal-skin products. When they
returned home from India, nomads from Kham and Amdo cheerfully
set about burning coats trimmed with otter, leopard and tiger.

This interview has bounced across the Tibetan plateau from Bhutan to
Amdo, and now it bounces back to those mysterious towers. 'Ah yes,
I didn't get round to it, but Frédérique followed it up, you know,' grins
Peissel. The towers come up as he shows me a picture of himself in
Tibet with an arm around the lovely Frédérique and sighs—she obviously brings back some exciting memories. 'I would have gone for her,
but Ted Turner had her,' he confides, wistfully. He means Ted Turner
of CNN fame—some tough competition. The free-spirited Frédérique
Darragon is a wealthy adventurer and a top polo player—a woman
who can rough it in the field but is quite at home in an elegant restaurant in Paris too.

Peissel sent Darragon off at a tangent: originally she set out to study
the snow leopard, but got sidetracked by the towers. She spent some
five years on-and-off wandering to collect material on them. Peissel and Darragon combined skills to produce a one-hour documentary for the Discovery Channel, aired in 2003. Some towers reach up
to 200 feet—as tall as modern 15-storey buildings. And some are up
to a thousand years old. Darragon has discovered the towers are able
to withstand violent earthquakes over the centuries because of their
star-shaped corners. Nobody had ever studied them until Peissel and
Darragon. But their exact function? Still a mystery.

Mustang, Bhutan, Ladakh, Changtang: all of his expeditions to the
Tibetan Plateau come together in his book, *Tibet: the Secret Continent*
(published in 2002). This large-format hardcover, illustrated by Peissel's fine photography, is about the Tibetosphere, the Tibetan sphere
of influence. A forgotten empire in the heart of Asia, this once-mighty
realm covers an area the size of western Europe. Peissel has logged a
lot of miles on the Tibetan Plateau. In fact, he has seen more of Tibet
than any living explorer—or indeed, explorer of any age. It's an unusual

calling in our time—to be an explorer. Peissel has succeeded in carving out a niche—doing exactly what he dreamed of doing. In the course of all this he has written over 20 books and been involved in the production of more than 20 documentary films and videos. And there are a number of other projects in the works. One of these is a book about the temple and fortress architecture of Tibet—which he intends to illustrate with his own watercolour sketches. Peissel discovered that he could get a better feel for buildings and the process of construction through time-consuming sketches rather than instant photography. 'The artist must learn and analyse what the lens of a camera cannot see,' says Peissel.

He says he's a lucky man to have been able to fulfill his dreams. How many people these days get to write 'Explorer' on their business card? So I ask him: Do explorers retire? And potter round the garden? Pore nostalgically over maps?

Peissel stops in his tracks, at a loss for words. He looks bemused, incredulous. He has not even contemplated such a prospect. Not any time soon, he responds. He has put on weight, he has a bulging stomach, he has grey hair—but he's in good shape, and his energy levels have not diminished. And his burning curiosity, he explains with an impish gleam in his eyes, grows stronger with the passage of time.

The Dome of Inspiration

In the footsteps of the explorers

BOOKS ARE PORTALS to other worlds—they fire up the imagination, open doors to magical new realms. Alexandra David-Néel was inspired by the impossible adventures of Jules Verne fantasies. And having overcome incredible obstacles herself, Alexandra in turn became a role model who inspired many others—particularly female travellers intent on following in her footsteps. If not on her real route, then at least in spirit. I once shared a Landcruiser in central Tibet with a backpacker crew that included a woman from Belgium—in her late forties—who was stubborn as a yak. Then I got a glimpse of the book she was reading: *Voyage d'une Parisienne à Lhassa*. That explained everything.

The explorers profiled in this book have all inspired me to go further than I ever imagined possible. They have pushed me to the limits—and damn the cost. I have not only followed Alexandra David-Néel's path, I have thundered along in Eric Bailey's hoof prints, trekked in the caravan tracks of Tucci and Rock, and huffed and puffed on a mountain-bike from Tibet to Nepal—along a similar route taken by Peter Aufschnaiter. This chapter recounts some of those experiences, and fills in a historical gap by focusing on Tibet of the present day—under iron-fisted Chinese occupation. Today, genuine Tibetan religious rites and culture survive outside of Tibet itself—in the regions of Himalayan India, Nepal and Bhutan. I hope that this book will inspire the reader to go and see the Tibetan world—to get right off the beaten path. Because the ancient Tibetan culture has much to offer—and much to discover.

Inspiration is a curious thing—it can strike out of nowhere. Two writers who have inspired legions of travellers to go to Tibet never actually set foot in the place. They got no further than the Reading Room in London. I am referring to the Reading Room of the British Museum—once the premier library of London, now downscaled to a showpiece after the British Library relocated to bigger premises. The Reading Room is a cavernous domed structure built along classical lines: lining the walls are row upon row of books; in the central area are row upon row of comfortable wooden desks with leather covers.

The two men? James Hilton, author of *Lost Horizon* (1933) and Lobsang Rampa, author of *The Third Eye* (1956). Both books were huge bestsellers—still in print today. And they have had a great impact on how Tibet has locked onto the Western imagination. *Lost Horizon* is presented as fiction—but many today try to link it to a real place. *The Third Eye* claims to be a real biographical account—but is fictitious. It was at the Reading Room that Rampa boned up on his sources—most likely Madame Blavatsky, Alexandra David-Néel, Nicholas Roerich and other mystics. He stole from these authors—and then outsold them many times over. James Hilton came to the Reading Room to absorb the lives of early missionaries to Tibet, and to crib from the works of Alexandra David-Néel. He may also have tapped into National Geographic feature stories by Joseph Rock when crafting the utopia of Shangri-La that appeared in *Lost Horizon*.

And the genesis of the book you are now holding can be traced to Lobsang Rampa. The idea started in a hot shower at Kathmandu Guesthouse. For a week or so in Kathmandu, I had baulked at buying an old book because of the cost. The book was a 1960s first edition called *The Rampa Story*: it was for sale next door in the rare book section of Pilgrims Bookhouse. I was about to fly out of Kathmandu, so now the decision would have to be made. It was during the shower that I hit on an idea: I could justify this purchase if it was research for my own book. What book? *Something to do with bizarre biography.* Now I had the justification. I quickly towelled dry, rushed down and bought the book, grabbed my bags and hopped a taxi to the airport.

On the plane, I started to read *The Rampa Story*—an outrageous 'autobiography', full of masterful hokum, poppycock, balderdash, mumbo-jumbo. I was thoroughly transported. And up in the clouds, an idea started to take shape. Rampa was a total nutcase. What about putting together more just like him—more oddball explorers of Tibet?

All between the covers of a single book? And call it *Eccentric Explorers*. I did not know then that this project would lead me on a wild goose chase lasting a number of years. Nor did I know that Rampa's profile would be the most difficult to nail down. But Rampa is here, in the book on eccentrics that I envisaged on that flight out of Kathmandu.

Rampa didn't need airplanes—he claimed to indulge in astral travel. And if the mood took him, to indulge in time-travel as well. Can you travel back in time? Teleport yourself to another era? Sure you can. Just watch the movie. If the movie is set in 1900, you can empathise: in the darkened theatre, cinematic sleight of hand transports back to that era—bridging time and space. You become a temponaut—a virtual time traveller. I went one better: I was actually in such a period movie, hired as an extra, on location near Gyantse, central Tibet. And I can tell you exactly how Eric Bailey felt in 1903: breathless, but exhilarated. Because I was dressed up myself in pith helmet and dashing around firing a .303 rifle at everything that moved—mostly Tibetans (who were in fact Chinese PLA troops dressed up as Tibetans).

We're on a film-set about twelve miles south of Gyantse, for the shooting of a movie called *Red River Valley*. The director is Feng Xiaoning from Shanghai Film Studios, and this is the second-biggest-budget film ever made in China up until this date (1996). The top film, I later find out, is *The Opium War*, which is about China's humiliation at the

The Union Jack, somewhat tattered, flies again in Gyantse, central Tibet —with PLA troops dressed as British troopers on the movie set

hands of the British during the original loss of Hong Kong in the 1830s. Both movies are slated for release to coincide with the 1997 British handover of Hong Kong.

Big budget means our director can even indulge in importing two professional Hollywood actors, one of whom plays a character who bears an uncanny resemblance to the British commander, Colonel Younghusband—goatee and all. Along with a motley crew of backpackers in Lhasa, I was recruited as an extra to play a British trooper.

The director's problem is how to rewrite history to suit the theme of heroic Tibetan resistance to the British barbarians, who also happen to be the military victors. Feng Xiaoning has done this by fictionalising the story, but still leaving it with highly recognisable elements. Initially, two British officers enter Tibet on a mission to collect butterfly specimens (shades of Eric Bailey). Later the same two return at the head of an invading British army, hell-bent on bringing 'civilisation' to the backward Tibetans. One of them is a Younghusband look-alike; the other is a sensitive army photographer who is horrified when British troops slaughter the Tibetans in battle. Besides which, he has fallen in love with a Tibetan chieftain's daughter. The two represent polarised points-of-view on invading Tibet. At the end of the story, everyone gets blown up—the heroines are blown up, the Tibetans are all blown away, most of the Brits die, and the Younghusband figure is also killed. So that takes care of the anomalies of history.

All the troops—Tibetan and British alike—are played by PLA 'extras' who arrive in a convoy of military trucks. Wardrobe and make-up artists transform them into their respective roles. The female roles are filled by well-known Chinese actresses, decked out in Tibetan jewellery—with the heroine played by the alluring Ning Jing. The PLA-Tibetan troops put on cloaks and are supplied with rattan shields,

Postcard from 1904: on the set of the movie *Red River Valley*, near Gyantse, the author (at right) is dressed as a British trooper

swords and blunderbusses; they wear wild hair-pieces. PLA-Brits don khaki uniforms, pith helmets, wigs and moustaches. As big-nosed Western extras, our job is to march past the camera in close-ups, while the PLA-Brit soldiers rumble along behind, slightly out of focus.

The eerie thing is that if you ignore the film crew, the illusion of being with the British expeditionary force of 1903 is complete. Long lines of horses and riders saunter through desert terrain under cobalt-blue skies; in the background, the imposing ruins of a Tibetan fort command a hillside. Adding battle atmosphere, an assistant runs amok with a sizzling censer that billows black smoke everywhere. *Action!* We mount an infantry charge, wildly firing blanks. I trip over my sword. We have to do the scene again. And again. Half a dozen times. I discover sprinting up a hill with a .303 rifle at this altitude can easily cause you to keel over, totally winded. Better off being a mounted officer, like Bailey.

On this set, I feel more than just empathy with Bailey and the 1903 expedition. I am undercover—on the inside of the making of a Chinese propaganda movie. I have never felt more like a spy in my life. This is great! Never, ever, invite a writer along as an extra on a film shoot: they come up with their own script on the proceedings.

Red River Valley was released in early 1997 to coincide with the handover of Hong Kong, as planned, but it bombed in theatres there. In

mainland China, it was a hit—it won Best Picture and Best Director
at the 20th Hundred Flower awards in 1997, and Best Music and Best
Editing at the 17th Golden Rooster awards, also in 1997. In the wake
of the June 1997 British handover of Hong Kong to China, the Chinese launched a major round of Brit-bashing. This included not only
making anti-Brit movies, but beefing up the rhetoric in Gyantse itself.
Gyantse fell into the spotlight as the heroic city where, in 1904, the
Tibetans staged their last stand on the road to Lhasa. In what was then
history's highest-altitude battle, the British stormed the fort and blew
up the powder magazine, leaving many Tibetans dead.

After everything had been blown to pieces, and all the mayhem
and shooting was over, and the PLA actor-troops had all boarded
their trucks and headed back to their bases, I found the opportunity
to wander off and explore Gyantse—looking for traces of Eric Bailey.
His presence was there—but his story somewhat skewed by Chinese
propaganda handiwork. Nothing survives of the British Trade Agency
compound in Gyantse that Eric Bailey commanded. It was swept away
by severe flooding in the 1950s. However, oddly shaped mud-packed
posts can still be seen on sections of highway in this area—remnants
of the British telegraph line from Sikkim to Gyantse. After a lot of dickering, the line was extended in 1922 to Lhasa, linking the capital of
Tibet directly with the outside world for the first time.

You won't find a statue of Francis Younghusband or Eric Bailey in
the town square of Gyantse today, but there are bas-reliefs of British
soldiers in pith helmets gracing the Hero Monument, just off the main
roundabout on Hero Boulevard. The Hero Monument is a huge three-
sided obelisk with text on each side—in Chinese, Tibetan and English. The English side reads: *Gyangtse Mount Dzong Monument to Heroes.*
Around the base of the obelisk are bas-reliefs: the front sections show
the battle of 1904 with Tibetans throwing down rocks, British troops
(easily identified by pith helmets and guns), and what appears to be
characters with Chinese dress and swords (not historically correct,
as there were no Chinese soldiers or advisers in Gyantse in 1904). A
side panel shows the British with heavy machinery; the back panel
shows PLA troops waving Chinese flags and people holding portraits
of Mao Zedong. The monument is set in a small park with a curious
entrance—a large wooden doorway guarded by Chinese imperial lions,
not Tibetan snow lions.

Towering in the background is Gyantse Dzong—the 500-year-old colossus where the Tibetans made their last stand against the British. The Tibetans lost the battle of Gyantse Fort to the British, but Chinese propaganda overlooks that detail. Up inside the fort is a small on-site museum called 'Memorial Hall of the anti-British'. Centre-piece for this hall is a bronze statue of Tibetans striking heroic poses while fighting the imperialist British. On the walls, the text cites 'Tibetan patriotic soldiers safeguarded state sovereignty and territorial integrity—defending the China-Tibet Motherland.' Also overlooked is the fact that the fort lies in ruins because the buildings and battlements were blown to smithereens at various points by Nepalese invaders, then British invaders—and finally by Mao Zedong's fanatical Red Guards. There is lots of rubble lying around—the Chinese blame it all on British cannons. Even so, it is one of the best-preserved forts in Tibet. I make my way up to the topmost battlements, which offer superb 747 views over Gyantse. From here, looking over the old quarter with its narrow lanes, you can almost imagine Gyantse as it once was.

That's much harder to do in Lhasa. Peter Aufschnaiter would barely recognise the Lhasa he so carefully surveyed in the late 1940s. A China Mobile poster broadcasts its vision of Lhasa's future: the Potala still dominates the skyline, but glass skyscrapers and telecom towers intrude—and in the foreground is a sleek futuristic-looking train (which arrived in 2006, against all geographic odds). Marking the arrival of the railway on Lhasa television, Chinese railway engineers and the PLA soldiers perform a kind of victory dance—army officers in green uniforms and white gloves prance around with women in Tibetan costume.

Thomas Manning (visiting in 1811) and Colonel Younghusband (invading in 1904) were disappointed with Lhasa, feeling cheated of the mystique they had expected. And the same phenomenon is true of Lhasa today—for quite different reasons. In the 21st century, Lhasa has turned into a humdrum Chinese town—it has the air of a Chinese theme park: Peking has come to Lhasa. The Chinese population is an occupying force: military, para-military, police and bureaucrats. Opposite the Potala is a vast square, modelled on Peking's Tiananmen Square, with the same lamp-posts with speakers attached to them. Potala Square is designed for military parades. Ominously, one of the tallest buildings in Lhasa today is the 13-storey police office tower, on the Sera Road. Ringing Lhasa are scores of military bases; there are several jails whose sole purpose is the incarceration of Tibetan political prisoners under dire conditions.

Down by the Kyi Chu River is a 17-floor tower, the Tibet Trade Centre. The structure shimmers with a green-tinted glass facade—strikingly out of character with old Lhasan architecture which used very little glass (sheets of glass had to be carried in over the Himalayas from India on animal-back). The Tibetans never used concrete in traditional structures—not even to bind stonework together. Concrete is the favourite Chinese building material, with a factory devoted to its production in Lhasa. Rows and rows of faceless Chinese concrete apartment blocks and government buildings and shops stretch west and north of the Potala. Major traffic roundabouts feature garish golden statues, built by the Chinese to commemorate their reign of terror. At night, glowing neon signs or lanterns with Chinese characters denote restaurants, bars, and karaoke salons. And, more discreetly, mini-brothels—of which there are many in Lhasa, catering to Chinese troops and settlers.

A throbbing Tibetan pulse is still found at Barkor Bazaar, where pockets of traditional buildings are clustered around the Jokhang Temple. This quarter is a riot of action and colour. Scores of pilgrims make the rounds, walking a sacred circuit of the Jokhang Temple. Six-foot-high conical incense burners billow clouds of smoke: the smell of juniper fills the air. Vendors lining the route loudly broadcast their wares. Pilgrims mutter mantras as they circumambulate the Barkor. Arriving on pilgrimage from far-flung regions are nomads—Golok women with hair done in 108 braids, Khampa men with red yarn tasselled through the hair. Among the crowd are beggars, just as in Manning's day: they are often pilgrims who have simply run out of money on their long journey. Today, monasteries in Lhasa valley are kept open and running purely because of their tourist appeal: men from the Chinese Religious Affairs Bureau keep an Orwellian eye on monks to make sure they don't step out of line. This is how a bunch of atheists handle Tibetan Buddhism: they sell it. The Potala is one of the main targets on the pilgrimage rounds, but it is a haunted castle—a lifeless museum that has not seen its rightful masters since 1959, when the 14th Dalai Lama fled to India.

When Chinese authorities first opened Tibet up to individual travellers, I jumped at the chance. At that time, you could go just about anywhere you wanted. Chinese authorities figured you would be hampered by a complete lack of transport infrastructure. But enterprising backpackers hitched rides on trucks—and the authorities underestimated the range of a mountain-bike. You can go a long way on a mountain-bike. All you need is a good dirt road, one that is dry because of little rain. Tibet is perfect for that. Back in the saddle, I am following Aufschnaiter's rough escape route out of Tibet in 1951, via Mount Everest and Mount Shishapangma. But he was on foot; I'm on a mountain bike. And at this slow pace in the saddle, I soak up the majestic mountain vistas, the silence, the honking of the wild geese.

In the 1920s and 1930s, in Maurice Wilson's day, British mountaineering expeditions marvelled at the great herds of wild animals they encountered on the approach to the north face of Mount Everest. That wildlife sanctuary has completely disappeared today. There's no trace of wildlife at Rongbuk except for the odd marmot. Rongbuk Monastery was razed during the Cultural Revolution, but partially rebuilt. In 1959, the abbot fled to the other side of Everest—to Nepal. He established a monastery at Junbesi, where contemplation of the peak continues. In the early 1960s, the Chinese and Nepalese wrestled over who owned the mountain—with claims and counter-claims—but the dividing line today still runs through the summit of Everest. Half the mountain belongs to Tibet, the other half belongs to Nepal.

The mountain itself? Awesome, towering, deadly. It's difficult to convey what it feels like to be in the presence of this colossus. It summons up all kinds of contradictory emotions. It's such a powerful place, and yet you feel so insignificant. It's a magical place—and yet an alien world, at the end of the earth. It's a place you know you wouldn't survive in for very long, a place where you feel menace in the air from the hostile environment. Half of you wants to scurry back to safer ground, but the other half is drawn to the wondrous poetry—the symphony of ice and snow and rock—of this great peak. You can feel the pull of the peak, but you know this spells danger. And for Maurice Wilson, the sighting must have been exhilarating—but at the same time, chilling.

At Rongbuk Monastery, the chanting at the modest main hall catches my ear: deep chanting of the monks, but offset by higher-pitched singing. That comes from nuns—they are conducting joint prayers until the reconstruction of an outlying nunnery can be completed. As I explore around the fringes of Rongbuk, looking for a vantage point to take photos (monastery in foreground, north face of Everest in background), I spot a simple stone hut on a ridge. The wind picks up, at times bringing my progress to a standstill. Totally out of breath, I reach the stone hut. A monk, somewhat surprised, invites me in, gives me butter tea. I look around. The hut is bare. The monk has nothing, but he has a few glass windows—offering the finest mountain view in the world.

On another foray to the western side of the Tibetan Plateau, I travel in the tracks of two explorers—Giuseppe Tucci and Michel Peissel—searching for ancient kingdoms. This has to be the all-time favourite explorer pursuit. The trip unravels with this theme—two fantastic kingdoms, back-to-back—lost kingdom, hidden kingdom. First up is Tsaparang in west Tibet. As the Landcruiser bumps over a rough dirt road on the final leg to Tsaparang, I wonder how anybody could possibly survive out here—it's hard to imagine an entire kingdom making it in such a barren and desolate place. Then up in the distance looms the long-abandoned citadel of Tsaparang, the base of the Guge Kingdom.

Tucci was the last European to see and record the fabulous artwork of the Guge Kingdom before Tibet fell to the Chinese. The murals and statues were well-preserved by the extremely arid climate when Tucci saw them. The art escaped plundering by Western treasure-seekers and museum collectors, but not the Chinese. In the mid-1960s, Red Guards ran amok and trashed the temples of Guge, smashing precious statuary, but miraculously leaving the murals largely unscathed. The temples suffered some water damage, but since this is a desert, things are kept freeze-dried naturally. It's an odd juxtaposition of clay ruins, destroyed statuary and intact murals on temple walls.

To reach the top of Tsaparang Citadel you must scramble through a long spiralling tunnel that is bored out of clay, with steps cut out. This tunnel could be completely sealed in times of siege. At the uppermost reaches is Tsaparang Dzong, with various structures thought to serve as palaces for the king, queen and high officials. The finest artwork of Tsaparang is found in a tiny building here—the *gonkhang* or protector chapel. A three-dimensional mandala within has been smashed to pieces by Red Guards, but exquisite miniature murals still grace the walls—of voluptuous female dancers who represent guardian angels, and of gory disembodiment scenes from hell realms. The view from the top of the citadel is phenomenal—dramatic desert landscapes stretch to the far horizon, dotted with snowcaps. From this perch, Tsaparang seems like a fantastic, mythical place—so far removed from anything you've known that you cannot help feeling like an explorer. It is an encounter with a culture that is at once alien yet highly imaginative, with bold design and vibrant use of colour. Tucci's arduous approach to this place, on foot and horseback, could only have enhanced that feeling of great wonder.

Although it was once within the Tibetan orbit, on a salt-trading route, the medieval kingdom of Mustang must now be approached from Kathmandu in Nepal. Returning from Guge, I cross overland from Tibet to Kathmandu, and fly to Jomosom to join a trekking group headed for Mustang. Because of its political sensitivity and the presence of the Khampa warriors, soon after Michel Peissel's visit, Mustang was closed down to outsiders—for over 25 years. When it re-opened in 1992, Peissel made the trip back to Mustang on horseback. I was among those who later followed—with a trek in 1996: Peissel's book on Mustang was my inspiration and my guide.

The only way into Mustang is on foot—all supplies must be moved by packhorse or mule. Access is restricted to guided groups. Our small group of Canadian trekkers follows the Kali Gandaki valley for several days, and then climb out of it, up a route hacked out of yellowish rock—poetically known as the Golden Staircase. Once you scale this obstacle, you enter the realm of Mustang, which actually lies on the Tibetan plateau. The ethereal snowcaps of the Himalayas float high above, dominated by the majesty of Annapurna.

Six days of arduous trekking brings us to the citadel of Lo Monthang, the only walled Tibetan town in the Himalayas. The town consists of 200-odd houses crammed together. It has only one gate, at the north. Close by is the king's palace, a fortress-style white building rising four storeys. We discover the king is open to receiving foreign guests for an audience, and soon we are making our way up the dim palace stairs. A Tibetan mastiff on a chain growls menacingly. Suspended from the ceiling is its predecessor, a giant stuffed Tibetan mastiff. We are ushered into the Tibetan-style tea-room of King Jigme Parbal Bista, who sits with one hand twirling prayer beads, the other stroking his Lhasa Apso. As is the custom, we each present the king with a white scarf, which is then placed back around the offerer's neck as a blessing. We present goods brought in from Kathmandu and then settle down on the low carpeted couches, feeling like envoys from a distant place. Some awful butter tea is served; a Sherpa acts as interpreter for question and answer.

Apart from a change of kings, little seemed to have altered in Lo Monthang since Peissel's book was first published. In fact, Peissel's key contact in Mustang—Pemba—lives in the centre of town, running a souvenir shop—which sells copies of Peissel's book. His son shows us around. But this isolation will not last. Electricity is snaking its way up the valley, and the last I heard, there are plans in the works to build a motorable road all the way to Lo Monthang.

In the 1960s, when Michel Peissel set about exploring the region of Mustang, his greatest obstacle was Khampa guerrillas, engaged in a secret war with the Chinese in Tibet. The quick-tempered warriors of eastern Tibet—the Khampas and the Goloks—were the greatest impediment to exploration of these regions. Alexandra David-Néel managed to win them over through her command of the local dialect and her extensive knowledge of Tibetan rites—the Khampas even venerated her as a female incarnation.

Who are the Khampas? And the Goloks? And the other warrior tribes of Amdo? You can see all of these clans if you are lucky enough to witness a full-moon festival with a horse-racing fair. These take place in the summer, in the grassland areas of northern Tibet and the peripheral areas of Kham and Amdo. When a chance came up to one, I jumped in a Landcruiser and headed out.

For this horse-racing fair, an impromptu tent-village is staked out for a period of four or five days; nomads stream in from surrounding areas. Horse fairs are the year's premier social events—nomad clans congregate to compete in races and archery, to swap news, and have some fun before the approach of winter. In former times, horse-racing fairs were considered 'marriage markets'—pretty, marriageable women decked out in their finest would gather while men of other tribes sized them up. Then the women would gallop off with the men in hot pursuit. Catching a woman was tantamount to keeping her, even if she happened to be the daughter of a rival, or enemy.

This kind of chase is rare today, but horse-racing fairs definitely have elements of match-making. Young Khampa women arrive

Khampas getting ready to compete in horseback archery contest in Kham

dressed in their finest costumes, loaded down with coral, amber, turquoise and silver jewellery—the more flamboyant, the more available. The women eye the competitors, checking out their horse-handling skills. In these remote grassland regions, a fine stallion is a sign of status, wealth and social position: a nomad will not part with a strong, fast steed no matter what the price.

In the warm-up to the main racing events, riders whoop and holler, launching their mounts at full gallop and perform acrobatics and trick-riding: letting go of the reins, reaching down from the saddle to scoop up ceremonial scarves from the ground, even riding the horse backwards (the horse still goes forward, but the rider sits backward). Spicing up the atmosphere are games, and rounds of communal drinking, singing and folk-dancing. And then the main event—the horse-race final. There are no dividing lanes, just a flat piece of grassland. The riders jostle for the lead in a wild thundering pack headed for the finish pole. Deciding on the actual winner is cause for heated debate, but eventually the lucky winner and his horse are wreathed in ceremonial white scarves. And after spending five days at this horse-racing fair—seeing the Khampas in action—I have a much better idea of who they are. They are tall, fearless, bold—and above all, proud people. Proud of their warrior-and-brigand descent, proud of their horses, proud of their traditions.

Joseph Rock adopted his own solution for keeping Khampas and assorted native bandits at bay—he travelled with a posse of reliable men, armed to the teeth and bristling with guns. But even Rock gave up in Golok territory—he was forced to turn back. Goloks are renowned for their stubborn streak—they are called 'those with their heads turned backwards.' The threat of banditry in these areas has been muted today by heavy Chinese military and para-military presence in these peripheral areas of the Tibetan plateau—the area formerly known as Kham, and today carved off into the Chinese provinces of western Sichuan and upper Yunnan.

Stephanne Sutton, Rock's biographer, said she would have loved to travel in Rock's footsteps but the Tibetan borderlands were closed to foreigners in the 1970s, so no chance. In 2001, the entire area of Ganzi in western Sichuan opened up to foreigners without any permits—for the first time in recent memory. I was determined to take advantage of this 'offer': with Chinese permits and regulations you never know when the doors are going to slam shut again. I manage to wrangle magazine assignments in Hong Kong—one for *Time Asia*, the other for an inflight magazine called *Silkroad*. I promise to write about the discovery of Shangri-La in southwest China, said to be connected to the writings of Joseph Rock.

This trip is quite different from the others in the footsteps of the explorers because retracing Rock's steps was my sole object. For the first leg of the journey, I team up with two feisty Australians—Tony and Peta. We take a series of buses, rattling over a high alpine route from Chengdu, headed for the remote town of Daocheng, the gateway to the Konkaling range—passing through a sparsely populated region that is home to yak herders who live in triple-storied stone farmhouses. In Daocheng, two days hence, we discover a wonderful Tibetan-style B&B to stay in—a castellated structure on the edge of town where we can recover from the jarring bus rides and marshal our forces for the road ahead. Sorting through his supplies, Tony turns suddenly and says *Fuck it! I've left the Vegemite in Chendgu!* The loss of the Vegemite, the essential black substance spread on toast by Australians, is a serious setback. And then, as if by way of apology for his strong language, Tony follows up with: *Pardon my French*.

The next morning, he has a lot more reason to say *Pardon my French*: a heavy snowfall throws all our plans into disarray. But the snow suddenly stops and the skies miraculously clear. We pile into two jeeps with some Chinese tourists and head for the hills. A lengthy kidney-jarring ride brings us to the fortress-like monastery of Gongaling, with over 300 monks—the same one that pops up in Shangri-La-type brochures from Sichuan. Then we push on to Yading village, where we spend the night in a tented camp.

Yading Nature Reserve occupies close on 400 square miles of rugged terrain: gushing streams, luxuriant forests of larch, pine, cypress, fir and oak, and majestic snowcaps with cascading glaciers and odd-coloured glacial lakes. And this day, the beauty is magnified because everything is blanketed in fresh snow. I am taking in these vistas from horseback. Like the Chinese visitors, we have rented horses for the nine-mile ride to another tented camp at the base of the sacred peaks. Turns out to be a wise choice, because underfoot is all slush and mud. Horsing around in Shangri-La: we move in a caravan as long as Rock's, but all Chinese tourists—armed to the teeth with cellphones and cameras.

Our guide to the area is, in fact, Doctor Rock. Failing to find any more recent descriptions of this area, Tony has brought along the July 1931 issue of National Geographic that details Rock's expedition to the Konkaling range—a whopping 65 pages of text and photos. Rock would have hated this tourist invasion in an area so remote, so pristine. But he would've marvelled at the high-tech equipment of the well-heeled Chinese visitors—their digital cameras, video cameras and knock-off North Face jackets. If you ignore the fancy jackets and the cellphones, you can experience the illusion of really following in Rock's footsteps—horse caravan and all. Back in the saddle again: right now, I am sitting exactly where many of the profiled eccentric explorers have sat—on a Tibetan-style saddle on a sure-footed Tibetan pony. The saddle is ingeniously constructed using very simple materials. First a brightly coloured carpet is placed on the horse's back, then a rudimentary wooden saddle, and topping this is a thinner handwoven Tibetan blanket to soften the ride. I have ridden on this kind of saddle in many places across the Tibetan world—the saddle speaks of the cohesiveness of Tibetan culture. Saddlebags are traditionally made of musk-deer skin.

If you come from the polluted urban core of Shanghai or Nanjing, then Yading indeed must appear to be a slice of paradise. From a tented camp at Luorong, we admire stupendous panoramas of Jambeyang and Chanadorje, two sacred peaks. Jambeyang, just under 20,000 feet, is a conical classic, with razor-edged snow precipices leading to the summit. For mountaineers, it presents a tantalising challenge: it has never been scaled, though expedition attempts have been launched.

I bid goodbye to Tony and Peta, who are turning back to Chengdu—and the Vegemite—and carry on with new-found Chinese travelling companions, who are heading in the same direction. We rent a jeep for the next leg to the sizeable town of Zhongdian, formerly known as Gyalthang in Tibetan. *Welcome to Shangri-La!* proudly proclaims the town map. Nobody with marbles intact could mistake Zhongdian for Shangri-La: it's a bland Chinese city full of concrete and karaoke, which doesn't fit the bill. But Zhongdian is being spruced up with construction of fresh neo-Tibetan architectural monstrosities in preparation for its role as gateway to Shangri-La. And this is all linked to Joseph Rock, posthumously. Rock's National Geographic stories are cited by Chinese spin-doctors as the main source of James Hilton's novel *Lost Horizon*. One small problem: while Rock wrote about the Konkaling Range in his 1931 feature for National Geographic, he didn't write anything about Zhongdian or Deqin for that magazine. He wrote about those regions in a mammoth two-volume academic work *The Ancient Na-Khi Kingdom of Southwest China*, published by Harvard in 1947—which was long after Hilton's *Lost Horizon* appeared.

Ignoring this anomaly, Zhongdian authorities have forged on in their goal to be recognised as the real Shangri-La (later, in 2002, three counties in the region were officially renamed Shangri-La County). To bolster their claim to paradise, in 2001 authorities in Zhongdian unveiled some irrefutable evidence: a vintage flush toilet—imported, used and finally abandoned by foreign missionaries (the mythical Shangri-La has state-of-the-art plumbing, as well as a High Lama from Europe). You can purchase a bottle of Shangri-La Red, a wine made in Yunnan, supposedly based on a recipe concocted by Jesuit missionaries. A number of businesses in Zhongdian blithely use the Shangri-La logo without rhyme or reason.

Coming down to earth: starting the grand descent off the Tibetan plateau. Down, down, down from Zhongdian to the ancient town of Lijiang, in southern Yunnan. The place exudes character. Sensibly, the Old Quarter of Lijiang is closed to motor traffic, but is besieged by Chinese tourists in tour-groups. Lijiang's designation as a World Heritage site has preserved its ancient architecture. Everything is capably run by Naxi women—they operate the restaurants, the shops, all the tourist venues. They are dressed in exquisite costume— embroidered white chemise, maroon velvet waistcoat, and ruffled white skirt. Though a compromised version of matriarchy is practiced today, Naxi women still make the family decisions, control the finances and do much of the labour in the house or in the fields, while men idle time away with poetry, music and calligraphy.

The Naxi lay claim to the oldest dance score in the world—and the world's oldest orchestra. At a performance, we see an octogenarian group in action: these are the only ones who can remember the music. During the Cultural Revolution, the music and culture of the Naxi was banned. The orchestra conductor, Naxi musicologist Xuan Ke, spent 21 years in jail for the crime of trying to preserve Naxi culture—and is now hailed as a hero for reviving it. He is also the mythmaker who started up the Shangri-La link.

Lijiang: Rock's old stamping ground. Jade Dragon Snow Mountain featured as backdrop in his expedition departure photographs for National Geographic, and the same mountain was prime ground for plant hunting. Today, getting to the snowy upper reaches of Jade Dragon Snow Mountain is a snap: buses unload Chinese tourists at the base of the 18,360-foot peak. From there, the highest cable car in Asia—nearly two miles long—whips them up to a viewing platform at 15,000 feet. The wiser tourists have rented down parkas and small canisters of oxygen. The unwiser ones lurch and slip around unsteadily in suits and platform shoes. For most, it's a thrilling encounter with ice and snow. Coming back from the peak, heading for Lijiang, I ask the driver to make a detour at this sign:

FOLLOW ROCKER'S STEP TO SHANGRI-LA

Here, at Rock's former residence, I finally catch up with the man. The Naxi-style villa encloses its own courtyard, where Rock once directed loading of mules for an expedition. The villa has been converted into an on-site museum, with a modest display of Rock's photos, his gear

沿着洛克足迹
走进香格里拉

FOLLOW ROCKEB'STEPEP
TO SHANGRI-LA

and his rifles. Upstairs is Rock's bedroom and study. The atmosphere in this room is eerie. It is like stepping into a National Geographic picture: Rock took a self-portrait seated in this room that appeared in a National Geo issue. But in three dimensions, the room is tiny and dark—and spartan. The bed is made of wooden planks; above it hang glass photographic plates—which probably would have dripped onto the bed when drying. Which must have been a bit disconcerting. I look at the writing desk—and the chair where Rock sat. No-one is around: I go and sit exactly where Rock parked himself for his National Geographic self-portrait. To my surprise, the chair almost collapses. This is not because of my weight—it's because this is a rickety folding chair, similar to the ones Rock used in the field. I examine the table: it is also folding. Rock's fold-up world—always ready to hit the trail in his caravan, with his folding bed and his folding rubber bathtub.

On sale at the museum is Rock's hefty history of the Naxi, translated into Chinese. The large-format hardcover runs to over 500 pages, including 160 pages of Rock's photos—the thing must weigh about four pounds. A monochrome print displayed at the villa shows Rock impeccably dressed in the silk and brocade of a Mandarin, while another shows him draped in a Tibetan sheepskin cloak, with fox-fur hat and Tibetan boots. Yet another shows him in a dapper suit, which he sometimes wore to a regal reception from a local official or fiefdom ruler. Rock revelled in his celebrity status in these remote parts: he was a short-tempered reclusive loner, but here he was in his element—his wanderlust and sense of adventure were more than sated.

One more stop: the village of Baisha. I've dropped in to see Doctor Ho. The doctor resembles a *dongba* wizard—sporting a long white beard, like Gandalf. He's wearing a surgical frock coat—a well-worn one at that. He tells me that he met Rock when he was a child in this Naxi village. Rock inspired him. In more ways than one, it seems. He darts around, extolling the miraculous benefits of the medicinal plants that grow in his garden—dominated by showy sunflowers. The medicinal herbs make up the ingredients of his fabulous cure-all tea, which he duly proffers—it is redolent of aniseed. The doctor claims this tea can cure or alleviate all kinds of diseases, from cancer to diabetes. He burbles on energetically in English, smiling through his wispy beard.

The wallpaper in his 'office' consists of newspaper clippings from foreign journalists about himself. Among them is a New York Times piece by Bruce Chatwin, titled: 'In Lijiang: Rock's Kingdom', which includes a vivid description of Doctor Ho. I know this should all be taken with a grain of salt—is he really a doctor at all? But I have enjoyed my cup of cure all tea immensely. Doctor Ho is a crafty devil, asking only for donations—and foreign visitors are prone to over-estimating the value of such donations. The good doctor at Baisha is a bit of a quack—and a prize eccentric.

I left the wizard behind—a spritely man full of vigour and wit, despite his advanced age, and happy in his eccentricity. And on the way back into Lijiang, something popped into my head. Doctor Ho's cure-all tea—the elixir for all ailments—somehow triggered thoughts of Alexandra David-Néel. She was suffering from quite another malaise—a malaise of the soul—and she found a startling cure. She made a great discovery on her travels—she found her own elixir. Alexandra described one of her 'little excursions' in a letter to her estranged husband Philippe thus: 'I walked forty-four days, crossed a dozen peaks with snow up to my knees, slept in icy caves like a prehistoric woman, without food, almost barefoot, the soles of my moccasins being worn out by the rocks in the road.'

Tough going? Maybe, but Philippe must have rubbed his eyes in wonder. What happened to the demure and flirtatious woman he had married 20 years earlier—who would suffer from one undiagnosed malady after another, stretched out languidly on a chaise longue? How on earth, at the age of fifty-plus, had she suddenly acquired the vigour of a teenager? The clues are scattered in Alexandra's writing. She found herself getting depressed and claustrophobic in her marriage to Philippe, installed in a villa in Tunis, feeling trapped in a life of endless cocktail parties and bridge evenings.

It was actually Philippe who suggested that she take a journey to the Orient to see if that would cure her malaise. Boarding a ship to India, her outlook instantly improved. She was like an animal released from a cage—off on a new adventure. Her health recovered in the Himalayas—she no longer suffered from depression, and long walks made her very fit. Another kind of liberation: she no longer wore the tightly corsetted dresses she used to. 'During these last years I have lived like a wild woman without a corset, high necks or real shoes,' she noted.

After her exhausting trek to Lhasa, Alexandra summed up the experience in these words: 'There is no more effective fountain of youth'. She had transformed herself—changing her personality, acquiring a new language, experimenting with new spiritual paths. Long years of study, meditation, yogic practices, long walks, fresh mountain air and a simple diet kept the fountain flowing. And the greatest gusher of all was that she dared to follow her wilder instincts. She not only realised her dreams—she eclipsed them.

Basecamp

A mountain of research is involved in putting together a book like this, and you have to watch out for the occasional avalanche of information—meaning you may get buried under a pile of books. Like any expedition, getting started entails setting up a basecamp for planning and strategy. In this case, it means a large and unwieldy database, and a constant supply of tea, wine and other nutrients. Following are some brief notes from 'basecamp'— timelines, sources, background notes and credits—for those interested in the fine detail and in further reading.

❖

Glossary of Tibetan & Sanskrit Terms

bodhisattva—one who compassionately refrains from entering Nirvana in order to save others; one who is on the way to becoming a Buddha

Bon—pre-Buddhist religion of Tibet, involving shamanist practices and sorcery

chang—fermented barley-beer, a potent milky liquid

chorten—inverted bell-shaped shrine containing relics, or the ashes or embalmed body of a high lama (*stupa* in Sanskrit)

chuba—cloak-like outer garment, usually made of sheepskin, also used like a sleeping bag by Tibetan nomads

dakini—a voluptuous female deity or 'sky dancer' who personifies the wisdom of enlightenment

Dalai Lama—one in a series of incarnate lamas dating to the 14th century; head the Geluk sect of Tibetan Buddhism, recognised as manifestations of the bodhisattva Avolokitesvara; supreme rulers of central Tibet since the 17th century; the current Dalai Lama, Tenzin Gyatso, is 14th in the lineage

dharma—the word of the Buddha and his teachings, also called 'Buddha Dharma'

dzong—castle or fort, usually grafted onto a high ridge and seat of local government

dzongpon—governor of the dzong, or district magistrate

gompa—active monastery

gonkhang—protector chapel at a monastery, and site of special initiation and other ceremonies

Kanjur—sacred text, part of the Tibetan Buddhist canon that contains discourses attributed to Buddha Sakyamuni

khata—white greeting scarf, made of cotton or silk, presented on ceremonial occasions or offered at monasteries

kora—clockwise circuit of a sacred temple, lake or mountain

lakhang—chapel or inner sanctuary

lama—master spiritual teacher or guru

Losar—Tibetan New Year, usually celebrated around February

mala—prayer beads or rosary, constantly carried by Tibetan pilgrims

mandala—mystical circle, often enclosing a square, representing the Buddhist cosmos—used as a meditational aid

mani stone—stone tablet inscribed with mantras, often included as part of a mani-wall, composed of many such stones

mantra—sacred syllables repeated many times as part of spiritual practice, such as *om mani padme hum*

momo—Tibetan meat dumpling

Monlam—the Great Prayer Festival, around the time of Losar

nirvana—release from the cycle of mortal existence and rebirths

Panchen Lama—head lama of Tashilhunpo Monastery in Shigatse in a reincarnate lineage, recognised as a manifestation of Amitabha Buddha

prayer flag—small flag printed with sacred prayers, activated by the power of the wind

prayer wheel—large fixed wheel or small hand-held wheel containing mantras, activated by the spinning of the wheel

prostrator—pilgrim who measures the distance to a sacred destination with the length of his or her body, flung prone along the ground

rinpoche—'precious one'—a reincarnate lama, also known when young as a *tulku*

sang—currency unit of Tibet under 13th and 14th Dalai Lamas

sirdar—head Sherpa on expedition, in charge of porters

sutra—sacred text, written or spoken teachings of the Buddha

tanka—painted portable scroll, usually depicting a deity, on fine cotton or silk; can be used as a teaching aid

Tantra—or Tantrayana, is the form of Buddhism most often associated with Tibet—it employs radical steps to seek enlightenment within a single lifetime

tantric—using secret techniques or practices from Tantrayana

Tashi Lama—alternate title for the Panchen Lama

Tenjur—sacred text, part of the Tibetan Buddhist canon that contains commentary on Buddha's discourses

torma—ritual 'cake' sculpted from tsampa and yak-butter

tsampa—ground barley-flour, a Tibetan staple food

tulku—reincarnate lama

yak—hairy high-altitude cattle, 'cow with a skirt'

yabyum—tantric sexual pose of deity and consort, symbolising fusion of opposites—often misconstrued by Westerners

Cameos

Other intrepid Explorers, barmy Visionaries & bizarre Characters making an appearance in the chapters, in the rough order that they appear (some surface in several chapters)

Manning chapter
George Bogle, East India Company envoy who returned from Tibet with a glowing report & an STD, 22

Huc & Gabet, French Lazarist priests—whose balls froze in the Changtang, 42

Kintup chapter
Captain Nicholai Mikhailovich Prejevalsky, Russian explorer who was stopped by hundreds of warrior-monks close to Lhasa, 54

SCD, aka Sarat Chandra Das—headmaster, spymaster, plus Sherlock Holmes' sidekick for his missing years (maybe), 58

Dr Laurence Austine Waddell, aka Colonel or Major, whose books stirred up rumours of a huge waterfall, 65

Bailey chapter
Brian Houghton Hodgson, pioneering naturalist who described many species from their skins alone—animals he never saw alive & kicking, 83

Captain Henry Morshead, British surveyor who was so indifferent to leeches that he ended up covered in them, oozing blood, 87

Frank Kingdon Ward, British botanist who would turn white as chalk when faced with a cliff-drop, 89

Wilson chapter
Captain John Noel, who greatly upset the Tibetans when he smuggled out monks to supply a live orchestra for his silent movie, 121

Tenzin Norgay, who went from being a porter to international celebrity—who never learned to read or write, but spoke up to ten Himalayan dialects, 146

George Mallory, legendary British mountaineer who said he climbed Everest 'because it is there', 122

Goran Kropp, Swedish climber who said he used elevators 'because they are there', 150

Rock chapter
Chote Chaba, the chubby King of Muli, who asked Rock about Puss in Boots, and if the Americans could fly to the moon, 168

Edgar Snow, upstart American journalist who took Rock to the Rose Room in Shanghai—which outraged him, 171

David-Néel chapter
Annie Taylor, missionary & nurse who set out to convert the Dalai Lama, 188

Ekai Kawaguchi, Japanese monk who set out for Lhasa with two sheep for company, disguised as a pilgrim, 196

Gertrude Benham, pioneering mountaineer who walked vast distances with an umbrella & three books for self-defence, 208

Tucci chapter

Aufschnaiter chapter

Rampa chapter

Peissel chapter

Timelines

Eccentric Explorers

Quixotic quests, key encounters

1811   Thomas Manning reaches the fabled city of Lhasa in the middle of winter—by accident

1880   Kintup sets out to solve the riddle of the Tsangpo's possible link to the Brahmaputra river—an epic mission that winds up lasting four years

1913   Eric Bailey explores the Tsangpo region—bagging 2,000 butterfly species and the rare blue poppy—and getting close to a colossal waterfall

1924   Joseph Rock encounters the High Lama of the Muli Kingdom—his passport to hunt for new plant species in the bandit-ridden region

1924   Alexandra David-Néel realises her dream of reaching Lhasa—the culmination of more than a decade of study and planning

1933   Giuseppe Tucci stumbles into lost world of the Guge Kingdom in west Tibet, a treasure-trove of rare artforms

1934   Maurice Wilson reaches the base of Mount Everest to begin his incredible solo attempt on the virgin summit

1946   Peter Aufschnaiter and fellow POW Heinrich Harrer reach the sanctuary of Lhasa, spending four blissful years there

1956   Lobsang Rampa's book *The Third Eye* is published in the UK, becoming an instant bestseller—thus making Rampa an instant guru

1964   Michel Peissel enters the remote kingdom of Mustang, near the Nepal-Tibet border, dodging Khampa guerrillas

1994   Peissel announces discovery of the source of the Mekong

Tibet

Historical context of relevance to this narrative, in particular, Tibetan-British & Tibetan-Chinese relations—19th century onward

1800   Proposal made for the Great Trigonometrical Survey of India, as the British consolidate their hold over the Indian subcontinent. The bizarre mapping mega-project is to last for eight decades.

1862   Captain Montgomerie of the Survey of India proposes training native spies to collect information for the mapping of Tibet and other parts unknown to the north of India.

1903   Using these same maps, a British invasion force of 3,000 troops and 10,000 pack animals marches into Tibet on the pretext of opening the place to trade with the British. The 13th Dalai Lama flees to Mongolia.

1904   British force pushes through to Lhasa, concludes a useless treaty and withdraws. As a result of this military action, British trade agencies are set up in Gyantse, Yatung and Gartok. Bhutan is carved off as separate entity.

1910   Chinese Army invades Tibet—13th Dalai Lama flees to India

1912   Tibetan uprising against Chinese oppression

1913   The 13th Dalai Lama returns to Lhasa to declare Tibetan independence

1920   first British mountaineering attempts on Everest are permitted by 13th Dalai Lama

1933   The 13th Dalai Lama dies in December, leaving a prophecy about great holocaust in Tibet

1935   The 14th Dalai Lama is born in Amdo

1939   Tibet remains neutral during WWII, a real Shangri-La at the time, but peace is not to last

1940   The 14th Dalai Lama is enthroned in Lhasa

1947   India gains independence from Britain. The partitioning of India with creation of Muslim nations of Pakistan and Bangladesh costs millions of lives. Ladakh is absorbed into the Indian states of Jammu and Kashmir. Though officially independent since 1923, it is only after the British withdraw troops in 1947 that Nepal becomes truly independent.

1950   Chinese troops invade Tibet, crossing into Tibet proper in October

1951   Under duress, Tibetan officials sign a 17-Point Agreement, which promises cultural autonomy but forfeits independence

1959   National uprising against the Chinese on March 10th. The Dalai Lama escapes Tibet into exile in India through Sikkim. Khampa guerrillas attack Chinese troops across southern Tibet from their base in Mustang.

1965   The Tibet Autonomous Region (TAR) is created, effectively reducing the area of ethnic Tibet by half

1966–76 Madness of the Cultural Revolution hits Tibet hard, with wholesale destruction of temples

1971   CIA withdraws support for Khampa guerrillas due to US rapprochement with China

1974   Due to pressure from China, the Khampa guerrilla threat in Mustang is eliminated by Nepalese troops

1975   Sikkim annexed by India; monarchy is abolished

1974   Jigme Singye Wangchuck enthroned as fourth king of Bhutan

1989   In March, severe rioting breaks out in Lhasa; in December, the Dalai Lama is awarded the Nobel Peace Prize

1996   Anti-Dalai Lama campaign is launched in Tibet following fiasco over the choice of the 11th Panchen Lama

2002   A concrete monolith is erected in Potala Square to mark the 50th anniversary of the 'liberation of Tibet'

2006   Railway from Golmud reaches Lhasa, enabling economic exploitation of Tibet's resources on a large scale

2007   The Dalai Lama is awarded the Congressional Gold Medal, the highest honour bestowed by US Congress

2008   Widespread protest erupts against Chinese rule across the Tibetan plateau—triggering vicious crackdown by Chinese troops

2009   Marks the 50th year in exile for the Dalai Lama

Sources

The following is a brief selection of sources consulted by the author: it is by no means exhaustive, as some unpublished and highly obscure material was used. In the following listing, books may be out of print or hard to find: the focus is on publications in English—more material can be sourced in other languages (French, Italian, German).

Background Reading
Tournament of Shadows by Karl Meyer and Shareen Blair Brysac (Counterpoint, US, 1999) is a lively and superbly researched tome about Great Game politics and skulduggery in Central Asia: Part III of this hefty tome focuses on Tibet. *The Story of Tibet*, by Thomas Laird (Grove Press, NY, 2006) is a fascinating account of Tibet's history and culture through the eyes of the 14th Dalai Lama (interviewed by Laird). Ian Cameron's *Mountains of the Gods* (Facts on File, NY, 1984) is a splendid account of exploration of the mountain ranges of the Himalayas and Central Asia, with illustration from the archives of the RGS. Also consulted were Peter Hopkirk's *Trespassers on the Roof of the World* (John Murray, UK, 1982), Graham Sandberg's *The Exploration of Tibet* (first published 1904) and Kenneth Wimmel's *The Alluring Target* (Trackless Sands Press, US, 1997).

Thomas Manning
Manning's Tibet diary is collated in *Narratives of the Mission of George Bogle to Tibet and of the Journey of Thomas Manning to Lhasa*, edited by Clements Markham (published in London, 1876, with a facsimile edition reprinted in New Delhi, 1971). Other writing can be found in *The Letters of Thomas Manning to Charles Lamb*, edited by G. A. Anderson (published 1925). Excellent material about Manning is written up as a chapter in George Woodcock's *Into Tibet: the Early British Explorers* (Faber, UK, 1971) and as a chapter in John Keay's *Eccentric Travellers* (John Murray, UK, 1982). Kate Teltscher's *The High Road to China* (Bloomsbury, UK, 2006) is a great source about the earliest British encounters with Tibetans via George Bogle's expedition.

Kintup
A good source on the pundits and their Himalayan intrigues is Jules Stewart's *Spying for the Raj: The Pundits and the Mapping of the Himalaya* (Sutton Publishing, UK, 2006). Derek Waller's *The Pundits: British Exploration of Tibet & Central Asia* (The University Press of Kentucky, US, 1988) is a superb scholarly source about these little-known heroes. Intriguing snippets about the pundits surface in the following two books: *A Journey to Lhasa and Central Tibet* by Sarat Chandra Das, and *Lhasa and Its Mysteries* by Laurence Austine Waddell (London, 1905).

Eric Bailey
Bailey wrote a number of articles about Tibetan wildlife, birds and butterflies that were published in both popular and scholarly magazines. He wrote about his Tsangpo expeditions for the Scottish Geographical Magazine. He is author of three books about his adventures, published in the UK: *China-Tibet-Assam* (1945), *Mission to Tashkent* (1946) and *No Passport to Tibet* (1957). Drawing on the diaries

and letters of Bailey is the biography *Beyond the Frontiers: Biography of Colonel FM Bailey* by Arthur Swinson (Hutchinson, UK, 1971), but material for this work was sanitised by Bailey's wife, Irma. An excellent source of fine detail on the exploration of the Tsangpo is *Frank Kingdon Ward's Riddle of the Tsangpo Gorges*, edited and annotated by Kenneth Cox, Ian Baker and Ken Storm (published by the Antique Collectors' Club, UK, 2001). Alex McKay's *Tibet and the British Raj* (Curzon, UK, 1997) provides an in-depth look at the British in Tibet from 1904 to 1947: in the book, McKay advances the theory that Bailey was involved in a coup in Lhasa. Background material on the British invasion of Tibet was sourced from *The Unveiling of Lhasa* by Edmund Candler (first published 1905) and *Duel in the Snows* by Charles Allen (John Murray, London, 2004), while Mark Cocker's *Loneliness & Time* (Secker & Warburg, London, 1992) provided good anecdotal material about Bailey.

Maurice Wilson
Wilson's Everest diary is held by the Alpine Club, UK. A section of the diary is reproduced in Matt Dickinson's *Everest: Triumph and Tragedy* (HarperCollins, US, 2002). Drawing on original letters and diaries is Dennis Robert's biography of Wilson, entitled *I'll Climb Everest Alone* (published by Hale, London, 1957). A more recent account is *Maurice Wilson: A Yorkshiremun un Everest* (Ruth Hanson, UK, 2008). For material on early Everest climbs, the author drew on John Noel's classic book *Through Tibet to Everest* (originally published in 1927) as well as Sandra Noel's *Everest Pioneer* (Sutton Publishing, UK, 2003). Material on Tenzing Norgay derives from Jamling Tenzing Norgay's *Touching My Father's Soul* (HarperCollins, US, 2002).

Joseph Rock
Rock wrote a number of stories for magazines such as the London Illustrated News. His most striking contributions were to National Geographic, with some ground breaking colour-photo inserts (marked with an asterisk * in the following listing): Hunting the Chaulmoogra Plant (Burma) (March 1922); Banishing the Devil of Disease among the Naxi (November 1924); Land of the Yellow Lama: National Geographic Society Explorer Visits the Strange Kingdom of Muli (April 1925); Experiences of a Lone Geographer (September 1925); Through the Great River Trenches of Asia (August 1926); Life among the Lamas of Choni (November 1928); Seeking the Mountains of Mystery: An Expedition on the China-Tibet Frontier to the Unexplored Amnyi Machen Range (February 1930); The Glories of the Minya Konka (October 1930); Carrying the Colour Camera Through Unmapped China*; Konka Risumgongba, Holy Mountain of the Outlaws* (July 1931); Sungmas, Living Oracles of the Tibetan Church—Demon-Possessed Tibetans and Their Incredible Feats* (October 1935).

Among Rock's scholarly works are: *The Ancient Na-khi Kingdom of Southwest China* (two volumes, Harvard University Press, 1947) and his two-volume Naxi encyclopedic-dictionary (published in Rome, 1963 and 1972). Rock's classics on the botany of Hawaii are *Indigenous Trees of the Hawaiian Islands* (Honolulu, 1913) and *The Ornamental Trees of Hawaii* (Honolulu, 1917). Drawing on Rock's diaries and letters is a biography by Stephanne B. Sutton, entitled *In China's Border Provinces: the Turbulent Career of Joseph Rock, Botanist-Explorer* (Hastings House Publishers,

NY, 1974). An article about Rock called *Our Man in China* appears in National Geographic's January 1997 issue (National Geographic also based a documentary special on SW China around Rock). The author consulted *Lamas, Princes and Brigands* by Michael Aris (NY, 1992)—a hefty catalogue to accompany a public exhibition of Rock's photographs—and Bruce Chatwin's *What Am I Doing Here* (Penguin, UK, 1989), which has an entertaining chapter called 'Rock's World'.

Alexandra David-Néel

Alexandra wrote in a handful of genres and different styles. Apart from her numerous magazine articles, she is author of 40-odd books—a number of them not translated from French. Her most influential works published in English are: *My Journey to Lhasa* (1927), *Magic & Mystery in Tibet* (1931), *Initiates & Initiation in Tibet* (1931) and *The Secret Oral Teachings in Tibetan Buddhist Sects* (1967). A thorough biography of Alexandra is *The Secret Lives of Alexandra David-Neel*, by Barbara and Michael Foster (Overlook Press, NY, 1998), though it adopts a tone of reverence and is given to fanciful conjecture. Less reverent in tone is Luree Miller's *On Top of the World: Five Women Explorers in Tibet* (Mountaineers Books, Seattle, 1984). Elizabeth Booz has a good sketch of Alexandra as a chapter of National Geographic's *Into the Unknown* (Washington DC, 1987). A fine pictorial record is showcased in Tiziana and Gianni Baldizzone's *Tibet, on the Paths of Gentlemen Brigands: Retracing the Steps of Alexandra David-Neel* (Thames & Hudson, London, 1995). Superb for context on Buddhism is Stephen Batchelor's *The Awakening of the West* (Parallax Press, Berkeley, 1994). For the final word on Alexandra, go to her official website, run by the Alexandra David-Neel Foundation, at *www.alexandra-david-neel-org/*. Accessed from the same foundation is a CD-ROM about Alexandra.

Giuseppe Tucci

Tucci was a prolific author, but with a highly specialised audience: works are mainly specialised scholarly tomes that have little appeal to the average reader, but some were written with a more general audience in mind—and thus are more likely to be found translated into English. He contributed numerous articles to journals and anthologies. He was also a translator of works from Tibetan to Italian. Among his expedition chronicles are: *Secrets of Tibet, being the Chronicle of the Tucci Scientific Expedition to Western Tibet*, co-authored with E. Ghersi (published in Italian 1934; English translation 1934) and *To Lhasa and Beyond* (based on his 1948 expedition, but not published in English until 1956). Scholarly works are many, embracing subjects from Tibetan folktales to erotic Nepalese art. Tucci's magnum opus is *Tibetan Painted Scrolls* (two volumes of text, one folio album, published 1949). Published by the Royal Italian Academy over the period 1932–1941 is Tucci's *Indo-Tibetica*, which comprises seven volumes—examining subjects such as the stupa, temples of West Tibet and interpretation of their mural paintings, and Gyantse and its monasteries. Very little is published in English about Tucci the man: Fosco Maraini's *Secret Tibet* (originally published in 1951, with a revised edition by the Harvill Press, London, 1998) is a key source on the character of Tucci, as seen by Maraini—who accompanied him on two trips to Tibet.

Peter Aufschnaiter

For quotations from Peter Aufschnaiter's diaries, letters and other writing, the author relied heavily on *Eight Years in Tibet*, edited by Martin Brauen (English edition published by Orchid Press, Bangkok, 2002—the book was originally published in German in 1983). Heinrich Harrer's *Seven Years in Tibet* (Rupert Hart-Davis, UK, 1953), his story in National Geographic (July 1955 issue), his photobook *Lost Lhasa* (Harry Abrams Inc, NY, 1992), and his hefty biography *Beyond Seven Years in Tibet* (Labyrynth Press, UK, 2007) all proved highly useful. Other fine detail was culled from Lowell Thomas Jr's *Out of This World* (first published in 1950), Christopher Hale's *Himmler's Crusade* (Bantam Press, UK, 2003), George Tsarong's *In the Service of his Country* (Snow Lion Publications, NY, 2000), Namgyal Lhamo Taklha's *Born in Lhasa* (Snow Lion Publications, NY, 2001) and Robert Ford's *Wind Between the Worlds* (David McKay, NY, 1957).

Lobsang Rampa

Rampa's bestselling title was his first, *The Third Eye*, though he went on to pen 19 titles in all (actually 21 titles if you include the unauthorised booklet *My Visit to Venus* and the dubious posthumous tome *My Visit to Agharta*). Among the cult titles are *Doctor from Lhasa*, *The Rampa Story*, *Cave of the Ancients* and *The Hermit*. Cashing in on Rampa's fame, the guru's wife Mama San Ra-Ab Rampa added three more gibberish titles of her own—*Pussywillow*, *Autumn Lady* and *Tigerlily*—all handled by Rampa's key British publisher, Corgi Books. And then, some 25 years after Rampa's demise, his former secretary Sheelagh Rouse came out of the woodwork with a book titled *Twenty-five Years with T. Lobsang Rampa* (self-published, Vancouver, 2005). Encounters with the elusive Rampa are described in several books: Eric Newby has a chapter about him in *A Traveller's Life* (Picador, London, 1982) and Alain Stanké wrote a book on the subject, entitled *Rampa—Imposteur ou Initié?* (Editions Stanké, Montreal, 1980). *Prisoners of Shangri-La* (University of Chicago Press, 1998) by Donald Lopez has a chapter called 'The Eye' devoted to Rampa. Of course, Rampa is still around: he's out there in cyberspace somewhere: *www.galactic.to/rampa* is one among a number of websites devoted to Rampa. Another one, *www.karenmutton.com/rampa*, is more of fan website.

Michel Peissel

Peissel has directed more than 20 documentaries for television—a number of them about Tibet, including specials on reaching the source of the Mekong, expeditions to Changtang, and about the mysterious towers of Kham. Peissel has written hundreds of magazine stories in English and French, and dozens of books. Key works include *Mustang: A Lost Tibetan Kingdom* (Collins & Harvill Press, London, 1968), *Cavaliers of Kham: The Secret War in Tibet* (Heinemann, US, 1972), *The Great Himalayan Passage* (Little Brown & Company, Boston, 1975), *The Last Barbarians* (Souvenir Press, London, 1998) and the photobook *Tibet: the Secret Continent* (Cassell Illustrated, London, 2002). Other sources consulted for this profile include Thomas Laird's *Into Tibet* (Grove Press, NY, 2002) for CIA background material. For someone who has spent a major part of his life revealing Tibetan secrets, Peissel is highly secretive himself—very little has been written about him, as he rarely grants interviews.

Research Assistance & Insights

Research is the backbone of a project like this: for assistance in tracking down hard-to-get details many thanks to Alex McKay, who provided insights on the British in Tibet, particularly Eric Bailey. Victor Chan and Kate Saunders set up valuable research contacts. Bradley Rowe of Glastonbury provided tips on Tucci and other explorers. Roger Croston assisted with material useful for several profiles in the book. Martin Brauen provided follow-up detail on Peter Aufschnaiter, as well as some of his photography. Alain Stanké provided insights into the character of Lobsang Rampa—and pictures of him too. George (Dadul Namgyel) Tsarong befriended Harrer and Aufschnaiter while they were in Tibet: he generously provided access to archival photos of pre-1950 Tibet. Geoffrey Flack provided a host of illustration from rare sources—postcards from old Tibet, stamps, seals and other arcane material. Naz Ali drafted the maps. Teresa Nightingale created graphics and artwork, including several portrait sketches. Kandit Xivivadh optimised archival photos. For polishing drafts, *merci* to Patsie Lamarre, who reads me well. Special thanks to Jack Joyce of ITMB for taking care of business. And my gratitude to Peter Sevcik, Irene Holman, Lesley Thomson, Tashi, Sonam and Kalsang for their input.

Illustration Sources

Front cover: (top image) Riders approaching the pyramidal peak of Jambeyang (MB photo). Central panel, three explorers: (at left) Joseph Rock © President and Fellows of Harvard College, Archives of the Arnold Arboretum; (middle) Michel Peissel in Paris with foxfur hat (MB photo); (at right) Maurice Wilson (Alpine Club, UK). **Back cover:** (top image) Pack-horse caravan, plus old binoculars, prayer-wheel and compass: iStockphoto.com. Central panel: (at left) the deity Yama holding the Wheel of Life in jaws, temple fresco, east Tibet; (middle) fresco of White Tara, ruins of Tsaparang, far-west Tibet; (at right) riders en route to horse-racing fair, central Tibet (MB photos)

Inside Art: A number of line drawings, other artwork and archival photographs derive from the author's personal collection. All photos in this book were taken by Michael Buckley (designated MB in some photo credits) except for the following pages. Pages 207, 285, 287, 290, 291, 292, 306, 312, 338, 400: archival photos of Tibet courtesy of George Tsarong, Kalimpong; 44, 72, 101: Royal Geographical Society, UK; 62, 63, 67, 111, 112: Sharyn Smith and Chris Jones; page 116: Alpine Club, UK; pages 154, 162, 163, 166, 175, 176 © President and Fellows of Harvard College, Archives of the Arnold Arboretum; 264 courtesy of Dr Martin Brauen, University of Zurich; 282 courtesy of David Appleby; 302, 320, 323: courtesy of Alain Stanké, Editions Stanké International, Montreal.

About the Author

MICHAEL BUCKLEY has travelled widely in Tibet, China and Central Asia. In the course of numerous journeys to the Tibetan plateau, he has hitchhiked overland from Chengdu to Lhasa, trekked around Mount Kailash, mountain-biked from Lhasa to Kathmandu, and mountain-biked from Leh to Kashgar. Buckley is author of *Shangri-La: A travel guide to the Himalayan dream* (Bradt, UK, 2008); *Tibet: the Bradt Travel Guide* (UK, 2006); and *Heartlands: Travels in the Tibetan World* (Summersdale, UK, 2002). He has also contributed to the anthologies *Travelers' Tales Tibet*, *Travelers' Tales China* and *Travelers' Tales India*.

Author website: www.himmies.com

Cryptic Cover

How sharp is your eye? As sharp as that of the Himalayan Griffon, which can soar in 'blue-thermals' over Everest? For those who like riddles, hidden in the cover of this book are some clues associated with the explorers:

* What is the Sanskrit name for the Tibetan rosary on the inside flap? (clue: part of the word lies close by). Which explorer is the rosary associated with and why?

* What explorer name can be found embedded in the background map used for the flaps?

* The butterfly on the front cover would catch the eye of which explorer? What's the common name for this butterfly—and why the large circular shapes on the wings?

* White Tara, the deity of compassion, is identified by the presence of extra eyes where? And the explorer who discovered this particular mural?

* The snowcapped peak on the front cover was first sighted by a Western explorer also pictured there. Who?

* Which explorer launched expeditions to research horse breeds in Tibet, like the hardy ponies seen on the back cover (middle panel)?

* The three-blue-eyed deity on the back cover has eyebrows made of what element? And the ability to generate this element within the body would be associated with which explorer?

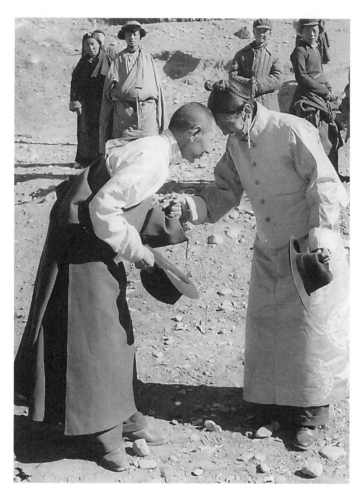

TOUCHING FOREHEADS

The traditional Tibetan salutation of touching foreheads takes place between high lamas—or between high-level officials (as in this photo from the 1950s). The gesture is a kind of 'spiritual handshake'—connecting the highest chakras. Hope you have 'touched foreheads'—making a connection with Tibetans—while reading this book. They are remarkable people with an extraordinary heritage—a heritage that is in danger of vanishing. To find out more about the current situation in Tibet, go to:
www.savetibet.org